W9-BCG-995

John Kobal
A HISTORY OF MOVIE MUSICALS
Gotta Sing Gotta Dance

John Kobal

A HISTORY OF MOVIE MUSICALS
Gotta Sing Gotta Dance

Exeter Books

NEW YORK

For Eleanor Powell
In spirit and in heart she was a true Ariel

Who's Who

Fred Astaire (Actor, dancer, choreographer)
Busby Berkeley (Choreographer, director)
Hans Bertram (Director), Joan Blondell (Actress)
Rene Clair (Director), Jack Cole (Choreographer)
Dan Dailey (Actor, Dancer), Bebe Daniels (Actress, singer)
Irene Dunne (Actress, singer)
David Essex (Actor, singer)
Bob Fosse (Director, choreographer, dancer)
Arthur Freed (Producer, lyricist), Kathryn Grayson (Actress, singer)
Karl Hartl (Director)
Lena Horne (Actress, singer), Madison Lacy (Stills photographer)
Fritz Lang (Director)
Laura La Plante (Actress), Lois Lindsay (Berkeley Girl)
Bessie Love (Actress)
Ben Lyon (Actor), May McAvoy (Actress)
Rouben Mamoulian (Director)
Melba Marshall (Berkeley Girl)
Jessie Matthews (Actress, dancer, singer)
Ann Miller (Actress, dancer), Vincente Minnelli (Director)
Walter Plunkett (Costume designer)
Eleanor Powell (Actress, dancer, choreographer)
Sheila Ray (Berkeley Girl), Richard Rodgers (Composer)
Victor Saville (Director, producer), Gwen Seager (Berkeley Girl)
Donald Ogden Stewart (Screenwriter),
Pete Townshend (Rock musician, composer)
King Vidor (Director), Charles Walters (Director, choreographer)
Mae West (Actress), Robert Wise (Director, producer)

Gotta Sing Gotta Dance
First published 1971

Revised Edition 1983

© Copyright John C. Kobal 1983

First published in the USA 1983
by Exeter Books
Distributed by Bookthrift
Exeter is a trademark of Simon & Schuster
Bookthrift is a registered trademark of Simon & Schuster
NEW YORK, New York

ISBN 0-671-06063-5

Printed in Spain

Contents

How Fred and Ellie began 'Begin the Beguine'

'I will never forget, – Mr Mayer saying to me "Ellie, how would you like to dance with Fred Astaire?" I idolized Fred Astaire! Back in New York when we were both working on Broadway I'd had opportunities to meet him, but I never wanted to because I'm an idealist, we'd meet and he might do something or say something and all illusions would go away. I said, "You gotta be kidding!" Mr Mayer said, "He likes the script. The money's fine. The only thing is you might be too tall for him. You meet him and we'll see if your height is alright. Mr Astaire will be in Mervyn LeRoy's office at eleven o'clock tomorrow morning."

I was so nervous I couldn't sleep. I got there early. I said to Mervyn, "I'm so nervous I took a bath in LUX last night hoping I'd shrink or something. I just hope this goes through." Suddenly the buzzer went.

"Quick, Ellie," said Mervyn. "Go hide."

In saunters Mr Astaire and his agent.

I'm hiding behind the door.

They sit down. There's a bit of chit-chat about the weather and the races and then Mr Astaire says, "Boy, I'm so nervous. Do you know how she works? Does she standard record or pre-record? How long does she rehearse?"

"Well, why don't you ask her" said Mr LeRoy. "Come on out, Eleanor." I slunk out, but the important thing is I heard him say almost the same thing I had said. Next thing we know the door opens and one by one in walks Mr Mayer, Mr Mannix, Mr Cole Porter. All the big ones. We're chatting politely till finally they say "Alright. Rise."

We stand back to back. Well, believe it or not Fred is taller than I am, not a lot, but – he's about 5' 8". So I fit.

Mr Porter hands us both a piece of paper – just a lead sheet in his own handwriting – "Begin the Beguine". He plays it. We listen. Marvellous. He plays it again. This is to be our first number. Now Fred was to go on vacation before we started and I wanted to reassure him so he wouldn't worry about anything. I said, "Mr Astaire, I know how important it is for you to have your own pianist, so feel free to bring whoever you want." (Your pianist, you see, becomes your everything when the only thing you have is an empty hall and a piece of music.) And because he was a stranger on the lot I told him I'd meet him at the east gate near the little bungalow Mr Mayer had built for me to rehearse in.

Before leaving I asked Fred at what time he liked to rehearse and he answered "anytime *you* desire." "No, no, no," I said, "*you* select a time." "No, no, whatever you . . ."

"Well, it was like out of *Mr Alphonse* you know. So finally I said, "Well, is eight o'clock in the morning too early for you?" "No, that's fine."

In the meantime we found out Mr Astaire cannot have his pianist because the musicians' union won't allow a man from another studio to come over. Meanwhile I have "Begin the Beguine" played backwards, forwards, inside out, and I have a general idea about what I would do.

The morning comes. He's back. I meet him at the gate and we saunter down to the bungalow. I introduce him to my pianist, direct him in to change into his work clothes, and he comes out and there are two little canvas chairs and we sit. We know we have all these numbers to get, but here we are, sitting. He says, "Would you like to hear the music?" I say, "Oh yes, thank you." So we play the music and I'm thinking, "We gotta get going. We gotta start. Who's going to start . . ."

"Would you like to hear it again, Miss Powell?", he asks. I say, "Yes, very much." Well, to everyone around the studio it was like a heavyweight boxing match – two champs in the ring. They expect POW!!! And here we are sitting an hour and a half listening to a piece of music we know backwards.

Up to the time that Fred worked with me he had always had a young lady that he could teach. And of course they would never say that they didn't care to do this or that, because that was *it*! In fact Hermes Pan used to take the girl's part. He would work with Fred, two men together, and Hermes would be whoever the girl was – Ginger Rogers, Joan Fontaine, or whoever. Then, when they'd got it all mapped out Hermes would go teach the girl her part, then he'd do it with her, with him taking Fred's part. Then when she'd be all rehearsed she and Fred got together for final rehearsals. But with me being my own choreographer because nobody could do what I was doing but me, and Fred being his own, who was going to tell who what to do? I thought of something to get us on our feet. I said, "Mr Astaire, I have a number and there's something wrong in the middle of it. If I did it for you, would you please help me? It just doesn't feel right." So I did it, got to the middle, and stopped. And he jumped out of his chair real quick and said "Oh, I see what you mean," and he did a little something and then he stopped and ran right back to the chair. So I said to him, "Mr Astaire, what are we going to do?" And he said, "Maybe if you go over in that corner and I go over here and we just take a couple of bars and improvise – and if you see something you like, stop me. And the same if I see something."

Well, you'd be amazed at how many things we did like. Not the same steps but the same syncopation. Finally he stopped, and I fooled around and ad-libbed. "What was that!" he'd go, and I'd have to define what I was doing, and vice versa. But it was three or four days before we started melting. Still it was Mr Astaire and Miss Powell.

One day we did the exact same thing on a difficult

piece of music in "Begin the Beguine" and he forgot himself and he ran over, lifted me in the air, said, "Oh, Ellie!", then put me down and said, "Oh, I beg your pardon." And I said, "Look, basically we are just two hoofers who started off in vaudeville, right? Please let's get down to Fred and Ellie." And he said okay. The ice was broken.

If you remember "Begin the Beguine", we did that thing in the circle, counter-rhythm – we went in a circle, he went this way and I went that. Well, we had more fun working on it! We started at eight, remember. My tummy made the worst growling noise – I was so embarrassed – and he said, "What time is it?" But we had no clock. D'you know, it was four in the afternoon! We had gone from eight right straight through to four, over and over. The poor piano player, he was absolutely dying! He had a cigarette hanging out of the corner of his mouth and the two ashtrays were full. So we got a Big Ben alarm clock and we set it at one, and we promised no matter where we were, we would stop to allow this man to have time.

We were crazy.'

You Ain't Heard
Nothin' Yet!

August 6th, 1926, is a landmark in the history of the movies. On that steamy summer evening in New York trumpets blared. Audiences rose enthusiastically. They were back with the same excitement that had met Lumière's train. In the box office the cashier was the last to leave the cinema. Sound had brought with it the clink of new coins and they would be heard for a long time to come.

But what of the entertainment fare that memorable evening? To whet the appetite for the main feature one could thrill to famous opera stars like Martinelli, Anna Case and Marion Talley. And if that wasn't enough for the memories of a lifetime, well there were always the piano and violin solos by Harold Bauer, Efrem Zimbalist (Sr.) and Mischa Elman, not to mention a Spanish dancing troupe called the Cansinos. Finally came the moment everybody was waiting for, *Don Juan* and John Barrymore with Sound. *Cinema Art* was excited enough to print '. . . the music was reproduced with such perfection that it was difficult to believe the artists were not in front of the audience . . . there is a scene where John Barrymore has a sword fight and it is an interesting fact that the swords can be heard swishing with a startling clarity and that as soon as the duel is over the swishing stops. There was not one swish too many.'

The startling clarity applauded by *Cinema Art* had been very much in the mind of cinematographer turned inventor, E. B. Du Par. When he had the first soundproof booth built to his own specifications 'The noise incident to the taking of a motion picture made it necessary to shut the camera in a special chamber. With the camera I was locked in the booth. I shot *Don Juan* through a small aperture, and looked out through a small peek hole. However, the construction of the booth did not permit of the booth's occupant to hear anything from without. It was necessary to depend entirely on light signals for starts and fades. The camera is run by a motor which is synchronized with the recording machine motor. Instead of running at the regular speed of 16 pictures per second, we exposed at the rate of 24 per second. The recording machine was located so that it was in another part of the building far enough away so that no sound could get to the actual place of photographing.' He did not add that it was as hot as hell in there but it must have been.

This cumbersome if ingenious device was, as we shall see, to play havoc with many a performer and director to come. The talkies lost the simplicity of the silents and gained the stifling booth, but it worked even if it was a necessary evil.

Gone with the silent film went the special effects of the Giant Wurlitzer which, with its gleaming rows of keys, was capable of producing almost any sound under the sun. Gone too were original scores by Saint-Saëns and Honegger and the actual experience of seeing it performed right in front of your eyes. But it was all in the name of progress. The miracle now was that sound came from behind the screen and not from the orchestra out in front. For the audience on that night in 1926 the effect was electrifying.

Perhaps in the deeper recesses of lyricist Al Dubin's mind (in partnership with composer Harry Warren he supplied the bulk of songs for the Warner musicals of the 30s) lay the lyric the Warner Brothers may well have been singing at the time – 'We're in the Money, We're in the money, We've got a lot of what it takes to get along.'

The curious thing is that the Warner Brothers did not necessarily play it safe with the sound device they were to use – the cumbersome sound-on-disc (Vitaphone) process. What could the Warner Brothers have known about sound? What was it that made them plonk for Bell Telephone Laboratories special turntable with its thirteen-to-seventeen inch records? The history of sound is exciting in itself and well worth relating briefly here. Thomas Alva Edison* (that great delegator of inventors such as W. K. L. Dickson) gave to the world the first sounds it was ever to hear when he patented the original tinfoil phonograph in 1877. One can imagine the excitement, not unlike that of 1926, when Edison was to enter his Long Island Studios and hear a voice welcoming him, as if there was a ghost in the laboratory. While there were other inventors on the road to discovering sound it is not important to argue here over who did what but rather to revel in man's ingenuity.

Today we can buy the wax cylinder as marketed by Edison at the time, and as primitive as they are, we can sense the miracle. If we had never had the good fortune to see Bernhardt her voice would still have been immortalized. It was the beginning of things to come. Back in France, Clément Maurice, favourite photographer of the great French stars of the day, persuaded them to take part in his experiments with sound on films. These were shown at the Paris Exposition of 1900 where he opened his Phone-Ciné Theatre and, as primitive as these short (one minute) synchronized recordings undoubtedly were, they became a successful novelty throughout Europe. He was to bill it his 'undying theatre'. Later, longer films like Sarah Bernhardt's *La dame aux camélias* (1908) and Caruso's *I Pagliacci* (1914) were added.

When the Warner Brothers took their hands out of their empty pockets in a grab for sound, nothing was perfect. It was not just a pioneering spirit, or even the thrill of adventure that prompted the Warner brothers to take the gamble with Bell, but simply greed, cunning, a desperate need to survive, and the desire for power. In short, the basic ingredients for success. With 'The Vitaphone' as their very own, if it succeeded, they would possess something their rivals needed, and with this possession as their key, they would be able to unlock the doors of the cinemas presently closed to their products.

Warners had been in business since 1912 as producers of short subjects and also as exhibitors. Their first real success as producers was in 1917, with *My Four Years in Germany*, but though John Barrymore, Ernst Lubitsch and Rin Tin Tin were among those who kept them solvent the Warner brothers had not managed to acquire a nationwide circuit of cinemas to show their films. They owned several prestigious showcase houses in the big

* For who really did it first, and where, and how, read *Edison, The Man Who Made the Future*, by Ronald W. Clark. Macdonald & Janes, London, 1977.

cities, but they ran into trouble when it came to the thousands of suburb and small-town houses where the real money was, but which were controlled by the four majors – Fox, Metro, Famous Players and First National. They had to offer their popular films to these exchanges at low rates to get them on to their screens. The profits were not enough to survive on. To do so they needed a gimmick. The Bell engineers came up with the goods. They were still far from perfect and some of the major problems would only start to show up as more and more films were made. One of the worst of these had to do with the difficulty of starting the disc and the film simultaneously. And if the film broke (as it often did) one heard the leading man accuse his lady love of unfaithfulness after they had both left the screen. Yet, having little left to lose, Warners decided to risk their all. It paid off. In so doing they revolutionized the entire industry, made themselves a fortune, and, just by the bye, put thousands of musicians, organists and pianists out of work, the usual casualty of progress.

The talkie revolution was to create another unhappy situation – for the community's disabled. The silent film had provided a unique bonus for the deaf. They not only saw the same things as their more fortunate neighbours, but were able to lip-read. Since the title writers often wrote quite a different conversation from the one between the actors, it must have given rise to some delighted amusement. For instance, in the silent *Three Weeks*, the Queen (Aileen Pringle), being carried to her bed of roses for a romantic *tête-à-tête* with her lover (Conrad Nagel), could be understood by the deaf to be telling Nagel what would happen to him if he dropped her, while she was supposedly whispering sweet endearments into his ear.

Cinema Art, that perceptive and short-lived film magazine of the 20s, cast a more critical, practical eye on the Vitaphone in their prophetic editorial of September 1926: 'While as yet it has not been applied to a cinema play, except for musical accompaniment, it seems evident that it will soon be used to reproduce conversations. . . . Some of our most decorative actors do not have good speaking voices. Our hierarchy of stars would go smash. Secondly, the present method of filming pictures in crowded studios with scores of directors and carpenters working nearby, would have to be done away with. Expensive soundproof rooms would be required. Finally, the present motion picture technique would be junked.'

It is only fitting that the final word should be Jack Warner's, who, with his brothers Harry and Sam, had gambled so much: 'In Hollywood . . . the reverberations from the New York premiere triggered a panic, as though the Black Death had struck the land. No one had openly discussed the potential crisis of talking pictures, nor were there any schedules, but the pros knew that Armageddon was at hand. There would be suicides, mental crack-ups, emotional illnesses. Men and women whose names were known around the world would disappear as suddenly as though they had been lost at sea.'

But the transition to sound was only fully clinched after the landmark film premiere that took place the following year at the Warner Theatre in

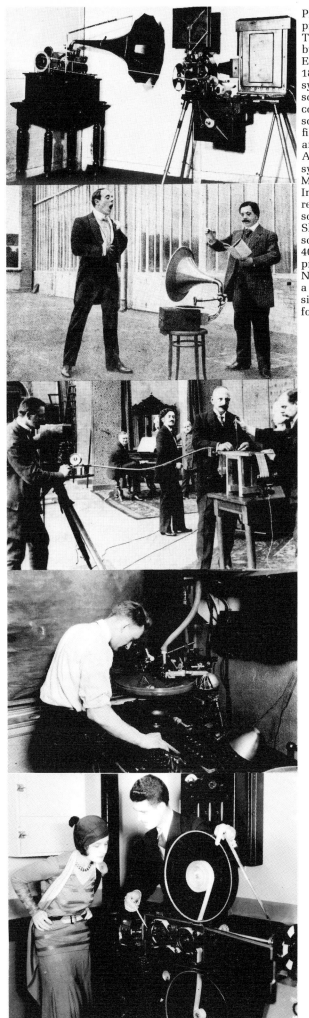

Progress towards talking pictures. From top of page: The Kinetoscope, invented by William Dickson in Edison's laboratory in 1894, offered a method of synchronizing film and sound. A singer – with a conductor – making a sound record for an earlier film. Oskar Messter and his assistant, Alfred Lewandowsky, synchronizing an early Messter film in 1913. In the Vitaphone recording studio. The soundtrack; Douglas Shearer, head of MGM's sound department for 40 years, explains the process to his sister, Norma Shearer, who was a front-rank star in both silent and talking pictures for more than 20 years.

13

Many great artistes appeared on film before the coming of sound. Far left: Anna Pavlova, in 1916, played *The Dumb Girl of Portici*, based on the opera by Auber. Left: Geraldine Farrar was more famous as an opera singer but she acted in several silent films, and played an opera singer in De Mille's *Temptation* (1916). While the orchestra in the pit is for the scene in the film, it serves to show what going to silent films was like.

New York. The night, October 6th, 1927. The brothers Warner unveiled *The Jazz Singer*. The songs and a brief piece of dialogue, sung and spoken by Al Jolson (*The Jolson Story*, starring Larry Parks. Columbia, 1946) in the context of a story whose drama was furthered and heightened by these, changed the nature of the medium and the course of the film industry. And it eliminated radio as a threat.

The story behind the making of *The Jazz Singer* was not, for George Jessel, the best of fates. It goes that Harry Warner had seen Jessel in the part-musical Samson Raphaelson play on Broadway, and the corny heart-tugger about the cantor's son who chooses to sing jazz on Broadway instead of *Kol Nidrei* in his father's synagogue, must have struck a chord in his emigrant's heart, for he was desperate to get Jessel and the play for his Vitaphone films. Desperate as Warner was, he wasn't a fool and Harry got the hit play for $50,000, while George Jessel's services were to cost $30,000. This was before Jessel heard it was to have sound sequences, at which point he held out for more money, and the deal was called off. Warner had a property but no star.

There may have been another reason besides cash, for Jessel was going to have to bare himself to the infant sound and that could have made him feel vulnerable. Consider that the bulk of stage-trained performers were dependent on the live audience to help them gauge how they were coming across, when and what to change, and to elicit from them those impromptu moments that become magic in the theatre and are achieved only from the live contact with an audience. What might have had a tightrope appeal on the stage and has an audience at the edge of their seats, would photograph as shameless hogging when enlarged a hundred times its size on the screen.

Next they offered it to Eddie Cantor, but he too entertained doubts, and rejected it. At last they turned to the man who was already being billed as 'Mr Show-Business' himself – Al Jolson. High time, one would have thought, since the character in the play was based to a large extent on incidents in

Above left: Giovanni Martinelli brought his heroic tenor to films in a Vitaphone short in which he sang an aria from *I Pagliacci*. The studio boss, Sam Warner, on far right.

Above: One of the earliest films with sound, *Don Juan* had a score and recorded action noise. On Broadway it was supported by a short featuring soloists from the Metropolitan Opera and celebrated instrumentalists.

Jolson's own life, which had led this Russian-born, Jewish immigrant (Asa Yoelson) to becoming a quintessential American entertainment phenomenon. If Jolson had entertained any similar doubts about exposing himself to this new medium, his ego, and a fee of $75,000 removed them. The rest, as they say, was for the history books.

'It's ironic,' wrote the only surviving Warner brother, Jack, in his autobiography, 'that *The Jazz Singer* qualified as a "talking" picture only because of a freak accident. Sam [Warner] was supervising the song recording when Jolson, in a burst of exuberance, cried out: "You ain't heard nothin' yet folks! Listen to this!"'

Another witness to the making of this film was its leading lady, May McAvoy, star of such silent classics as *Sentimental Tommy*, *The Enchanted Cottage*, *Ben Hur* and *Lady Windermere's Fan*, who had gained enough experience to be ready for the big talkie.

May McAvoy: When we first started on those Vitaphone shorts they tried to keep it a secret, so they'd be first, I guess, but by the time we started on *The Jazz Singer* everybody knew because there'd been so many Vitaphone shorts by that time. I did so many of those shorts they began to call me the Vitaphone Girl. When I first heard about sound, I thought it would be a great thing. It was one of the reasons I decided to sign a three-year contract with them. But when I heard these Vitaphone records, that sounded like a scratchy old Victrola – it was all done on enormous flat records and there was no synchronization with the film. Oh, it was very, very difficult working like that. You had to do your whole scene in *one* take. And that meant they had to have a camera for the whole long shot, a camera for two people on one side, another camera for people here, and close-up cameras and you were doing the whole thing in one long take; and you were surrounded by microphones hidden in any place they could find, and you were permitted to move only a little bit one way or the other because if you moved too much you got out of range of the camera that was directed at you; and you weren't playing to the kind of camera we'd been used to, because now the camera was put in what looked like a telephone booth, sound-proofed to keep out the clicking noises the camera made. Oh . . . *you* try to play a scene looking and sounding anything other than mechanical in a situation like that.

When I first met Jolson I thought he was the most nervous man that ever lived. He had never done a movie before. He was at home on the stage or in nightclubs or any place else where he could do his own stuff, but to follow a script and do camera work was very, very trying for him. Every time we did a

15

scene together he would say, 'How was I? Did I do that right? Shall we try it again? Let's try it over again!' He would ask to do things over and over and over again. Each time he felt he could do it better. I knew what he meant, because when you are very new at something, you freeze, you're more mechanical. I felt this in certain scenes at the start of the picture. It was the sort of thing he had done on stage, particularly the musical things, but in drama it was all quite different. Not that there was a great deal of dialogue. That wasn't hard for him. But he was afraid of the camera; he was afraid of how he looked, and acted.

We used to have to work at night, because Warner Bros were right on Sunset Boulevard where the traffic was awful all day long. So we waited until night time, when the traffic died down. Sometimes we'd start shooting at ten o'clock at night – but if a noisy truck went by, that destroyed the take. Usually we didn't start till midnight. One time, 'Mother and Father' Warner came over to the studio; they wanted to see how sound was being done. So, they were put into a couple of rocking chairs on the set where they wouldn't be too much in the way. Right in the middle of a very important take, dear little Mrs Warner started rocking back and forth, and the chair began squeaking, so of course the take was destroyed.

I remember the first sound sequence we shot took place in the café where Jolson is working as a waiter, and I come down the stairs with a party of people and sit at a table. Myrna Loy did a little bit in that scene with me. And he was singing and we were all pounding on the table. Of course he wasn't giving it all he had, in the way of voice, like he would have on the stage, since he was really miming to a playback*. He was still special even so. Most of us connected with the film were disappointed when we first saw it. I don't know if Jolson was or not except that I think he always felt that he could have done better. And then, as I say, the recordings were so squeaky and unreal. They didn't sound like the people who were talking. Of course his singing was something else again . . . because that was a voice that couldn't be mistaken. But the speaking voices, that's what was so bad about it.

It was to take a few more years for this voice to rise to the expectations aroused by it, and for the new cameras to find the flexibility and reclaim the poetry that had been the achievement of its silent parent. But film-makers appreciated that the screen's ability to talk was not necessarily the same as making sense, or being entertaining. More than one of them must have felt like shouting out Lina Lamon't immortal lament, 'I cainnnt ste-e-end it!' But they learnt. The novelty became a necessity.

May McAvoy: Of course after that film came out, and it was such a huge success, everybody realized that they had to know how to talk for pictures, talk dramatically, and there was a great, great *rush* by the studios to sign up everybody who had ever been in the theatre, and many of those of us who had

* Gloria Swanson's memories differ from McAvoy's. Swanson recalled that for *The Trespasser* and *Indiscreet* the orchestra was on the set, and it was not lip-synched.

never done anything but picture work were just eliminated from doing any picture work practically. Everybody knows about Jack Gilbert, but really, women's voices suffered much more than men's, because they sounded just so screechy. Fortunately sound-on-film came along pretty soon after the Vitaphone thing, and that was a great improvement, or maybe there wouldn't have been any stars left. You see, we were all used to dialogue. We had had it in silent pictures; all of my career you had to speak dialogue, and with feeling. The trouble we had wasn't being able to talk, it was with the sound, and the equipment, and because of our limitations as to movement, and the *dialogue* we had to say. The dialogue wasn't exactly what you would like to say. There were times, oh so many, when we rehearsed a scene and the dialogue sounded so stilted and so awful . . ! We would have to sit down and have it all re-written before we shot the scene. Particularly with *The Lion And The Mouse* (WB 1928) which I did after *The Jazz Singer*, and which was an all-talking picture for which they had a lot of stage actors like Lionel Barrymore, Alec Francis, Buster Collier, all of them with stage training except for me, and it was terrible for all of us. You had to work with it until you felt comfortable with it. You had to say, 'I don't like saying that . . . it doesn't mean anything.' You would go into a conference with the writer and they would re-write it till it made a bit more sense.

The companies were rather harsh on some of the people who had worked for years and years and helped build a business for them, and here found themselves used as the guinea pigs of that era. Many of them could have improved by study, or time, or simply with better equipment. That was the worst thing for us – I made seven talking pictures but none with the right kind of sound equipment. You can't blame the studios for wanting to sign up stage names, people who can do dialogue and remember lines, and are used to it; you can't blame them for wanting big names . . . theatre people . . . But they could have been a little bit more patient with their own and given them better breaks because the way it turned out, a lot of the stage stars they brought out to Hollywood didn't do any better. But it was panicky, and it was unfair, because most of the people had fairly normal voices and were intelligent enough to realize that if they didn't know how to project their personalities through their speaking, they could be taught easily enough. At the end of my time at the studio, I was having difficulty with one of the bosses, with Zanuck. I had a great deal of trouble with him, as many people did. I was very unhappy there for that reason, and I wanted out even though my contract still had six more months to go. I didn't want to get into a scandal of any nature, which could have happened because his wife thought that I was trying to get him or something, when all I was trying to do was fight him off all the time. I could tell you stories . . .

Early in 1928 another enterprising American producer, William Fox, had bought a rival sound process along the lines of the sound-on-film technique pioneered by Lee De Forest, which Fox called Movietone. Before the end of the summer the

revolution had taken place. Every studio was busy tearing down old stages and building new ones to accommodate sound equipment. There was to be no turning back, though for the next few years, until the conversion of cinemas to sound could be completed, the studios still released so-called silent films, but which were merely the appalling silent versions of their visually static talkies. These abortions put the final kibosh on any memories or nostalgia people might have retained for the achievements of the silent films. Having made the change at such great and traumatic cost to itself, Hollywood could not allow for any lingering doubts.

When, as late as 1930, Charles Chaplin declared that he would make his new film, *City Lights*, as a silent picture, he spoke as a popular genius unique in his field, who could afford such idiosyncracies. Though many a silent star and director shared his feelings, no one else could afford to risk their belief at the box-office. By 1930 even Garbo had spoken. The argument was purely academic.

In the fiscal year ending 21st August, 1928, Warner Brothers had not yet begun to feel the full financial benefits. However, by the end of 1929 they had the record net profit of $17,271,805 or an increase of 745% over the preceding year. Despite the financial success there were problems to solve. To deal with these, a new figure was introduced to film-making, the sound specialist. It was he who concealed the microphone in the vase of flowers on the boudoir table, who dictated where the camera must be placed in order to keep the microphone out of vision. He was the final arbiter on what could and what could not be done. He controlled the knobs that lowered or raised an actor's voice to an acceptable pitch. Constant adjustments were required due to the microphone's sensitivity; without them, a sudden outburst from a performer could quite easily blast the equipment, a not uncommon occurrence. Stage star Jeanne Eagels' deep tremolo reached a pitch of high emotional intensity for a scene in *Jealousy*, which knocked the equipment completely out of function. Another famous instance had the whizz-bang-wow 'It' girl Clara Bow enter a dormitory and say: 'Hello, everybody.' It recorded as a shattering, fortissimo 'HELLO EVERYBODY!!!'

The Microphone Didn't Kill John Gilbert—

The classic casualty of sound historians cite is John Gilbert. Gilbert, MGM's top male star, had, by the last years of the silent era scaled a phenomenal peak of popularity, comparable to the madness that had surrounded Valentino. Silent, passionately romantic, 20s flappers swooned over him as their children were later to swoon over the Gables, Flynns, Brandos, Presleys and Beatles. The fan magazines, all sixty of them, reported monthly that Jack was fearless, reckless, impetuous, boyish yet virile and mad for love of the mysterious Swede, Garbo. His eloquent silence heightened his gay appeal as audiences were left to imagine the passionate words of love with which he wooed his leading lady, *and* the tone of voice in which he did so. It is doubtful whether any voice could have lived up to the expectations the poor man aroused. The emotional atmosphere surrounding him was too intense not to carry the risk of disaster. It wasn't a voice they were waiting for but a climax to their fantasies.

The role selected for John Gilbert for his talkie debut in *His Glorious Night* (MGM 1930), was that of a stiff, noble, self-effacing, highly romantic Ruritanian lover, a type he had played with great success in a number of his silent hits (*The Merry Widow* as Prince Danilo, *Love* as Vronsky, or the title role in *Bardelys the Magnificent*) where looks and gesture were the all-important requirements needed to convince. But, clearly, it was a type totally unsuited to his basic mid-American, flat, twangy, accent. Irregardless of whether or not one found his voice high or nasal, problems which are correctable, essentially it was a miscasting blunder, on a par with Clark Gable as Parnell, John Wayne as the Mongol war-lord, Genghis Khan, in *The Conqueror*, or Charlton Heston as Michelangelo. Had Ronald Colman, Gilbert's major rival for the title of Great Lover, the English actor remembered today for his reserved, romantic mellifluous English inflections, made his talkies debut in a similar role he might have got away with it, even though the type was no

Above: How they 'sounded'. John Gilbert's, Norma Shearer's and Lon Chaney's voice patterns illustrated in a fan magazine.

Left: Robert Montgomery, MGM's new leading man, receiving instructions about the voice and the sound camera in 1929. Montgomery was one of a number of stage players who went to Hollywood following the advent of talkies.

longer flavour of the year in 1930, even in operettas like *The Vagabond King*. But Colman's boss, Samuel Goldwyn, took no chances with his valuable investment and Colman's first words on the screen were those of hard-hitting Bulldog Drummond, with the audience's sympathy with him from the start, and the type of voice of secondary importance. Colman, of course, went on to become one of the greatest male stars in the history of movies. The question remains why Gilbert's bosses at MGM failed to take more care with their property.

As Gilbert's voice was, had he been presented as a cowboy, a convict, or almost any contemporary American type, his career and his reputation might have taken a very different turn. The mistake in the first place was the role; and then the dialogue he was asked to deliver – a bunch of high-flown sentimental flutterings at a time when a new breed of men were sweeping across the nation's screens, the arrogant, macho gangster who slapped his woman around, drilled holes into his rivals, and spoke faster than his getaway car. As an operetta Prince the cards were stacked against Gilbert. So, why was nothing done? Well, Louis B. Mayer, powerful boss of MGM's west coast studio operations, had a long-standing personal grudge against Gilbert that was no secret. When MGM's east-coast head office, headed by Marcus Loew, signed Gilbert to one of the most lucrative contracts in the studio's history, even before he had made a talking picture, and against the advice and without the knowledge of Mayer, it became a personal challenge to Mayer's authority and aggravated his hatred of Gilbert. But Loew's decision was also based on his knowledge of Gilbert. He had heard Gilbert talk often enough. Gilbert was a very gregarious, outgoing fellow. It suggests that Loew found nothing wrong with Gilbert's voice and didn't want to make the mistake other studios had with valuable stars they had let go, only to find them making a great success in talkies for other studios. But it was a creative decision that went to the heart of the place Mayer considered his own. For Mayer, Gilbert's disaster would confirm his wisdom and forever remove all attempts at outside interference. It would be a blow against the powerful star he hated, against east coast dominance, and a warning which the studio's other employees could not fail to note. Why else would he have OK'd the release of the film when it was clear after the first out-of-town screenings that it would be a disaster? Mayer didn't have to give an order to the sound department to alter Gilbert's voice. All he had to do was to stand by and let the film go out. And nobody could blame him. He hadn't signed the contract for Gilbert's services. He hadn't directed the film. Gilbert was finished as audiences across the nation laughed where they should have swooned.

Further, Hollywood pictures were earning up to 40% of their take in the foreign market. When Garbo's American popularity started to slump soon after 1932, the studio still kept her on the payroll at increased salaries because her films earned so much abroad. And, her voice, in Spain, France, Italy, Russia, even in her native Sweden, was dubbed by other actresses. Those countries never heard *Garbo* talk! Presumably they wouldn't have heard John Gilbert talk either, so his voice, good, bad or indifferent, wouldn't have mattered there.

More typical, yet every bit as final, were the cases of silent stars who seemingly made the hurdle but did not stay the course. Gloria Swanson, another of the legion of diminutive powerhouses to reign in the 20s as a star of the first magnitude, had a triumphant sound debut in *The Trespasser* (1929). The euphoria in *Photoplay* (Dec. 1929) was typical: 'You'll paste this baby in your memory book. Gloria Swanson, in her first all-talkie, is a sensation. The glorious one never looked more beautiful. Her voice does every trick demanded of it and she sings two songs like a meadow-lark! . . . it's an achievement!' Yet, within a few years, Swanson could not get work in a film, and her luck did not change until 1950 and *Sunset Boulevard*. A superb actress and even more enthralling as a personality, she played, brilliantly, a silent star who had already lost herself in delusions before sound came to strand her career in an old house by the wayside. But no one, at the time Swanson's own film career ground to a halt, considered her a casualty of the talkies – just lack of public interest. Or little Mary Pickford (it was an era of little giants), the world's sweetheart, greatest of all silent stars, who even won an Oscar for her sound debut in *Coquette* (1929) but made her last film in 1933. She was considered Hollywood's Queen, but there were few returns at the box-office for her in the talkie era, whether in Shakespeare, in musical roles or in romantic sagas. What might have given some of these fabled careers new life required more than a voice, demanded rather, as with Garbo and Ronald Colman, the revelation of a new personality. Garbo, the sexy challenging temptress of silent films, going about her work of destroying sticky lovers like flies, had little in common with the doom-laden and much-imitated passive creature sound transformed her into. With a voice dipped in the darkness of her soul, loving too much and none too wisely, she was to become one of the most quoted woman of the century, whose threatened 'I tank I go home' and her plaintive, 'I vant to be left alone' were quoted by shopgirls and college professors alike. This role reversal played a vital part in Garbo's continuing popularity. While other silent favourites also survived into the 30s, only Garbo became sublime. Certain fast-rising stars in the last years of the silent era – Joan Crawford and Norma Shearer for instance – moved from carefully chosen talkie debuts to surpass their popularity as silent favourites, because they were still fresh to the public. This applied to such other youngsters as Loretta Young and Constance Bennett, who would become hugely popular stars in the 30s and beyond. Like all the ones who made it they succeeded because they leapt at the new medium with the same eagerness as their public. Their personalities were capable of mirroring the shift in the public's mood. They evolved, filling the slots left by old favourites, with voices whose suitability never even became a question.

Less has been written about the directors who failed to make the transition such as Griffith, Herbert J. Brenon, Marshall Neilan and von Stroheim. While there are other factors too complex to elaborate here, they, like the stars, were to suffer. Time would take care of Griffith and von Stroheim but not so the highly successful Herbert J. Brenon. Every director around was wary of the changeover. One can imagine their minds working overtime in an effort to understand a totally new way of working. It is as if they were suddenly in strait-jackets.

King Vidor, in his autobiography *A Tree is a Tree*: 'The American camera, having just arrived at great flexibility, through the general use of perambulators and counterweighted booms, was being frozen . . . Cinematography had retrogressed to the nailed-down tripod of the early days. The casual spirit of the silent movies disappeared. Draperies were hung in the rafters to muffle sound; to achieve any mobility, cameramen would run four cameras for one take, set at different angles and distances, so that the finished film would seem to have some flow. Sometimes this necessitated ten or twelve changes on the close-up camera in the course of one ten-minute recording.'

Later, directors like Vidor, René Clair, Ernst Lubitsch, and Sergei Eisenstein were to create some of their finest work in sound. The Russian director Pudovkin formulated his thoughts on paper in the autumn of 1929 '. . . It is a new medium which can be used in entirely new ways; sounds and human speech should be used by the directors not as a literal accompaniment, but to amplify and enrich the visual images on the screen. Under such conditions, could the sound film become a new form of art whose future development had no predictable limits?' His conclusions must have been based to a large extent on seeing musicals. What else was there!

100% Talking, 100% Singing, 100% Dancing

Just as 'talkies' were becoming the talk of the country, the Broadway musical had emerged from its doldrums with such hits as *Whopee, Show Boat, Rose Marie, Rio Rita* and the lavish girlie revues. On the tried if not always true principle that nothing succeeds like success, Hollywood latched on to this box-office tonic. Not only were musicals a priority on every studio agenda, but every film, whether a musical or not, had to have a theme song. Costly films completed just before *The Jazz Singer* were pulled out of release and returned to the laboratories for an added musical track to cash in on the vogue.

Laura la Plante, the popular, blonde, bobbed, bubbly silent comedienne of Universal studio, was given her most mature role to date as shy, demure Magnolia Hawks when Universal bought the landmark Jerome Kern musical, *Show Boat*, soon after its opening in 1927, to make it as a lavish, albeit silent, film. Although the songs had become instant classics and might have seemed indivisible from the show's success, the decision to buy it was not that unusual. A lot of musicals and operettas formed the basis of very successful silent films, like *The Merry Widow* and *The Student Prince*. *Show Boat* was a huge hit, orchestras would still be playing the melodies and the story, adapted from Edna Ferber's river-boat saga, was a strong one even without music. But then came sound, and the subsequent decisions, even in the light of the panic of the times, look like examples of dazzling stupidity. Miss la Plante recalled the experience half a century later.

'We had almost finished work on *Show Boat* when we heard that Warner Brothers were coming out with sound. None of us at Universal knew anything about that. Our film had been made silent but it was still in the cutting room, when the news about WB came out. Everybody went to see *The Jazz Singer*, and we realized our film would be lost without sound. And of course it had been a very expensive film to make. So we went back and re-made the last half of it with sound. When the film was released, it was shown with an intermission. The first half was silent, and after the intermission, after you'd have your cup of coffee, or cigarette, you'd come back in and the rest of it was in sound. We couldn't re-shoot it all because in the meantime we'd lost two of the people in the film. One of them, Otis Harlan, our Capt. Andy, had died, and the other, (Alma Rubens who played Julie), was in a mental institution.* The second half wasn't filmed in sound, it was dubbed, using all the people who were available. Of course they had to write special dialogue to fit what we were saying because it wasn't the play exactly. But this was still cheaper than re-shooting it, and re-casting it. I did most of my own singing, though I know they got a woman in to dub some of the songs.

'I don't know now if it wasn't Helen Morgan they were trying to get to dub my singing of 'Bill', because they wanted to mention in the publicity that they had Helen Morgan's voice, and even though I sang 'Bill' in the film, I don't think the studio cared that on the stage that had been Julie's song, and here I was

Laura La Plante and Joseph Schildkraut in the 1929 version of *Show Boat*. The film, a silent, was nearly completed when the success of *The Jazz Singer* persuaded Universal to add sound to the second half.

singing it, and my voice wasn't anything like Helen Morgan's voice. They just wanted to be able to mention that you could hear Helen Morgan's voice. That was all. It didn't make much difference whether she was singing her original part or mine.

'I remember very well spending hours on the sound stages, trying to match up my voice with the movements of the lips on the screen. Of course we all looked a lot more relaxed on the film than a lot of people who were making talkies because we didn't worry about how we sounded while we were making it, and as film was shot as a silent picture we moved easier. The singing didn't worry me that much from what I can remember, because Magnolia wasn't supposed to be a trained singer, she was just this girl on her father's boat, and even in the silent version we did shoot the musical numbers. I mean, I'd be strumming a guitar and singing, except of course if we hadn't added sound you would have heard only the orchestra playing.'

So far so good but ironically, or rather idiotically, with the exception of 'Ole Man River', all the songs dubbed into the film were new, specially written for the film, by Gene Austin ('Look Down That Lonesome Road'), Joseph Cherniavsky ('Love Sings

* Alma Rubens subsequently died of a drugs overdose. According to historian Miles Kreuger, some if not all of Laura La Plante's singing was dubbed by Eva Olivotti. This version was released while the play was still running to packed houses on Broadway and on the road. Ziegfeld, needing money, sold it to Universal, and Universal, also needing a hit, bought it when they thought it would have to be silent. By the time the film was ready for release, and to capitalise on the fame of the Broadway musical that had made stars of its cast (including Helen Morgan, the original star, and Lill La Vene, the coon singer), Universal decided to add an eighteen-minute long prologue which was shot on the Movietone system, and featured five selections by members of the original company. (This may have been where Miss La Plante got the idea that Helen Morgan was connected with her version, though she did not dub for anyone in the film.) It also had short speeches by Universal's chief Carl Laemmle, and the show's producer, Flo Ziegfeld.

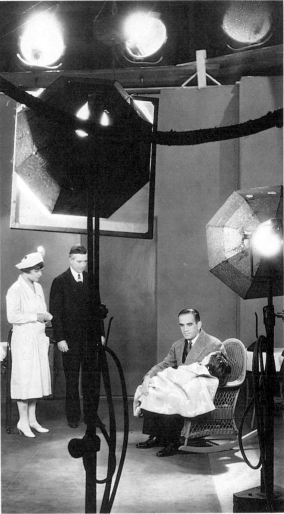

Above: Clara Bow. HELLO EVERYBODY!!

Above right: Al Jolson, with Davey Lee on his lap, in *The Singing Fool*. The star's second film contained 'Sonny Boy' (Jolson sings it in this sequence) which became one of the biggest-selling hits in the history of popular music.

a Song in My Heart') and Billy Rose ('Here Comes That Show Boat'). That such an incredibly stupid decision could arise says more than anything about the naiveté, stupidity and greed motivating the studio chiefs at this unsettled, hair-raising time. It's one thing not to use any songs, it's another to replace the immortal Kern score with totally forgetable, forgotten songs by second-rate composers. The story goes that the fast-talking, bantam theatrical impresario Billy Rose convinced Old Man Laemmle that the public was tired of the songs and he should get himself a new score, with new hits. And Laemmle believed him. No wonder the studio only survived the rest of Laemmle's tenure at the top by producing horror films.

Another, more plausible but equally meretricious reason for the new songs was to do with the majority of the studios' affiliation with music publishing houses, which meant that royalties from songs written specially for films were paid to the studios. If that was the case here, Laemmle still came a cropper since the new songs failed to find an audience. Nevertheless, here was another gold mine. Not only did the addition of a musical score on the soundtrack help unreleased silent films, but the songs would have a life of their own apart from the film.

Wings, a superior aviation drama starring Clara Bow and Gary Cooper, was generally conceded to have added an extra million dollars to its box office takings through the addition of a musical score. Others benefited enormously from having

such songs as 'Diane' *(Seventh Heaven)*, 'Charmaine' *(What Price Glory?)*, 'Jeanine, I Dream of Lilac Time' *(Lilac Time)* written for them. Many, like 'Ramona', from the film of the same name, became standards outliving the fame of the films that fathered them. No one had been too wild about the film of *Ramona* when it was made. Then the publicity man on the picture came up with the idea of a special song. What he wanted was a special melody, with special words, titled after the picture, dedicated to the star, Dolores Del Rio, and to be used with the showing in such a way as to become part of it. The result was the Wayne and Gilbert song which got much of the credit for the film's million-and-a-half at the box-office. From popular standards to the ludicrous was a short step. The song for Ronald Colman's talkie, *Condemned* was 'The Song of the Condemned'; for Clara Bow's *The Wild Party* audiences got 'My Wild Party Girl'; Mary Pickford got Irving Berlin to write her a song of the same name for her first talkie, *Coquette*. For Corinne Griffith's 'silent with sound' costume drama, *Divine Lady*, Joseph Pasternak, later to gain fame as the producer of Deanna Durbin and Kathryn Grayson musicals, wrote 'Lady Divine'. For Cecil B. DeMille's directorial sound debut, *Dynamite*, a story set in condemned cells and the bottom of coalpits, somebody suggested 'Dynamite, Dynamite, Blow Back My Sweetie To Me', which mercifully was not used. Instead he had Dorothy Parker and Jack King pen the standard 'How Am I To Know?', though its insertion into the film was

almost as funny as the song he didn't use. While the condemned man gets married to a rich socialite the night before his electrocution, a prisoner in the adjoining cell, with convenient guitar, sings the song. The singer was Russ Colombo, making his unbilled film debut. For Norma Talmadge's sound-adapted silent flick, *Woman Disputed* (1928), the tunesmiths penned 'Woman Disputed, I Love You.' At the height of the craze, Hollywood wags suggested that the song for Norma Shearer's talkie debut, *The Trial of Mary Dugan*, should be 'Mary Dugan, You're a Trial to Me.'

Songwriting for pictures turned every Hollywood writer into a 'production writer'. Instead of groping for ideas before turning out a number, the writer was given situations by the film's director and the scenarist, who could tell him in advance what they wanted the lyrics to convey. Even so, definite ideas were not always available, or else the producer could not express them. A Paramount producer, for example, simply told Al Bryan and R. Whiting, 'We've got a picture called *Wolf Song*. It's all about a man on a mountain; write a song for it.' From this came 'Yo Te Amo', warbled by Lupe Velez and 'Wolf Song' roared by Gary Cooper and the mountaineers. Lyricist Arthur Freed also recalled '. . . they came to us' (Freed and Brown) 'and asked us for a song for this picture which was called *The Pagan* (MGM 1929), so we called the song 'The Pagan Love Song' for Ramon Novarro to sing. Our music publisher, Jack Robinson, said: "What the hell is a pagan?" It sold 1,600,000 copies in the US alone.'

There were other profitable spin-offs to musicals. The first song written to be sung as part of a film was 'Mother, I Still Have You' for *The Jazz Singer*. It was written by Louis Silvers and Al Jolson. Had the number been released a year later, by which time the studios had learnt to exploit this new gold mine, its sheet music sale could easily have been from 300,000 to 500,000 copies instead of 30,000. The reason for the small sales was the small number of theatres equipped for sound at the time of the picture's release.

But a year later, 'Sonny Boy' (sung by Jolson in *The Singing Fool*), swept the country and became one of the greatest sellers in the history of popular music. Everybody made money out of this song which originated when Jolson called De Sylva, Brown and Henderson (*The Best Things in Life are Free*, starring Gordon McRae, Ernest Borgnine and Dan Dailey. 20th Century Fox, 1957) long distance to tell them that he needed a heart-tugging song to sing to his child. Four hours later they sang this number to him on the phone. Repeated use of it, (especially the emotional climax that had Jolson singing it in the hospital to his dying 'Sonny Boy', helped boost the record sales over the two million mark in only a few months.* Warners quickly bought up a major publishing firm, Whitmarks Inc., lock, stock and barrel. For the complete rights to the firm's catalogue of past hits and rights to future publications, Warners paid over $5,000,000. Fox signed up composers De Sylva, Brown and Henderson and bought out their publishing company. MGM made similar deals with the Jack Robbins Music Co.

* For most Europeans, the first Jolson 'talkie' they saw was not *The Jazz Singer*, but *The Singing Fool*. The film's impact, or rather that of Jolson's personality, would remain for an age part of their lifelong memories. When Simone de Beauvoir wrote her autobiography, she would recall seeing the film with Sartre, and when it was over, deeply moved, she turned to Sartre and found that there were tears in his eyes.

In spite of perplexing difficulties with sound apparatus and the resultant shortcomings in the films, Will Hays, Czar of Hollywood, could announce that picture attendance in the USA had increased by 15,000,000 weekly in 1929, due to the enormous popularity of sound films. For a time it seemed as if every second film was a musical as studios outdid themselves in proclaiming their films to be ALL TALKING – ALL SINGING – ALL DANCING – ALL COLOUR.

Faces with *voices* were brought from the Broadway stage. The actress Ruth Chatterton, whose career had been tobogganing, became, overnight, the screen's first lady because of her beautiful voice. Fan magazines devoted articles to voices: 'The Screen Goes Baby Talk' (Helen Kane's Boop-Oop-e-Doop) and 'The Sexy Voice' (actress Ann Harding). Fredric March, Miriam Hopkins, Bette Davis, Spencer Tracy, James Cagney and Joan Blondell were some who went West and stayed to become screen idols. That old cry, 'Where will all the new stars come from?' had found an immediate and prosperous reply. But no other area of the legitimate stage was as depleted by Hollywood offers as the musical-comedy. For a giddy time it appeared as if a pretty face and voice were all that was needed to make a movie star.

Among those recruits were Alexander Gray and Bernice Claire, Vivienne Segal and Walter Pidgeon, Irene Bordoni, Jack Buchanan, Maurice Chevalier, Jeanette MacDonald, George Jessel (who, after turning down *The Jazz Singer*, then made a similar though not as successful film, *Lucky Boy*, in 1929), Ziegfeld favourites like Eddie Cantor and Fanny Brice (*Funny Girl*, starring Barbara Streisand. Columbia, 1968). John Boles, who'd left Broadway three years earlier for silent films came into his own with musicals and seemed to be in every film that

George Jessel, the star of the stage play, *The Jazz Singer*. He was to have repeated the part in the film but Al Jolson replaced him. Jessel is seen here in a Vitaphone short, *The Lyin' Tamer*.

didn't have Joe E. Brown or Jack Oakie. Ethel Merman and Ginger Rogers made features and shorts in New York studios long before either one admitted to being in films. Jimmy Durante, who co-starred with Helen Morgan (*The Helen Morgan Story*, starring Ann Blyth. Warner Bros, 1957) in *Roadhouse Nights* (1930), was a recruit from the night clubs. So were Texas Guinan (*Incendiary*

Blonde, starring Betty Hutton. Paramount, 1945), Harry Richman and Sophie Tucker. Radio sent Kate Smith, 'The Songbird of the South'. All of these had a brief go at musicals.

Whatever their merits, and most of them are justly forgotten, these films provided a great deal of work. In one musical hundreds of extras, including 150 dancing girls, worked steadily for five months . . . in another nearly 500 ensemble girls were used. *The Film Daily Year Book* for 1930 stated that the American Film Company employed more people than Ford and General Motors. Commenting on the Broadway capitulation to Hollywood money, *Photoplay* (Oct. 1929) gloated: 'With every train pulling into Los Angeles, several carloads of New York stage people, actors, playwrights, songwriters, or what you can offer, shake the dust of the Mojave from Fifth Avenue habiliments, hop into a taxi and start for Hollywood. There are more than 2,000 Broadway-ites here now, and every day brings in a new invasion . . . Not since the days of '49 has there been such a rush to the coast.' When even the master showman of the American Theatre, the legendary impresario Florenz Ziegfeld (*The Great Ziegfeld*, starring William Powell. MGM, 1936) left Broadway to go to Hollywood, it must have seemed as if New York's day as the nation's arbiter of the arts was truly over.

When Hollywood beckoned, Ziegfeld greeted the opportunity with open arms and grandiose plans inspired 'by all that great outdoors there for sets . . .' His deal was with the equally astute, and creative film-producer, Samuel Goldwyn. Ziggie was to supervise films based on a number of his great successes and to maintain the high standard he was famous for on Broadway. An interview Ziegfeld gave to the critic of *Dance* magazine prior to his departure makes it apparent that he saw movies as nothing more than more lavish opportunities for his sort of thing. 'This will be largely because I will have the whole outdoors at my disposal for backgrounds. Besides, my sets will be larger than could be placed on any stage but I am not going to follow a similar scheme in fixing up the size of my company and go in for numbers that might properly be classed as mobs . . . As in the past I am not going to rest content with the beautiful girls who have already danced for me. I shall always be on the lookout for new girls who possess the good looks

Right: Samuel Goldwyn greets Florenz Ziegfeld upon his arrival in Hollywood.

Broadway stars flocked to Hollywood to appear in musicals. Left to right: Sophie Tucker in *Honky Tonk*. Helen Morgan, star of *Applause*. Gertrude Lawrence in *The Rage of Paris*. A brunette Ginger Rogers, hardly out of her teens. Fanny Brice in *Be Yourself*.

my standard demands. Some very beautiful and talented girls have come to me from dancing schools. I expect to obtain many more from the same source. And you can expect, repeat, they don't have to be able to sing a note.'

Goldwyn had bought the successful Eddie Cantor stage musical *Whoopee!* (UA 1930) from Flo Ziegfeld. Cantor, *(The Eddie Cantor Story,* starring Keefe Braselle. Warner Bros, 1953), who had already appeared in several talking shorts like *That Party in Person* (1929) was to repeat his Broadway success. Although musicals were on the downward swing of the pendulum Cantor, like Jolson, was an enormously popular musical and comedy star, and this was to be his launch in the Talkies. His musical had been a gigantic hit when it opened in 1927. Songs like 'Making Whoopee' and 'Love Me or Leave Me' (which wasn't in the film) were on everybody's lips, and it was to have the touch of the legendary Flo Ziegfeld. If that was not enough, the film was also to be shot in colour, although by now that too, like musicals, had begun to pall on the public. The early two-strip Technicolor had created some aesthetic and beautiful surrealistic moments but on the whole, with the colour fluctuations from orange to green at any given moment and on any part of the screen, colour had ceased to seem wondrous and became an irritating distraction as one saw a red-

faced performer switching to Martian green and back again. On the adage 'In for a penny, in for a pound' Goldwyn added to his million-dollar production by bringing the Los Angeles born Broadway dance director, Busby Berkeley, back out to stage the numbers for the film.

It is the colour, Eddie Cantor, the songs, and to a lesser degree the production numbers that make the film more than a passing curio. The colour camera revealed a succession of breathtaking Maxfield Parrish sunsets and skies of vermilion hues, saffron yellows and periwinkle blues, across which scantily dressed maids on horseback, trailing lavish feather head-dresses down their bare backs to the ground beneath their ponies' hoofs, rode up a mountain path for the sake of a ravishing tableau.

Berkeley's contribution to his first film effort was, on the whole, a muted forerunner of what he was to become famous for. His imagination needs the gigantic sets and acres of girls and gadgets to stun and dazzle. Ten people on the march is a rag-bag. One thousand coming at you is an army – powerful, imposing, threatening and . . . dazzling. Berkeley understood that when he took away the threat and simultanously upped the exhilaration by turning men in uniforms into platoons of half-naked, soft, smiling playgirls, undulating in precision towards the camera. Added to this restriction was the fact that the camera, with which Berkeley dances, was then still in its box, able to photograph movement but not to move itself. All Berkeley could do was to have his girls (including a nubile pre-teen Betty Grable and willowy Virginia Bruce) moving before the camera, into the close-up, and then stepping smartly out of frame. Although the effect was a bit jerky, it was the forerunner of the time when his camera was mounted on a monorail and moved in smooth, long, flowing takes along endless rows of girls, standing on different levels and grouped in intricate patterns. Even so, most of Busby's effects, such as the overhead shots of girls to resemble flowers opening out to the dawn, were included. Movies were clearly his scene.

The film's other plus was Cantor, the only member of the cast who didn't speak his lines as if translating from a foreign language – with vowels round, consonants sharp, voice teachers proud and drama dead. And if there's one thing musical comedy plots need more than anything, it's speed. *Whoopee!* is quite silly, shockingly racial and allows for flagrant and very gay sexual innuendo, especially in the Cantor character, a hypochondriac who goes west with a wagon load of pills to cure himself, but who leaps in terror, rolls his eyes and flaps his wrist at the tread of a boot and the sight of a gun. He's a compendium of Jerry Lewis clichés, but with a singing voice that allowed him to go solo. The woman to catch this man was the energetic, high kicking, Ethel Shutta, with a face like a friendly blonde slab of concrete. The subplot concerns an Indian half-caste who loves a maiden but renounces her because of his drop of Indian blood. When the old Indian chief who raised him as his own tells him that he was actually a foundling, the son of white parents, thus not an Indian and so eligible to marry a white girl, his joy is unconfined. Not very nice.

The musical slump was not halted but *Whoopee!* was a great success and Eddie Cantor, Busby Berkeley and Samuel Goldwyn were all to go on to greater fame, which shows that if you do something you believe in and do it well, there'll always be an audience to appreciate it. For Ziegfeld it was the end of a great career, for he died before he could work on any more films. Meanwhile at studios run by executives less imaginative than Goldwyn, the lavish all-star revues they were turning out, (*Hollywood Revue of 1929: Glorifying the American Girl* (1929) . . . and all the *Broadway Melodies, Big Broadcasts, Vogues, Fashions* and *Follies* to come), were based on the Ziegfeld formula. Flo, always the showman, had in fact gotten his idea as a result of a visit to the Folies Bergère but on his return to the States he made of it a totally American art form. It was this highly-charged mixture of ravishing, statuesque girls, comics, and sets to dazzle the Sun King himself, which Hollywood adopted. The

Above: Musical numbers took some strange forms in the early sound days. A production shot from MGM's *March of Time*.

Right: Paramount's *Glorifying the American Girl*, à la Ziegfeld. The American boy gets a fair showing too – note pre-Tarzan Johnny Weissmuller, the boy holding the net.

principle was that bigger was better. Unemployment was rife. Salaries were low. The unions were weak. Like the Pharaohs in good old pre-Moses Egypt, they built a lot of pyramids.

The Irish concert favourite, John McCormack, who had never made a film, was paid $80,000 for ten weeks work on *Song o' My Heart* (Fox 1930). Though beautifully directed by Frank Borzage, it failed with the public, whose romantic fantasies when hearing McCormack on records were dampened by the vision of a nice, beefy middle-aged man.

Warner Brothers brought out another Ziegfeld superstar at $100,000 dollars per film. Her name was Marilyn Miller (*Look for the Silver Lining*, starring June Haver. Warner Bros, 1947). Marilyn, a Broadway legend in her own right and the highest paid dancer in the land, was to repeat her stage success, *Sally* (1929), for the grand fee of $1,000 dollars an hour for a 100 hours of work. Although *Sally* was a success of sorts her next two, *Sunny* (1930) and *Her Majesty Love* (1931), were not. They were typical of the kind of films that were to bring Warners to its knees again. On the evidence of *Her Majesty Love*, her last film, one will never know what made Marilyn Miller such a hugely popular star on Broadway. But star she was. So what went wrong? She had the likeable Ben Lyon and another Ziegfeld star, W. C. Fields, (*W. C. Fields and Me*, starring Rod Steiger. Warner Bros, 1976), for support. No, the curious thing is that Warners, having fetched out the dancing star, gave her, unbelievably, one dance, a tango and not a very good one at that. What did *Her Majesty Love* have to offer? Part of the trouble lay with the all too literal adaptation of the successful German film, *Ihre Majestät die Liebe*, directed by Joe May, and redirected in Hollywood by the German emigrant, Wilhelm Dieterle. The story opens in a Berlin nightclub. The feel of the scene, indeed of the whole film, is stolidly Germanic because Dieterle copied the original version shot by shot but lost its charming insouciance. The latter was often the case with foreign films re-made in Hollywood. But the

object of the exercise was to eliminate any competition from the original when it was released in America.

Far left: Marilyn Miller in the film of *Sunny*, one of her stage successes. *Her Majesty, Love* was adapted from a German musical, *Ihre Majestät, Liebe*, but it realized none of Miss Miller's particular talents and she made no more films.

Above: Corrine Griffith in the sound remake of one of her silent successes, *Lilies of the Field*. In a ballet-mechanique sequence Miss Griffith graced a gigantic automobile as a radiator cap.

The finale of *Gold Diggers of Broadway* (1929). Winnie Lightner, Ann Pennington, Lilyan Tashman and chorus. The original sequence was in colour.

As situation comedies go *Her Majesty Love* was tyical Lubitsch fare, with the sort of characters he would have loved, and the dialogue his films sparkled with. Says the grandmother to her spend-thrift grandson when he complains about his lack of funds: 'In my day, young men with debts married women with money.' Or the father, a juggling Fields who has to put on his glasses to hear, reassuring his worried daughter about marriage to a rich bald-headed old rou: 'One rich old man is worth two rich young men.'

But Dieterle, who was to make his mark with the verbose biographical film series, was no Lubitsch. It is hard to understand why WB wasted the talents of the expensive Marilyn Miller on *Her Majesty Love*, and ended her film career with it. Perhaps they saw the light. Perhaps the public's lack of interest in so many of their dull, stagebound musicals and in high-priced stage stars made them panic and cut the songs and dances so necessary to her appeal. Whatever, despite some radiantly lovely close-ups, here again is one of those cases of a Broadway legend whose unique and special gifts didn't ignite on the screen. Surprisingly – especially to the heads of studios – some of the most successful early sound stars proved to be silent film favourites like Bebe Daniels and Bessie Love, whose careers had been almost written off by the industry.

Miss Daniels, a star since her early teens, had quickly progressed from being Harold Lloyd's leading lady in one and two-reel comedies to become one of the most popular comediennes of the twenties. When the mike panic hit Hollywood, the studio executives disposed of many of their high-priced stars without even testing their voices. Paramount's production head, B. P. Schulberg, failed to pick up options on Thomas Meighan and Richard Dix (both of whom would continue their careers in films) and Bebe Daniels. Justifiably hurt and furious at the treatment from her home studio, she bought out the remaining ten months left of her contract and accepted an offer to work for former Paramount producer, William Le Baron, now the production head at the newly-formed RKO. She had a triumph. In an interview with Miss Daniels and her husband, Ben Lyon, in London, 1966, she recalled:

'I was waiting for a script to start working under my RKO contract when I heard that they were pre-paring *Rio Rita*. So I asked Bill to let me have the part. He was completely taken aback by this. "But you can't sing," he said. "How do you know I can't? Try me. Give me a test." I had the same voice teacher as Jeanette MacDonald – Grace Newell. They were pleased with the test, and I got the part. I wasn't afraid of sound. I knew I could talk.'

According to Ben Lyon: 'RKO couldn't afford her for the part at her contracted salary – which had

Right: Sound had arrived but the perfection of details took some time. Jean Arthur as a young Paramount contract player scrubbing clothes for the microphone.
Below: Betty Compson's talents as a violinist proved useful in the new medium. They also helped her emote; here she plays favourite airs while her producer reads her lines from the script.

been for Bebe to make comedies like the ones she had been doing at Paramount, in which her salary was often the biggest budget item. To play in *Rio Rita*, a lavish and costly production for the new company, Bebe took a terrific salary cut, but in turn was to be paid a percentage: 10% above the first one-and-a-quarter-million gross. Nobody expected it to do much more than $750,000 or $1,000,000. The film turned out to be one of their highest-grossing productions and made a fortune for all concerned.'

Press and public were enthusiastic: *Photoplay* (November 1929): 'In practically every respect, it is the finest of the screen musicals . . . Despite very strong competition, Bebe Daniels is the most glowing personality. Her voice, untrained as it is, has a rich quality which an experienced prima donna might well envy. Her performance is colourful, and she appears lovelier than she has for years. *Rio Rita* will revive Bebe's great popularity.'

Bebe Daniels: We shot it in twenty-four days. Now they take six months to shoot a film and are pleased when they get a minute-and-a-half of screen time at the end of the day. Half of the film was shot in an early colour process, the first half being in black and white, and they had an intermission between the two halves when they road-showed it. We shot some of it on location, which created its share of problems. They had mikes planted all over. We'd be sitting near a potted plant, inside which they'd hidden a mike. We'd say our lines, then get up to move, not saying anything else until we had walked over to the next spot where a mike had been placed. The musical numbers were shot ordinarily like the rest of the film. My second cousin was Lee De Forest, the father of sound, and he used to come on the set and was always doing things to the microphone, moving mikes around to better positions and that sort of thing.

We did have some problems with the mikes! It was all direct recording. Watching the results of a day's shooting, we thought that a humming bird had got into my mike; whenever I opened my mouth out came this hum. Since I was no good at synchronizing my voice to the movements of my lips, we had to re-shoot the scene. The thing that threw me at first, working with sound, was the absence of noise. We were so used to the whirring of the cameras and the small orchestra playing nearby to provide mood music while we worked in silent films. Sometimes, when we were rehearsing a scene for a silent film, we'd ask the cameraman to turn on an empty camera so we'd have the whirring sound we were used to. Of course with the early sound films the mikes could not be directed to pick up only what sound was wanted; they'd pick up anything, so we had to be very quiet unless we were doing a scene.

Working behind the scenes on *Rio Rita* was the dress designer, Walter Plunkett, who had begun a career that was to make him one of the greatest in his field. His credits include: *Mary of Scotland*, *The Gay Divorcee*, *Little Women*, *Gone With the Wind*, *Duel in the Sun*, *The Story of Vernon and Irene Castle*, *Madame Bovary*, *Summer Holiday*, *An American in Paris*, *Singin' in the Rain* and *Seven*

Above: The camera crane for Universal's spectacular film set for the stage hit, *Broadway*. It weighed 28 tons and was noiseless in operation. The scene was not.

Left: Bebe Daniels was not only beautiful and a versatile actress – she could sing. Paramount didn't know that when they dropped her in the early panic caused by sound. RKO reaped a rich reward when that studio starred her in the musical, *Rio Rita*.

Brides for Seven Brothers.

'Well, anything with music went. Betty Compson could play a violin, so she never stopped making movies in the early sound days. She used to finish a film on one lot, pack her bags and go on to the next studio. She had it in her contracts that her shooting time should never exceed two weeks so that she could go on to the next film. Of course, Betty was also a very talented actress, and she originally came from the stage, so she had no trouble talking. But they tried everything if it made sound. They were also experimenting with colour then.' (In 1929 there were colour sequences in at least sixty feature films, mostly in musicals like *On With the Show* and *Gold Diggers of Broadway*). 'Half of *Rio Rita* was in this two-tone system, and since the colours consisted of either a very bright red or a deep shrill blue tone, it made designing for them difficult. There were so many colours you couldn't use because they wouldn't come out right. We couldn't use yellow because it turned out looking like muddy brown. They only had one colour camera at RKO and they were already shooting another film in colour, so they had to shoot *Rio Rita* sequences at night. I was in charge of the wardrobe on both films, so I just moved into my bungalow on the lot in order to be on hand. *Rio Rita* had been a smash on Broadway, and had cost them quite a lot. To us humble workers, Bebe Daniels was a big star from Paramount. Nobody, as far as I recall, knew that she had had a tiff with them. That sort of thing doesn't always travel as quickly as people might think.

'The effect of the mikes could be felt all over, right down to the wardrobe. We had to use special fabrics for the costumes, because these mikes would pick up any sound and distort it terribly. Beaded dresses had to be kept to a minimum and couldn't be full. We could only use them on very tight dresses and even then, often a thin net was sewn over them to make certain they didn't clang or anything. We couldn't use taffeta because it made such a noise. Instead, by rubbing it together under a mike, they used it for simulating earthquake sounds and fires. With hoopskirts which were needed for *Dixiana* we had great troubles. Petticoats made from silk would rustle too much, so they had to be made out of felt and wool. It was really just like *Singin' in the Rain'* (MGM 1951).

'Shoes had to be specially covered with felt and rubber, since without them Bebe would have sounded like an onrushing herd of buffalo when she tiptoed on the set. We had trouble with fans. *Rio Rita* had Bebe using one often as a Mexican señorita. We had to make one specially, so that it wouldn't clatter, and shatter the mike every time she closed it or tapped John Boles with it. When you walked on those sets, and we only did when we were called to account for something, the tensions were fantastic. You had to remain absolutely silent so as not to spoil a take. If you moved at all, there'd be nasty glances from everybody. It was continuous chaos. The expense of converting old stages was great, and the sets were closed down while this was happening. In the middle of it the Depression came. Budgets were slashed. Salaries halved. A lot of stars priced themselves out of the business back then.'

Rio Rita's real success meant that during 1929 and 1930 the market would be flooded with more of the same, though not always as thoughtfully made: *The Vagabond King, The Desert Song, The Rogue Song* (Lawrence Tibbett's spectacular debut), *Sunny, Sally, Golden Dawn, Viennese Nights, New Moon* (Lawrence Tibbett's spectacular flop), *Married in Hollywood, Song of the Flame* . . . with neither end nor progress in sight as production heads remained happy to sell films on the legend, 'From the Broadway hit of the same name', long after the public had grown weary of them.

However, a musical cycle evolved at this time that was indigenous to film – the 'back-stage' musical. While it revolved around Broadway and the music business it came from the movies and dealt with the mystique attached to these arenas in wholly cinematic terms. The man responsible for launching

Left, above: Bebe Daniels and John Boles in *Rio Rita*.

Below: Bebe Daniels and Douglas Fairbanks, Snr. in *Reaching for the Moon.*

Right: Song writers Arthur Freed and Nacio Herb Brown with stars Anita Page and, sitting on the piano, Bessie Love. Miss Page was to become Mrs Brown. The plot of *The Broadway Melody* simply developed from conversations between Freed, Brown and Irving Thalberg.

this trend was MGM's creative production chief, Irving Thalberg, when he gave two young song-writers, lyricist Arthur Freed and composer Nacio Herb Brown, the go-ahead to write a number of original songs for Metro's first sound film, *The Broadway Melody* (1929). In keeping with the studio's high opinion of itself, it had to appear to be not only bigger and better but more original than anything anybody anywhere else was doing. The truth was more charmingly improvisational. Although it grossed more than $4,000,000 (at a time when the average admission was 35 cents, compared to more than twenty times that amount today) it had cost a mere $280,000 to produce and, irregardless of the publicity hype, it was never considered by the powers that be to be anything more than a trial run.

To show just how little MGM thought of its chances, the film's only name player, Bessie Love, whom critics singled out for 'giving the most astounding performance in months' and who was nominated for an Oscar for her role as the elder of the two sisters in love with the same man, had been considered washed up in Hollywood. She was still only in her twenties, a veteran whose notable career as leading lady of silent films began with a role in D. W. Griffith's *Intolerance* (1915), and continued over the next fifteen years in a number of other celebrated films, including *The Lost World, Human Wreckage,* and *Lovey Mary.*

'When the offer came from MGM I had just done a sixteen-week variety tour. I had a very clever agent who decided to try me for the stage during one of my down periods in films. I had had quite a few of those and, instead of trying to get me parts in films, he thought it might be a good idea to take a different direction altogether, and do a musical comedy in New York. The variety tour was a break-in, testing ground for that. At about this time, somebody at MGM, Thalberg possibly, wanted me to do a test for *The Broadway Melody.* My agent and I both refused. I had done enough films for them to know

my work, and if they wanted to hear me they could see me in the variety show. Still, Metro insisted on the test, and while I was against it, my agent wisely booked me into Grauman's Egyptian Theatre for a week, and they saw me there. In the meantime, I did *The Swelled Head,* a two reeler with sound, for Warner Brothers with Eddie Foy Jr., and subsequently did the test and got the part.

'Our director, Harry Beaumont ("tickled, teased and whipped it into a fast, funny, sad little story, alive with titters and tears" wrote a critic in *Photoplay),* had already directed a few sound films for Vitaphone [Warner Brothers]. Arthur Freed, who wrote the songs, had been a beau of mine a few years before. Of course, at this point a great many of the sound problems with the mike hadn't been ironed out. I remember listening to the playback of one scene, and we heard this echo in the background. So the sound experts said, "Everybody out!" They laid carpets and covered the entire area with nails. Back we went and reshot the scene; listened to the playback. The echo was still there. So out we went, in they came, hanging the place with heavy curtains and material to drown the echo. Playback, echo, out; they added something else, until finally they got it as good as they possibly could. Mind you, all this time, the sound equipment was being improved literally week by week, so that the end of *The Broadway Melody* sounded much better than the beginning, but Thalberg decided against any more reshooting because of the cost and time.'

Like Bessie, her old beau was another of Thalberg's strokes of genius. Arthur Freed, who would eventually found the most celebrated musical unit in Hollywood and who displayed a genius for spotting talent that made him a legend in his own time, was then earning a living around Hollywood as half of a successful song-writer team with composer Nacio Herb Brown. Thalberg heard of Freed through one of his top writers, Ralph Spence, who was also a friend of Arthur's. In one of his last interviews, Freed took time out from his orchids to tell me:

'Irving was talking about doing a musical and had asked Ralph to bring Herb and me over to the studio to discuss some ideas. It was all that simple – we talked, he liked our ideas, and we started working on the film. It was supposed to be called *Whoopee,* but we couldn't use that title because Ziegfeld had it, so I came up with *The Broadway Melody,* which was the title for one of the songs we wrote him for the film. Then we wrote the project around it, about those two sisters in love with the same song and dance man. A funny thing – Irving told us that since none of us knows anything about making musical motion pictures we'll just experiment with this and not spend much money. It ended up playing fifty-three weeks at the Astor and winning the first Academy Award. I used a lot of the problems we had while making it when we made *Singin' in the Rain* years later. We didn't know how to get the sound in – we were on step ladders – everything you could think of – holding mikes over people's heads while trying not to be seen until some guy fell from his perch into the set. The cameras weren't quiet, so

they had to be kept in an airtight box and you couldn't pan or move the camera. So we came across the idea of prerecording, otherwise you would have had the sound coming from the camera and the music from the orchestra at the same time and the whole thing making such a ruckus. This way we could get a bit of movement into the pictures. The whole thing was ad-lib. The script was pretty much like that – we just went along day by day and tried what we thought was right for the story. We didn't see too much of Irving because he was doing so much all over the studio, and you couldn't ever get to see him, least not when you thought, but he was wonderful. Whenever there was a major decision to make, he made it. He was in New York when we were shooting the big number, 'The Wedding of the Painted Doll'. When he got back and saw it and didn't like it, he told us to reshoot it, and since colour was also being tried out, he told us to do it in colour – so that's the only colour sequence in the film. But basically his feeling about the picture was that it was an experiment, and if we got it all right, why then we'd make a good one. With all the song hits we had from that and our next one, *Hollywood Revue*, for which we wrote 'Singin' in the Rain', we made so much money out of royalties that year, probably more than anyone else in the studio, that we took a year off and I went to Europe. Before I left Irving took me aside and said, "Arthur, you can be here as long as I'm here."'

Bessie Love recalls: 'Things were happening so fast. When we were doing the musical number for *The Broadway Melody*, the orchestra was playing right along with us; it was all direct recording. By the time we got to the end of the film we recorded the musical numbers first and then acted to them on playback, like they do now. Word had come down to us that

Above: Bessie Love in a dramatic scene, having sacrificed her chance of happiness to her sister, from *The Broadway Melody*. Sound may have been primitive, the camera may have been static; but Miss Love as the self-sacrificing half of a sister act overcame all problems with her tremendously effective performance. The human factor remains timeless.

Left: Broadway shows *The Broadway Melody* at the Astor, where it ran for over a year.

Stage and cabaret performers continued to augment the movie talents in film musicals in the early years. Left, below: *The Cocoanuts* saw the debut of the four Marx Brothers (Harpo had appeared briefly in a silent, *Too Many Kisses*). Zeppo is on the left, next to Kay Francis. Far right is the gallant Margaret Dumont, the sublime foil for the brothers' anarchic humour. Left, bottom: Alexander Grey and Bernice Claire in *No, No, Nanette*. Far left: Walter Pidgeon, baritone, in *Bride of the Regiment*.

Thalberg and Mr Mayer had seen the rushes and were very pleased with the film. The first rushes we saw were of a scene where I opened an envelope with a card inside, and after reading it, ripped it in half. When we heard the sound of the card being torn we were surprised and excited. It was all still such a novelty, hearing the noises one made on the screen.

'After the success of *The Broadway Melody*, I was cast in nothing but musicals [*Good News, Chasing Rainbows. They Learned About Women, Hollywood Revue of 1929*]. In *Hollywood Revue,* we all just did sketches and bits. They wanted everybody at MGM to do something they had never done before. They asked me if I had ever done an acrobatic dance. I told them I hadn't. So they said, "O.K. You're doing an acrobatic dance!" And it was fun! Charles Reisner directed it all, to the best of my knowledge, and Sammy Lee staged the musical numbers, as he had for *The Broadway Melody*.

'At the same time we had no unions, and we were worked all hours. That was really terrible; to get the film out before anybody else could beat them to it, we worked day and night. The film had a four-week shooting schedule, and we would have to be on the set ready and made-up to shoot at 9 a.m., and we wouldn't finish till about 9 or 10 at night. They just didn't know anything at all about making films. They would move us about like so many pieces on a chess board. I remember hearing that one of them, supervising a sequence being shot for a film on the next stage, yelled, 'Would you tell that blonde lady to move away from there. Tell that blonde to move!' *That* blonde was Garbo.'

Hollywood Revue (director, Charles Reisner) was also nominated at the time of its release for an Oscar. Another screen first, though hardly original, it was instantly carbon-copied by every other studio in town. The all-star movie has always been a sure formula for success. MGM boasted more stars than are in heaven and *Hollywood Revue* featured most of them; otherwise it was like *Fox Movietone Follies, Show of Shows* (Warner), *Paramount on Parade*, and Universal's spectacular *The King of Jazz*, for which they filmed the introductory dialogue sequences in *seven* languages including Japanese. Besides the all-star casts, they all had colour sequences, incredibly large and sometimes imaginative sets – such as the Erté-inspired Jewel Box number in *Hollywood Revue of 1929*, and the black and white Larry Ceballos-created dance number in *Show of Shows*, and of course the hundreds of pretty young things.

For the first of the big *Hollywood Revue* numbers Bessie Love is pulled out of master of ceremonies Jack Benny's pocket, and with Bessie sitting in his hand they chat before singing 'I Could Never Do A Thing Like That!' Another sketch with trick photography has teeny-weeny Marion Davies in travesty, stepping gaily out from under the legs of a male chorus decked out in the uniforms of the British Household Cavalry, singing 'Tommy Atkins On Parade'. Jack Benny is the link between the acts that parade everybody of note under contract (including songwriters for one of the numbers), except Lon Chaney and Garbo. As it was one had Marie Dressler, Polly Moran, Buster Keaton and

Jack Benny in a comedy number entitled 'For I'm The Queen'; while another elaborate number features the great stone face at the bottom of the ocean, doing a hootchie-kootch before the elaborate tableau of jewels that preceded it.

Whatever the content, the camera varies little beyond close-up, medium-long shot and long shot. Most of the sequences appear to have been filmed in a single set-up. There are some awkward though encouraging attempts at unexpected angles that must have had the sound-experts up in arms, including overhead shots of the Albertina Rasch ballet company that achieves the effective flower patterns popularly credited to Busby Berkeley, whose first film work came after. The spectacular two-tone technicolor finale begins with Charles King's rendition of 'Orange Blossom Time', with the Rasch girls wearing green tutus and thus partially obscured by dancing in front of a green orchard dotted with brilliant oranges.

A dramatic shift swings us up on to Mount Ararat (the sets were large), and as the storm clouds clear and the sun emerges, MGM's parade of stars, fetching in transparent raincoats and hats, are led by Ukelele Ike in front of Noah's Ark, to sing 'Singin' in the Rain'. It was the great hit of the film and would reappear in countless MGM films over the next two decades until it finally came to rest as Gene Kelly's finest moment and the title of one of the most celebrated of all musicals.

Much of this film's pleasure, and that of films like it, remains in seeing famous faces doing the unexpected, such as Bessie Love's furiously acrobatic dance, climaxed as she is swung about by her legs like a human pendulum; and Norma Shearer and John Gilbert, in the first of the technicolor sequences that has them flush wildly across all the shades of red, doing the balcony scene from *Romeo and Juliet* (Shakespeare was another casualty of early sound). It gets better when it turns out to be a film within a film and stage-trained Lionel Barrymore in the director's chair advises Norma and John to give the scene a contemporary feel and do it as a slangy send-up. Since it wasn't meant to be serious, John Gilbert, looking and sounding relaxed, is fine.

These films, for all of their awful nothingness, were to provide a format that would find its slot on television. In recent years, the almost monthly 'all-star' industry-sponsored Award shows, and similar tributes to past giants with one foot in the grave, follow this early Film Revue format to a T. One has the sight of famous people walking on or standing up, to indulge in some silly chit-chat, sing so-so, and walk off or sit down to applause from their peers who are glad to see them alive and know just what it feels like to make a fool of oneself on this sort of occasion.

Meanwhile, over at Fox, De Sylva, Brown and Henderson wrote an original score for the musical comedy *Sunny Side Up* (1929), starring the nation's film sweethearts, Janet Gaynor and Charles Farrell, which was another huge hit and pointed the way musicals were wise to take. And still they came: Jerome Kern (*Till The Clouds Rolls By*, starring Robert Walker. MGM, 1946), Rodgers and Hart (*Words and Music*, starring Tom Drake and Mickey Rooney, MGM, 1948) and George and Ira Gershwin

Right: A production
number from *The
Hollywood Revue of 1929*.
The elaborate sets were
less effective in the film
than in stills because of
unimaginative camera
work.

Right, below: Marion
Davies in the 'Tommy
Atkins on Parade' number
in MGM's *The Hollywood
Revue of 1929*.

Janet Gaynor was another
of the silent film
favourites who went on to
greater success in talkies.
Her all-colour musical,
Sunny Side Up, helped
her on the way.

(*Rhapsody in Blue*, starring Robert Alda and
Herbert Rudley. Warner Bros, 1945) were new
arrivals. At the height of the boom every important
songwriter in the business seemed to be in Hollywood, contributing to the shape of the film musical
we admire today. There were a few exceptions, like
Cole Porter (*Night and Day*, starring Cary Grant.
Warner Bros, 1944).

In an interview for *Cinema* (1930), Richard
Rodgers expressed Broadway's initial attitude
towards movies: 'We had all sorts of ominous
warnings before we came out. All the routine fables
about stars who ate peas with their knives and
producers who couldn't read or write. We were
good and scared.

'Herb (Fields) and Larry got here first. When they
saw how wrong the advance reports had been, they
had Jack Warner frame me. The first day in, I went
to the studio for lunch to meet Mr Warner. He was
just like the producers in the funny stories. He
sprawled over the table and said: "Well, now you're
here, you got to get to work. And I don't vant none of
your highbrow song-making. Musik vit guts, ve got
to have – songs vit real sentiment like 'Stein Song'
and 'Vit Ters in My Eyes, I'm Dencing'."

The working conditions were another source of
amazement. 'My God, offices with oriental rugs, and
studio cars at your disposal, and people to carry
your papers so you won't strain yourself . . . we are
fortunate here. Our supervisor on *Hot Heiress*
(1931) never interferes and we have almost *carte
blanche*. They gave us the cast we wanted; they've
put every facility at our disposal, given us intelligent co-operation. These gags about Hollywood
slavedrivers must be myths.'

Rodgers explained how they planned to tackle
the film medium: 'The dialogue, the action and the
story progression are kept in quick tempo. As for
the songs, the point is not that they be logically
'planted'. The very planting of a number is false.
The heroine kidnapped by Arabs and, in the middle
of the desert, singing an aria to the accompaniment
of a fifty-piece orchestra is ridiculous. But it doesn't
become any more reasonable if there is a short
interval of dialogue preceding it – "Let me go, you
beasts, or I'll scream for help!" "No one will hear
you." "Yes, they will; why, there's a caravan passing
now! Who can they be?" "Why, it's the great
Toscanini with his orchestra on his way to Tunis.
Hark at how the infidel dogs do play!"

'Most important in songs for the screen is their
relevance. We are not making them numerous. They
are seldom reprised. And they are all definitely
connected with the story, pertinent to the actors
and the action. We ease into them in the dialogue, so
that before you know it, you realize that the
characters are speaking lyrics and their gradual
entry into the song appears very logical.'

Ben Lyon had already made his transition into

sound with the spectacular aviation drama, *Hell's Angels* (1930), and was cast in *Hot Heiress*. He has congenial memories of the experience: 'It was an original story which, for that time, was rare for musicals. Herb Fields wrote the story. I was a riveter, and I remember a song I had ['The Riveter's Song'] that went something like this: "A girl loves a soldier, a butcher, or a baker, but nobody loves a riveter like his mother." That was Hart for you. He was an amazing character. He changed styles in lyrics for a number like Gershwin did rhythms. None of this rhyming "moon-swoon" thing for him. At times, when he wasn't satisfied with the way we did a number, he'd leave the set, and come back ten minutes later with lyrics that fitted what we had to do like a glove. Playing the riveters, Tommy Dugan and I had to learn to walk those steel beams, and we were about two storeys off the ground most of the time. It was all about an heiress (Barbara Hutton type, played by Ona Munson) who lives in a plush apartment house alongside a new building being put up. When the new building reached her level, we saw each other and fell in love. At the hero's lunch-time, I'd drop a wooden plank from one of the steel beams to her window, and while she had her expensive three-course menu served inside her apartment, I'd be sitting on my plank, with my little lunchbox of sandwiches and coffee. As the building progressed in height she kept moving to the flat above so we could keep meeting. I had some songs to sing, but you didn't have to be a Gordon MacRae or a Nelson Eddy to sing them. I'm not a singer, but I do have an ear for pitch. I remember I was sitting with Rodgers at the piano one day, and he said that some of the greatest singers in the world couldn't stay on key, whether they started with or without accompaniment. Give them the first key, let them sing, and at the end, when you play the key they should have finished on, they're usually a tone off. I told him I was sure I could keep on key, so we tried it, and I was right!

'The camera was still in the booth then, and one day, Fields was in the booth while Ona and I were sitting on the set with a mike boom hanging over us.

Ben Lyon and Ona Munson in *Hot Heiress*. The songs for this romance between a rich girl and a riveter were the first contribution Rodgers and Hart made to movies.

You know what those booths were like; about four or five feet square, and absolutely sound-proofed once the door was shut, with no ventilation, so that no noise of the camera would get out and into the mikes. Well, some of the sequences would last up to three minutes, and in the booth you'd have Fields, the cameraman, sound engineers and the director. When they emerged after a take, they'd be covered in sweat.

'I completely forgot that Walter Pidgeon was in *Hot Heiress* as well. He was in at the beginning when they were making all the musicals. But he didn't click then. Warner was very unhappy that he wasn't pulling his weight at the box-office, not even a plus, and they wanted to drop him, to break his contract. Walter was getting something like $1,500 a week in his second year under contract, and he refused to break it. So Warner sent him on the sets, to appear as an extra. Of course, when he arrived on those sets the directors said, "Walter, what the heck are you doing here, you're not on this film!" He'd tell them that he was called to go, but they'd tell him to go home. After this had happened several times,

How it was done. Opera singer Lawrence Tibbett enjoyed a brief success in Hollywood when talkies arrived and singers were in demand. In this *The Rogue Song* production still he is being made up for a scene in which he is mercilessly whipped. But a stand-in does the cries of pain for him.

35

The success of *The Hollywood Revue of 1929* led to a number of imitations. Top left: Warners offered *On With the Show*, and Universal the better-remembered *The King of Jazz*. Above: Paul Whiteman and his orchestra on a huge piano. Left: The Rhythm Boys trio included Bing Crosby, the one on the left. Bottom: Jacques Cartier performed a Voodoo dance on a huge drum. The production still, left, shows the cameras ready to film it.

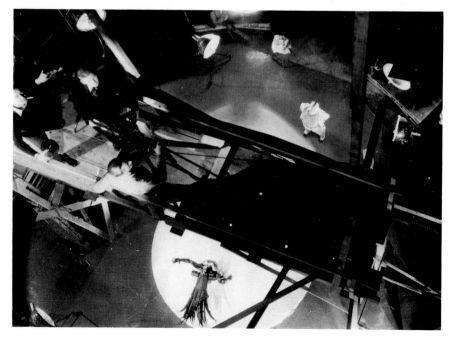

Above: A production shot of the gallows scene in Ludwig Berger's *The Vagabond King*. This film of Rudolf Friml's operetta boasted Jeanette MacDonald in her second film, stage star Dennis King as Villon – and colour.

Right: Ernst Lubitsch breaks for coffee. On the set of *The Merry Widow*.

Below: *The Love Parade*. The wedding of Queen Louise of Sylvania (Jeanette MacDonald).

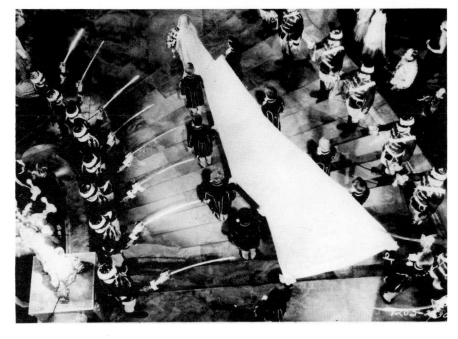

Jack called him into his office and told him they were so pleased with him that they were giving him a raise in salary to $1,750 a week, which he accepted. A week later, they fired him. Under his contract, which was for $1,500, they could let him go if he got more or less than the contracted amount.'

Throughout its brief life, the magazine *Cinema* was ahead of its time and usually had its tongue in its cheek when dealing with Hollywood hyperbole but it unfailingly treated the public with respect. Its February 1931 editorial summed up the revolutionary changes that had taken place so far and gave credit where credit was overdue – to the directors:

'The musical comedy field yielded a bountiful crop to the talkie-singie-dancies. Very expensive productions of stage successes have been made. Their success is due, apparently, to some favourite in the cast, because they amount to very little as motion pictures, and usually their stories are very old, without any attempt to enliven them with new twists, and the best of their music is not new. The best of them have been either written directly for the audible screen or so freely adapted from some old play that they are practically originals. *Sunny Side Up* (1929) and *The Love Parade* (1929), each in its special way, are among the year's leaders in finding out how sound and action can combine on the screen in a special form of its own . . . If we were making our own list (for the yearly top ten polls), there is no doubt about what two pictures would head the sound section of it. They are *Hallelujah* and *Applause*. As drama, they were exceptionally free from falseness and sentimentality and triviality – qualities practically inescapable in motion pictures that pretend to be serious. On the other hand, they had depth and dignity and beauty.'

Pioneers in Sound: Lubitsch, Vidor and Mamoulian—

It is to the credit of artists like Ernst Lubitsch, Rouben Mamoulian, and King Vidor that they had the vitality and ingenuity to circumvent the powerful and feared sound experts, and to lift the medium out of the rut. As film historian Arthur Knight put it: 'They had no rules to go on, no precedents to quote. They had the opposition of sound men to contend with, and the indisputable fact that at the box-offices across the nation almost any film made money if it talked. But these men sensed that talk alone was not enough and that the public would soon tire of the novelty of sound for its own sake and demand to see a "movie". It was their pioneer work that brought forth the techniques to make the movies move again.'

In 1927 Ernst Lubitsch and King Vidor were at the top of their profession – Lubitsch with a dazzlingly influential string of sophisticated sex-comedies and King Vidor with classics like *The Big Parade* and *The Crowd*. Rouben Mamoulian was working in the theatre where his revolutionary productions were making him one of the most talked-about young talents in America. They were among the major contributors to the awakening of the American cinema from its talkie sleep, and each one with a classic musical.

Lubitsch had been certain that sound would rob films of their magic, mystery and charm. However, *The Love Parade* (1929), his first talkie, was a model of how these films should be. The biographer Herman G. Weinberg '. . . its pictorial eloquence, visual wit, cinematic innuendo, and simultaneously making full use of the resources offered by the new medium – contrapuntal sound, dialogue, music, sound effects. So fluid and

malleable was the combination that from these many strands emerged a homogeneous whole. Everything that was right in the way a sound film was made then remains as right as anything done today.'

Besides its many other pleasures the film also served to introduce the enchanting Jeanette MacDonald as the Ruritanian Louise the First, Queen of Sylvania, whose main affair of state is to find a husband. The young Queen, presiding over a meeting of her ministers, ends their fuzzy debate on the need for her marriage. To demonstrate that she doesn't need their help she raises her skirt to display a shapely gam, and informs them, 'There is only one leg in all Sylvania to match this . . .', and, following a delicious pause – she reveals the other one.

Lubitsch's *The Love Parade* gets off to a fine start with two bottles of champagne, a high-kicking chorus line and 'Paris'. Cocky straw-hatted boulevardier Maurice Chevalier, whose film debut in the inferior *Innocents of Paris* (1929) had overnight made him a sound super-star, was used by Lubitsch to advantage as count-about-town. In an opening joke that establishes Maurice and his need to get out of town he is accused of being unfaithful by a hysterical woman we suppose to be his wife until her husband bursts in, pointing a gun.

Fade-out. Fade-in: Dawn in Sylvania! An American coach party are sightseeing and obviously bored until their cynical guide revives their interest by giving a price tag to the historical antiques. Inside the palace (which cost 'two million dollars'), the sleeping Queen, roused by her ladies-

Queen and Consort in *The Love Parade*. Jeanette MacDonald and Maurice Chevalier.

Lubitsch, seated between the camera booths, directs two scenes at once for *The Love Parade*. A counterpoint duet between Maurice Chevalier and Jeanette MacDonald (right) and Lupino Lane and Lillian Roth (centre) was accompanied by an orchestra on the far left. Many sound experts of the time (1929) believed that this sort of complicated filming was not possible.

in-waiting (including Ziegfeld beauty Virginia Bruce) inquiring after her majesty's sleep sings to them about her 'dream lover', imploring him to '. . . fold your arms around me . . .' while getting up and slipping into something a little more comfortable, a transparent negligée. Lubitsch touches abound: for the lavish marriage ceremony, he reintroduced the tracking shot so that the camera regains its ability to flow, moving back slowly during the wedding to include the whole sequence in one continuous movement. This he achieved by the simple expedient of shooting it as a silent scene – simple enough, one thinks now, but something literally unheard of or unthought of. And so he freed the camera from its control by the sound-box. Later he laid a soundtrack over it. He conducted this and similar sequences to the beat of a metronome, thus ensuring the musical harmony of the whole, and breaking more new ground.

Married but not harnessed, Maurice is eager to be a good lover and king. But while Louise wants him to treat her as merely a woman at night, she sharply reminds him that during the daytime only she rules and leaves to review her troops. Like her ladies-in-waiting, the guards are ever ready for a royal sing-song. Lubitsch simultaneously underscores the sex-war between Queen and frustrated consort with a parallel state of affairs between the Queen's maid (Lillian Roth) and the master's valet (Lupino Lane). The dialogue, 'Forget that I am Queen Louise the First of Sylvania. Tonight I am just a woman,' is not always up to Lubitsch's standard (which revived in top form with his next films – *Monte Carlo, The Smiling Lieutenant*,* and *One Hour With You*) – but his controlled use of it, the injection of songs that contributed to the story line, and especially his use of silence (when most directors were concerned with getting all possible mileage out of sound) were daring and different. He already used sound to underscore his visuals – as when Chevalier tells a risqué story where the punch line is rendered inaudible by slamming doors. Here was a director not in awe of technology and showed that a song could be used as a plot link, instead of an intrusion.

The Love Parade, which Lubitsch had intended as a parody of the genre, gave an enormous boost to the popularity of filmed operetta in Europe, especially in Germany where they would bring these to a very fine art indeed. Admittedly the film also suffers from many of the faults of the time. The task of returning movement to the screen was bound to cramp even a master's style. But there remains in *The Love Parade*, and in King Vidor's work, a current of excitement flowing through

A classic moment from Lubitsch's *Monte Carlo*. Jeanette MacDonald sings 'Beyond the Blue Horizon' from the train window.

them that has lost neither in the telling nor the seeing. No allowance is needed for Lubitsch's next musical starring Jeanette, opposite the musical comedy star, Jack Buchanan, who was as much the archetypal English *bon vivant* as Chevalier was a French one, and who proved an adroit foil for Jeanette's charming huffs. The film was *Monte Carlo* (1930), and *Cinema* wrote: 'Monte Carlo has no chorus ladies tripping gaily in and out of boudoirs, no Albertina Rasch girls appearing miraculously at the little informal party of the Countess So-and-So, and very few instances when you feel, with a certain sinking in the stomach, that the principals are about to give birth to a song.'

Lubitsch's genius for creating a mood quickly and then sustaining it for the entire length of the film was superbly realized with one pokerfaced wedding guest dryly remarking to another on the invisible but irresistible attractions of the chinless groom: 'He's rich, he's wealthy, and he has nothing but money. He's everything a woman could desire.' Later, when the count, masquerading as her hairdresser, strips off his apron and asserts his masculinity by taking her in his arms, Jeanette looks up from a passionate embrace and says: 'That's what you get for being nice to the servants.'

For Herman G. Weinberg, *Monte Carlo* excels for its exhilarating 'Blue Express' train sequence. Jeanette, in a train compartment, sings 'Beyond the Blue Horizon' (Lubitsch intercuts the sound of the starting train and transforms the characteristic

* *The Smiling Lieutenant* was to be the third, and so far last, adaptation of the hugely successful Oscar Straus operetta, *Ein Waltzertraum*. Directed first by Ludwig Berger in Germany in 1925, it was one of the USA's most successful importations, released by MGM in the US, and prompting them to produce *The Merry Widow* (based on the Franz Lehar operetta) and Sigmund Romberg's *The Student Prince* (dir. Lubitsch) as silent films. Next it became one of the first, equally successful, German-made talkies, *Der Liebeswaltzer*. Only they didn't use the Oscar Straus score, but one written especially for the film by Werner Richard Heymann. Lubitsch returned to the Straus original, but with the changes that made it very much his own.

tempo of the wheels gaining speed into the opening bars of the song), and as the train hurtles on its way, Lubitsch underlines the exuberance and freedom of the song with a visual orchestration of flying rails and whirring train wheels, which builds to a grand-slam, breathtaking ending.' (Unforgettably aided by the chorus from peasants at work in the surrounding fields.) 'These few moments of film have been enshrined in the film history books as an example of Lubitsch's virtuosity in combining image and sound. With this film, the last vestiges of the operetta stage have disappeared from Lubitsch's

King Vidor directing *Hallelujah* in 1929. 'I've thought of all my films in terms of music. I choreograph the scenes. I've never been able to think of a film without music.' (King Vidor, 1972).

work. Here the director has achieved the same absolute fluidity and freedom that marked the camera movement in the best silent films.'

What Lubitsch did for boudoir affairs, King Vidor did for earthier passions. While Lubitsch was making *The Love Parade* for Paramount, Vidor was at work on MGM's *Hallelujah* (1929), a subject as far removed from Ruritanian romps as can be imagined. He had long wanted to film an all-Negro story. The studio bosses had vetoed the idea before, but with the beginning of sound he convinced them that the music of the Negro spirituals was ideal for the screen. (Regrettably, some illogical Tin Pan Alley songs by Irving Berlin were imposed on the finished film, against Vidor's wishes.) Even so, fear of a boycott by Southern cinema owners of a film starring Negroes provided solid resistance until Vidor offered a sporting proposition which MGM president Nicholas Schenck could not refuse. He, Vidor, would make the film without a salary; he offered to invest his guaranteed salary, dollar for dollar, with the company's investment. Schenck's gambling instincts were aroused. As Vidor relates it, Schenck's reply was: 'If that's the way you feel about it, I'll let you make a picture about whores.'

The cast was mostly found in the Negro districts of Chicago and New York. Negro actors were few and scarce in Hollywood, where their parts were commonly played by white actors in black face. Daniel Haynes, the leading man in the film, was a Broadway understudy in *Show Boat*. Nina Mae McKinney, a pert seventeen-year-old, had been in the chorus of *Blackbirds* on Broadway.*

The film was a mixture of silent shooting, which accounts for its photographic eloquence, and studio sound. Vidor had grown up in the South, and this was a personal, artistic evocation of his childhood memories, like 'hearing my sister rocked to sleep each night by one of the best repertoires of Negro spirituals in the South'. Vidor wanted to evoke the

* Nina is arguably the first black star in a major film produced for a white audience. Subsequently she appeared in everything from Vitaphone shorts, films made for black audiences, co-starring in British films like *Sanders of the River* (1935), and small parts in films like *Pinky* (1949). She died in 1969.

Above: The revival meeting in King Vidor's *Hallelujah*.

Right: The baptism ceremony in *Hallelujah*. The inclusion of Tin Pan Alley songs in the completed product was bitterly opposed by Vidor, as contrary to the values of his film.

sincerity and fervour of the black man's religious expression. At that time, a film with an all-Negro cast made by a major studio was something unheard of, whatever its treatment of the subject. Vidor's sincerity and affection for the people was genuine, and his directorial genius made *Hallelujah* into a true and deep experience – an American masterpiece.

The filming was beset with difficulties. 'On location in Memphis, there was no portable sound equipment; the hoped-for sound tracks did not arrive in time. We just had to go ahead and shoot as for a silent picture, and the sound was put in later. The difficulty of matching sound tracks recorded in the studio with scenes made on location proved almost insurmountable. Negro sermons and baptisms were photographed without benefit of sound equipment. Later, in the studio, a wild recording was made; then the editor went to work and through the most tedious and maddening process had to fit the two together . . . There were as yet no 'moviolas' in use, so that the editor had no way to tell by looking at the film what the actor was saying. They had to effect the synchronization by showing the film in the studio projection room with a push-button signal to the operator, who would immediately make a grease mark on the rapidly moving film. This served as the best guide for the editor who would then accomplish an accurate bit of synchronization. It was a remarkable feat, matching word to lip movement. Unlike today's method, in which the artist records his song, and in the filmed sequence, mouths the words to a playback of his recording.'

Having shot the climax of the film – a relentless pursuit through an eerie swamp – they got back to the studio and set about adding sound. 'To a motion picture studio in 1929, this was a fresh and unexplored adventure. We found ourselves making big puddles of water and mud, tramping through them with a microphone . . . rotting branches and fallen trees were crawled over; strange birds flew up from the morass. Never one to treat a dramatic effect literally, the thought struck me – why not free the imagination and record this sequence impressionistically? When someone stepped on a broken branch, we made it sound as if bones were breaking. As the pursued victim withdrew his foot from the stickiness of the mud, we made the vacuum sound strong enough to pull him into hell.' A bird call becomes a hiss, a threat of impending doom. 'In my first desperation with sound, I believed that this non-factual use of it was ideally suited to my film.'

The studio was right in one respect. This magnificent film, exulting in its Americanness, received few bookings south of the Mason-Dixon line. Vidor never again directed a musical, although his lyrical blending of image and sound elevates all his best work, never more so than in the climax of that astonishing western opera – *Duel In The Sun*. In that, the rush of ravishing images – emotional, fervent – the creative editing, the cumulative force of its overheated passions scored by Dimitri Tiomkin's fiery music, came together to fuse two people on a mountain top amidst a hail of bullets from their guns. It was Wagnerian in an emotional impact that was first signalled by the musical.

The third member of this early triumvirate was the Armenian-born stage director, Rouben Mamoulian, who had found his way to America in the late twenties. Of the three, his were the purest musicals, acting as beacon lights to the Golden Era which was to follow a decade later. With *Applause* (1929), Mamoulian not only revealed sound's gifts, but his own – a director who recognized the difference between stage and screen. These gifts were very well appreciated by Lewis Jacobs in *The Rise of the American Film*: 'His awareness of pace, rhythm, movement, and music has made his musical films his best; in these more than in his dramatic pictures he has blended the cinematic elements into an excellent whole. In a day of readjustments, when the proper relation between the film and the microphone was being groped for consciously, or, in many cases, unconsciously, *Applause* spoke in favour of camera mobility first, talk second.' Mamoulian's use of mobile sound was then novel: for instance, a chorus continues through this second scene, being modulated so that a conversation can be heard above it. The camera moved freely, daringly, and even enthusiastically – sometimes in fact too much for the spectator's comfort.

'One of the most effective moments in *Applause* comes when the lover of the fading burlesque queen tells her she is old, ugly, finished. The camera hovers for a moment over Helen Morgan's face, moves slowly to the framed picture of her in her lovely youth, and then comes back to her. The movement of the camera and the continuing bitter voice over it combine to intensify the effect enormously. In another scene, as the dancer's daughter in a restaurant lifts a glass of water, the music fades slowly and the picture dissolves to the identical movement of her mother's arm, lifting a glass of poison to her lips. Such touches were uncommonly good in the early days of sound.'

In an interview for this book in the summer of 1968, Mamoulian explained his philosophy of film-making: 'On the stage you have one action only – that of the actors. On the screen, you have three: 1)

Two shots from
Mamoulian's *Applause*.
Helen Morgan in her
memorable film debut as
the pathetic, fading
burlesque star, Kitty
Darling.

into a rhythmic whole, it would be great theatre.'

In 1922, at the age of twenty-three, he directed a play to excellent notices at the St James's Theatre in London. 'I had directed it in a thoroughly realistic manner and I discovered the realism on the stage gave me no satisfaction at all. It was much too limited in scope, a near imitation of life. I preferred poetry and rhythm. Since then I have never used a naturalistic method in directing. I found from experience that imagination and stylized action combined with psychological truth makes a much greater aesthetic and emotional impact on audiences. In fact it seems to add to the truth of what they see on the stage, making it more real than realism.'

As a result of the play's success, he received an offer from George Eastman who wanted him for his theatre in Rochester, New York. He accepted. At this theatre, newly-built by the multi-millionaire owner of Kodak film, Mamoulian founded a new opera company, and the operas he produced there soon spread his reputation to New York and Broadway. His desire to work in the dramatic theatre – where his ideas of combining all the elements of movement, dancing, acting, music, singing, decor, lighting, colour, etc., would find a proper outlet – led him to join the Theatre Guild, then one of the most stimulating and progressive theatrical groups in America. It was the first to première many of the major works of the top American playwrights. Mamoulian soon directed many of these, including Eugene O'Neill's *Marco Millions* and *Porgy*. His ideas for the latter, subsequently to be used by composer George Gershwin for his classic opera *Porgy and Bess* (also directed by Mamoulian), was possibly Mamoulian's greatest theatrical triumph, as innovator and director of dramatic visionary sweep.

'In it I tried all my ideas of a dramatic integration of many elements.' He created a scene, not in the original play, which made theatrical history – the famous symphony of sound. Mamoulian again employed this idea in *Love Me Tonight* (1932). It was not, as is often said, taken from René Clair's first sound film, *Sous Les Toits de Paris* (1930).

The curtain rises on Catfish Row in the early morning. All is silent. 'Then you hear the Boom! of the street gangs repairing the road. That is the first beat. Beat two is silent; beat three is a snore, z-z-z-z-z- from a sleeping Negro; beat four is silent again. Then a woman starts sweeping the steps – Swish – and she takes up beats two and four so you have: Boom! – Swish! – z-z-z – Swish! A knife sharpener, a shoemaker, a woman beating rugs, all join in. The rhythm changes 4:4 to 2:4, then 6:8, and then goes into syncopated and Charleston rhythms. It all had to be conducted like an orchestra!'

Arriving at Paramount in 1929, Mamoulian's first film was made at a time when most directors were still perplexed by the new camera which had overnight gained a voice and through the shock lost the use of its legs. Lubitsch was about to make *The Love Parade*, and von Sternberg made *Thunderbolt* (both for Paramount), doing things with the camera that seemed staggeringly daring at the time. Paramount expected a stage director who knew how to direct dialogue. They never expected to get a

the action of the actors, 2) the action of the camera, 3) the action of the editing. All three should be rhythmically integrated. Add music to it and you have one cohesive whole to which you can apply Michelangelo's definition of a perfect sculpture: Roll it down the hill and nothing will break off. I ask myself, what is more powerful emotionally than music, dancing and rhythm? Rhythm has always dominated me, probably from the time of my school days. I felt rhythm really belonged to the theatre and if I could combine dancing, drama and music

Rouben Mamoulian. On
the set of *City Streets*
(1931).

man who put all the ideas that had made him a theatrical sensation to work for him in this new medium immediately.

Applause was filmed at the New York Astoria studios. (At that time, some major companies still kept their New York studios operating, enabling many a stage star to work in films during the day while working in the theatre at night. But most of these New York studios were closed early in the Depression to cut down on costs.) 'Initially, Paramount had wanted me to sign for seven years; learn the business of film making for two years, and in that time work as a dialogue coach. I countered by signing for one picture and no options. I watched the shooting at Astoria, asking questions about lenses and things. After five weeks of that I felt I had mastered it. As far as the camera goes, I feel it's like singing; if you have no voice, you give up. If you have no camera eye, you can't learn it. If you have an eye, it doesn't take long to learn.'

For Mamoulian, tales of what the camera couldn't do were of no interest. 'In those early sound days, people just thought of films as being all dialogue – talk, talk, talk. I wanted to do things you couldn't do on stage. I wanted to use a mobile camera, but that was impossible because the camera and the cameraman and the director and the assistant cameraman and probably the assistant director were all squashed together in a sort of house on wheels! All the sound was recorded on a single track; the mike picked up everything you didn't want it to. If you had a letter in a scene, it had to be soaked in water. Like that it didn't make a thunderous crackle, but of course, it looked like a Dali watch. The blow-up came on the third day. I wanted to shoot a scene entirely in one shot. It's where the girl, who had come to New York from a convent, is lying in bed in a cheap little hotel room. Her mother, played by Helen Morgan, sits beside her and sings to her the only kind of song she knows, a burlesque number, but she sings it as if it were a lullaby. As she sings, the daughter fingers a rosary and whispers a prayer. They said we couldn't record the two things – the song and the prayer – on one mike and one channel. So I said to the sound man, "Why not use two mikes and two channels and combine the two tracks in printing?" Of course, it's general practice now; but the sound man, and George Folsey the cameraman, said it was impossible. So I was mad. I threw down my megaphone and ran up to Mr Zukor's office. He was with Jesse Lasky and Monta Bell when I barged in: "Look," I said, "nobody does what I ask . . ." So Adolph Zukor came down and told them to do it my way.

'After that, the crew was hell! They refused to help with anything, letting me do it all. By 5.30 we had two takes in the can. Next day I went to the studio very nervous. But as I went in, the big Irish doorman raised his hat and bowed. It seemed they had had a secret 7.30 viewing of the rushes in the studio the night before and were so pleased with the result that they had sent it straight off to a Paramount Sales Conference.

'"Well," said George Folsey, very cheerful when I went in, "where would you like your cameras today?" "Today," I said, "I'll have four cameras and I want them shooting up from the floor." This meant they had to send out for men with pneumatic drills, because the studio floor was concrete, two feet thick. I waited till they brought the men in, then said: "O.K., that's enough. I've had my revenge!"

'None of the cast had made a film before, including me. Now the film had had great reviews, but it didn't do well at the box-office. For a year, I didn't hear from Paramount.' (In the meantime, he continued to direct plays for the Theatre Guild in New York.) 'Then they offered me another one-picture-no-option contract. After I'd signed, they told me (Wanger, Lasky, etc., who worked out of the New York office) that Ben Schulberg, the studio head on the coast, hated me and had fought the decision to sign me. I met Schulberg on the train to LA' (nobody was yet flying) 'and for the next five days I never saw a tree or a town; we were playing poker the whole way. I lost the first five weeks salary, but we became good friends.'

'It is for the superfluous that we live,' said Brecht, who was not given to superfluity. Oscar Wilde said, 'No civilized person ever regretted a pleasure.' Pleasure is the first law of the musical. Nothing needs less justification. The musical, the art form of the 20th century, became a focus for dreams, for ambitions, and the source of so much else no one could have foreseen. They were the magic toy bound by neither the traditions nor the pretensions of the past. They had nothing to live up to, escape from or lose, thus enabling them to take extraordinary risks with a triumphant audacity. There was no age barrier, no language barrier, no cultural barrier to their enjoyment. Their growth overpowered all reason. Audiences, drawn first to a novelty, became addicted to an art.

Louise Brooks in *The Canary Murder Case*. Her refusal to chirp for sound meant she had to be dubbed; it ended her career as a Hollywood star. Fifty years later she has the last word – as a celebrated writer.

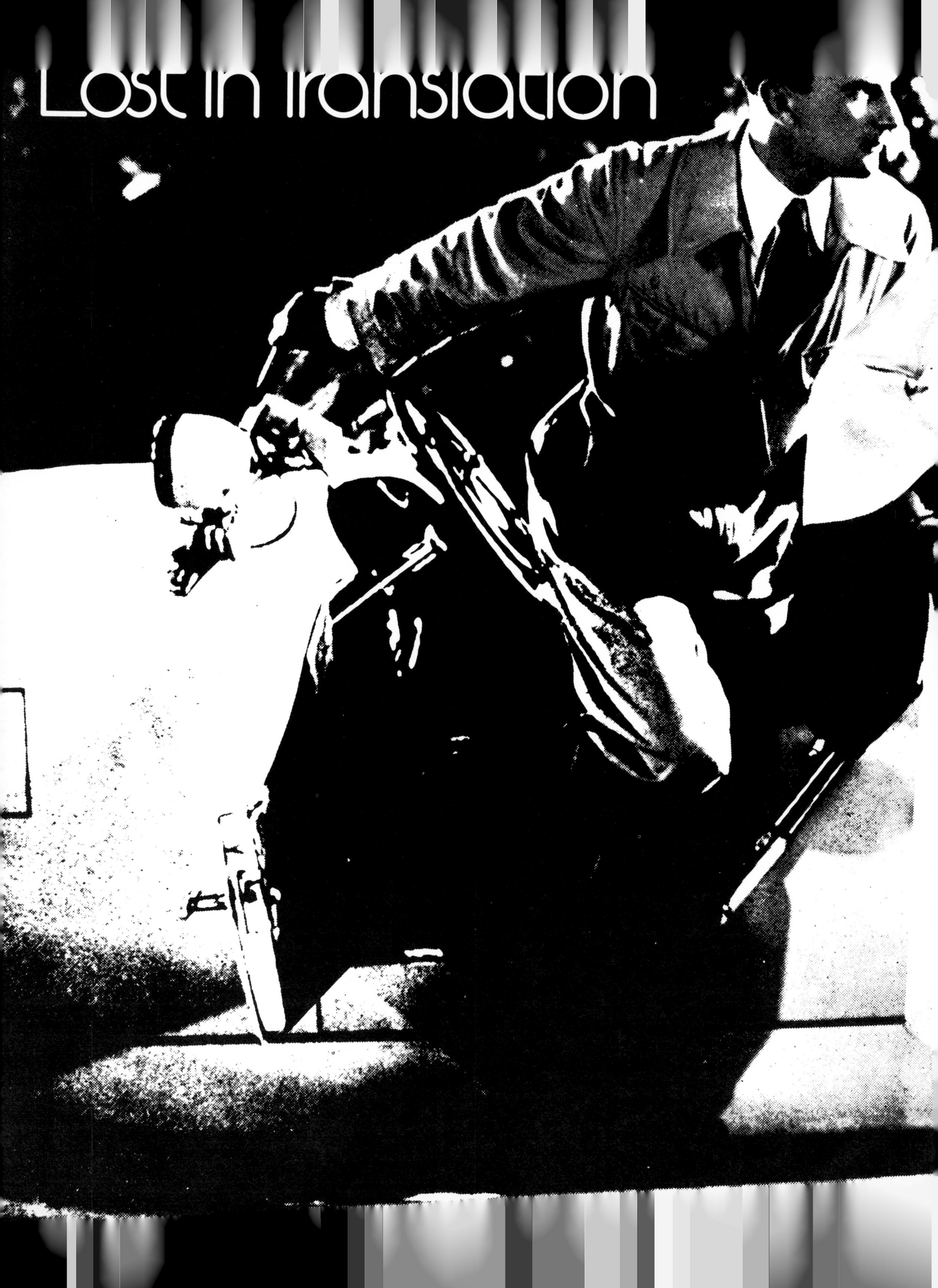
Lost in Translation

In a business notoriously beset by false starts, stops and accidents in a quest for survival, one of the strangest of all occurrences in the history now occurred. Even as the American musical, due to public apathy, disappeared into a two-year-long retirement and further development with sound techniques shifted to other areas. The European film makers were themselves to make of the musical a real celebration of the spirit that is the cinema. By the time Hollywood woke up it found the European, and especially the German-made musicals at a peak. It would take them a decade to catch up. It is worth speculating as to whether or not the American cinema would ever have reclaimed its dominance over a genre one thinks of as exclusively its own if political and economic events hadn't called a halt in Europe. For in taking the lead the German film industry made musicals of such witty inventiveness, lightness of touch and charm, in which image, sound and song were blended so artlessly that, had they rolled them down a hill, not a bit of them would have broken off.

Hungary had Tokay, the puszta and glamorous and amusing Hungarians who sang and looked good wherever they filmed. They made films that pleased those for whom they were made but none of them had wide audiences outside their borders. The Italians filmed a lot of operas or their own versions of German musicals. I know neither well but the beautiful Maria Cebotari, the Romanian-born soprano who starred in Italy, made a moving Butterfly in *Il Sogno di Butterfly* and other films. Her brilliant career was cut tragically short when she died at the age of thirty-nine.

France, though not a major contributor to the genre, managed to produce some musicals that broke across national borders. French inventors, film pioneers and directors had in their day made the silent cinema world renowned, aided by the intellectuals whose regard for the medium was commendably different from most other countries in treating it as an art equal, even superior at times, to music, literature and theatre. The arrival of sound and the adjustment to it, coming as it did at a time of a severely depressed economic climate that placed them under the financial domination of the monolithic American and German film companies, halted their advancement and isolated them in an ethnic corner which few of their films were able to surmount. For much of the 30s they produced little better than domestic versions of foreign films, or the most dismal 'all-talkie' adaptations of French plays. Yet the French public, then as now, were avid filmgoers. Paris, where so many émigrés hope to die, was already famed as a centre in which films from all over the world received a screening. But musicals were never a part of their staple diet, even on the stage. Their legendary singing and dancing stars came from their music halls and revue theatres like the Moulin Rouge and the Folies-Bergère. Renoir immortalized them in *French Can-Can* (1955) with Edith Piaf, Jean Gabin and Patachou amid the finest evocation of the colour and vivacity of the can-can and its dancers on film. The silly story is merely an excuse for the marvellous atmosphere. So it is that French film musicals are a rare species and famous ones even more so. Their impact on the culture of the nation can be gauged in a pleasant pictorial record produced in conjunction with Henri Langlois of the Cinémathèque Français, *Images du*

Previous pages: Lilian Harvey and Willy Fritsch in *Die Drei von der Tankstelle.*

The musical has never been a notable feature of French cinema – in spite of the success of René Clair – but the occasional success has appeared. Left: Annabella and Albert Prejean in *Un Soir de Rafle* (1931). Left, below: the Folies Bergère favourite Josephine Baker in *Zouzou* (1935). Below: Abel Gance's *Un Grand Amour de Beethoven* – with Harry Baur (1936) – and *Paradis Perdu* (1940). Bottom: Yvonne Printemps and Pierre Fresnay in *Trois Valses* (1938) and *La Valse de Paris* (1949).

The musical in Italy was, inevitably, directly influenced by the form in which Italians excel, the opera. Right: Maria Cebotari in *Il Sogno di Butterfly* (1939). Far right: Gina Lollobrigida in Leoncavallo's *I Pagliacci* (1948). Right, below: Nelly Corradi and Tito Gobbi in Donizetti's *L'Elisir d'Amore* (1946). Far right, below: Sophia Loren miming the title role in Verdi's *Aida* – the singing was contributed by Renata Tebaldi, no less (1953).

Cinéma Français in which every subject and theme is handsomely covered by a host of pictures *except* the musical.

Of course there are exceptions. France, after all, was the home of Offenbach, Saint-Saëns, Bizet and hordes of musical emigrés. There was a brief wave of operettas in 1931-32, inspired by the success of the ones from Berlin. To prove these were not isolated instances Claude Autant-Lara directed a frothy film version of Reynaldo Hahn's operetta *Ciboulette* (1935) starring the Opéra Comique favourite, Simone Beriau, as a country maid on her way to the Paris market with her uncle's produce and discovering her future husband under a load of cabbage. The dialogue was sung and spoken mostly in verse, the music was pleasant, the adventures were slapstick, and the period costumes (1860) superb. The popular lyric soprano Yvonne Printemps was in her element in Ludwig Berger's spirited soufflé, *Trois Valses*, made in 1936 during Berger's flight out of Germany on his way to England, and as the sparkling inspiration of Jacques Offenbach in the otherwise stagey *La Valse de Paris* (1949), directed by Marcel Achard and set in the times of and to the melodies of the operetta composer.

Yet, out of a period of national poverty the golden years of the French cinema would rise, helped by a state of free competition opened up by the Depression and box-office fluctuations, with films by Abel Gance, Marcel L'Herbier, Jean Renoir, Marcel Carné, Julien Duvivier, Jacques Feyder. And while the musical would play no part in this, ironically it would be musicals that helped to launch this resurrection, the work of René Clair.

René Clair was the first French film maker to tackle the problems of sound head on, with results that affected the style and look of musicals elsewhere. As ex-journalist, actor, writer, critic and a leading silent director of already international repute, he utilized sound – to which he had been strongly opposed – to create a quartet of sparkling musical-comedy fantasies. *Sous les Toits de Paris* (1930) was the first important sound film to originate from France, followed by *Le Million* (1931), *A Nous La Liberté* and *Quatorze Juillet* (1932). Speaking of the past, he said: 'Despite the excessive use of noises in the early sound films, most directors retained the literal techniques of the silent film, showing each source of sound in turn. If people were eating, one would hear every chomp and swallow. Every bird would sing; no farm animal would pass by without going through its entire vocal routine; no clock would be seen without striking. If it had a sound, it had to be heard.'

Being his own scriptwriter as well as editor, Clair was in control of all the elements, and had learnt the pitfalls to avoid from the early Hollywood sound films. His imagination kindled those of American directors, who could point to the commercial reception of Clair's films as an argument for achieving their desired end.

René Clair with Adele
Astaire, Maurice Chevalier
and Jack Buchanan in
1937. Adele Astaire was
the original choice for the
feminine lead in Clair's
Break the News.

'Two or three pictures with sound were being made in France in 1929. *The Jazz Singer* was a success here as well, of course. The great thing in silent films was that we were obliged to find something to make up for the absence of words. We were compelled to invent new things. Since the coming of sound, the American comedy – like Mack Sennett – had practically disappeared; that great time of the American comedy was really pure genius. As soon as sound came, visual gags weren't necessary. In Russia both Eisenstein and Pudovkin had the same negative reaction to loss of visual invention; in the States, Chaplin and Stroheim did this, too. I was in rather good company! Though one obviously couldn't start making silent films again today, I am still against the big use of words; not sound, *words*! We have already got the theatre for words. Why cannot we explore another medium? Every time I had to make an important scene in dialogue I was ashamed, because it is a proof of weakness.

'I was told that American directors were particularly bewildered by the way I had coped with the sound during the long travelling shot going from the roof to the street singer in *Sous* . . . On each floor, you can see somebody doing something: one man washes his feet, another is smoking, and they finally sing the title song. We filmed it silently with very, very poor mechanism. We had a little elevator to carry us and the camera, and that was very dangerous to shoot from! Then I had to add the sound track. Rather than follow the sound engineer's advice and plant a mike beside everybody, which they would have to turn on and off so as to get the sound of a voice fading as the camera moved on (which had a lousy result), I attached the mike to a moveable pole. At that time, to move the mike was blasphemous. It stood still, and *you* had to move around it. We did it my way, and the result was perfect. Technicians are very careful and don't like experimenting. I have never since rediscovered the joy and excitement that we (the crew) had at the beginning of sound, when everything was being discovered. We were lucky to be working at that time.'

In *Sous les Toits de Paris*, Clair took the ingredients of reality and transformed them into a distinctive world of his own, in which the street singers, shopkeepers, petty thieves, and all the people of Paris become as puppets in a ballet. The story line is little more than a series of charmingly romantic and humorous sketches of Paris life, a street singer (Albert Préjean) and his two friends, and there is the girl Pola (Pola Illery) whom they all love.

'At the time I was shooting my second or third silent picture, I heard a circle of street singers on my way home from the studios. As I listened to them, I

Right: The rooftops of
Sous les toits de Paris.

Opposite, top: *Le Million*.
Irony and wit meet
merrily in romance. In the
foreground the tenor
(Constantin Stroesco)
struggles to get his arms
around a lavish soprano,
(Odette Talazac) as they
sing 'Nous sommes seules'
(We are alone), unaware
that the audience's
laughter is caused, not by
their own awkwardness
but by the discovery of the
pair of real-life lovers
(Annabella and René
Lèfevre), who had thought
themselves safely hidden
behind the flats.

Centre: The phonograph
factory of Clair's *A Nous
la Liberté*.

Bottom: Inside the factory
in *A Nous la Liberté*. The
still conveys the labour
atmosphere which the film
satirizes.

thought how sad it was that I had no sound with which to make a picture. Four years later sound came, and I returned to my street-singers idea. For the opening of *Sous* I had Albert Préjean walking through Paris in the early morning, and his song is picked up by the people living there. It was not strictly speaking a musical; it was not conceived as musical comedy.

'I filmed for a branch of a big German-owned film company called Tobis. Tobis had, in fact, the first licence for printing sound on the film itself, dating from around 1908. We had terrible problems with the sound crews on *Sous*. . . The crew they sent us was from Germany, and they didn't even speak French. I was the only one who could speak a little in German with them. They were absolute masters over sound. The microphone had to be just there, on a sort of perch in front of me! This made me furious, because when I was directing a scene, it prevented me from doing the camera movements I wanted. At the time, the sound engineer was not on the stage, but in a cabin above the stage, rather away from us. Once, while he was inside his cabin, I moved the mike – for a certain technical reason – about two metres from where he had put it. We had a rehearsal, and I called the sound engineer to ask him how it was. "Perfect," he said. So I said, "The mike was two metres farther away than where you had put it. So get the hell out of here, this is my stage!" They were not motion picture people, they were sound engineers and had nothing to do with making films. They didn't care about the camera. All they wanted was that their sound be as perfect as possible.

'So it was made, but it wasn't much of a success in Paris, because people didn't really understand it. It had a kind of success, because everything with sound was a success of sorts at that time, but the critics were not good. Then the German manager of the company wanted to show it in Berlin to prove that they had made sound in Paris as good as that in Berlin. Well, the success of *Sous* . . . in Berlin was such that its entire cost was reimbursed in one cinema alone! After that, all the countries bought it. Before Berlin, I thought I would never direct another picture. After Berlin I decided to make *Le Million*, and was given a free hand. *Le Million* was such a very big hit at the box-office that they finally let me do *A Nous La Liberté*. At the time of *Sous* . . ., it was absolutely impossible to mix the sound. In the film, every time the music comes, it is interrupted either by applause or something else, because I had to cut the sound; I could not mix it. I wrote a report to the German manager, saying that I had seen American pictures in which they must have done it on two tracks, and my old friend, Robert Florey, who was directing films in Hollywood wrote me to confirm this. So I started to shoot *Le Million* at the end of 1930, thinking they would have to find some way, for I made no provision for sound links, applause and such things, that we could have cut. When the picture was finished, I told the distribution manager that it could not be released before the sound was mixed. The sound engineers repeated that it was impossible, and there was a terrible row in German, at the end of which the manager shouted at them to get out. A week later, they could

Street scene from
Quatorze Juillet.

revealed more of Clair's private pessimism than his romantic elegance, more at any rate than a contemporary audience wanted to be made aware of, or at any rate not by a man to whose films they flocked for the charm with which he dealt with the everyday and lightened the lot of the ordinary men and women of France. *A Nous*, an elegant satire, was of course a Frenchman's view of Fritz Lang's disturbingly futuristic world in the silent classic, *Metropolis*. But a public with their shoulders pressed against the poverty and unemployment caused by the Depression found little to amuse them in a story which mocked labour and called for them to lay down their tools, bundle their possessions into a kerchief and head for the life of the open road. In restrospect, Clair could sympathize with their attitude, and at the time he understood what the public's reaction meant to him as an artist who made films for a living.

'Unfortunately, *A Nous* was a great critical success but not with the public. They didn't like it too much. I think now it was too audacious for that time: I treated the subject too unrealistically within a realistic background – factories, jails, labour, things like that.'

It's hard to do a Clair film justice with stills, as it is one of Mamoulian's or any other director who uses his camera like a musical metronome, always moving, gliding, its delights found in the rhythmic flow of action set to music. But pictures enable one to appreciate his mastery of composition and design, to delight in his unpretentious borrowings from the old master painters to create the right mood for his subjects: one can sense the influence of pre-Raphaelite painters like Holman-Hunt in *Le Million*; and that of the Flemish school of painters like Rogier Van der Weyden in *Sous les Toits*. For *A Nous La Liberté* the inspiration is the architecture of the pervasive Bauhaus movement – all deco angles, new graphic lines cutting across old horizons, complex, fascinating, aesthetic, hectic but finally dehumanizing shapes and boxes in which one is almost deco'd to death. Since Clair's subject is the evil of totalitarianism, whether from the left or the right, the film's look, with sets by Lazare Meerson and camera work by George Perinal, is in keeping with the theme. Because Clair's touch is deft, he pulls off an otherwise heavy subject with laughter, style and charm. Whereas Lang's *Metropolis* still frightens with its cold vision of the future, *A Nous* leaves one feeling affectionate good humour. Till one starts to think about its implications. The film contains several classic sequences, such as the afore-mentioned joke with the girl whose voice, first heard by the man in his cell (he is locked up for vagrancy) inspires him to break out so he can meet her, only to discover it wasn't her voice but that of a singer on a record. And the classic chaos on the factory floor begins when the mechanized routine for the mass manufacture of record players is thrown into turmoil when one man forgets to put in his cog on his turn, thus upsetting the routine of the man next to him, and they upsetting the third man, and so on and so forth, till the resulting pandemonium was good enough for Charles Chaplin to lift it virtually wholesale for re-use in his first use of sound in *Modern Times*

mix sound! The distributors backed me up, of course, as it would not have been possible to release the film the way I had shot it.

'*Le Million* was definitely conceived as a musical. The idea of people singing without reason was a real novelty then. In films like *The Jazz Singer* people sang because they were singers in the story. *Le Million* was based on an old vaudeville play, written in 1908 or thereabouts. I thought it was a very good idea for a film; in fact, the mechanism was very close to my silent film *The Italian Straw Hat* (1927).

'I started working in the south of France, and was very disappointed when I realized that there was no way of imitating the mechanism of craziness of that kind of farce without using the dialogue. I became so desperate that I sent a telegram to my company saying that I didn't want to do it. They answered that they had just bought the rights for me, so I was obliged to do the damn thing. The solution to the problem came when I realized the only possible way of making that craziness right for the film would be to make it unrealistic: instead of speaking the dialogue, I would have them singing it without giving any reason. I wrote the script but no dialogue. I never wrote dialogue at that time. I preferred the actors to improvise dialogue and then cut it if I didn't like it. I returned to Paris, excited with the idea and ready to shoot, when I went to see a German picture that was playing. It was *Die Drei von der Tankstelle* and I found that the German director, Thiele, had had the same idea. He didn't explore the sound the way I did, but there were a lot of things which were the same. I was a little mad to discover I was not the first one to do it. I made *A Nous La Liberté* on the same principle, but going a little farther, and I intended to continue in that manner with my films.'

All of Clair's good films, as it is with all good art, possess that touch of venom, the dash of spirit that gives good work its bite, but *A Nous La Liberté*

(1936). The film ends with out two heroes setting out for the life of the open road (ditto *Modern Times*), the one having sacrificed his love, the other his business empire; and the workers, replaced by machines, are seen singing while fishing, down by the riverside. No wonder Clair's capitalist friends thought it was communist, and his communist friends thought it was anarchist. In fact, it was Utopian, but you can't please everybody.

'For me, and for most of us I think, the beginning of the creative use of sound in pictures came in with the German director Walter Ruttmann's *Melody of the World* (1928). It was a long documentary, but with a marvellous use of natural sounds. I don't think much has been done with sound since that he didn't do, if still primitively. For me that film was the real basis in my change of attitude when I saw how one could cut and change the sound. I don't know whether that picture was seen in America at the same time as we saw it here. We had seen very few musicals from America when I made my first sound film. Even in *The Broadway Melody*, which was quite good, there was not a particular use of sound, and the first Lubitsch film, *The Love Parade*, one must admit, was technically not very imaginative. Everything on *Le Million* was written down before I began shooting; the music, and where it was going to go in the script. Some things were shot silent. At that time, I didn't write the dialogue, though since then, I write practically everything.

'If I had to drop one of the three operations of making a film – writing, directing and editing – I would drop direction. The personality and the value is more in its writing; and, as the editor, you control everything. Even if I write and direct a film, the editor can do what he wants and perhaps destroy the entire effort. Some people in America like Preston Sturges, Lubitsch, and Frank Capra did all three things. In Hollywood it is very clear who did what: script by . . . directed by . . . produced by . . . edited by . . . , but here in France, they confuse everything because they don't understand. Actually, it's a little my fault. I was one of the few directors who also wrote his own scripts, and so they assume everybody did. Since then, how many new sound-effect inventions have been made in the cinema? Practically none. Maybe world of sound is very limited.'

Thereafter Clair worked all over: a satirical comedy for Alexander Korda, *The Ghost Goes West* (1935); also in England a musical teaming Jack Buchanan and Maurice Chevalier, *Break the News* (1938), and some nimble comedies in America. He resumed work in France with *Le Silence est d'Or* (1947), and worked there until his retirement in 1965.

More typical of the French musical output were vehicles for stars like Tino Rossi, Frehel, Chevalier, Suzy Delair, and for the glamorous, romantic stars who usually found time for a song, like Danielle Darrieux *(Premier Rendez-vous)*, Jean Gabin, Simone Simon – and Florelle. Florelle was not glamorous, she was not a star – but she was a singer out of a drawing by Toulouse-Lautrec. Her voice was rough, matching her appearance. Not romantic or soulful but earthy, full of grit and pebbles; the sound of cars in the rain splattering worn clothes. In *L'Amour aux Sixième Étage* she is asked to sing a newly-composed song: 'No. I can't sing. What do you mean, you want me to sing? Eh.' She shrugs her shoulders and sings. In life those moments are unavoidable embarrassments. On the screen it is magic.

There were occasional musicals, really little more than revues, with long-stemmed Folies girls like black American-born Josephine Baker, Mistinguett, Zizi Jeanmaire, and the kind of operettas I have already mentioned. These made up the bulk of the French contribution to the genre. A few of these players sang. None of them really danced. Until Jacques Demy.

The Russians were among the last to start making sound films. Once they began, however, some superior early musical shorts and more dynamic musical films can be found. *Romance Sentimentale* for instance, an appealing short film, though filmed in Paris in 1929, was suggested by Sergei Eisenstein and made by G. Alexandrov and E. Tissé. In a room a woman sings a sad old gypsy melody, while outside her window, nature weeps in sympathy.

The early use of sound in Russia provoked extraordinary bursts of the imagination. Long before America discovered (i.e. with the Broadway première of *Oklahoma*, 1943) that the farmer and the musical could be friends, the Russians who weren't likely to look for proletarian heroes and heroines from the ranks of showgirls and musical performers, roped in not only the farmhand, but the tractor driver, the cowherd, the animal breeder, the postmistress and all those others whose labour provided the backbone of the socialist revolution. The subjects of these musicals were a proletariat deriving their happiness from their dedication to the state. The trend started in 1934, the first year of serious sound production in the Russian film industry, where among the 19 talkies made that year, they had their first international success with the Alexandrov musical, (one of two produced), *Vessiolie Rebyata* (Happy Fellows), which is

Ljuba Orlova as the heroine of Russia's first musical, *Happy Fellows* (Vesiolye Rebyata). The film, called *Moscow Laughs* in the USA, was directed by Grigori Alexandrov and enjoyed international critical success.

A still from Disney's *Steamboat Willie*. Alexandrov acknowledged the influence of Disney's cartoon shorts in his musicals.

Below: A droll moment from *Happy Fellows*.

Bottom: A production shot of the climax of *Happy Fellows*.

probably the most famous musical in the history of the Russian cinema. To date, 5737 copies have been printed up to meet the never-ending demand.* The idea was suggested by the enormous popularity of the Leningrad Jazz Orchestra under the direction of Leonid Utessov. It was initially planned to call the film *Jazz-Comedy* (but that sounded too much like capitalist bourgeois propaganda for it to be kept). The film's score was by a popular composer named Isaak Dunayevski, who now began a career as probably Russia's most successful popular composer. His songs for this and other films have become part of the Russian orchestra and choir repertoires ever since. Amazingly (natch!), considering its almost immediate triumph with the Soviet public, the film became the centre of a gigantic vindictive controversy which ran through the film industry, raged in the press, and was to reach up to the highest office of the Politburo before it received official clearance. It was only when a desperate Alexandrov showed it to the distinguished author, Maxim Gorki, and received his approval and support, that it was saved. Alexandrov's strongest critics were fellow film directors who considered it light, frivolous, and totally alien to their culture. Gorki, on the other hand, thought it was the life and soul of Russia. Thereafter the film went on to triumph far beyond its own broad borders after it was shown at the 1934 Venice Film Festival.

Said the critic of *The New York Times*: 'When the Muscovites produce a film which does not mention Dnieprostroy, ignores the class struggle and contains no hint of additional Marxism, it immediately becomes one of the great events of the international cinema. The new Soviet jazz comedy . . . is not more politically minded than a Laurel and Hardy picture . . . Yet the fact of the matter is that the film bursts with vitality and is sometimes uproariously side-splitting.' While the always socially-conscious Charles Chaplin sent his friend Alexandrov a telegram in which he wrote that, 'Alexandrov opened a new Russia for Americans. Before *Moscow Laughs*' (US title) 'Americans knew the Russia of Dostoevsky, now they can see a great transformation in the psychology of the people. The people are jolly and carefree. That is a great victory . . .'

Alexandrov's success, aided immeasurably by the catchy melodies of his collaborator, Dunayevski, was to lead to three more musicals with Dunayevski, whose roots were in the everyday, inevitably starring the popular blonde allround musical comedy actress Orlova. In *Zirk* (Circus, 1936) she played the American circus artist Marion Dixon, 'the human cannon ball', on a tour of Russia. The film's biggest song hit, 'Pesnja O Rodina' (Song of Home) became almost a second Russian national anthem, and reappeared in Lewis Milestone's anti-war propaganda film, *The North Star* (1943). In *Volga-Volga* (1938), which Stalin sent Roosevelt as a present, she played Strelka (the arrow), a carefree, bike-pedalling postal lady who delivers the mail to a small town where everybody, except the local bureaucrat, plays an instrument.

* Source of this and other factual information on the Russian films, Michael Hanish, *Vom Singen im Regen*, Henschelverlag, Berlin, DDR, 1980.

In their last film together, *Svetly Put* (The Happy Road, 1940), she was Tanya, a contemporary Cinderella in the Lilian Harvey mould.

Alexandrov, who'd spent some time in Hollywood with his friend Sergei Eisenstein, claimed that his inspiration came not from seeing American musicals (he was in London at the time of *The Broadway Melody*) but from seeing the early Disney Silly Symphonies and certainly, judging from some of the scenes, his films owe more to the eccentricities of these shorts, and to silent comedies, than to the American film musical. In a sequence from *The Happy Fellow* Kostya, attracted by a flute concert, temporarily locks his animals in a stately mansion. Pretty soon we have a flute concert with animal accompaniment. Before it's finished the animals are all over the house, eating the food laid out on a table, the cows drinking the water out of the aquarium, and after their meal, the happy and sated pigs collapse exhausted underneath the table where the waiters, caught up in the madness, start to pepper and salt them. Only when the befuddled humans start to cut them up do the pigs spring back to life!

Alexandrov's success failed to unleash a wave because, innately, these sort of non-political, good-natured escapist films were against the grain of a lot of serious-minded and much more politically powerful artists, writers and bureaucrats. But they did have some follow up. Most notably in the work of Ivan Pyriev, who, starting in 1938 with *Bogataya Nevesta* (The Rich Bride), also began to specialize in musicals, and introduced another musical favourite, Marina Ladynina, as the star of his films, always as an optimistic, energetic and enthusiastic workaholic. For his first film, with a score by Dunayevski, she was the rich collective farmer, Marinka. In *Traktoristy* (Young Life, 1939), she was the cheerful tractor driver Mariana; in *Svinarka I Pastuch* (They met in Moscow, 1941) she was highly honoured animal breeder Glascha who meets and falls in love with a farm labourer from the Caucasus at the annual All-Union Farmers'

Exhibition in Moscow. The themes in Pyriev's films met with official approval since they concerned the problems of increasing crops and livestock. One of their last films, *Kubanskie Kasaki* (Cossacks of the Kuban), made in 1950, still harped on the national drive to increase productivity, as two Kuban Cossacks vie with each other to raise the biggest of corn, not all of which came from the soil. Besides these excursions into trying to make people believe that breaking your back on a collective farm for your country was a regular songfest, there were the

Above: Ljuba Orlova in a Busby Berkeley style number in Alexandrov's *Circus* (Zirk).

Below, left: Marina Ladynina as the heroine of Ivan Pyriev's *Young Life* (Traktoristy).

Right: The Russian musical, 1950 style. A scene from Pyrjev's *Cossacks of the Kuban* (Kubanskie Kasaki).

more exportable musical excursions of the Russian cinema, filming their sanitized national treasures in ballet, opera and circus. The Russians have shown remarkable ingenuity in utilizing film for staging operas like *Boris Godunov* as large musical spectacles, and, as a means of perpetuating the art of their great classical artists, like Galina Ulanova (*Romeo and Juliet*, *Giselle*, *Swan Lake*) and Maya Plisetskaya. Opulent sets, and a Russian penchant for magical fantasy and simple-minded but mythical heroics, have found a colourful ally in filmed ballets and operas, e.g. *Glinka* and *The Stone Flower*.

Spain, Mexico and South America were latecomers to talking pictures, though Hollywood produced numerous Spanish-language features especially for this market long after it ceased

making foreign-language films. The Latins filmed stories beating and swirling to the rhythm of the flamenco, the tango, the samba and the rumba, and to the sound of castanets. They had their own, very popular, singing and dancing stars who shone though their films were made on shoestring budgets: dancers like Antonio, Ana Esmerelda and the great Pilar Lopez; hugely popular singers like Estrellita Castro, Antonita Colomé in the 30s; Juanita Reina and Lola Flores in the 40s and 50s; Mexico's idolized Jorge Negrete, Pedro Infante and Luis Aguilar, charro singers. José Mojica, Hugo del Carril and Argentina's celebrated Carlos Gardel were among the most famous tango singers of their day, their popularity taking them to Hollywood where they starred in a number of films for

Left: Carmen Sevilla, a favourite of Spanish filmgoers since the 1940s.

Left, below: Margarita Mora and Tito Guizar in *Amapola del Camino*.

Left, centre: Tango singer Hugo del Carril in *A Media Luz*.

Opposite, left: Argentine-born Libertad Lamarque in *Eclipse de Sol*. A favourite of Latin American audiences, Lamarque continued her career in Mexico after the rise of the Peróns – Evita (Eva Duarte) had played a small part in one of her films.

Bottom: Spanish-born Sara Montiel in the Mexican film *Piel Canela*. Montiel appeared in several Hollywood films without singing or dancing.

Far right: Imperio Argentina in the Spanish-German co-production *Andalusische Nachte*, which was shot in Berlin. It was based on Merimée's *Carmen*.

companies like Paramount and Fox, and which were then distributed in their own countries and to the large Spanish-speaking population of the United States. Libertad Lamarque is best known outside of her native Argentina and Mexico not for her singing but because she had to leave Argentina pronto when Perón came to power. Evita, who had played a supporting role in one of Lamarque's films, could afford to bury the hatchet – in her rival's neck. Lamarque was as great a star in Mexico as she had been in Argentina and outlived the Peróns.

The Latins had their musical child stars: Marisol, a sort of Shirley Temple, and Joselito, a sort of Bobby Breen. But of them all, only two of the Latin stars had careers whose impact reached beyond the borders of their own native language markets – Sara Montiel began in Spain, went to Mexico, and moved to Hollywood, where her four films included the lead opposite Mario Lanza in *Serenade* (1956). She returned to Spain to star in the most successful film ever made in the Latin countries, *El Ultimo Cuple*. Its success made her Spain's foremost female box-office star of the 60s, though her appeal leant heavily on the cleavage and pouting look so popular at that time. But even with her success she could not rival the artistry and popularity of the passionately throbbing-voiced Argentina-born Spanish star of the 30s and 40s, Imperio Argentina, whose songs carried her name far beyond the boundaries of her language and enabled her to star in films made all over Europe. These included Sardou's – not Puccini's – *Tosca* (directed by Jean Renoir in Italy, 1939), and *Andalusische Nächte* (1938), filmed in the UFA Berlin studios during the Spanish Civil

War. It was loosely based on Merimée's *Carmen* and had music by José Munoz-Molleda and Juan Mostaza-Morales. Certainly, the music and dances of Latin American countries – if not their stars – contributed a large and colourful addition to many American films during the 40s, based on their own appeal and not on any benevolent good-neighbour policy the US government might wish to promote.

Where France had its René Clair, England had its Victor Saville. They were the only directors outside of Germany whose work in musicals made any impact on the American public, who saw their films, if they could get to see them, because they enjoyed them. But on the whole England's musicals, considering the English affinities with the American genre and the renowned gallery of their music hall and stage artists, are an embarrassment. It wasn't to be the English film makers who took the lead then, nor, with a few exceptions, since. Few of their films and fewer still of their musicals ever achieved the standard set by the English theatre. Paltry imitations of Hollywood all-star revues like *Elstree Calling* (1930), for which even Hitchcock directed a few sequences, hardly helped, although the novelty of West End names 'talking' helped it to get its money back. It is impossible to think of one memorable English musical starring such wonderful musical artists as Cicely ('There's Something About a Soldier') Courtneidge, her husband, Jack Hulbert, Noël Coward, Ivor Novello, Gertrude Lawrence (*Star*, starring Julie Andrews. 20th Century-Fox, 1968), Beatrice Lillie, Gracie ('The Biggest Aspidistra in the World') Fields, George ('When I'm Cleaning Windows') Formby, Vera ('We'll Meet Again') Lynn, Evelyn ('When I Grow Too Old to Dream') Laye, Tommy ('Little White Bull') Steele, Julie (*My Fair Lady*) Andrews, Petula ('Down Town') Clark – all of these artists of international calibre. They all made films in

England and, carried by the stage reputations and personalities of the stars, those films were popular in the British Isles.

Admittedly for most of its years the British cinema seemed forever to be behind what the rest of the world was doing. In the 30s, as with most European countries, this was partly due to the lack of finance. *Sunshine Susie* made in 1932, cost only £30,000, and the average Jessie Matthews musical which boasted of the best in sets, costumes and music, was made for between £50,000 and £70,000. But more important than the lack of money was the lack of writers, directors and producers who respected or understood the genre. It isn't that one wanted English producers to do American-type musicals but for them to have found a cinematic equivalent of the Gilbert and Sullivan operettas or the sophisticated Noël Coward musicals.

Yet one of the brightest dancing stars in the international firmament was Jessie Matthews, the posh-voiced Cockney who made all her musicals in English studios. So appealing and high-spirited was her personality that the films of this saucer-faced musical nymph had the same impact on American audiences as they had on her British fans. It was only because the US cinemas were tightly controlled that her films did not achieve the great breakthrough everybody rightly expected. Throughout the 30s her films, carefully mounted, lovingly made, proved immensely popular. *The Good Companions*, her vignette in *Friday the 13th*, *Evergreen, Gangway, First a Girl, It's Love Again,* etc., were skilfully woven around her artistry, highlighting her exquisite dancing and empha-

Richard Tauber as Canio in *Pagliacci* (1937), a misguided British attempt to film Leoncavallo's opera (Tauber was the only opera singer in the cast). The girl in his arms is Steffi Duna.

sizing her appealing blend of 30s sexiness, sentimentality and piquancy. She worked with several directors, including her husband, Sonnie Hale; Alfred Hitchcock, who on a sabbatical from suspense directed her in his only musical, *Waltzes from Vienna* (1933), and Carol Reed in a comedy *Climbing High* (1939). But it was the five memorable films she made with Victor Saville that assured her place in film history. He it was who best understood her unique qualities and summed them up for me by saying, 'She had a heart. It photographed.'

George Formby, a great British film favourite of the 1930s.

Jessie Matthews rose from being one of André Charlot's young ladies (during which time she understudied Gertrude Lawrence) to starring in the celebrated Charlot Revues, and in 1930 co-starring with Lupino Lane in Cochran's celebrated production of the Rodgers and Hart musical *Evergreen* at the Gaiety Theatre – which sent her to the top of her profession.

'It was while I was doing *Hold my Hand* that Albert de Courville, the director of *There Goes the Bride* (1932) saw me on the stage and told Michael Balcon that I had a flair for comedy and could give a sustained performance. Balcon didn't believe this and was all against my being cast for the part. They finally let de Courville have his way. When Balcon saw the first week's rushes, he signed me for a long-term contract.

'Albert de Courville was one of the best directors I worked for, but he could be unpredictable. I would be on the set at 6.30 in the morning, and at 3 a.m. the following morning, I would still be there! One time the sound man came over and asked me if I couldn't do something about the rumbles in my tummy. I said, "I sure can. It needs some food! And then it will stop rumbling.' The director came over and told me not to get temperamental. I asked him if he had any idea what time it was. "It's half-past three, and I've been on this set since six in the morning. The sound department is complaining about the rumbling noises in my stomach, and I want some food. It's not unreasonable at half-past three to want some food . . ." He said, "I made a film once with some flyers, and during that film, two men were killed!" I went beserk. "That's all you ruddy care about. Well you're not killing this girl off." And I raced off the set, pushing anyone who tried to stop me out of the way. I didn't realize until later that two of the people I'd nearly knocked down the stairs were Michael Balcon and his brother who were just coming to watch the filming. I locked myself in the dressing room, crying and sobbing. I was completely exhausted.

'The important collaboration in terms of my film career was with Victor Saville and Michael Balcon at Gaumont British. We began with *The Good*

Everything stops for tea. Jessie with Victor Saville, the director of her best films, on the set of *It's Love Again*.

Right: Jessie Matthews, the British star who became an international favourite in musicals during the 1930s. A still from *Friday the 13th*.

Below: Jessie Matthews in *The Good Companions* (1933). Her leading man was John Gielgud.

Companions (1932), from the play by J. B. Priestley, and co-starring a singing(!) John Gielgud.

'The breakthrough into the overseas market really began with that film. It spurred Gaumont on to spending even more money on my films, and getting technical talent in from America to work on them. This gave them the polish that so many of our other musicals of the period lacked.

'The British film producers then relied on a really good story, but eventually found that they had to go to America for the technicians to do the filming. Unfortunately we were very stubborn. We would not learn from the Americans. It's sad, as we might have been better technically then. For instance, they had great difficulty in photographing me when I first went into films. I have this tilted nose. We used to have terrible trouble with it, because nobody knew how to go about photographing it. They used to make it worse by highlighting it, so that it came out like a bulb. Then Sir Michael Balcon decided to make me into an international star and got Glen MacWilliams, an American photographic expert, over to work on my films which Victor Saville was to direct. On the first day's shooting when Glen arrived I was in tears in the make-up room. I was a bundle of nerves. I thought here's another cameraman who won't know what to do with my face. I began at once saying to him, "Look at my bulbous nose; look at my long upper lip; look at my big teeth and small chin!" He looked at me and said, "Anybody who says they can't photograph you, baby, is alibi-ing their own damn bad photography!" Glen shot a few feet of me with no make up at all, then took me back to the German make-up man. He said to Heinrich, "Put the thinnest of make-up possible on her; no shading at all, and concentrate on her eyes." When I saw the first few shots, I went straight out and bought him a gold cigarette case. I wouldn't move in any film after that, unless I had Glen MacWilliams as my photographer.' (MacWilliams photographed *Lifeboat*, with Tallulah Bankhead. A man who can find enough different angles in a lifeboat to make a film in it interesting must be brilliant).

'My films had more of a gloss than most English films of that time, because they were international. We had Americans, Germans, and English working on them. When I first began, the technicians, camera and make-up men made me feel so self-conscious that I began to have the biggest inferiority complex about my looks. I dreaded doing close-ups. But Victor Saville used to say to me, "Darling, you look beautiful. Look that camera straight in the eye and say – I am beautiful, and my God you'll be beautiful!" With his magic and the lighting, there was no doubt about it, I looked beautiful!

'I had a lot of American composers for my songs' (Rodgers and Hart, Irving Berlin; Cole Porter first wrote 'Let's do it' for her and her husband, Sonnie Hale) 'and the English writers picked on me for preferring them. I'd say, "I simply choose the best songs." I had the choice of songs then. I didn't know whether they were English, French, Italian, Russian, Jewish, German or what the hell their nationality was! The songwriters were introduced to me as ordinary human beings; they would play

enabling you to strive for perfection, which I always wanted. I collaborated on most of my own dance numbers, literally 50/50, with the choreographers I worked with.'

The film of *Evergreen* (1934) was a free adaptation by Victor Saville and Emlyn Williams of the stage hit, with new songs added to the original Rodgers and Hart score. They couldn't be on hand to write additional material as it might be needed, so they gave Saville the right of interpolation and it resulted in the song that virtually became Jessie Matthews' signature tune, when Harry Woods wrote 'Over My Shoulder' for her finale. *Evergreen* is the story of a 1909 music-hall actress, who was

Jessie Matthews in her most celebrated number, 'Dancing on the Ceiling' in *Evergreen*. In this she was her own choreographer.

their songs, and sometimes I would start to sing a song with them, from which they had accidentally pinched eight bars. They'd stop dead in their tracks, look at Louis Levy, who was the musical conductor, and ask, "What gives?" Louis would tell them that's what I was there for. I had a very good musical ear. They used to hate my guts!

'For a London play, rehearsal time would be four weeks for the entire show. In films, however, I'd spend six weeks just on the big dance numbers to get them perfect before the actual shooting. I've always preferred films to the stage; I've always been terrified of an audience, afraid I wouldn't be able to give my best. In films, the fact that you can always do a scene again takes a load off your mind,

blackmailed into retirement, and the subsequent success of her daughter, who exploited her fame. Singing 'Over My Shoulder' she did a strip to show the audience that she wasn't her own mother. The early part of the film affords an opportunity for excellent period settings of music-halls and so forth, and the latter for cheerful modernism – for both the apartment interiors as well as the stage productions. Towards the end, a restless Miss Matthews, in love with the man who must pretend to be her son, executes a particularly fine, long solo dance through the rooms and up the stairs of her home. The technique of this production and its presentation rise well above the material itself.

Remarkable then that after having scaled such a peak they maintained that level. Admittedly their next collaboration, *First a Girl* (1935), wasn't another *Evergreen*. The songs by M. Sigler, A. Goodhart and A. Hoffman were very good but the plot, a much watered-down version of an earlier German film, Reinhold Schünzel's *Viktor und Viktoria*, had become airy. It was still about the girl who goes through much of the film disguised as a boy. But men's tails only emphasized her sexuality and not even a stuffed shirt could disguise her femininity, not with those large, heavily painted lips, those soft, delicately shaded doe-like eyes and that boyish hair cut that is far too fetching to be anything but a girl's. Saville draws his jokes not from the disguise but from the story itself, while using the whole charade for lavish production numbers that matched anything Hollywood was doing, as where Jessie, in glamorous beaded chiffon and bird of paradise feathers is discovered asleep in a gigantic birdcage.

'It's Love Again', wrote John Gillet, 'was the last of Saville's British musicals of the 30s and one of the most lavish, in terms of settings and musical numbers. It is quite clearly American-influenced' (with several trans-Atlantic talents like Lesser Samuels, later to collaborate with Saville in America), 'but it also has echoes of the European musicals which Saville had adapted. Yet it remains a recognizably personal film, due to its defiantly English sense of humour (which, in the case of Sonnie Hale, now seems dated and repetitive) and in the sheer flair and warmth of the playing. The idea of a publicity stunt which creates a mythical exotic lady big-game hunter who descends on London society is made for musical comedy, and Saville and his scriptwriters wring some splendid situations from it, managing at the same time to integrate the numbers logically into the plot, like Jessie as a big-game huntress performing bizarre, hotted-up temple dance at the reception. This is followed by a fast-and-furious slapstick shooting scene which, Saville recalls, was later reworked by Preston Sturges for the 'Ale and Quail Club' shoot-out in *Palm Beach Story*. One remembers the intimate numbers as well as the big ones, like the charming song and dance between Jessie Matthews and Robert Young on the landing, and the later 'non-dance' in the restaurant where everything is conveyed through shots of tapping feet. (The songs are by Coslow and Woods). Like other Saville films, everything finally revolves around Jessie Matthews and how triumphantly she carries it! Whether

A number from *First a Girl*. The risque German musical, *Viktor und Viktoria* (1933) was adapted for Jessie Matthews without the risk – but the numbers were good.

Jack Buchanan in *Brewster's Millions*.

gliding into 'It's Love Again' before Ernest Milton's bored producer, or belting out 'Gotta Dance, Gotta Sing' in the Park, she exudes extraordinary charm and a kind of innocent tenderness and makes the dialogue sound even wittier than it is. And in the final production numbers, dressed in shiny sequins, she pulls out all the stops in a great display of star power, followed by the beautifully staged scene of her returning quietly up the theatre stairs past the hurrying crowds to start all over again – as Elaine.' After this collaboration Jessie continued successfully for several more years on her own while Saville took his talents further afield, to Hollywood.

Another debonair musical comedy star of the period was Jack Buchanan, 'Mr West-End'. Before

Gracie Fields in *We're Going to be Rich*, the first of three attempts by 20th Century-Fox to promote her as a glamorous international star. The attempt failed in spite of her enormous popularity in Britain.

A scene from *Keep Smiling*, Gracie Fields' second film for 20th Century-Fox.

musical comedies like *Man of Mayfair, Yes, Mr Brown, Brewster's Millions, Break the News* and others, some of which he also produced and directed. The films were trifles, popular in England, but they never carried much weight abroad, even though his personality, his ability as a song and dance man and his stage reputation on both sides of the Atlantic put him almost on a par with Fred Astaire. Fittingly, Buchanan's finest film moment was opposite Astaire in Vincente Minnelli's loving satire of Broadway cranks and shysters, *The Band Wagon* (1952), for which Buchanan pulled out all the stops with ineffable finesse. Never more in control even at his most outrageous, and if it weren't for the fact that one can't steal the show when the show is so good, he would have.*

The highest-paid stage, film and recording star in the world was the singing Lancashire lass, 'Our Gracie' Fields. Most of the money spent on her predominantly British films, popular only in her own country, went to her and it showed, but since audiences flocked to see her anyway, it obviously didn't matter. At the time of her film debut in *Sally in Our Alley* (1932), the title song of which is one of the numerous standards associated with her, she was already a long-ranking music hall and stage star. She had a plain, down to earth personality and a powerful carolling voice. These were the film's virtues and this is virtually the only thing to make these films viewable today. The titles of some of her films are the clue to what people saw in her: *Looking on the Bright Side, Shipyard Sally, Keep Smiling, Love, Life and Laughter, Sing as We Go* and *The Show Goes On.* Since people seemed to like her in anything — 20th Century-Fox signed her to a lucrative contract in the hope that they could make her an international draw. For their first deluxe attempt at glamorizing her, *We're Going to be Rich* (1938), they gave her two Hollywood-type leading men, set the story in 'exotic' turn-of-the-century South Africa and attempted to launch her as a Mae West type! This rouged and corseted Gracie was not 'Our' Gracie — nor was she anybody else's Gracie in the less ambitious films she made in Hollywood during the war to finish her contract. But she was better made-up than she'd been in her other films, and she remained a leading recording and stage star with her devoted British public, up to the time of her death, aged 81.

It so happens that the English cinema began and ended the 40s with a masterpiece and that the same man was connected with both. For the first I beg indulgence, for it's not strictly a musical, but its joys are so many and so woven in with the music that it takes its place here. It was conceived, produced and partially directed by the Hungarian, Alexander Korda, aided by his production designers, brother Vincent and William Cameron Menzies; by Georges Perinal's dazzling camera work; by an utterly beguiling script by Miles Malleson, and by a cast that was drawn from many nationalities in wartime England and could not be faulted. It had as Princess, June Duprez (English), as King, John

producing, directing and starring in British film musicals he had appeared with great success in several made in Hollywood, including *Paris* and *Monte Carlo.* He had already starred in several silent British films and continued throughout the 30s giving delightfully deft performances in

* The song, 'By Myself', sung by Astaire, was originally sung by Buchanan — in *Between the Devil* on Broadway.

Justin (Maltese descent), as the little thief, Sabu (Indian), and as the evil wazir, awesome in his power and obsession, Conrad Veidt (German). All these help to make the film an exciting adventure. Perinal's rainbow hues make it a technicolor tour-de-force of teeming bazaars that sparkle with a thousand colours, marbled palaces in the dusk, the red sails against the blue-black ocean, the brightly-woven turbans, swirling cloaks, the fantastic treasures of the Arabian Nights – all with colours to rival them. So far its success is assured as romance, adventure, spectacular oriental fantasy. But it is Hungarian composer Miklos Rosza's stirring, sinuous, sensitive score, spun in to accompany and add a ravishing shimmer to the story, that gives this film its place among musicals. The slave's song, 'Be Still, My Heart', (sung by Adelaide Hall) to a Princess awakening to love on a hot afternoon in a garden, whose gardener is Death; the little thief plucking up courage in the bowels of the terrifying, one-eyed goddess, with a song of bravado that scatters the skeletons; the glittering, chilling dance of the silver maiden (directed by Ludwig Berger), and our first glimpse, a flood of colour and movement, of the teeming port of Bagdad (directed by Michael Powell), where the sailors and slaves unload the newly-arrived ships and sing of their mistress, the cruel, eternal sea. It is wondrous. It is *The Thief of Bagdad*, and it takes its place with *Fantasia, The Wizard of Oz* – and the film it inspired forty years later, *Star Wars*. One of the directors employed on the film (the others included Ludwig Berger, Tim Whelan and, uncredited, Korda himself), was Michael Powell, a highly imaginative artist with a great bent for the fantastic, who would be responsible for the musical masterpiece, *The Red Shoes*, that climaxed this decade.

Michael Powell, who had begun his career as an assistant to Rex Ingram in Nice, became a writer, then directed for Korda, and teamed up with another Hungarian, Emeric Pressburger, to form a company to write, produce and direct their own films. In that capacity they made *The Red Shoes* (1948) from an original screenplay by Pressburger. It is the first and, for most students and lovers of ballet, still the only film to capture the dance world's atmosphere with its strange allure and consuming passions. With a radiant new star, the Royal Ballet's Moira Shearer in her film debut as the ballet-crazed Vicky Page. ('Why do you want to dance, Miss Page?' 'Why do you want to live, Mr Lermontov?'). Designed by Heinz Heckroth, photographed in beautifully dreamy colours by Jack Cardiff, and with an original score by Brian Easdale conducted by Sir Thomas Beecham, Powell's film achieves an almost third-dimensional atmosphere. The story, inspired by the Byzantine world of the Ballets Russe and the tortured relationships of Diaghilev with some of his dancers, takes its last inspired stroke from Pavlova's career, when the performance that great artist was scheduled to dance the night of her death went on as announced, ends on the shot of Vicky's follow spot taking her place, dancing her part. Like Pavlova, she was irreplaceable. The film was an enormous success in its day and went on to become a cult. The central ballet, created by Robert Helpmann, perfect for film, is unsuitable for the stage and has never been adapted for the theatre, but generations of awed and enamoured youngsters have come to ballet as a result. It inspired others to try and integrate full-length ballet numbers into their films: *An American in Paris, Invitation to the Dance, Black Tights*, and Ben Hecht's fruity *Spectre of the Rose*, with exchanges like this one: 'Love me with your eyes,' the hero tells the heroine. 'I am', she replies. 'Harder!'

What Powell and Pressburger had done was something more than show that a mass audience would sit still for classical ballet. They made their audiences share and enjoy a world that was more notorious for cutting people out of it than for letting

Above, left: Michael Powell at work, directing the opening scene of *The Thief of Bagdad*. More than forty years later it remains the standard by which all subsequent tales of romance, fantasy and adventure must be measured.

Above: One of the many exquisitely-composed shots in a visually memorable film. The colonnade of the Sultan's palace in *The Thief of Bagdad*, one of the many memorable moments when music not merely accentuates the mood but creates images independent of but in harmony with those from the film – and every bit as spellbinding.

Opposite, top left: A scene from Michael Powell and Emeric Pressburger's *The Red Shoes*. The ballet master is Leonide Massine; at class can be seen Robert Helpmann, behind Ludmilla Tcherina, and fourth behind him the film's sensational discovery, Moira Shearer.

Right: Classical ballet on film. Tcherina and Helpmann in the second act pas-de-deux of *Swan Lake* in *The Red Shoes*.

The shoemaker (Massine) and the girl who accepts the fatal red shoes (Shearer). A scene from the full-length ballet in the film *The Red Shoes*.

Far right: Moira Shearer in *The Red Shoes*.

any but the most obsessed into it. That still remains this work's unique achievement. To appreciate the uniqueness of Powell's achievement one has only to recall the more recent attempt to film the great Nijinsky's life and his destructive relationship with Diaghilev (*Nijinsky*. Paramount, 1979).

Spurred by their triumph, Powell and Pressburger went further. This time it was to be not just a chunk of culture made accessible by the melodramatic parts of the story binding it together, but Offenbach's fantastic opera, *The Tales of Hoffmann* (1951). It reunited most of the creative production team and artists who had become international stars since *The Red Shoes* – Moira Shearer, Robert Helpmann, Leonide Massine and the ravishing brunette ballerina Ludmilla Tcherina, used here not to dance, but to vamp Hoffman on his Venetian interlude. This time they failed to pull it off, for

Above: The Prologue, *Tales of Hoffmann.* Moira Shearer in the dragonfly ballet.

Above right: Ludmilla Tcherina as the seductive Giulietta in Powell and Pressburger's *Tales of Hoffmann.* Many of the principal parts were played by ballet dancers; they mimed the words which opera singers contributed to the soundtrack.

Opposite, top left: Anna Neagle in *London Melody.*

Right: Anna Neagle on more familiar ground. *The Courtneys of Curzon Street,* made in England and one of many films in which her co-star was Michael Wilding.

people can be wearied by an excess of splendid, ravishing, opulently beautiful sights and sounds that leave one no space to reflect on what has been going on and to catch one's breath, a discovery which those other masters of the fantastic, von Sternberg in the 30s and more recently Federico Fellini, made to their cost. But its effect is memorable and has influenced many subsequent attempts at filming opera including, most recently, Joseph Losey's version of Mozart's *Don Giovanni* (1979), and Franco Zeffirelli's glamorous *La Traviata* (1982).

About that time there was another attempt to film an opera, this one English, and it arose from a burst of patriotism lit by the dawn of a new Elizabethan age – John Gay's *The Beggar's Opera* (1952). Prestigious talents set to work on it. It was to be the greatest of its kind. Christopher Fry adapted it and wrote new lyrics as well. The bright hope of the British theatre, Peter Brook, selected this for his directorial film debut, and none less than Sir Laurence Olivier chose to reveal his light but undistinguished baritone in the role of Macheath, the romantic 18th-century highwayman. Most of the other actors were given suitable dubbed voices. The film moves, it thrives, it over-teems with ideas and action, drowning singers and songs. Peter Brook, one of the most cinematic stage directors is, sadly, a very stagey director of films.

Apart from these films, the British musicals of the 40s and subsequently differed little, their defects

proliferating, from their predecessors. There was Anna Neagle in the 40s – a popular performer whose films were riddled with stereotypes and caricatures. Under the guidance of her mentor – husband, producer and director – Herbert Wilcox, she also became an important dramatic box-office star. In the 30s musicals she was *The Little Damozel* (1933), and had a success when she chanted the 'Jingle of the Jungle' on the nightclub floor in *London Melody* (1937) but suffered because of the hero backstage. Wilcox had such faith in her that she replaced Jeanette MacDonald in *The Queen's Affair* (1933) when the American star fell out, and starred in the film version of Noël Coward's *Bitter Sweet* (1933), opposite Fernand Gravet before Jeanette re-made it in Victor Saville's 1940 production. All similarities between the two stars cease there.

Anna Neagle's popularity in modest musicals and historical slices began with *Goodnight Vienna* (1932) and continued into the 50s on the screen, and seemingly forever on the stage. In 1939, having had her greatest success as Queen Victoria in *Victoria the Great* (1937), she went to Hollywood, where she appeared in three RKO remakes of earlier musicals, *No No Nanette, Irene* and *Sunny.* Back in England during the war she became a favourite star in a string of technicolor fantasies which partnered her with Michael Wilding or somebody who looked like him. She was usually the servant girl who married the son of the house on the hill against family opposition. She would leave her husband (for his sake), pressured by his snobbish family, and quickly make a great career for herself on the London musical stage. In the meantime, husband, pining on the inside but stiff upper lip on the outside, has joined the army to carry on family tradition. He rises in the ranks and she in the theatre without their running across each other for the next half a century, until, unchanged by the passing years, he discovers her entertaining his

troops. A dramatic reunion ensues, and then possibly a flashback to the good old days when they first met, loved and danced as *The Courtneys of Curzon Street*, *Spring In Park Lane*, *Piccadilly Incident*, *Elisabeth of Ladymead* or *Maytime In Mayfair*.

Miss Neagle had returned from Hollywood, well-coiffured and made-up, looking more Greer than Garson and all the other English 'lady' lookers who had made their mark on Hollywood. She was a conscientious actress, and an attractive and like-able dancer but moon-faced Michael Wilding was a liability.

In vain one looks for one musical to match the sentiment of a Novello melody, the sparkling elegance of Noël Coward, or the wit and bubble of Gilbert and Sullivan. Instead one gets the funereal Bryan Forbes Cinderella story, *The Slipper and The Rose* (1976). About films like it and others, hind-sight may prove a kindlier judge but, once, in Jessie Matthews, the British musical had a Cinderella and Victor Saville was a director who could fit a film to a star whose foot fit the slipper. Their work was good in its day, and grew better in the meanwhile. Now it is simply marvellous. It can be done.

The Japanese didn't start to make talkies until 1932, and those they did make were propaganda and not musicals. China filmed a few native operas, rarely seen by anyone from the West and so hard to judge. Although a great many films were produced in the Far East, few if any made an impact on the American or European market until the breakthrough in the 50s.

India's output is too vast and complex for more than the most passing glance here. For a daily audience of 12,000,000 people and an average of 700 new films a year, the Indian cinema usually contains numerous and very long musical

sequences irregardless (by Western standards) of subject and plot. Modelled as their industry is on the outrages of the American and European studio systems of the 30s and before, it's not surprising that so many of their films and whole genres (i.e. Westerns, serials, musicals) are little more than neatly-pirated adaptations of American, French, English and Italian successes. Chaplin's *Limelight*, de Sica's *Shoeshine* and Cukor's *My Fair Lady* were

Anna Neagle in *Sunny*, one of the four films directed in Hollywood by her husband, Herbert Wilcox.

Sid Field and Kay Kendall in *London Town*, an expensive disaster made by the Rank Organisation and released in 1946.

Right: Anna Neagle and Michael Wilding in *Spring in Park Lane.*

Indian cinema commands a huge audience which loves song and dance interludes. Left: *Aan* (1952) had its world première in London. Right: *Apna Desh* (1945) looks forward to independence – note the map of India, in chains, and the portrait of Gandhi.

all popular with Indian audiences. So the ninety-minute *Shoeshine* became a four-hour *Awara*, and the long *My Fair Lady* became the very long *Manpasand*, the story of a little twig seller who makes a rich marriage in Bombay society with the help of a Henry Higgins. The history of talkies and musicals in India was briefly this: *Alam Ara*, an Arabian Nights subject released in March 1931, was India's first talkie – made after the film's director had seen the part-sound American musical *Show-boat*. Sound triumphed in India on a wave of music. It was nothing for a film to have anything from 42 to 70 songs – but music has always been an essential part of Indian theatre and it proved to be the Indian cinema's sure-fire way of unifying its diverse cultural and linguistic groups. Thus, from the outset, the song-and-dance formula unified the fabric of the nation, even if for only a few hours. But until the mass immigration of Asians to make new lives for themselves in Europe and America few of their enormously popular movies were known to a Western public, and none had any influence.

Finally to the star of the show – Germany. This is the cinema that produced Dietrich, *Congress Dances*, Anton Walbrook, *Faust*, Conrad Veidt, *Caligari*, Emil Jannings, Elisabeth Bergner, Ernst Lubitsch, Pola Negri, *Nosferatu*, Luise Rainer, *Siegfried*, Peter Lorre, *M, Metropolis*, Asta Nielsen, *Die Drei von der Tankstelle*, Billy Wilder, Lilian Harvey, *Tartuffe*, Lil Dagover, Hedy Lamarr and many more. But first to re-cap a little. By 1932 Hollywood woke up to find itself trailing behind. The film capital would take a decade to catch up. Here was a musical cinema full of witty inventive-

ness, lightness of touch and enormous charm.

I cannot think of a better example than one of the triumphs of 1934, and incidentally, actor Willi Forst's directorial debut, *Leise Flehen Meine Lieder* (Unfinished Symphony), depicting the early life and unhappy love of Franz Schubert. It was written by Walter *(Ninotchka)* Reisch, and starred Hans Jaray as the day-dreaming composer and a very glamorous Hungarian soprano, Marta Eggerth, as the high-born excuse he finds for not finishing the Unfinished. Schubert, a young, struggling composer, is eking out a living teaching maths at a boys' school. He has difficulty holding down a job since his thoughts are forever off on another tangent. During a walk through a meadow separating his home from work the seeds of one of his best-known melodies, 'Heidenroslein' (common to every English schoolboy as 'By the wayside growing — Rosebud, Rosebud, Rosebud, red, By the wayside growing'), begins to take root. Arriving late in his unruly classroom, his mind is almost completely in the thrall of his inspiration, so that he is oblivious of the boys' mockery as he keeps turning the signs on the blackboard into musical keys, and the lines separating one maths problem from another into double and triple bars of music. The students, who

are taught by repeating the solution out loud, start with two times two and end up by singing the melody.

This inspired device for introducing a song, the beauty of the clear melody, the purity of the boys' voices, the innocence and wit of this scene fuse into a sequence of extraordinary joy. The film is passionately, sweepingly, unashamedly romantic. It is also very lovely. Beneath the window the headmaster, already on his way to reprimand Schubert, stops dead when he hears the maths class in song. Of course schools were never like that. They should have been.

As the film made its triumphant progress across Europe and America, a whole spate of Schubert vehicles followed (including Richard Tauber in the British-made *Blossom Time,* Bernard Lancret in the 1939 French-made *Sérénade,* and a 1941 American remake of the Forst film, retitled *New Wine.* With Alan Curtis as Schubert and Ilona Massey as his love, this was Reinhold Schünzel's last film.) None could match it. Long after, when the German cinema was being written off because of the policies of its leaders, Forst's talents with films like *Bel Ami* (1939) and *Operette* (1941) were continuing to refine themselves. Forst, along with screen writer Walter Reisch and writer-director Karl Hartl formed one of the German-speaking cinema's most dynamic, creative triumvirates. By the time I made contact with Willi Forst he was living in embittered self-exile in Switzerland, and though touched by my interest, and courteous, he had no desire to relive the past. The third member of this youthful group of collaborators, the director and subsequent production head of Wien films, Karl Hartl, then still living in Vienna with his actress wife, Marthe Harell when we met, was fortunately more forthcoming.

As a teenager during World War I, Hartl started

Top left: Willi Forst, the Austrian actor who became a director and was responsible for some of the best musicals made in Germany.

Left: Forst's *Leise Flehen Meine Lieder,* with Hans Jaray and Marta Eggerth. This romance about Schubert's life was shown in England and the USA as *Unfinished Symphony.*

Above: Anton Walbrook (then known as Adolf Wolhbrück) and Paula Wessely in soft focus framed by the palm fronds. A scene from Forst's stylish *Maskerade.*

Top: Lizzi Waldmüller in the vibrant *Bel Ami*.

Above: Willi Forst acted as well as directed. He is on Maria Holst's right in *Operette*, which he made in 1940.

his film career at the thriving Sasha Film Co. as an assistant director – a glorified title for what was in fact a catch-all job that consisted of carrying cans of film and equipment from one end of the city to the other, and all the other odd fetch-and-carry jobs the company's top director, Alexander Korda, might need him for. Hartl struck up a close friendship with a teenage screenwriter, Walter Reisch, and a young ambitious film editor, Gustav Ucicky.

'We used to meet at a little coffee house, The Film Club, where we'd get to talk about movies and exchange ideas. We knew we wanted to work together, so when Reisch came up with the idea for *Pratermizzi* (1927) with Ucicky as the director and me as editor, we took the idea to Baron Sasha

Kolowrat, a marvellous human being who was mad about racing cars and engines and owned Sasha Film. Lucky for us he was a keen gambler and we talked him into it. We were all in our early twenties when you have the nerve to believe everything is possible. Billy Wilder was around too, writing for *Die Stunde*, a real boulevard tabloid. He was what we'd call a shotgun journalist, the kind who is always found lurking in other people's bedrooms – but very amusing. Later we all worked together at UFA. Billy wanted to be in films for as long as I knew him.

'*The Singing Fool* had been a sensation everywhere in Europe, including Germany and Austria. UFA planned four experimental films to test audience reaction. It's easy now to wonder why they hesitated so long before starting, but then you couldn't be sure it would last and a lot of important people were saying that sound would be the end of the film and it was better to leave things as they were. So UFA planned these four films: the first was the operetta, *Der Unsterbliche Lump* (Dir: Gustav Ucicky. 1930), based on a script I wrote with Robert Liebman, starring Gustav Fröhlich and Liane Haid; the second film was *Der Liebeswalzer* with Harvey and Fritsch; the third was *Die letzte Kompanie* (Dir: Kurt Bernhardt. 1930) with Connie Veidt and Mady Christians, and the fourth film in this group was *Der blaue Engel*. That was UFA's first all-talkie programme. Not a bad one. Virtually every film was a success and ensured the breakthrough of the sound film in Germany. At the same time Tobis Klangfilm, who had their own sound patent, were making *Die Nacht Gehört Uns*, for which Reisch and I wrote the script. Hans Albers starred in it and it was previewed in Berlin at the end of 1929, shortly before the UFA films, because Froelich worked faster. Sternberg, for instance, took about three months to make *Der blaue Engel* while Froelich shot his film in one month.'

Die Nacht Gehört Uns (The Night is Ours) was based on a French play (and also filmed in French) produced and directed by the silent film pioneer, Carl Froelich, who remained one of most distinguished of German directors until his death. The script, the direction, the enormous popularity of its "Hoopla! Here I come" star Hans Albers, and especially its fresh use of sound, made the film a sensation. A girl speeding her car over Sicilian mountain passes requires sounds to match: cars starting up and crunching along winding, gravelly roads. Sounds taken on location, while she's recovering in a hut after her crash – the wind, the birds, the memory of the screech of brakes: the mysterious rescuer, introduced as a voice from off-screen.

Karl Hartl: On top of which we shot all four films with simultanous English versions. The prestige film was [*Der blaue*] *Engel* of course, because it had Jannings, and *Der Liebeswalzer* also cost a good deal more than the other two. A lot of the people couldn't speak very good English, some not at all, but they could mouth the words well enough to be dubbed. It made the lip-synch easier of course if they had some knowledge of the language.

We didn't have the problems they had in

Hollywood – we didn't have to worry about people's voices for one thing because most of our major silent stars were also established stage favourites whose voices grew with their personalities. Most of the stars who didn't make the transition had already been *passé* in silent films. The men did better than the women. One of the biggest stars, Brigitte Helm (*Metropolis*), had difficulties at first because she had no stage experience. The studio was very concerned that she wouldn't make the transition. She had an incredibly powerful optical presence which would have been suited to a resonant sonorous voice, like Garbo, but she had a very squeaky little voice. But we overcame that. We wrote a story for her (*Die Gräfin von Monte Cristo.* 1931), in which she played a little movie extra who drives off the set in the limousine she's supposed to be getting out of, and doesn't stop till she gets to Monte Carlo, where they mistake her for the clothes she's wearing, the car she's driving and the labels on the empty movie luggage. This way we used the impact of her presence and also accounted for her voice.*

We spent three days experimenting with every way for a scene that would only run about 50 feet on the screen, just so we could get the effect of a quiet flowing brook behind our lovers, the way we wrote it. By then we'd gone too far to tear the page out and try something else. Four months later we're sitting in the screening room at the Neubabelsberg studios where the scene was being synchronized with Haid and Fröhlich, and next to them sat one of the gaffers with his feet in a tub of mud. While they were talking he was squirming around in the tub, and the sound he made was so exactly that of a little brook that we couldn't have gotten it any better with the equipment we have now.

I started directing more by accident than design, because of this silly policy in the German studios as a result of one of those moral waves that shot through the hierarchy forbidding husbands and wives from working on the same film, when the

* As *The Countess of Monte Cristo* it was re-made several times in America, once with Fay Wray, and another time with Sonja Henie – her last American film.

* The German film industry was notorious for its husband/wife teams – Joe and Mia May, Fritz Lang and Thea von Harbou, Elisabeth Bergner and Paul Czinner, Richard Eichberg and Lee Parry, Anny Ondra and Carl Lamack.

husband was a director and the wife an actress.*

Years later. Hartl's long string of commercial and critical hits, including the futuristic *F.P.1 antwortet nicht*, which he not only co-wrote with Reisch, but directed and adapted for all three language versions, and the monumental *Gold* (UFA 1934) were to result in an invitation by Goebbels to return to Austria as head of production of the moribund Wien Film, and to regenerate the Austrian film industry. For most of the war Hartl and Willi Forst managed to confound Berlin's propaganda chiefs by making a series of popular musicals, too light to carry a message, which were aptly described as 'a flight into the past!' After the war, Hartl's old ties with Korda resulted in collaboration on films like *The Third Man* but all this was still a long way off, not to be known in 1930.

UFA, the largest of the German companies, took their challenge straight into the opposition's home base by opening a flag-ship theatre of their own in New York, for the exclusive showing of their product. Other New York cinemas also specialized in German features shown to large and enthusiastic audiences right up to the outbreak of the war*. In 1930, of all foreign films shown in New York, more than half were German, the remainder were divided

Above: Hans Albers, the box-office king in Germany, in *Heut Kommt's d'rauf an*.

Above left: Karl Hartl on the set with his star, Johanna Matz, while making *Mozart – Wenn die Götter Lieben*.

Left: In 1930 the German company, UFA, released four sound films to test audience reaction to talkies. All of them were successful – but one of them became a film classic. Marlene Dietrich in *Der blaue Engel* (The Blue Angel).

director, Wilhelm Thiele, who began in films in the mid-20s but wouldn't make his mark until sound when, in quick succession, he directed a string of hugely commercial and imitated musicals. His first *Ton-film* was in the operetta mould, *Der Liebeswaltzer* (The Love Waltz, 1930). UFA's first declaration of war against films in technicolor with songs à la Hollywood. An ambitious director, experienced authors and a hit songwriter (Werner-Richard Heymann) made up the crew'. This film, opening in 1930 with a brilliant Berlin première, and the quick follow-up *Die Drei von der Tankstelle*,

Above: Wilhelm Thiele, whose *Liebeswalzer* contributed much to the success of UFA's venture into sound films, shooting an exterior for *Die Drei von der Tankstelle*.

Right: Lilian Harvey and Willy Fritsch in *Die Drei von der Tankstelle*.

Far right: A scene from Thiele's *Die Privatsekretärin*, a musical in a modern setting which was so successful that versions were made in three other languages.

Far right, below: Renate Müller, star of *Sunshine Susie*, Victor Saville's English version of *Die Privatsekretärin*.

Opposite, top left: The success of sound persuaded producers, for a few years at least, that other-language versions of their films should be made simultaneously. Gilbert Roland, second from left, is one up on his fellow actors here, having two languages at his command. The film was MGM's *Man of the North* (1930).

between ten other countries.* By the end of 1931, despite the terrifying reports of economic crisis and the popping of banks on every side, the privately owned UFA was able to pay 6% dividends on its stock for the first time in four years. This meant that, not only were they a money-making proposition, but the movie business in general, despite the still lingering sighs of critics for the silent days, was a worthwhile business proposition for investment.

In the 20s and early 30s Erich Pommer, head of Universal Film AG, known as UFA studios, was a key figure in creating an enviable environment for stars, writers, composers and directors to work in. The silent films he produced had helped make the German film world renowned. The musicals he produced boosted that reputation. Marlene Dietrich, before von Sternberg but already fascinating, had the female lead in the first German film with an added synchronized sound score, *Ich Küsse Ihre Hand Madame* (I Kiss Your Hand Madame, 1929), in which the title song was dubbed for the film's star, Harry Liedtke, by Richard Tauber. The following year, Dietrich, whose career had promised much for so long but never quite delivered, was to star and to exceed the brightest promise in the Pommer production that was to become a milestone in movies – *Der Blaue Engel* (1930). 'Falling in love again, – Never wanted to, – What am I to do, – I can't Help it.'

Another Pommer protégé was the young stage

* As late as October 1940 New Yorkers could see German films, like the anti-Bolshevist *Henker, Frauen und Soldaten*, starring Hans Albers, Zarah Leander's *Das Lied der Wüste*, or the Austrian musical *Der Opernball*.

* In 1934 the *New York Times* reviewed 64 German-language films, not counting all those Hungarian films produced by Germany.

reuniting Willy Fritsch and Lilian Harvey as the lovers, this time in a modern setting, ensured the trend by their phenomenal success.

The film's sweethearts had worked together in silent films without creating much of a stir, but sound made them the classic screen lovers, idols of the Germans. (For the French and English versions, being less ambitious than Lilian and not wanting to learn to speak in other languages, Fritsch's role was usually taken by the French actor Henri Garat.) Lilian, able to skip through her roles in three languages, became the German cinema's most important international drawing card.

Most of Thiele's musicals were set in the present and dealt with identifiable types, not out-of-work chorines or runaway princesses, but office secretaries and garage mechanics. These energetic proletarians and their simple interests and ambitions were the novelty that convinced the public to go along with the musical illogicalities. Along with his producer Erich Pommer, Thiele decided that *Die Drei von der Tankstelle* (1930) had to go even further in the dramatic integration of music, song, dialogue and picture, so that the story and characters would continue to develop while the plot flowed through each of these elements.

Before Thiele fled Nazi Germany to near oblivion in Hollywood as a director of jungle fantasies (*The Jungle Princess, Tarzan Escapes . . .*) he directed several more popular musicals, the best known perhaps being *Die Privatsekretärin* (1931) starring Renate Müller. It belonged to the moment, less restricted by the sentimentality that dates the operettas of that period where characters, stuck in turn-of-the-century sentiments and traditions, came in two types – princes and waitresses or waiters and princesses. So popular was this musical relating the love affair between the boss and his secretary that UFA also used the amenable Fräulein Müller in the French, Italian, and English adaptations of the film. Despite few accommodations except for the different language and a familiar supporting cast, the film was to have an enormous popular success, nowhere more so than in England where audiences made *Sunshine Susie* (Dir. Victor Saville) and its song 'Today I feel so happy' one of the big hits of the

year. Of course Saville, an old hand with several successful sound films behind him, brought some touches of his own that benefited the film. He restaged the song hit that Susie first sings in her courtyard apartment. Overheard and joined by the other dwellers in the block, Müller waltzes out of her room, along the streets of London into her office where neat, row upon neat row of fellow secretaries are pounding their typewriter keys in harmony with the refrain 'So happy, so happy . . .' Like a number

Lilian Harvey as a dancer in silent films. Top: *Die Kleine vom Bummel* (1925) and above, *Die Tolle Lola* (1927).

of German stars who made a personal hit with the English public (Gitta Alpar remade her great stage and screen operetta hit *Die Dubarry** in England as *I Give My Heart*), she followed it up with *Marry Me* (1932), the English version of another of her German successes, *Mädchen zum Heiraten*. This time it was directed by Wilhelm Thiele and shot in the Berlin studios, with an English supporting cast including music-hall favourite George Robey, brought over from London for the occasion. The spark failed to ignite a second time, which brings us to the central problem talkies created for European film producers and the subsequent marketing of their product abroad.

In Europe, as in the States, the biggest problems were not technical but human ones – an audience's national characteristics and interests. What a German finds funny might not necessarily make a Parisian laugh, or a man in Salt Lake City. One of the first victims of sound was comedy. There was no verbal equivalent for the international appeal of a pratfall. Ironically, while the talkies brought the public back they appeared to threaten the industry with the loss of its lucrative foreign-language markets. In Hollywood appearances have been enough to launch panics. One solution, still with us today, might have been inspired by one of the classics of the theatre, Cyrano de Bergerac, the hero of which mouths the words with which the handsome lover wins the girl – in movies they called it dubbing – "The Cyrano Method" by another name. But there were other attempts, and for a time some of the cleverest were made in Europe.

Hollywood worked out a simple model. Scenario writers developed a story which it felt would have an international appeal: French, German, Italian and Spanish actors were engaged and, in addition to the original American version, foreign-language versions were made with the foreign casts using the same sets, costumes and technical staff. Over at Elstree, for example, E. A. Dupont made the first German talkie, *Atlantic*, with a simultaneous Eng-

lish version. However, there were problems with this talking sea epic, since director Dupont, ill-acquainted with the English language, had his English cast talking as if they were German. It was nevertheless to receive ecstatic acclaim by the British critics and public.

Of course the subject matter, a sinking luxury ocean liner, and water gurgling, rushing, crashing in, had universal appeal, which helped it to overcome the weakness in this system. Obviously, this plan failed to take into consideration the mentality of the different populaces. It wasn't only language that separated people of different nationalities (or else anything American would be equally popular in England), but attitudes of mind, backgrounds and national concerns. But at first this was how they did it, and for a few years it worked.

The German studios, without the huge resources of the American companies, felt obliged to go along with the trend. Having neither funds nor, as yet,

* On Broadway Grace Moore introduced the popular *Dubarry*, and its success took her back to Hollywood for a triumphant film career.

established international box-office stars capable of handling roles in three languages, they set about recruiting young, inexpensive talent from abroad. Many of these artists who made their film debuts in these German 'versions' went on to become world stars: Annabella and Charles Boyer (French version of *Brand in der Oper*), Laurence Olivier (English version of *Hokuspokus*), Jean Gabin (French version of *Das Schloss im Süden*). Conversely, the silent German star, Camilla Horn, who had found herself adrift in Hollywood when sound came in, returned to Europe and steady employment for the first few years in Paramount's new studios at Joinville, re-creating many of the roles Nancy Carroll, Clara Bow and Sylvia Sidney had played in the States.

If anything was needed to show that the public went to the movies to see the stars rather than the stories they appeared in, these vehicles proved that. They didn't want to see Lily Damita or Nora Gregor wearing Norma Shearer's clothes in French or German versions of a Norma Shearer role (types for which they might never have been cast in their own countries); it was Norma Shearer herself they wanted, even if it meant dubbing her voice. Of course, if Norma or Joan or Greta had spoken for themselves in the foreign version that would have been something else, as Jeanette MacDonald's career showed. For it was her enormous popularity with the French public, who heard her speak and sing their language in the French versions of the Chevalier films, which kept her screen career alive

in Hollywood until Thalberg and MGM, teaming her with Nelson Eddy, finally made her a great star.

Actually, given all the pitfalls of 'version' filming the Germans, especially UFA, managed to deal successfully with this problem for a number of years by building up a repertory company of interchangeable, international, and equally popular stars who possessed the ability to speak their roles in more than one language. This way they had star appeal in every language. Of course in the end, even Pommer's foreign 'versions' had their limitations. What was light and frothy to Germans could become a heavy piece of *strudel* when translated into English, unless the English version was considerably reworked, rewritten and edited. So, by the end of 1933, despite some triumphant exceptions, this practice was abandoned. Only the songs could be counted on to retain their international appeal in any tongue, but then music travels on a different passport while Merry Widows need none at all. But the success of Ingrid Bergman's American debut, re-creating her role in the Swedish film, *Intermezzo* (1939), is the exception that proves the rule.)

Hokuspokus (1930) had music by Robert Stolz. The English title was *The Temporary Widow*, with Lilian Harvey, and was shot at the huge Neubabelsberg studios outside Berlin. This report from a German fan magazine on 'version' filming gives a glimpse into the problems and the excitement of the times:

'Only the hundred lamps remind one that this is a scene for a film and not a real courtroom, and the tyrannical, all-powerful microphones covered over with a green cloth and looking like presents on a Christmas tree, hang from gigantic beams over the heads of the main actors. The director, Gustav Ucicky, is there with the writer of the English version, Benn Levy.*

'The scene is over. It's O.K.! From the jury box and the seats in the courtroom the extras get up. They weren't in the scene but provided the sounds of laughter, comments and coughing that will be heard frequently in the background between the questions and answers. Now it's time for the scene to be shot for the English version. Ucicky discusses it with his English writers; he gives an order for the German cast to be replaced with a new set of actors brought over from London.' (In one of his first screen roles, the young English actor, Laurence Olivier, played the Willy Fritsch part – a young unsuccessful painter who pretends to be dead in order to sell his work.) 'But not only the actors are different, the behaviour in the courtroom, down to the smallest detail, is modelled on English procedure. Outside, Lilian Harvey is taking a break with her co-stars from the previous scene, when the assistant director comes rushing after them to bring Miss Harvey back, since she is playing in both versions. She's not joking when she says: "Being a linguist can get awfully tiring when you're making talking pictures," and disappears into the sound stage. The fluidity of the English version is remark-

*1 *Filmwelt*, June 8 1930. Benn W. Levy was responsible for writing the classic Rodgers and Hart stage and film musical *Evergreen* (1934).

able in its difference from the German one. Even the direction, the order of sequences, are quite different from the German version. The script was quite freely adapted by Benn Levy for the English while the German script by Walter Reisch and Karl Hartl adhered much more closely to the stage original.' The film floated along on such an air of romance and fantasy – passing lightly over marriage vows and other conventions – that overturned moral issues were beside the point. The lovers were clearly well suited, and would make a go of the match.

The so many brilliant, original touches strewn throughout these German musicals reappeared virtually intact, but unacknowledged, in the American musicals of the 40s, many of them written by the men and women who grew up in the New York of the 30s, where they could easily have been influenced by these films. A fantasy number in *Einbrecher*, taking place in the toy manufacturer's private puppet gallery, which has the puppets come alive and comment in song and dance on the antics of their human owners, was reused virtually intact for a scene in Harvey's Hollywood film, *I am Suzanne* (Fox, 1934), and would form the memorable high spot of *Lili* (MGM, 1956). In *Ein Burschenlied aus Heidelberg* (Student Song from Heidelberg, Music by Hans May, 1931), the German student who teaches his American girl friend to conjugate German verbs through the lyrics of 'Ich liebe, du liebst, er liebt *(Amo, amas, amat)*,' turns up seventeen years later as the celebrated French lesson Comden and Green wrote for MGM's *Good News* (1947) that has bookish student June Allyson teaching campus hero Peter Lawford the French he needs for his exams using much the same method.

The commercial success and pioneering inventiveness of the German output ensured that their impact on films everywhere, and particularly on other musicals, would not go unnoticed. The excitement that went into making them became the element which gave the films their timelessness and their delight. Many of the films I speak of here have been forgotten, even in their own countries, their era having been so short, and the time elapsed since then having been so long, and Hollywood rapidly absorbing their best parts into its own films. Rediscovering them, all these years later, one is constantly rocked back with delight at the excellences which, until very recent times, it was believed only the MGM musicals of the 40s and a few early Lubitsch and Mamoulian films possessed.

There was the film directed by Lilian Harvey's Hungarian protégé, Paul Martin, *Ein Blonder Traum* (1932), a wicked satire on Hollywood, whose chinchilla lightness, delectable tunes by Werner Richard Heymann, dances staged by Franz Rott, and finely-honed sophistication bring Lubitsch to mind. This was almost inevitable, since the script was by Reisch and the young tabloid journalist who had become his collaborator, Billy Wilder. The story was original enough, about the friendly rivalry between two window cleaners (Willi Forst and Willy Fritsch), for the affection of the starry-eyed little acrobatic dancer, Jou-Jou (Harvey), whose dream is to have a big career in movies – a profession the wittier of the two rivals (Forst) describes as being 'Not fit for adults.' Of course the witty Willi loses the girl and she ends up in Hollywood. Everybody's goal. In that respect the film was like a group visa since Harvey, Martin, Wilder, Reisch, Erich Pommer and Richard Heymann were all about to set sail for there – and Reisch and Wilder would end up writing scripts for their idol, Lubitsch.

Another master farceur, the popular actor/director Reinhold Schünzel, who scored a great triumph with *Ronny* (1931), which boasted a score by the operetta king, Emmerich Kálmán, directed one of the most audacious musical comedies of them all, a memorable mixture of sexual confusion and confetti sex, *Viktor und Viktoria* (1933). (Fifty years later it served as the basis of Julie Andrews' film of the same name. By those who never saw the original, Blake Edwards' film was considered masterful). Viktor is Viktoria, a second-rate little actor (Herman Thimig) paying his rent between engagements by working as a female impersonator. He meets a starving actress (Renate Müller) outside the labour exchange, in the middle of a downpour that brings him down with a cold. So he won't loose his meal-ticket, he talks her into taking his place on the stage for a performance. Just till he gets his voice back. Though she still has grave doubts, hunger speaks louder than reason. Though still hesitant, she goes on and enjoys a triumph! The public had seen lots of female impersonators who weren't much as a man, but few who were this superb as a woman. Given the nature of most female impersonators, nobody becomes suspicious of her as a man either. With no other job in sight, and Viktor as her manager, she is soon off on a triumphant European tour. The problem of course is that she has to keep pretending that she's a man off-stage, which becomes a crisis when she falls in love with a man (Anton Walbrook), whose date (Hilde Hildebrand), convinced that Viktoria is a man, also develops signs of romantic interest. The

songs by Franz Doelle (who would do the score for Schünzel's *Amphitryon*) are intricately scored and consistently melodious as events and incidents pile on top of each other with no time for second thoughts and everybody falling in love with everybody else. It's Shakeseare's *As You Like It*, served as the Germans liked it! Some years later, as has already been mentioned, Victor Saville made the English adaptation (*First a Girl*, 1935) as a vehicle for Jessie Matthews. While it had all the stunning visual elegance that was a hallmark of Saville's work – sets by Alfred Junge, superb production numbers, etc. – it lacked the cutting edge of the original. The sexual double-entendres were watered down to pantomime dames and principal boys. Jessie, in tuxedo and laminated hair, was delicious to look at but always the nymph errant. Thus her success as a man never makes real sense, as with the 1982 Julie Andrews remake. Julie's just too asexual in the part. The female characters interested in

Above left: Renate Müller and Anton Walbrook in Reinhold Schünzel's *Viktor und Viktoria*.

Above: Jessie Matthews in *First a Girl*.

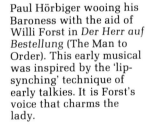

Paul Hörbiger wooing his Baroness with the aid of Willi Forst in *Der Herr auf Bestellung* (The Man to Order). This early musical was inspired by the 'lip-synching' technique of early talkies. It is Forst's voice that charms the lady.

Jessie (or Julie) as a boy, and the male characters interested at all in Jessie (or Julie) make sophisticates into myopics.

Of course musicals are made by music and all the films I've mentioned had great scores, memorable tunes that became international hits. Perhaps the crisis of identity running through a lot of the plots in the films I've recounted hints at something deep in the German subconscious or so some historians would have us believe.

Popular escapist entertainment does offer up a mirror to a generation, but the state of reality (which at times seemed more unreal than in the films) in the outside world, was a spur to the imagination of the writers and directors of that era, and never more so than in the case of Erik Charell's *Der Kongress Tanzt* (1931). In all of its three language versions the cast glittered; besides Fritsch and Harvey, there was voluptuous Lil Dagover, and Conrad Veidt as the Machiavellian Austrian statesman, Prince Metternich. Ignoring the serious overtones of the Vienna Congress (met to discuss the division of Europe between Austrian Emperor and Tsar Alexander of Russia), Charell uses the occasion to create the glittering background for an adult's fairy tale. Beautiful women, waltzes and sparkling wine seemed to be the only things that interested the Viennese. Christel (Lilian Harvey) is a young glove salesgirl who falls in love with the Tsar (Fritsch), on the town and incognito, to escape from the tedium of Metternich's court ceremonials. A good-natured simpleton, in his employ because of his resemblance to the ruler (also played by Fritsch), is along to take his place and pull the wool over Metternich's eyes. In musicals like these, set in the past, the audience's sympathy and joy lies in the fact that the real world (Tsars and Congresses) is trivial, and the private (a little glove-girl's romance . . . with a Tsar) is far more important. She was the one the viewer identified with (unless there were any Tsars in the audience) and loved all the more for being so silly and trusting. One thinks of all the mothers who packed their daughters off to beauty contests, dancing schools – and all in the belief that Hollywood awaited them. The essence of so much that is good about the film can be found in what has become one of the most imitated sequences in musicals – Christel's drive in an open carriage through the city and out into the countryside to the fairy-tale castle given her by the Tsar as a token of his affection. It was a musical film find – an emotional state expressed musically in choreographed exhilaration to flow to Heymann's international hit, 'Das gibt's nur einmal, das kommt nicht wieder' (It only happens once in a lifetime). The jubilant refrain is taken up by the merchants in the market places, the people in the streets, the farmers in the fields, the soldiers on parade, the washerwomen, the children and the world outside the walls of the cinema. Even before Hitler made emigration a necessity, Hollywood brought out its chequebooks – buying up the film's stars, producers, directors and composers. (Henri Garat repeated the double role of Tsar and valet in the French and English versions and made his Hollywood debut opposite Janet Gaynor in *Adorable* (1933), a role he'd played in the French version of the

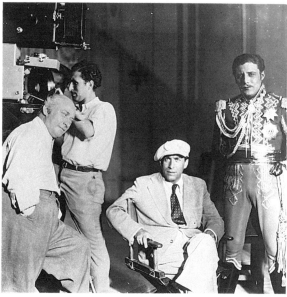

Above: An overhead shot of the ballroom scene in *Der Kongress Tanzt*.

Left: Erik Charell, seated, on the set of *Der Kongress Tanzt*. Henri Garat in costume as the Tsar for the French and English versions.

Top right: *Der Kongress Tanzt* (Congress Dances). Lilian Harvey in the coach.

Right: Loretta Young and Phillips Holmes in *Caravan*, Erik Charell's unsuccessful Hollywood venture.

German film *Ihre Hoheit Befiehlt*, opposite Lillian Harvey. In the German version Fritsch had been teamed with brunette Käthe von Nagy for a change of pace.)

Kongress was Charell's film debut. Known as the Ziegfeld of the German Musical Comedy Theatre, his productions at the Berlin Grosse Schauspielhaus, like *White Horse Inn*, were the most successful theatrical enterprises of post-war Berlin, as well as of Paris and London. But film gave him even better opportunities to spread his taste for the lavish and spectacular all around the world.

In France, *Le Congrès s'amuse*, was responsible for a wave of gay, light French operettas. *Il est charmant* (He is charming, 1931) with music by Raoul Moretti starring Henri Garat, and *Paris-Mediterranée* (1932), directed by the German, Joe May, with Annabella and Jean Murat and a score and script by the Viennese, Bruno Granichstaedten, were two of these. They even made a German version of *Paris-Mediterranée*, *Zwei in Einen Auto*, with Magda Schneider – Romy's mother – and Karl-

Ludwig Diehl. The films had all the tricks, turns and faults of the standard operettas, and the public, turned on by *Congress*, adored them. England shared in the madness, and launched a spate of its own operettas, as well as copies of most of the German ones. *Goodnight Vienna* (1932), directed by Herbert Wilcox, had an appealing score by George Posford, and gained footnote fame for launching Anna Neagle. But its original popularity in the British dominions arose from a hankering for kitsch and kisses. Songs were there to plug the leaky plot and lead the lovers to the happy clinch. In fact it wasn't as silly as it sounds, not to contemporary audiences, who not only identified with her pluck, but who knew of plenty of duchesses who'd begun like Miss Neagle as one of Cochran's young chorus ladies.

In Hollywood, Charell, who had been signed by Fox to repeat his triumphs, spoke out about his dissatisfaction with what the Americans had been doing with musicals, and of his plans to revolutionize things. To hear him talk of his ideas suggests that he believed *Caravan* to be a film years ahead of its time, with camera movements and individual scenes in the film which run as much as 300 to 400 feet without a cut, for which directors like Max Ophüls, and later still, the Hungarian director, Miklos Jansco, were to be extravagantly admired.

'In *Caravan* I am using as few "cuts" as possible, and am trying to tell my story just as a spectator on the actual scene would see it. I believe that this makes the resulting picture much more realistic and plausible than if I made the audience dizzy by rapidly alternating the viewpoint.' A contemporary trade journal reported:

'Hollywood film experts have been considerably interested in Charell's application of this belief, and in his extensive use of "dolly" and "crane" shots to get his effects. On only two or three occasions has the director employed more than one camera at a time, even on the most elaborate scenes, but this camera usually follows an intricate path, carefully rehearsed and timed, through the set, and it has frequently taxed the ingenuity of the Fox Film technicians to arrange tracks and equipment so the instrument can be moved as he wants it.

'As a result, many of the individual scenes in the picture run as much as 300 to 400 feet in length, with the camera now making a long shot of a huge crowd of gypsies, hussars or Hungarian villagers: now bending to concentrate on a leading player or a significant movement, now wandering among a group of dancers, perhaps singling out one or two for a close shot, then following or preceding a certain character from the set.'

Without having seen the film, one can still perceive that Charell went against the conventions of the day, in Hollywood at any rate, by virtually outlawing the intercutting of close-ups of the stars, for a free-flowing endless camera movement. No wonder the film failed to find a public, who were used to seeing the stars in studied close-ups, or that he failed to find favour with the stars of his film. Loretta Young, to the apoplectic fury of her studio boss, walked out during the film's première; when it went on to become a total failure at the box-office, it vanished from sight.

Americans never really took to Ruritania, except when Nelson Eddy and Jeanette MacDonald brought their American fizz to those stories. Charles Boyer's powerful romantic style was out of keeping with the proud, curly-locked, violin-playing gypsy, Lazi, telling the haughty Countess Wilmar (a beauteous but bored Loretta Young): 'A hundred pengös is not enough, my lady. I may be a gypsy, but I'm not for sale. You may be a lady – you may be the richest lady in all Hungary, but you haven't got enough pengös to pay for my love'. That was the sort of thing that finished John Gilbert's career and sent Boyer back to Paris.

Charell returned to Germany, and non-Aryan Pommer had better luck in England. Only Heymann, whose songs had already been heard in *Adorable* (Fox, 1933), stayed on to write background scores for many films of the 30s and 40s. These include *Smilin' Through, The King and the Chorus Girl, Bluebeard's Eighth Wife, Ninotchka, The Earl of Chicago, The Shop Around the Corner* and *The Primrose Path*. But nothing tarnished the reputation of the film that had launched them all. *Congress Dances* remains for many the definitive European musical to come out of those halcyon days.

Time was running out for a lot of talented people working in Europe, but meanwhile no theme was sacred, no subject spared. Max Ophüls directed the ravishing international opera star, Jarmila Novotna, in Smetana's *The Bartered Bride* (1932), with an eye for telling composition, and G. W. Pabst brought his genius, coupled with his sardonic humour, to Weill/Brecht's *Die Dreigroschenoper* (1931). Like other secure giants who had already established themselves in the silent era, Pabst felt that the true mission of the screen was to present the story by images and music, with words to be used only as a last resort (which may have accounted for Brecht's fury with the project). This was not John Gay's London, on whose *The Beggar's Opera* Brecht had loosely based his work, and as far as Brecht was concerned it wasn't his London either; nor does it look like much of anyone else's London unless it was the London of Pabst's earlier film, *Lulu*, where Wedekind's child met Jack the Ripper.

In the 1935 operetta *Amphitryon* Reinhold Schünzel, with a score by Franz Doelle, used the free hand which his great popularity had gained him to recall the German musicals' glory (by 1935 it was fading fast in the memory of most) in this daring mockery of the high and mighty rulers of the land. In Leni Riefenstahl's paean to the Führer, *Triumph des Willens*, she opens with the famous shots of gigantic crowds of Germans gathered for the mass Nürnberg rally, their eyes raised reverently to the heavens from which the plane bearing Hitler will descend. This was undiluted gloriana. In *Amphitryon*, Schünzel has the lecherous old Zeus, King of the Gods, descend from Mount Olympus to try to bed the virtuous wife of a departed soldier, perched on the handle of an umbrella, while down in Sparta massed crowds of Greek women look up reverently to heaven. By the time Goebells got the joke and ordered the film withdrawn, it had already made its point. Schünzel's audacity was no longer acceptable and he started to think about America. There he directed several operettas, i.e. *Ice Follies of*

1939 – best known for Crawford as an unlikely Sonja Henie – *Balalaika* and *New Wine* – all delightful, but not very successful.

By the end of 1933, the kind of musicals I speak of were fading. So many of the people who made them were emigrating (not all for the same reasons), taking their talents to Elstree, Joinville, Vienna and Budapest, on their inevitable way to Holly-

The spirit of the times. Above: In Germany the organised adoration of Der Führer was caught by Leni Riefenstahl in *Triumph of the Will*. Top: Adoration satirized by Reinhold Schünzel in his film of the operetta, *Amphitryon*. Top right: In

America audiences could forget the Depression for a brief hour or two with *Footlight Parade*, banned from Germany by Goebbels – or feel encouraged to hope by the charm and optimism of Shirley Temple in *Stand Up and Cheer*

major film-producing centres, including America. As in Germany, a new government came into power in the US with the promise of a New Deal which would put an end to the chaos created by those who had gone before. With that end there would also have to be an end to the frivolous anti-establishment attacks that had made the establishment antics bearable.

But America was a democracy – free enterprise and all that. A people really had to show that they were fed up with things as they were before their government could implement laws that would make a change of direction possible and give power back to the censors. When Shirley Temple came along and the public flocked to see her, the pundits on Capitol Hill knew their moment had come, and took it. But that wouldn't be for two more years. Europeans are more conditioned to taking orders from their representatives. Instead of waiting for Shirley Temple, the Germans took Adolf Hitler's brand of optimism. Dr Goebbels, Hitler's Minister of Culture, made sure that the country's artistes wouldn't have the chance to prod the public's new consciousness into re-thinking their decision to vote Hitler and his party into power. One of his first preventive acts was to ban any films he considered subversive or immoral from entering Germany. Of course Goebbels was paying Hollywood the ultimate tribute: the American popular films were far more subversive for being irreverent than any amount of serious political propaganda from another country. The huge new musical sensation, *42nd Street*, so harmless, one might have thought – was among the first lot of American films to be forbidden by the new state censorship office. Naturally, the Führer, Miss Braun, his mistress, and members of his staff who loved American films and saw all the latest ones even long after Germany was at war, were exempt. But what Goebbels did was bound to meet with approval by the native film producers, for under the guise of moral rearmament he was boosting production, and the successful consumption of that product. Here was something which most European film producers, suffering under the American monopoly system dominating their native industries, must have secretly hoped and prayed that their Governments could do for them.

Consider England: the British Parliament, after heavy lobbying by its struggling film industry, tried to curb the Hollywood imports by imposing things like the quota system, whereby renters were obliged to sell, and exhibitors to show, a varying proportion of British-made films. What this created were the notorious 'quota quickies'. As long as 30% of the product made and shown was British, the rest could be foreign. The Hollywood studios, owning controlling shares in the British cinema chains, could afford to use some of their profits to finance British films made so fast (often shot at night on a set left over from the day) and so cheap (£2000 would pay for one) that cinemas, to get around the act which insisted a British-made film had to be shown, would put it on in the morning to an audience of cleaning women, and then, when the paying public came, there was another glorious Hollywood picture. Naturally this shrewd ruse to

wood. Many found safety there, but ironically not much work. Hollywood could now afford to be choosey, since the threat these talents had offered them when still working in Germany was gone, and thus the need to hire them. Sympathy was one thing, a job another. But there was another reason for the decline from these light, irreverent, but magistereal films, and it applied to all of the world's

Above, left: Gitta Alpar in *Die Oder Keine*. The Hungarian-Jewish soprano was a favourite with audiences in pre-Nazi Germany.

Above: Willy Fritsch in *Walzerkrieg*, and left, Arletty in the successful French version. Both were directed by Ludwig Berger, who used the French version to get out of Germany in good time. Arletty as Ilonka, the part played by the popular Hungarian soubrette, Rose Barsony, in the original version.

Left: G. W. Pabst directed Brecht's *Die Dreigroschenoper* in 1931, and made a Beggar's Opera in contemporary terms. Rudolf Forster as Mack the Knife.

get around a weak law did even more damage to the British film since these films employed a lot of British technicians, writers and directors.

It wasn't hard for Goebbels (anymore than it had been for the other companies in the States) to appreciate Busby Berkeley's eye-catching, mind-boggling, harmlessly extravagant production numbers, and to know that these would appeal to a German audience. The large mass-movement of crowds had always had a special attraction for German directors – Max Reinhardt in the theatre, Lang and Lubitsch, and later, Leni Riefenstahl, in movies. (An interesting footnote to this interest in the massing and controlling of crowds as 'art'. One of the last *new* American films to be released in the Third Reich was Cecil B. De Mille's *Union Pacific* (1939); and in 1940, among the tiny handful of American films still being shown, was De Mille's 1936 epic, *The Plainsman*.)

Goebbels made his top German producers and directors 'come and see these films, again and again, so they could learn from them, observe, absorb, and make ones like them', recalled Karl Hartl for me. Goebbels didn't want films with a message but ones that would stop the message from getting through. He supported the German film industry in the production of their own musical extravaganzas, after the scripts had been as sanitized as a baby's diaper. The results were all-star extravaganzas like *Es Leuchten die Sterne*, which for size (if not skill) were like the early Berkeley musicals, but for liveliness were more like the heavy ones made by others. (More of that later.) Highlights included a near naked lady wearing a wimple and veils dancing to rouse an Iron Man she finds standing in a hallway!

When MGM's 'New Deal' style musicals with Eleanor Powell started to arrive early in 1936, and

Above: Camilla Horn, the German star who made a successful transition from silent films to talkies by starring in German-language versions of Hollywood films.

The German musical in the 30s and some of the stars. Top right: Magda Schneider in *Die Katz im Sack*. Right: Pola Negri in the marvellously melodramatic *Mazurka*. Far right: Marta Eggerth and Hans Söhnker in the film of Kalman's operetta *Die Csardasfürstin*. Bottom, left: Erna Sack, a soprano with a phenomenally high range, in *Blumen aus Nizza*. Right: Lil Dagover in Oscar Straus's *Eine Frau die weiss was sie will*.

La Jana in an extravagantly exotic number in *Es Leuchten die Sterne*. Dancing to rouse an Iron Man.

A scene from *Königswalzer* (1936), in which Willi Forst appeared as an actor.

found an immediate and enthusiastic German public, Goebbels, who forgot to ban them* because he must have been too occupied looking for meaningful content in the background to notice that talent is far more subversive, decided just the same to provide the German public with its own industriously happy 'tap-tapping' Queen – and the short-legged but bouncy acrobatic Hungarian whirlwind, Marika Rökk, tapped up a storm to order. With competition controlled, their own product was bound to dominate and flourish accordingly. The only post-1936 American stars whose films were widely distributed in the country were Jeanette MacDonald and Nelson Eddy vehicles, and those starring Eleanor Powell, Loretta Young and Shirley Temple. Their films were still being distributed late in 1939.

But the German musicals of the Third Reich (except for those exceptions that only prove rules) no longer played a major part in the history of the genre. UFA, Tobis Klangfilm, and their other film-producing companies were little more than glorified fiefs of the Reichskammer. Still, while casts of thousands and large sets are within the reach of a

* There must have been some right old gnashing of teeth and breaking of heads after *The Jungle Princess* was released in Germany, and it was discovered that the director E. Lloyd Sheldon was in fact a pseudonym for the German-Jewish emigré director, Wilhelm Thiele, whose first Hollywood film this was.

Above and top: Two
scenes from the lavish
Marika Rökk vehicle,
Kora Terry (1940).

Top right: Marika Rökk in
Hallo Janine. The
Hungarian dancer was a
hugely popular star in
Germany before, during,
and long after the Nazi
era.

Zarah Leander, the
Swedish contralto who
became Goebbels' answer
to stars like Dietrich and
Garbo. In *Zu Neuen
Ufern*.

man in control of billions, certain things still
rankled with the man who wanted to rival the great
Hollywood moguls as film producer and star maker.
In vain did Goebbels try to lure two of his chief's
favourite stars, Dietrich and Garbo, to make films in
Germany. (One should remember that it was
Garbo's immense popularity in the countries Hitler
dominated which kept her one of Hollywood's
highest salaried film stars; and that Dietrich was, of
course, a native daughter.) Both ladies refused all
offers unless it meant they could get close enough to
the Führer – to shoot him. So, Dr Goebbels, astute
film buff and Minister of Propaganda, rebuffed but
not defeated, concocted a 'singing Garbo' in the best
Hollywood style. It was to be one of his most

successful coups. To begin with, he eliminated the
competition. 1936 was the last year German
audiences saw the two Hollywood divas. The new
star didn't need to worry; she was pretty special by
any standard. (MGM were desperately eager to sign
her up.) But Goebbels took no chances. 1937, the
year after *Camille* (Garbo) and *Desire* (Dietrich) had
made the rounds, UFA launched their 'discovery'
with impressive fanfare and graven invitations –
the film was called *Zu Neuen Ufern* (To New
Shores) – rather prophetic that. Voila! And there she
was. Larger than life. Saucy. Knowing. Mysterious.
Everything to every man but . . . Her name was
Zarah Leander, the Swedish contralto. Her voice
was thicker than a London fog, trailing all the

sadness her plots came up with (and, boy, her plots came up with a lot!) in its wonderfully rich, dark, deep timbre. What an undercurrent. While in carefully posed, dramatically lit close-ups she looked spookily like her Swedish compatriot, Leander had already been a huge success in her native Sweden, and in Austria, where Goebbels discovered her, and she had already appeared in several films, including the Austrian-made *Première* (1937, directed by Geza von Bolvary). *Zu Neuen Ufern* was a lavishly mounted turn-of-the-century story of Gloria Vane, the worldly chanteuse of Victorian England, who nightly delightedly shocks the shockable *beau monde* of London by singing the provocative 'Yes Sir! – I'm Gloria Vane, notorious and well known. Yes Sir! Not very popular with uncles and aunts. No Sir! Afraid I might meet their watched-over darlings in gambling saloons or in my bedroom. Well, yes, she didn't appear to be quite what the censors had in mind, but, if truth be told, it's all an act. She only loves one man, and he's the bounder, because of whom she is deported to an Australian penal colony, and there she sings another song, the archetypal blues about the woman left out in the cold 'Ich steh'im Regen' (I Stand in the Rain). These women always look their best when they've fallen, with the moonlight bouncing off the muddy little stage and throwing stars into their shimmering tatters. The songs were by Ralph Benatzky; the film was directed by Detlef (Douglas) Sirk. Sirk directed her next triumphant vehicle, *La Habanera* (1937), about an outwardly cool but inwardly tempestuous Swedish tourist who meets and falls for a rich, hot-blooded Spaniard. The marriage is doomed, maybe because he's not a blond Aryan, but the story was strong, the sets were exotic, the costumes glamorous; the plot included malaria, and her big song hit, 'La Habanera', told us that only

the wind knew what was wrong with her heart. Zarah Leander was what press agents love to call an overnight sensation. She then had many other triumphs. Leander's popularity spread far beyond the German market, to France (long before and all through the Occupation) and on into the Latin-speaking countries. Like Marika Rökk, with whom she competed for Tchaikovsky in *Es war eine rauschende Ballnacht* (Directed by Carl Froelich, 1939), Zarah Leander survived World War II, a spate of acrimony in her native Sweden for having worked in Germany (and in Germany for having walked out of her contract to go back to Sweden in 1942), several comebacks, to go on and on and on, to become, like her sisters, a camp legend.

And then there was the exotic dancer, La Jana (in fact, she was an Austrian, and caught cold and died from dancing on stage in so few clothes); the chanteuse, Lizzi Waldmüller, who first introduced the wonderful title song in *Bel Ami*, 'whose not handsome, but so bold, so gallant and never cold, he's no hero, just a man women love'. There was the snazzily sophisticated Hilde Hildebrand, and the whistling favourite, Ilse Werner, whose best musical was Helmut Käutner's *Wir Machen Musik* (We're Making Music). For a time even the emotional former silent star, Pola Negri, was back at the old stand (beautifully kept and refurbished for her German sound debut in Willi Forst's *Mazurka* (1935), wearily intoning her smouldering songs. And, until she left the country in 1939, there were still films starring Lilian Harvey, teamed with Fritsch in very smart, very fast-paced sophisticated comedies like *Glückskinder* (1936), and *7 Ohrfeigen* (1937) both directed by Paul Martin. And throughout these years there had been and still were a spate of popular musicals starring operatic and record favourites like Richard Tauber, the pocket-sized

Opposite, top: Zarah Leander as *Maria Stuart*.

Bottom left: A set design by Ernst Hasler for *Traummusik*

Far right, above: Hans Holt as *Mozart*, with Winnie Markus.

Below: Willi Forst's *Wiener Blut*, with Willy Fritsch.

Far left: Zarah Leander in *La Habanera*. Below: At Venice Airport in 1942.

Josef Schmidt (*My Song Goes Round the World*); Jan Kiepura, whether alone or co-starring with his wife, Martha Eggerth, Erna Sack, Jarmila Novotna, and Beniamino Gigli, the dumpy little unromantic Italian tenor with the gloriously beautiful voice, who had as his co-stars some of the most glamorous leading actresses in films – Isa Miranda, Camilla Horn, Marie Cebotari, Magda Schneider. When he sang, it was easy to be blind to his appearance. But increasingly the trend in musicals was to stories drowned in cloying sentimentality and delivering kitschy homilies about a good woman being the blonde one who wanted nothing more than to go home and raise the sort of large family that would please the Führer.

Yet from amidst the blinding prejudice and tragedy, and the horror of genocide, there came a life-enhancing musical film *Symphonie eines Lebens* (1942), that is unique, very beautiful, and deeply moving, not because of where and when it was made, but because of the man who made it, and why. It is the film of a man's life and his work, which

opens up through the movements of his symphony
as the camera records his dreams, his murderous
passions, his despair, and hope reborn. The great
French actor, Harry Baur, was brought over from
France to play the composer. Here was a Jewish
actor playing in a German film made in Germany in
1942. The director was Hans Bertram who wrote to
me from Germany in 1972: '*Die Symphonie eines
Lebens ist 1941/42 geschrieben und . . .*'

'. . . *Symphony of a Life* was written and filmed in
1941/42. I had the idea for this film, and from the
outset conceived it as a music film for which the
treatment and the music were to be written
simultaneously.

'I wanted the finest actor of his day for the central
role, and went to Harry Baur in Paris. His papers
were forged so that I could work with this
remarkable human being and sublime actor who
was able to convey the drama of the music through
his shoulders down to his fingertips.

During the filming they denounced him back in
Paris. They let us finish the film without our
knowing that he had been denounced. The day after
we finished shooting my friend Harry returned to
Paris; they were waiting for him at the station and
placed him under arrest. Though he was released
some weeks later, he died soon after. He never saw
the results of his great achievement.

'I myself was forbidden to work and it was only
because of a cleverly contrived operation coupled
with my departure from Berlin, that I avoided being
sent on a non-return military mission' *(Strafkom-
panie)*.

'My name was removed from the credits. I was
never able to attend a public screening. The
gentlemen of the day could afford to let *Symphonie
eines Lebens* vanish as if into thin air.'

The music, so eloquent, so vital, was by Norbert

Schultze, played by the Dresden Philharmonic and
sung by the Vienna Boys' Choir. There is little
dialogue – the film exists in the look, brilliantly
photographed by Carl Hoffman, and in the music.

By the end of the war what had become a mere
trickle, dried up. In *Illusion in Moll* (1952) Hildegard
Knef, who, it was widely hoped would go on to
become another Dietrich, sang a song about
illusions being the most beautiful thing in the
world. She did not become another Dietrich, though
she did go on to star in a Broadway musical, and
make a number of successful records. What German
producers revived in the 50s under the guise of
'Heimat films' left little room for any illusions about
a resurgence; they rocked no boats, left no waves,
and are best forgotten. The re-makes of their
classics don't even bear mentioning.

But, once there was a time. And what a time it
was.

The Great Depression

The Hollywood Musical in the Thirties

'Sawyer you listen to me, and listen hard. 200 people, 200 jobs, $200,000; five weeks of grind and blood and sweat depend on you. It's the lives of all these people who've worked with you. You've got to go on. You've got to give! And give! They've *got* to like you! They've *got to*! You understand! You can't fall down. You CAN'T – because your future is in it! My future – everything all of us have is staked on you. But you keep your feet on the ground and your head on those shoulders of yours and go out. And Sawyer – you're going out a youngster ... *but you've got to come back a star!'* says Warner Baxter as Julian, the show's director, to his shivering young chorine Peggy Sawyer in *42nd Street* (Warner Bros, 1932).

The 30s was Hollywood's heyday. Whereas previously Hollywood had skimmed off much of Europe's élite with the offers of fabulous wealth and glamour to be found there, after 1933 something more compelling than cash brought forth a torrent of talent to their shores. Amongst those who came out of a basic need to survive were Thomas and Heinrich Mann, Igor Stravinsky, Otto Klemperer, Bruno Walter, Sergei Rachmaninoff, Berthold Brecht, Kurt Weill, Leopold Stokowski, Arnold Schoenberg, Franz Werfel and Max Reinhardt. When we add to this the sheer numbers of others, some already there, some still arriving, we have what amounts to a Hollywood not unlike the Florence of the Medicis: such names as Chaplin, Garbo, Dietrich, Astaire, Lubitsch, Rodgers and Hart, Sternberg, Dorothy Parker, P. G. Wodehouse, Donald Ogden Stewart, Aldous Huxley, Anita Loos, Dashiell Hammett, William Faulkner, Robert Benchley and F. Scott Fitzgerald. And still they came. But, sadly, the gifts of many of these artists were either to be ignored or squandered, or left to their own devices; some faded to nothing in the shade of the citrus trees. For Hollywood did not have a Lorenzo de' Medici to harness the talents of all of them. What, in spite of these shortcomings, was being done during these dark Depression days? The poet and screenwriter, Donald Ogden Stewart, like most writers always more politically conscious than his employer might wish, and whose formidable screen credits include *Dinner At Eight*, *Holiday*, *The Philadelphia Story*, *Love Affair*, *Keeper Of The Flame*, and *Summertime*, remembers:

'Economically, the Depression had little effect on the people in Hollywood, most of whom never even got round to learning how to spell it. Some of us were disgusted when we watched the producers of lavish musicals spend more and more money on sets and things for films that completely avoided the reality of what was happening in the rest of the country at the time. Because Hollywood wasn't affected by the Depression, it wasn't prepared to involve itself. Almost any movie in the 30s made money. There were one or two attempts to try and face the real situation; but most films dealing with the Depression were made when it was nearly over, such as Frank Capra's social comedies in the late 30s. I thought, coming when they did, they cheated, like his *Mr Deeds Goes To Town* (1936). It skirted the real issues; who was responsible for the Depression and why; the lack of foresight; the fact that no one was prepared for the collapse.

'Certainly, as far as I knew, Hollywood never made as much money as they did then. Producers and studio heads have never been as sure – except during the last war – that entertainment was what the public wanted. Hollywood, as a social animal, didn't come of age until the Hitler threat rose in Germany.

'As for the Depression being responsible for any film trends, personally I doubt it. That would suggest that Hollywood created originals, when all they ever did to the best of my knowledge was buy a success, whether it was a book, play, song or personality. Then they'd set about handing it to us writers and their casting directors to formalize it.' Perhaps Donald Ogden Stewart did not equate

backstage problems of survival with those of ordinary people when he heard from the screen:

'Sawyer you listen to me, and listen hard. 200 people, 200 jobs, $200,000; five weeks of grind and blood and sweat depend on you. It's the lives of all these people who've worked with you. You've got to go on ...'

Be that as it may, *42nd Street* was a sensation. It went straight into the hearts of millions hungry for a little lightness. (Like Jolson's little missus, Ruby Keeler, whose growing success in the face of his diminishing popularity could have served as the model for all those *A Star Is Born* stories.) While the public was never to totally forget Jolson, there had to come a time when he was to have had his day. *Hallelujah I'm A Bum*[*], written especially for Jolson, and dealing directly, or as directly with the Depression as Hollywood could see it, was a failure at the box-office. Lewis Milestone and Ben Hecht, director and writer, both known and respected for their strong social and artistic commitment, brought to the screen a story set against a background of New York's Central Park, Wall Street, the tenement districts and the haunts of the rich. (It was shot in the parks of Los Angeles.) The hero, an amiable derelict (Jolson), and his friends, Acorn, Egghead and Sunday, form part of a group that has opted out of conventional society and its

[*] Al Jolson's *Bum* became a less ambiguously named *Tramp* when the title was altered for England to avoid any offence!

Previous pages: Warner Baxter as the producer in *42nd Street* being tough with the chorus girl, Ruby Keeler, who becomes his star. Behind Miss Keeler, Una Merkel; behind Baxter, George E. Stone. On Baxter's left is Ginger Rogers, as Anytime Annie ('The only time she said No she didn't hear the question.').

Top: Screen-writer Donald Ogden Stewart (sitting, left) relaxes from his acting chores between shots of *Not so Dumb*, with star Marion Davies and director King Vidor.

Above: Al Jolson in *Hallelujah, I'm a Bum*. Despite a script by Ben Hecht, songs by Rodgers and Hart, and direction by Lewis Milestone the film was a failure at the box-office. The Depression was all-pervasive – no one wanted to see a musical about it.

Above: Berkeley used forty girls with violins for 'The Shadow Waltz'. The violins lit up with neon and seemed to play themselves in the dark. A number for *Gold Diggers of 1933*.

Right: Ruby Keeler auditions for a part in a show in *Dames* (directed by Ray Enright). She gets the part!

attendant woes to live in the 'freedom' of Central Park.

The score was in the hands of Rodgers and Hart whose previous limited experiments with rhythmic dialogue had worked so exuberantly in *Love Me Tonight* and again in *The Phantom President* (1932), where their lengthy sequences of couplets and music wound effectively into the situation. With *Hallelujah* they expanded their experiments into a full-blown screen operetta much as Jacques Demy would do many years later with Michel Legrand, and as the Germans were already doing at that time. 90% of the dialogue was sung in rhyming couplets. Because the melodies were integrated with the rhythm of speech, it made the songs seem more like speeches. As Lorenz Hart explained in an interview:

'The dramatic action, the flow of photography and the humour and pathos of the characters in the story will be inherent in the music. We write lyrics and music especially for the camera.'

Despite their inventiveness and the talents of all concerned the film was not a popular success. The American public found the subject and its presentation simply not to their taste when there was so much else to choose from. *Hallelujah*'s box-office failure meant that further experiments in this direction were left to Broadway with shows like *Porgy and Bess*, and Rodgers and Hammerstein's *Oklahoma*. Both were directed by Rouben Mamoulian. *Hallelujah*'s failure also marked the beginning of the end of Jolson's film vogue. For a time he had reigned over the screen with a string of maudlin tear-jerkers that followed on the heels of one another – *The Jazz Singer* (1927), *The Singing Fool* (1928), *Sonny Boy* (1929), *Say It With Songs* (1929) and *Big Boy* (1930). But by then his screen popularity was already showing signs of waning. Had somebody at Warners taken Jolson's career in hand as Goldwyn did with Eddie Cantor or Thalberg with the Marx Brothers, had they cured Jolson's ham for film, extended his range, adapted his material or given him something or somebody to play off against besides himself, Jolson might have gone on. Instead, each Jolson 'special' became more repetitive until even a lavish all-star production like *Wonder Bar* (1934), or co-starring him with his wife, the hugely popular movie-star Ruby Keeler (*Go Into Your Dance*, 1935), couldn't turn the tide. What neither he nor those around him took into consideration was the unique qualities that set film apart from the other media. It is the most powerful medium for under-statement, with stunning emotional climaxes built on carefully accelerating, subtly observed minutiae. The eye of the camera has the ability to select those qualities in a person, often unknown to themselves and unnecessary in the other arts; it needed, and created a brand new type of entertainer to fulfill that need – the movie-star. Jolson, assaulting the subtly-probing lens with his whole bag of tricks, swung from one theatrical extreme to the next and gave the camera no chance to focus on the man within, nor to assimilate his contribution into the whole. This problem was not unique to Jolson and is with us still, i.e. Streisand, Mick Jagger, etc., but helps to explain the basic difference between stage and screen, and the failure of so many legendary stage favourites in movies. Then, ironically, Larry Parks, a movie actor playing the man Jolson, not only achieved the success in films which Jolson himself once knew, but, in the process, made Jolson a big name with the public again.[*]

As a result of the Depression, films in the first half of the 30s favoured a hard-hitting, anti-social, anti-establishment mood, while almost any attempt favouring the rich was greeted unfavourably at the box-office: only those antics of the monied class

[*] Al Jolson did his own dubbing for the songs mouthed by Larry Parks. An amusing aside occurred in the sequel, *Jolson Sings Again*, which had Jolson, played by Larry Parks, arriving at the studio to dub the songs for *The Jolson Story*, and being introduced to and congratulating Larry Parks on playing him.

caricaturing them as wilful, spoilt, manic and otherwise unsympathetic were accepted by movie-goers. By 1934 this mood had reached its climax with films like *I'm No Angel*, *Red-Headed Woman*, *Public Enemy*, *Little Caesar*, *Bed of Roses*, *Blonde Venus*, *Gold Diggers of 1933*, *Wonder Bar* and the like, and showed signs of turning. Franklin D. Roosevelt, elected to the presidency in 1932, had ushered in a 'New Deal' which was taking hold of people's minds and stabilizing the country with hope. Rebels, outcasts and other social malcontents who had monopolized the screen began to fade from favour. A cautious optimism could be felt in the way stories were now slanted, not towards reality, but to a straight-faced emphasis on the positive rewards to be gained through virtue and hard work. There were other changes – less drastic, less funny too: the economy that had forced the heroine out on the streets now offered her a recipe for pancakes, through which, in a series of quick dissolves, she became a huge success. (*Imitation of Life*, 1934.) Thus movies proved that hard work and honest sweat always triumph in America. By 1935, any actress found on the streets stayed there without benefit of soft-focusing street lamps and glamour. The gangster reverted to his role as society's vicious enemy and, accordingly, played by actors like J. Carrol Naish and Akim Tamiroff instead of by stars like Cagney, Raft and Robinson.

Homespun sentiments and child-actors spawned a listless cycle of films, but probably the saddest casualty was the gold-digger, so brightly portrayed by Aline MacMahon, Glenda Farrell, Ginger Rogers, Una Merkel, Toby Wing, Lucille Ball – not forgetting all those selfless slavies, the busy Berkeley blondes.

A cum laude graduate of the gold-digging class of 33 was Joan Blondell. Ever afterwards she continued as one of the screens consistently excellent all-rounders, first as star, then as character actress, in musicals, screwball comedies, sophisticated farces, or romantic dramas. To paraphrase Mae West, 'Joan Blondell good, is very, very good, but when she's bad, she's absolutely delightful.'*

Blondell was born in the proverbial trunk, and arrived in Hollywood in 1930 with James Cagney, having been discovered with him co-starring on Broadway. She wasn't really what one would call a

* Joan Blondell was working up to the time of her death in 1979.

'We're in the Money!' The opening chorus of *Gold Diggers of 1933*. But this is the Depression era, and lack of money stops the show.

singer or a dancer, though she was to do both endearingly, and said of herself, 'You can't be much of a glamour girl with chipmunk cheeks.' However, she had the knack of making any part she graced a pleasure by dint of superb professionalism, a fine natural sense of humour and a perfect pitch for comedy. Like Mae West, Joan Blondell could parody sex without ever losing her own sex appeal.

Like many a trouper before her she came up the hard way and with 'no regrets'. When I first met her she was working on a new TV series. She was warm and easygoing and compulsively likeable.

'I started work in my dad's act when I was three years old. That was when vaudeville was bad and he was touring in Sydney, Australia. Then my brother was born, and he went into the act. When my sister came along she was roped in as well and we all struggled in the act. We did everything –

Right: Joan Blondell leads the chorus in the memorable 'Remember my Forgotten Man' in *Gold Diggers of 1933*. The star is facing away from the camera, arms up-raised.

Below: Busby Berkeley and the legs of three of his showgirls. On the set, *Gold Diggers of 1933*. Most of the superb stills and innovative photo-montages we have of the Berkeley films at Warners were the work of that dare-devil stills photographer, Bert 'Buddy' Longworth.

sang, danced, did comedy sketches, everything. I did that till I was seventeen. Always on stage, always going, and always together! Eventually we had to leave vaudeville – we weren't getting any work, and I had to go make the rounds getting little punk jobs here and there. The small salary I made kept us going. Then finally, when the George Kelly break came, it was uphill from then on. The thought of making a living any other way never came up in my family. We were show people. When I finally came to Warner Bros. and was actually in one spot, it took me an awful long time to realize I'd see people again and that I could make friends, and not be hurt. But until then my life revolved completely around my family, and that bond of love has never been broken. I was educated without any schooling. Now and again, we'd have to go, when we hit some town where the authorities were alert; they'd come backstage and take us to school. I guess I've been to between forty and fifty schools altogether, for a week. When I first got into pictures, there'd be notices saying: 'Dallas's own Joan Blondell!', 'Battle-creek, Michigan's own Joan Blondell!', 'Chicago's own . . .' because someone would remember that I'd been to school there for a week.'

The chorus girls (one of whom is the fifteen-year-old Betty Grable) in *Palmy Days*. The star was Eddie Cantor. The dance numbers for his first four Goldwyn musicals were staged by Busby Berkeley.

For those who cherished *Gold Diggers of 1933*, there is one image that left its mark on their memories. Joan, a solitary figure, is standing beside a lamp post. As the whore, lonely, accusing, bitter, she sing/speaks the haunting:

Remember my forgotten man?
You put a rifle in his hand,
You sent him far away,
You shouted Hip Hooray
But look at him today!

Her bitter plaint is taken up by a black woman in a tenement flat above (Etta Moten) and transformed into a lament of the soul that knows no barriers to its suffering. Her cry, reaching out over the closed city, rises and melts in with a series of powerfully telling images: eager young men off to war and the promise of glory, cheered on by the crowds at the station waving them off; the misery of the front replaces dreams of glory. Hunger, unemployment and neglect are all that greet them on their return. The camera travels along queues of haunted, unshaven faces with frayed collars turned up against the cold, as they wait in silence, reduced to begging by the society they had gone off to protect, for the hand-outs that will enable them to survive.

The music is wonderful – plaintive, spiritual, martial, dirge-like, as the scenes unfold. Finally, the black woman's deeply stirring rendition is taken up by everyone on stage, men and women,

Forgetting him, you see
Means you're forgetting me
Like my forgotten man.

And facing out of a gigantic tread-mill, they look out over the heads of the audience and into the camera, to reach and stir audiences everywhere. And the film ends. It is an anthem that cannot be ignored. It

Berkeley's number, 'What a Perfect Combination', for Eddie Cantor's *The Kid from Spain*.

made for a powerful punch. Its cry reverberated throughout the land. The composers of the memorable number were Al Dubin and Harry Warren. The choreographer was Busby Berkeley.

Like Lubitsch, Sternberg and Mamoulian, Busby Berkeley also had his own signature. Shakespeare's Prologue in *Henry V* calls out for 'a muse of fire that would ascend the brightest heaven of invention'. Busby Berkeley, riding high on his specially designed giant camera monorails, became that muse to the musical, lighting up the sky with creations that left little to an audience's imagination, possessed as he was of an imagination that more than confounded and dazzled their own.

As a drill instructor with the American army in France his success in getting platoons of soldiers to march in precision, with the minimum of shouted orders, for the 1919 Peace Parade in Paris astounded his superiors and word got back to

Above: Eddie Cantor's 'Keep Young and Beautiful' in *Roman Scandals*. The numbers were staged by Busby Berkeley. Right: The slave market number, 'No More Love', in the same film.

Berkeley's classic 'The Lullaby of Broadway' number for *Gold Diggers of 1935*.

America. He wasn't a choreographer in the true sense of the word, but a dance director of the old 'one, two three, kick, kid!' school. In that capacity he worked on over twenty Broadway shows – starting with Rodgers and Hart's *A Connecticut Yankee*. Movies, without the limitations inherent in the theatre, were the obvious direction for him. His reputation spread to Hollywood, then in the first flush of sound. Along with dance directors Sammy Lee, Seymour Felix, LeRoy Prinz and Bobby Connolly, he received offers to work there but was the last to go, accepting because Eddie Cantor, who had known him on Broadway, suggested him to Goldwyn as the choreographer for Ziegfeld's *Whoopee* (1930). Although *Whoopee* was successful, the genre's appeal had already peaked. Other musicals completed but not yet released had most of their numbers cut out, removing rhyme from plots whose only reason had lain in their excuse for songs. Under contract to Goldwyn, Buzz created numbers for the annual Eddie Cantor vehicles (which relied more on Cantor's comic personality than the songs), including *Palmy Days* (1931), *The Kid from Spain* (1932) and last but best – *Roman Scandals* (1933). Buzz also did the numbers for the Mary Pickford musical *Kiki* (1930). There wasn't much other work around. By the end of 1932, with no prospects of a change, the discouraged Berkeley had decided to return to Broadway when he received the call from Zanuck.

Begining with *42nd Street*, Berkeley's wizardry with the camera created the most astonishingly beautiful sights set to music and ushered in a new era. Berkeley proceeded to take the threat out of army drills and military May Day march past parades by transforming soldiers in uniforms into star-spangled girls, and heavy armaments into ballrooms, crystal chandeliers and endless corridors of mirrors. To achieve his effects he freed the camera from its conventional positions of seeing and recording what it saw, and made it the all-seeing eye of the God of Dance.

Admittedly Berkeley had had a few predecessors for his sort of spectacle. Early in 1929 MGM's Viennese-born dance director, Albertina Rasch, grouped her troupe into floral arrangements which were photographed overhead à la Berkeley for *Hollywood Revue of 1929*, and *March of Time* (1930). The modernistic sets designed for Berkeley's fantasies by Anton Grot, (the brilliant Polish-born art director who was the driving creative force at Warners in the 30s), had their precedent in those devised by Mallet and Stephens for Marcel L'Herbier's film *L'Argent* (1929) and any number of German films. But Berkeley's genius lay in bringing the camera in close on the individual girls, expanding from their smiles into geometric patterns that grew delirious, and entered surrealistic dimensions.

Besides the perfectly shaped 'Remember My Forgotten Man', there stands another number which, besides being an Oscar winner and Berkeley's own favourite among his work of that period, is also a farewell to an era, 'Lullaby of Broadway', from *Gold Diggers of 1935*. Here Berkeley was also entrusted with the direction of the story part of the film, but this portion unfortunately lacks the flair that marks his numbers. Structured around Warren

Wonder Bar. Berkeley's 'Goin' to Heaven on a Mule', where bad taste reached a new low.

and Dubin's hymn to the glamour of show-biz and show-people, 'Lullaby of Broadway' – running almost fifteen minutes – opens with songstress Winnie Shaw's face as a pinpoint of light in a sea of black velvet, slowly enlarging with her low, husky rendering of the song until her face fills the screen. By tilting his camera, her facial outline is transformed into an aerial view of New York. Warner's technical department, second only to MGM's, creates a superb montage that speeds the action. Dawn: the clock in the steeple strikes 6 a.m. The streets are empty except for a lone milkman as the girl beds down for the day. The melody moves into the razz-matazz rhythms of the working city until dusk falls and her alarm calls her to another night on the town. While the city sleeps, the action moves high up over the rooftops into a nightclub with three bands and one hundred precision dancers, where the girl and her escort (Dick Powell) are the only guests. 'I used a cocked angle in the middle of the dance sequence, where I tilted the camera for a reason,' said Berkeley. 'The girls fell one after the other into the arms of the boys, after which I wanted the boys to throw them up again. Physically, it was impossible, but reversing and cocking the camera, thus changing the angle and making it appear natural to the eye, I could make it look as if they did it.'

For the climax of the precision routine welling up around the table, he cut out all sound except that from the tapping armada, costumed in a sado-masochistic Orry-Kelly fantasy of black leather and lace. Their pounding advance is an intoxicating, Bolero-like rhythm, escalating to a hedonistic crescendo of swirling percussion sounds, the call of which no one could withstand. The alluring throb of 200 heels pulls her in. Laughingly, she backs against the stylized sets. Suddenly she stumbles, tumbles backwards and crashes through the wall-high French window, plunging to a nightmare death on the asphalt below. The ritual sacrifice has been made, society has been appeased. The carefree gold-digger is dead. The frenzied tempo stops and the camera returns to its objective position, with the aerial view reverting to Winnie Shaw singing the last bars of the songs as she dwindles from sight. It is of course an inspired variation on Stravinsky's

The Rite of Spring.

What gives Berkeley's numbers such a lift is that the song always provides the spring-board for the lyrical transposition of music into images. Of course he was fortunate in that they were constructed on great melodic lines which could support his excesses, yet were capable of standing on their own. For these 'popular' song hits were the 'folk song' of the big city. They capture the feelings and dreams of its inhabitants and yet they also underline the irony of their existence. The Broadway and Hollywood tunesmiths were masters of this transient art: 'Lullaby of Broadway' is a classic. With its precise, rapid rhyming couplets it conveys the vitality and the restlessness of city life as seen through the girl. The irony is in the (Dubin) lyrics, the feverish restlessness in the (Warren) music, and its immortality is guaranteed by Berkeley's spectacular number which is not only a farewell salute to the good-time girls but a true song of the city. When he failed, he plunged into depths of perfect awfulness. A classic was his creation for another Jolson come-back, *Wonder Bar* (1934). It was, to be fair, a musical in which bad taste had already had a headstart. Having begun its life in Berlin in 1930 as a highly lauded, sensationally popular 'chamber musical', compared by critics to Kurt Weill's *Die Dreigroschenoper*, its success made it a natural for Broadway. The New York producers, who described it as 'a continental novelty of European night life', then proceeded to scrap what they had bought for its 'unique and special qualities', to make it suitable for an Al Jolson vehicle. Not content with this mutilation, the movie went further – because even the Broadway adaptation was still strong stuff and the country's moral climate was hardening. An echo of the original Montmartre milieu – haunt of gigolos and gigolettes and American bankers who feel that Paris is no place for their wives while they are there – occurs in a scene on the dance floor where a sleek, patent-leather gigolo cuts in on a couple, and spins off with the man in his arms.

As in all Berkeley's work the most important star was his camera, swooping down from dizzying heights, diving under water and between the legs of rows of girls, almost into their perfect teeth:

'I quickly realized that the camera had only one eye; I felt the camera intuitively. I said to myself, "Buzz, there are unlimited things you can do with a camera, so you might as well start now, in your first picture!" When I arrived on the set, I saw that four cameras had been set up for shooting, placed in different locations, to give a variety in angles. After you've shot the action you wanted, the cutter would take the sequences and put them together. Well, this isn't the way I'm going to do it. I told the assistant cameraman that I only shoot with one camera. That was a bit daring, because everybody knew I had only just arrived from New York and I'd never worked in films before! But I told them that I did my editing *in* the camera, and I always have ever since. I only use one camera in anything I have ever done.'

For most of the decade he had an almost free rein. The results could be as sumptuously extravagant as the one he concocted for *Roman Scandals*. In this the torch-singer, Ruth Etting, sings the Dubin/Warren number 'No More Love', while overlooking a slave market where nubile girls wait to be auctioned. Scantily-clad, slave girls are chained in graduated tiers around a towering block, on the top of which a brutish slave driver lashes his long snaky whip about. The bottom row of Cleopatras were respectable compared to the Godivas who iced this flesh cake, covered only by knee-length blonde hair. Since any form of fleshings would have shown in the close-ups, they were naked underneath. The girls agreed when Berkeley convinced them that it would be done in a beautiful and artistic manner, and shot it at night to avoid unnecessary visitors. (His Goldwyn girls included Lucille Ball, Betty Grable and Paulette Goddard in their earlier days!) The climax comes as a girl leaps to her death rather than be sold to a man she doesn't love.

For a number in *Footlight Parade* Anton Grot designed an aquacade in which 100 girls could slide down a studio-built waterfall into a forest lake that turned into a pool with gold spring-boards. This became 'By a Waterfall'. 'With the technicians, I designed the pool and made caverns underneath it with thick plates of glass that I could shoot the camera through. It was the first time an aquacade had been done on the screen.' (Not surprisingly, Berkeley was later called in to work with Metro's mermaid, Esther Williams, on such popular fare as *Million Dollar Mermaid* (1952) and *Easy to Love* (1953) where he had 100 people on water skis.' 'For *Footlight Parade* I designed a special bathing costume with rubber head pieces looking like hair, that ran down across the girls' bodies to give a semi-nude effect. We rehearsed it for two weeks and shot it in six days. It was my toughest number to film because of the camera set-ups under water, above water and the high shots, plus the physical stress and strain of the girls in the water. We had hydraulic lifts in operation that pumped 20,000 gallons of water a minute over the falls, and the set underneath the stage looked like the hold of some enormous ocean liner.'

For 'Don't Say Goodnight' in *Wonder Bar* Berkeley ordered sixty moveable white columns and an octagon of mirrors twenty-two feet high and sixteen feet wide, to create the impression of hundreds of people doing a minuet, when in fact there were only eight dancers. Never once was camera or operator seen in the mirror.

For *Dames*, he seemed to be throwing the girls into a close-up. 'I did that in reverse camera. I showed the girl in close-up first; then she went down to the floor on a wire. The girls reached for her and let her down to the floor. When viewed in reverse, it looks as though she was thrown right up from the floor into the lens of the camera.'

He claimed responsibility for the invention of the camera monorail, a special camera-crane device. It consisted of two rails up in the rafters of the sound stage and the rigging that came down from it like that of a frame. The camera car went up and down the side of the rigging. Before, a boom had to be used that required five or six men on the stage floor to push it, and another two or three operators to lower it. His monorail needed only two men and was smooth and fast.

Berkeley had a reputation as an expensive director, but there were no complaints from the

What a man of genius could do with mirrors. Berkeley's 'Don't Say Goodnight' in *Wonder Bar*.

Dolores Del Rio and Ricardo Cortez with the chorus in the sado-masochistic little 'Tango del Rio' for *Wonder Bar*.

Berkeley marshals the girls for the military precision number 'All's Fair in Love and War' for *Gold Diggers of 1937*.

front office as long as he brought in the patrons. The cost of his numbers at Warners was the equal of a small-budget film, averaging $10,000 a minute of screen running time. Since the average number ran from seven to ten minutes, they could cost anywhere between $75,000 and $125,000 each and there were usually three or more such numbers in any musical.

Speaking of Berkeley in an interview he gave Albert Johnson, Roger Edens, the composer,

Early Goldwyn Girls. From left to right: Paulette Goddard, Betty Grable and Lucille Ball.

arranger, producer and Arthur Freed's right hand during MGM's musical heyday, recalled: 'To cash in on the current dance craze, "The Conga", a song was written into the score of *Strike Up The Band* (1940) for Judy Garland and Mickey Rooney. They were ready to shoot . . . then Berkeley decided he wanted to make it a huge number with about five minutes of Judy singing, and with every possible type of camera angle; and he decided he wanted to do the entire song and dance number in one take. Nobody thought it was possible, but he rehearsed it with a complete camera crew for five days, laying out every movement step by step, with cameras taking all kinds of angle shots of maraccas and trumpets. It soon became like the opening number of a Broadway show. There was the same great tension, because the number could only be shot once. When the morning came to shoot, practically the whole studio was down there. Everyone was very tense and keyed up – and the result was a real giving performance. The scene went beautifully, without a hitch. Even now, it has an unforgettable

The 'By a Waterfall' number in *Footlight Parade* in 1933. Left: Berkeley's presentation of Esther Williams in *Easy to Love* twenty years later.

something extra about it.'

Warner Brothers' financial resurgence with the success of *42nd Street*, and *Gold Diggers of 1933* had the other studios exhorting their dance directors to similar efforts. Money was plentiful, so were girls. But what the results proved was that Berkeley, the Cecil B. De Mille of musicals, was a law unto his own.

As has been mentioned, Darryl F. Zanuck was to give Berkeley the call, thereby giving us *42nd Street*, *Gold Diggers of 1933*, *Dames*, etc. Zanuck, prior to forming 20th-Century Films with the semi-retired ex-UA President Joseph Schenck, was the 'whizz kid' manager of Warner Bros. Studios. The story goes that in 1932, against Jack Warner's own initial

Busby Berkeley at MGM. Judy Garland and Mickey Rooney, right foreground lead the exuberant 'Conga' line-up in *Strike up the Band*.

Far left: Airborne. The girls on the wings of a plane in *Flying Down to Rio*. Anything went, as long as it went far enough.

Below, and bottom: A carousel number from *Dancing Lady*. The stars were Clark Gable and Joan Crawford. Making their film debuts were Fred Astaire and Nelson Eddy. Joan Crawford in a frame close-up.

Fashions of 1934. Berkeley's style could be applied to many forms. A pattern of girls and feathers – and girls as human harps.

Opposite, left: *Transatlantic Merry-go-round*, a musical set on an ocean liner. Shades of Le Sacre du Printemps – but of course the selling point was the girls.

Right: Maurice Chevalier and Ann Sothern in the straw hat number for *Folies Bergère*. Busby Berkeley's influence was clearly seen in the musicals of other studios.

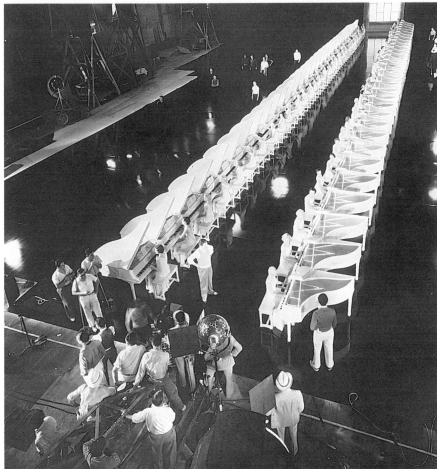

Above: 'The Words are in My Heart' required the use of fifty-six pianos in this Berkeley number for *Gold Diggers of 1935.*

opposition, he made the decision to revive the musical. He gave the go-ahead to start *42nd Street.* (The original choice for the direction of the film was Mervyn Le Roy, but he was too ill to work. However, it was he who persuaded Zanuck to hire Berkeley.) This was a dramatic move on Zanuck's part since musicals had been made taboo after their slump in 1930. Knowing a good thing when they saw it, Warners not only repeated the formula immediately, but kept the same cast and crew at it. These included, besides the stars' faces, the art

director, Anton Grot, who gave Warner films their look of splendour and who conceived those architectural eye-poppers for the numbers; Orry-Kelly who undressed stars as stunningly as he dressed them; directors like Lloyd Bacon and Mervyn LeRoy to keep the action at a brisk pace; and another team, besides Ruby and Dick, whose contribution to musicals, and the Warner ones in particular, was even more auspicious – the songwriters Al Dubin (lyricist) and Harry Warren (music). But what set this film cycle apart from anything that had gone before or would come after, was the master builder of the production numbers that were to be the heart and soul of these films. That was of course Busby Berkeley.

Few of Berkeley's competitors achieved his light-hearted blend and quite the same imaginative results. Typical was Metro's *Dancing Lady* (1933). The size and the quantities of everything, including the star power (Crawford and Gable, Franchot Tone, and 'introducing' Nelson Eddy and Fred Astaire) are impressive. But the handling is heavy. When at last the treacly plot, held together only by the close-ups, gives way and the production numbers by Sammy Lee take over, the camera, in the pay of the accountants, sits back and records Metro's lavish expenditure. The set revolves but nothing takes off, not even the platinumed Harlowites who sit astride mechanical horses circling a sparkling mirror-plated merry-go-round. The result is more a listless parody of what it hoped to emulate. Similarly with *Flying Down to Rio* (1933) – dances by Dave Gould) where dauntless chorus girls dance on the wings of an airborne plane: or the two independent Zanuck productions, *Moulin Rouge* (1934, dances by Russell Markert) and *Folies Bergère* (1934, dances by Dave Gould); or *Transatlantic Merry-Go-Round* (1934, by Larry Ceballos), or those for another of MGM's mammoths – *The Great Ziegfeld* (1936), with the Oscar-winning numbers by Seymour Felix. While these musicals contain pleasures,

rarely do any of them approach Berkeley's best. Of course men like LeRoy Prinz, Dave Gould, Seymour Felix and the rest were far more creative as dance directors, but here they were called on to imitate another man's ideas which isn't the same sort of thing at all.

But to get a real feeling of those days, here are the voices of the people directly involved. There is Madison Lacy, Hollywood's leading pin-up photographer in his years at WB, friend to most of these girls and husband to two of the loveliest of them. There is Joan Blondell, and supporting her on either side are the Berkeley girls, Lois Lindsay, Melba Marshall, Sheila Ray and Gwen Seeger. It was girls like these Al Dubin and Harry Warren had in mind when they wrote:

What do you go for,
Go see a show for,
Tell the truth
You go to see those beautiful *dames*.

Ziegfeld glorified them, Berkeley automated them: they were Goldwyn's follies and George White's scandals, they paraded for Paramount, and put the revue into Hollywood, and Warner Bros, who owe their economic survival to them, released these statistics about the 'ideal' movie chorine. She measured a $32\frac{1}{2}$ inch bust, 23 inch waist, 34 inch hips, $12\frac{1}{2}$ inch calf, $7\frac{1}{2}$ inch ankle, and added that Venus de Milo with her $28\frac{1}{2}$ inch waist couldn't get a job as a script girl on poverty row. (*Photoplay* Dec. 1929).

Sheila Ray

The difference between dancers and show girls was the dancers did the dancing, and showgirls were never asked to dance. They always had two left feet. That's a terrible thing to say, but they did, most of them. I was still in school when *42nd Street* came

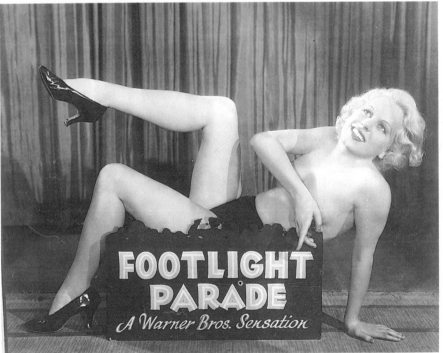

out. And when I saw that, I thought: that is for me. And somebody told me there was an interview out there, and I went. They had limited interviews. If your name wasn't on the list, they didn't let you in. But you'd go anyway because once you'd been at that studio it kind of helped. I'm 5′ 6″ tall. And when I first started in the business, it was the ponies – that's what they used to call them – about 5′ 1″ or 5′ 2″. Then all of a sudden when Bobby Connolly came out, he preferred the tall girls. And my friend and I were always front and centre.

Bobby and Buzz were there at the same time at WB. Berkeley didn't use Connolly's girls very much, but Connelly did use the Berkeley girls. They got along very well but there definitely was a rivalry

Eleanor Powell in the 'So Long, Sarah Jane' number in *I Dood It*. Sheila Ray is second from right.

A break in filming. Busby Berkeley's girls in costume for 'All's Fair in Love and War' in *Gold Diggers of 1937*.

there.*

We worked because we had to work, my father died when I was twelve, and I'm the youngest of eight children. And I had two sisters that weren't married, and the insurance money ran out that Dad had left, and my brothers' businesses weren't doing so well . . . And it was a wonderful way to earn a living. I just loved the smell of the studio. And the people there were the greatest in the world. It was always such fun. The only competition was when we went to an interview to be chosen. But once you started work there wasn't any competition. We worked incredibly long hours then. That was before SAG (Screen Actors Guild). When I used to work for Albertina Rasch over at MGM *(Rosalie)* I'd roll over out of bed on to the floor and then get up, because she'd have you using different muscles that you'd never used before! She'd forget to let you rest. After about the third day it would start getting better, but she'd have no patience with our moans and groans. I didn't enjoy working for her. On the other hand we all loved working with Busby and Bobby Connolly*, because he was so sweet; and then later on for Jack Donohue, because he was always kidding around.

We would rehearse for weeks on numbers. It would be about 10 o'clock call, then we'd have an hour off for lunch, and then work till about six. But during shooting, we'd have to go there about 7 in the morning. Eight hours a day without a break was

* On the other hand there wasn't any rivalry between the girls at all.

* Connolly shared the choreographic load at WB with Berkeley and even staged the numbers for some of the films Busby directed, like *Stars Over Broadway*, and later, when they both went to MGM, *For Me And My Gal*.

normal time. They could work us any hours. That was before the unions came in.. I was hanging on a harp in one film . . .

JK: That was *Fashions of 1934.*

Sheila: We were typewriters in *Ready, Willing and Able* [with Ruby Keeler and Lee Dixon]. We would lie there by the hour, and then our legs would go on cue to make the typewriter work. That was a funny time. In those days you didn't have pantyhose. It was just stockings. And little black panties would come over the top. And once in a while it would ruin a shot if a piece of skin showed between the top of the stocking and the other. The cameraman would have to go up and down on the dolly to see if there was any skin showing.

The nicest experience I ever had was on *Cain and Mabel.* Clark Gable and Marion Davies. I was a seventeen-year-old kid, and my mother got invited to go up to the Hearst ranch to teach Marion Davies her dance routine, over a weekend. We rehearsed about five minutes and all the rest was just goggle-eyed! She was the nicest hostess – you'd think I was the Queen of England, that's how nicely we were treated. And we actually got paid for it, and that just killed us – Mom and me!

There was no hoofer like Eleanor Powell. At that particular time. I know Ann Miller was around, but Eleanor's feet were just great. And the routines she used to work out with Buddy Rich . . . he'd play the drums and they'd work out the taps, and we'd work it out from that and put it together and that's how the routine would develop.

I worked with Greta Garbo in one picture. It was just a ballroom scene, you know. We were ballroom dancers, and she was in this ballroom scene. They wanted people who could actually dance nicely on the floor. That was in a comedy, *Two-Faced Woman* (1941). But, now, Eleanor Powell – she was just one of us. Fred Astaire has always been Fred Astaire, and I've worked with him, but he's always very quiet. Never liked anybody at rehearsal. After he knew his routines – great. But he didn't like you around when he was learning, and I don't blame him because it's pretty tough when you've got an image like that. Kathryn Grayson, now she's not a dancer, but I taught her many times. There were a lot of hours put in, there's just no doubt about it. But we were all thrilled to be on the picture, to have a job.

There were three complete close-up girls for Berkeley, his three favourites – we used to call them the three little pigs, they were so cute. One is Eleanor Bailey, she's got a bit heavy but she's still a doll; and then Lois Lindsay or Lois Lacey; and then there's Victoria Venton.

JK: I see you were in *The Great Ziegfeld* [Choreographer Seymour Felix] 'A Pretty Girl is Like a Melody'.

Sheila: Oh, yes, that was the big number. We were bats in that. We danced on the steps. We had quite a hard number coming down the steps. We'd just sit for days and days before they'd even get to our area. They had the girls up on top, and by the time they did a close-up, I think we shot that for weeks and weeks and weeks. We seemed to be on that for ever. Most of the girls used to knit. They would knit or write letters. Even I knit. And some of our dancing

boys knit. I was in the 'Lullaby of Broadway' number. We saw that just recently. And we just laughed at it, because of the dancing then and the dancing now. That just wasn't dancing. Technically, dancers are much better today than they were then. Each chorus girl you see on television now is better than most stars you saw then. The style has changed. Everything became modern. I think Astaire did an awful lot for that. He was the one that combined ballet with tap, although he never had a ballet lesson in his life, but he got the style.

JK: Did you work on the Garland films as well?

Sheila: We were in *The Wizard of Oz*, but in *Girl Crazy* I did the Apache dance with Mickey Rooney. I threw him around. That was the last time I was in a picture. Berkeley did that. But Berkeley was a cameraman – he was not a dance director. This is a terrible thing to say, but I think he did a time step and a break! We'd learn our numbers after they'd

Top: 'You're just too marvellous'. Ruby Keeler and Lee Dixon dancing on the typewriter keys. A Bobby Connolly idea for *Ready, Willing and Able*.

Above: Robert Alton, seen behind the star, arranged a rhumba and partnered Greta Garbo in her last film, *Two-Faced Woman*. It was supposed to start a craze. It didn't. But then, neither did the film – nor the star, in parts like this.

decided the music. Like 'Begin the Beguine' with Eleanor Powell.

There was a hillside, and Mr Connolly asked me to do turns coming down it. He didn't ask Eleanor Powell, he asked me – just to see if it could be done! So we did it. But you had to do it fast, 'cause if you did slow turns you'd fall over because it was very steep.

I'd been married close to eight years and I didn't have any children. So I was working for Eugene Loring out at MGM, and I worked out my contract and then gave it up. And you know what I did? Came home and went right over and took lessons. Went to class. I couldn't stand not dancing! So I went over and paid for it instead of getting paid for it. I think I was about 28 or 29 when I left. I didn't want to hit 30 as a dancer, because I wanted to leave with a good impression. I didn't want anybody to ever say: 'What's that old bag dancing for?' Nowadays I put on a few shows at schools, and I took a show to Camp Pendleton and it was very successful. Just amateur. Just for the fun of it. I danced and I loved it, and I loved every minute of it. I'd have done it again, I would, always, I could never have done anything else. It's the only time I wish I were younger. It was marvellous. I was doing what I liked, and I loved the people. People are so important. And we had the best.

Berkeley in *Screen Facts (No. 10)* said: 'I had sixteen beautiful girls under contract (during the mid-thirties) and I would supplement them with other girls on each picture.

'Every time I started a picture I would tell the studio I had a call for girls. Warners would say, what do you want a call for girls for? You've got sixteen under contract and you used twenty-five or thirty in your last picture. That was in the days when we used to throw open the studio gates and let them all come in for interviews. There was no extras' or dancers' guild or anything. Once I had 723 girls show up on a call for one of my *Gold Diggers* pictures. I was all afternoon picking girls out of this large number, and finally ended up selecting three girls out of the 723! My sixteen regular contract girls were sitting on the side waiting, so after I picked the three girls, I put them next to my special sixteen and they matched, just like pearls. Back in those days the word would get around that Busby Berkeley was going to have a call for his next picture and they would all flock to the studio with high hopes.'

Above: 'A Pretty Girl is Like a Melody'. The famous spiral staircase of *The Great Ziegfeld*.

Right: Gwen Seeger, one of the beautiful Berkeley girls. Photographs by Madison Lacy.

Gwen Seeger

When I worked in the Goldwyn Girls, I made around $200 a week. I mean, nowadays about $500 would be the equivalent. I began by winning a beauty contest, called Miss Prosperity. It came right on the heels of the Depression. I had a publicity mán, and he said why don't you go into the motion picture business? I was only about 17. So we went over to Paramount and I had been raised in a boarding school – I had gone to this girls' finishing school for 12 years.

I'm not what they call a gypsy type. I'm more the showgirl type. As a matter of fact, I was always classified as a showgirl. We call the hoofers the gypsies. But with Buzz, you were a combination of everything. You were a hoofer, a showgirl, you had to be able to appear and do scenes. You really had to be an actress. I mean, he called on you many times when you actually had to act. You weren't just a girl kicking up her heels. Nor, as a showgirl, just a beautiful dumb girl standing there.

I made more money than some of the dancers did. See, I worked with Sammy Lee at Fox – I worked in *Tin Pan Alley* in 1940, and I worked with Lee at

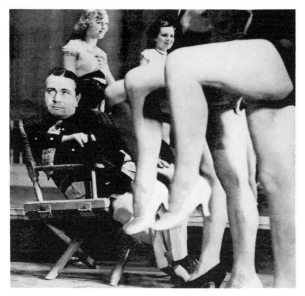

Choreographers at work. Left: Bobby Connolly and, right, Larry Ceballos and chorus girls, both at Warners. Below: Sammy Lee looking over the girls at MGM. Bottom, left: LeRoy Prinz with dancers rehearsing for *The Time, the Place and the Girl*. Right: Robert Alton puts the Goldwyn Girls through their paces for *Strike me Pink*.

MGM on *Dancing Lady*. The very first picture I worked in was at Paramount, and it was with Clive Brook and Miriam Hopkins. It was a little speaking role, just a couple of lines. As a matter of fact, the very first person I ever worked with was a boy named Bud Flanagan who later became Dennis O'Keefe. And he and I worked together in this scene.

It wasn't too hard to get into pictures if you were attractive and had a nice figure. I had always been able to dance. I had had dance training at school. Then after Paramount, the next picture I made *Speak Easily* (1932) starred Jimmy Durante and Buster Keaton at MGM. Then *Dancing Lady* (1933). I found that as I finished one I would be in demand for another. There was really only a handful of us that they wanted. We were trained and knew how to handle ourselves. There would be interviews. We had to go in bathing suits and parade around these people. And there might be 100 girls on an interview, and just 15 or 20 would be selected. The competition was very tough. We were all very pretty girls with excellent figures and there were thousand of girls who would come out here to try and get in the picture business. You had to have a good, well-proportioned figure. Some girls have a little opening there where the thighs don't meet. And your calves had to touch. This showed that your legs were in proportion. Because in our costumes – what there was of them – practically our entire leg was showing. Then you had to have very good photogenic features. And you had to be able to take on a part or a bit that they might throw at you.

In some of Buzz' large numbers, he used hundreds of girls. And men too. But in his basic numbers,

Some of the flamboyant costumes created by Adrian for MGM's *The Great Ziegfeld*.

maybe 50 or 60 was the top as a rule. He did this to achieve that effect where he could get his overhead shot. In his musicals we did do a lot of hoofing, and I wasn't as good a hoofer as some of the other girls. They were wonderful dancers, and they were always in the front in the numbers. But when there were close-ups we were usually used – myself, and Lois Lindsay was one of them. She's married to the head still man over at Warner Bros, Madison Lacy. She and I worked in a scene for Buzz. It was very funny; Buzz was a person who, if he liked you, you were in all of his pictures. He would have interviews because he would bring in new girls to add to the line, but his stand-by girls were always with him. I was always in his pictures, and Lois, and Vicki Benton . . . she was a blonde, a cute little girl. We were in *Gold Diggers in Paris*, we had quite a number in that. Lois and I played women of the streets in Paris. We were all done up with fancy hair-dos to look like street women . . . and then they had girls who were very sweet. Now, in *The Harvey Girls* I worked with Judy Garland – that wasn't for Buzz – I was one of the Alhambra girls, and she was one of the Harvey Girls. That wasn't exactly a musical and

we didn't do many numbers, but there were a lot of us in there.

I just went from one show to another. There were many studios that wanted to keep me under contract, but I preferred going with the different directors on different pictures. In the 'By a Waterfall' number I remember almost drowning! We had to dive and come up smiling and our mouths would get full of water! We were spouting around like whales!

We were water-logged at the end of the day – we were in there for hours and hours. And Buzz is a perfectionist. Everything has to be just so. If it wasn't just right, he'd take it over and over. And if you felt sick, there was always a nurse around!

Truthfully, musicals were a very, very hard grind. Seymour Felix, I think, was the hardest person that I ever worked for. He was doing *Kid Millions*, an Eddie Cantor picture, and we did a number called 'Mandy' – a musical number. Lucille Ball was with me on that. And George Murphy was in it – our ex-Senator, and Ann Sothern, Ethel Merman. And he would have us do that number over and over again until we almost dropped. He kept himself going with coffee and aspirins. And so he was just

keyed up constantly. He was just driving us and driving us till you would almost explode. He was very nice, he cared for us all, but we were young and he figured you can spring back. But he wouldn't let up and then, all of a sudden, one girl would go into hysterics and start to cry from being so tired. You'd go for six or seven hours without stopping. Not even a rest period! And you'd be in such a position that you couldn't get down. And in this one particular number you had to pass a tambourine on, and if you got it wrong you ruined the whole number. So, as a result one would get the hysterics again and this would start all the girls crying and it would get very dramatic and we'd yell and scream. It was funny as a matter of fact! Although it wasn't funny then! So Lucille Ball did something funny, that was very typical of her. There was this kid, it might have been her first big job, she took the tambourine and kept it. Just held on to it. Well you see she was so keyed up. Well Felix went mad. He screamed and hollered at this kid who started to pee in her pants. So Lucille got very angry at Seymour Felix. He was a little man. He was about 5' 1" I think. I'm only about 5' 4" but I build up with heels to about 5' 7". I'm really not the tall showgirl type. And Lucille Ball, who was about 5' 9" or 5' 10", got up and walked down and put her finger in his face and scolded him, and he said something to her, and she just picked him up and put him under arm, walked off the stage and took him outside, stood him up and said, 'You look here. You leave us alone for a while.' And dusted her arms like this, and walked back to her place! She carried him out like a suitcase! It really broke the tension. She was always doing something funny. It's why the girls liked her so.

I had opportunities of being a leading lady and stardom and so forth at different times. But there was a little price to pay and I wasn't about to do it. If you know what I mean. I don't say that everybody that's ever achieved stardom had to, but I just didn't care for the approach. And I would say, 'No, I wasn't interested.' You see, I'm in the cosmetic business now. I own two cosmetic firms, and I've been quite successful. Well, during the time I was in pictures, my mother – who is the creator of Pink Ice Home

Alice Faye and the chorus in *George White's 1935 Scandals*, the film in which Eleanor Powell made her screen debut.

Centre left: In *42nd Street* there were 200 girls taking part in the big numbers. Warner Baxter as the producer in this classic backstage story, choosing the girls for the chorus.

Bottom left: On the set of *Dames*. Harry Warren, the song writer, is at the piano. Also present are players Dick Powell, Guy Kibbee and Jim Ellis.

Left: This is not a mirror reflection. The girls above are strapped firm for a rare camera angle. Berkeley can be seen at the end of the tunnel. A production shot from *Dames*.

Below: First aid. The Berkeley girls sometimes needed it after a strenuous session during the production of *Footlight Parade*.

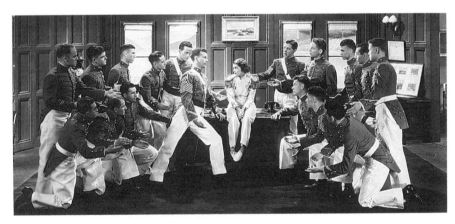

Top: The stars of *Kid Millions*, centre. In ascending order Eddie Cantor, Ethel Merman, George Murphy and Ann Sothern. Lucille Ball, still a Goldwyn Girl in 1934, can be seen far right, third row up.

Above: Ruby Keeler and Dick Powell in *Flirtation Walk*. The musical numbers were staged by Bobby Connolly.

just awful. It was so heavy and thick. It just penetrated our pores, and we would break out and look awful. We would go into close-ups and we had a big problem. Finally, I would just refuse to wear the make-up that they had and wore only my mother's make-up. As a result my skin cleared up and the cameraman used to say: 'What did you do? You look so much better than the other girls.'

We wore very scant attire. Of course, some of the pictures we see now go way beyond decency, which I'm very much against. I think it's hurt the industry terribly. In our days we were covered with a few feathers and beads, but we were covered! It was nudity, but it was covered! And it wasn't vulgar. And yet, when I got off the set I'd always run and cover myself up with a robe! I felt like I was too undressed to be wandering around. But I think the thing I hated most was the body make-up – I couldn't stand that. And it took hours after we got through at night to scrub it off.

In fact, I don't recall any of the girls who worked for Buzz being a vulgar or a bad girl.

JK: Were you aware of the Depression?

Gwen: Not really. It never seemed to touch me. My family didn't lose anything in the Depression, so as a result I didn't feel it. There seemed to be a lot of gaiety and laughter. Actually, from '32 right through '36 things seemed to get a little better. Everyone seemed to have an air of anticipation about them. The films portrayed all of the poor, downtrodden, sad experiences.

I was in *Gold Diggers in Paris* and *Footlight Parade* and *Varsity Show* and *42nd Street*. I was in some of the very good numbers. But we wouldn't be called for everything, when they only needed hoofers, say, to be with Ruby. Showgirls earned more and yet they did less. The good hoofers were put in the front line, regardless of whether they were good-looking or not. But when they'd go in for a close-up, they'd pick the showgirls. Or they'd pick the girls with pretty faces when they had to surround the star. And maybe when he was singing and you'd have to pose near him. The stars had their dressing rooms, but we only had hard benches or folding chairs. They didn't make us too comfortable. And we were bone weary because we would be going through these numbers. It wasn't so much the dancing but the routine . . . over and over and over again until it was perfect, and Buzz was a stickler for perfection.

We portrayed a gold digger type of girl, but really none of us were. It was a part to play. And it was part of the way the 30s were. There were lots of girls that were doing this. But they weren't working in chorus lines – that was their livelihood! They were real gold diggers, and we were merely portraying the type of girl that was actually doing this.

Lois Lindsay married Madison Lacy. He was the head still man. Today they own camera shops, and they're doing very well. Several of the girls married well. Lorena Layson married Mr Mayer later on. Others had their problems. One I know is working right now as a cashier in a health food store. It's been hard on her, but she's still making a living. A lot of them married men right from the studio. Not the actors. They would marry maybe sound

Facial, which is a very famous facial – was making these cosmetics. And when I was not in pictures, she was utilizing the fact that I was a starlet. And so I was learning the cosmetic business along at the same time I was in pictures. And Joan Crawford had taken quite an interest in me at one time. And she had lined up an interview with a big producer at MGM, and I guess was planning on grooming me really for stardom. And I didn't know anything about it. I got a leave of absence and took off for Canada with my mother, right at the time they were planning the tests and so forth. But I learned the cosmetic business, and you can't be an actress for ever.

You were exercising constantly in these numbers, dancing day in and day out. So your body was kept in good shape. Your skin had to be kept in good shape for close-ups. I was very, very careful about my skin. The make-up we wore in those days was technicians, the people we used to see at work all the time. One of the girls married one of the leading cameramen, Stanley Cortez. The technicians were very, very fine men and a lot of them got married to showgirls.

Joan Blondell

The kids working on TV today complain about how hard it is. Believe me, they don't know what hard is. We had no unions, then, and didn't even have Saturdays off. I did 27 films in 30 months at one stretch. At one point, Cagney told me to 'walk', go on strike for better pay and less hours. He said, 'Now is the time to do it, while we're both in the top box-office ten.' He did. But I didn't have the courage, what with so many people to support. So I stayed. I supose it might have done my career some good if I had put up a fight, better parts and that sort of thing. When I was doing *Dames* (1934) I was seven months pregnant. They squashed me into these costumes with all these tight girdles. I thought I was going to die, and they photographed me from the waist up as much as possible. I passed out a couple of times. They gave you ten days to have your kids, then, back to work! The studio made me do four films while I was carrying my daughter Ellen, and three when I was carrying Norm. Busby shot my big number, 'The Girl At The Ironing Board' after we'd nearly finished filming on *Dames*, when the baby really showed, with me in a large apron that hid most of the bulge. For the rest of the time he kept me behind the ironing board, or a clothes line.

'The Girl at the Ironing Board'. Joan Blondell in *Dames*.

Jimmy Cagney and I were given two great roles in a play written by George Kelly, who wrote *The Torch Bearers* and one Broadway hit after another. Cagney had been in musical comedy and I'd been in vaudeville. I started getting jobs outside of New York in little stock companies dotted here and there. Eventually we both auditioned for this play and it opened on Broadway the night of the crash in 1929. So the play didn't run but Cagney and I got wonderful notices. Nothing ran at that time because everybody was busy jumping out of windows. Then Marie Baumer wrote another play for us called *Penny Arcade*. Al Jolson saw us playing in it, bought it, and sold it to Warners with the stipulation that they take us. We arrived the same day and signed the same day for that one picture (*Sinner's Holiday*). I think they were kinda annoyed at having the law laid down by Jolson because they gave our roles to

Grant Withers and Evalyn Knapp and gave us two minor roles. But we were getting paid and we were happy and grateful. I'll never forget the day we saw the first day's rushes. It was a hot day on the back lot and all the bosses, Warner and Zanuck, came down and watched and signed us to a long-term five-year contract right there in broad daylight on the back lot! That's how it started. We made five pictures in a row but we were first teamed on Broadway. I'd done everything in vaudeville but my laundry!

We'd been doing the same sort of films for so long that we used to change our lines around or add to them, ad-lib during filming and nobody would be any the wiser. After that I was forever doing the same part – just a change of clothes. I'd try to vary the tempo, but there wasn't too much you could do with those dames I was always playing. I understood those gold-diggers. I was always a very observant person, and I saw plenty of them in my years in the theatre and vaudeville. They were so unlike me. I was a very introverted and shy kid in those days, and there I was forever playing these brash extrovert characters. One of the films I made around that time was something called *Convention City*. It didn't have much music or singing but it was so blue, I heard they had to end up using it for stag shows. The films we used to have to make! Cagney said that I must be the most sophisticated virgin the city had ever seen! The hours were awful because we didn't have unions then and worked any time they wanted. You could find yourself coming in at six o'clock in the morning and working till midnight and being back at six the next morning. You'd have breakfast at 6.30 and nothing till lunch at 3.00 pm. People were about ready to fall over. You'd work all day Saturday and into the night so that you wouldn't have to work on company time on Sunday. You got to sleep during the day on your own time! I think Warners specialized in that sort of toughness. They had something hot going for them in the musicals and the gangster films. They also had a whole bunch of us that were hot. They were going to wring it dry, and they did! At Metro, for instance, they took much better care of their people and they were guarded press-wise, and it's been told a million times – they actually made stars out of some people who otherwise would never have gotten there. Velvet glove treatment. I suppose I was a fool not to have fought then. Because I was under contract they only gave me the scraps – or the parts they couldn't get Carole Lombard for. But you see I don't think I was mistreated. I couldn't have worked for all that time feeling mistreated. I think only once did I run away and not start a picture on time. That was one year in the 30s when I did eight pictures and I was so exhausted that I got in my car and I drove home and had a bath and got into bed and stayed there for about four days. I mean, I was starting to stutter and my eyes were blinking! I couldn't even look at anyone steadily – that's how tired I was. After four days I went back to the set and of course they docked me for it – took part of my salary away.

You never could figure out why they cast people how they did. After a time I couldn't tell one part from another. Seeing them now, the story often surprises me because I have no recollection of it! But the pace was so fast and furious. You can't really bear down on the import of a story and live your own life too. I just *did* it. The only other vacation I had was in the middle of a picture called *Back In Circulation* (1937) with Pat O'Brien. My appendix blew up and they took me to hospital. Well, the shooting was nearly over and they wanted me to finish some shots but the doctor said I couldn't leave the hospital. They made a deal with the doctor to take me by stretcher to my house up on Lookout Mountain, and they had the set designer come and make what looked like the scene we were in when my appendix burst. There was a crew of sixty up there – sound and cameras and everything – and they changed the end of the story so I could be sick in bed! They didn't waste any time at all with me!

I've always been a very quick studier – read it once and I know it. You know, Cagney and I wrote a lot of our own funny lines. Lots of times you trip over a so-called comedy line and I know it's got to be right to the bone. Everything we did was in demand. The screen just ate up everything we did. We had marvellous people working, like Aline MacMahon, Allen Jenkins and Glenda Farrell. All those people were just great. In a way, Warners was the first home I'd had after my family. We were all like brothers and sisters. There was a camaraderie and professionalism that you just don't meet with today. Now it seems everyone is out on their own and preparing for this greatness they believe will happen.

It was just everybody's shoulder against the same stone. That, to me, is completely lost and over. I think acting and movies is as hard as any line of work because for one thing you've always got, on top of the hours and the strain, butterflies in your stomach. No matter how long you've been in the business. That isn't what the average man has to suffer with every day of his life. No matter how cool we looked we had that nervous strain all the time, even though the surroundings were pleasant and you felt you belonged. Your gut shrunk up when it was time to go. We were all like that. I know, for instance, that Jimmy Cagney who made such a hit the first show we did together, had to have a bucket in the wings so he could throw up every night before he went on stage. He was so nervous it was unbelievable and yet look at how cool he seems.

JK: Berkeley had a reputation for being a real tyrant – did you find him so?

Joan: Well, he was a wild man – he had to be. He had to do insane shots. Three storey-high stages were built for him, you know. You could hardly see him up there. He'd begin on an "S" with two little birds and then pull back and go round that set with 500 girls and 200 pianos, etc., and then come right back up again and sit down on those birds. But he was fabulous. He was strict, but he had to be because he had a mass of things to organize. He rehearsed crazily, like a general with an army. But I always liked him very much and found him fun. I remember in some picture I was very pregnant with my second baby. I was squashed to bits in this little tutu and had to sing, 'Try to See It My Way, Baby' (*Dames*, 1934). They had sound trouble, and something fell down, and I had to do this thing over and over again. It was driving me crazy. Then I slipped and

Joan Blondell and Dick Powell open the 'All's Fair in Love and War' number in *Gold Diggers of 1937*.

fell, and I was really frightened because I was expecting a baby, y'know. That stays in my mind because I thought it would never be done. It was one of those silly numbers in a musical y'know, where I'm supposed to play a dizzy girl.

I remember one of the big numbers involving rocking chairs – 'All's Fair in Love and War', it was. Buzz was already way in the ceiling getting ready for the shot. This was gonna be it, after endless rehearsals. One of the girls in the front line got desperately sick and dizzy, so they had to yank her out quick and not let Buzz know up top. They grabbed my stand-in, who can't dance a step. She hadn't even looked at the number. Buzz starts and makes this long tour with the camera and finally gets down to her. He nearly screamed blue bloody murder and almost jumped off the high stage and killed himself. He stopped this massive ninety-piece orchestra and all the whole thing and screamed, 'That stupid fool down there, she's out of step!' I think he was gonna come down and kill her because he thought she'd been rehearsing all along. They had to pull him off her and explain that she was put in at the last minute. Then, of course, he was furious because the assistant didn't tell him. Then too, there were a lot of scraped hips and knees, and people falling. None of it was easy but it came out right.

I don't have any regrets about my career. I was very lucky. I had acclaim. When I got married to Dick [Powell], I looked out of the fifth floor window at Paramount Theatre and all of Times Square was blocked with people looking up at me! That kinda thing made me feel, 'Wow, is that possible?' But I couldn't really take myself seriously or see the glory of being a star. I just felt, 'Wow, this is lucky!' But, my home has always been foremost in my life, be it husband, children, or whatever. They made jokes about it at Warner Brothers because the moment they said 'Cut!', I was out of the studio and into that car and zip, through the gate! Half the time I'd forget to put on my shoes! You see, to be a top dramatic star you've got to fight for it and devote your life to it 24 hours a day, thinking yourself a star, operating as a star. But making those pictures was a big teamwork thing to me. It's not a single soul who was the star – it's the team, production crew, the lot. A couple of times I almost got killed; things dropping from the flies and so forth. Some stars might have

had the person responsible fired, but what the hell, they didn't mean it. I kept my mouth shut. It was all in a day's work. Berkeley had a great sense of humour too, but he worked us to the bone. It was even worse for his girls. I don't think they had any time off. We did have a team spirit then, like a large family, which is lost now. I'm glad I was part of the 30s, the Depression years. People needed to laugh, to be released from despair. They needed to forget fear even for a few hours; they needed to sway, to hum, to gaze at the sort of things Berkeley did. I contributed. *Isn't that terrific!*

LeRoy Prinz, who had the longest career of any Hollywood dance director, with credits ranging from Cecil B. De Mille's *Madame Satan*, through *High, Wide and Handsome, Murder at the Vanities, Bolero, Yankee Doodle Dandy, This is the Army . . .* told of his method for hiring girls: 'I made my final judgement of a girl when the interview was finished, and she turns her back to me, and walks away. Her carriage in retreat tells me more about her style than anything she previously had done. Get the picture, fellas?'

Lois Lindsay, Melba Marshall and Madison Lacy

Lois: I think one of the most fascinating numbers I remember working on was not a dance number, but in *Hollywood Hotel* – with Louella Parsons and Rosemary Lane – and he did a shot which was the equivalent of a zoom lens today. Only there were no zoom lenses then. We were in a tremendous café and Louella Parsons was sitting way, way over there in the far corner. And we were all sitting at tables between her and the camera. Like we were dining and drinking, in evening clothes. And the camera came in on a dolly and went all the way over to her for a close-up and they talked, and then it came back out. And as it went in we all got up and moved our chairs and tables and everything for the camera to go through and as it came back out we put all of our chairs and tables back, and sat down and went dah-dah-dah just as if we had been carrying on all the time. But it was exactly the effect of a zoom lens today, only it was done the hard way.

Madison: In that connection, Louella had on her rubber pants under the table.

Lois: I'm not concerned about whether –

Madison: See, she had kidney trouble –

Lois: She sure did.

JK: Wasn't there a lot of competition to be a close-up girl, and didn't you get more money for that?

Melba: We didn't care. We never thought of it that way. And to this day I don't think of it that way.

Madison: You might say they were divided into

three classifications. There were the girls of very polite morals, putting it politely. What we'd call the professionals. Then there was the ambitious group, who had a combination of both to help them get ahead. Then there was the quiet group, that were fine and very sweet and lovely girls. Now each group more or less settled into its own clique. In other words there were the real gold diggers who only worked to be around the big shots; then there were the real semi-prostitues, who wanted to get ahead in films; and then there were the knitters, we called them. And during all the Berkeley era there were these three groups of girls. And they settled into their groups, and would compare their various affairs; and one would compare her possibilities regarding financial gain with another. And the others were just a bunch of nice girls who would knit.

Madison: We married the knitters.

Melba: You're darned right, and it's true.

JK: But there must have been a group who were used for those weekend specials for the business meetings in San Francisco.

Melba: Oh sure. PS, they weren't the close-up girls.

Madison: The close-up girls were the sweetest bunch, they were also the youngest. It probably went as high as 20 to 25 girls. And they'd sit in the corner in bunches and knit. Well, I'll have to amend that to some extent. At Warner Bros it was exactly as you say. But at Metro almost all the showgirls were mistresses – about to be or had been – of some producer or director. There was a group of about 20 or 25 that were kept there purely for that purpose. And at Warner's there only were about 5 or 6 in that group.

JK: Between showgirls and hoofers was there any rivalry?

Melba: No, we all mixed together except on the stage. The dancers were cliquish and the showgirls were cliquish, and the two never mixed.

JK: There was also a salary difference, wasn't there?

Lois: Yes, because some of the dancers were sore that the showgirls who we thought could do nothing, could come out for double the amount we were making. There was a definite resentment.

JK: How about Veronica Lake? She'd been an extra in *Forty Little Mothers*.

Lois: We couldn't stand her.

Melba: She was a real opportunist.

Madison: Her husband made the world's worst picture, with Barbara Stanwyck and David Niven –

JK: Oh, Erich Maria Remarque . . . *The Other Love*

Madison: A sort of 'Camille'. I shot it.

JK: Somebody killed it.

Madison: André de Toth.

JK: When you photographed a starlet, Madison, you must have had a different approach?

Madison: No, it was the same. With the exception of a few. Dietrich you were inclined to hold back, because she had a certain lighting and she knew damn well what she wanted. But the others you controlled.

JK: But then, what is the difference between the photograph of a star and a starlet?

Madison: None.

JK: Is it merely in my mind that I tend to think so

Madison: Yeah. You take Sheridan, or [Kay] Francis, or Lombard, they do what you tell them to and you have no problems.

JK: When you photographed a star, did the studio have any instructions on what they wanted?

Madison: Oh, yes. It depended entirely on what you were doing and when you were doing it. For instance, at WB you were left pretty well alone.

JK: But if they were selling Ann Sheridan as 'Oomph', you wouldn't shoot her wearing a nurse's uniform?

Madison: Well, [pointing to a photo of his] over there she's pulling a pistol out of her pocket.

JK: I often thought: 'Why would anyone want to become a show girl or a chorus girl?', since it seems you couldn't progress much beyond it once you became one.

Madison: Well, Buzz had ten or twelve girls that he called his close-up girls. You'll see Melba and Lois and Vicky and Ellie, and Ethelreda and Gwen and so on – always in the foreground. All the publicity pictures that I would take we'd invariably have the same group of eight or ten girls. They were by far the best-looking girls in the bunch. And in the big numbers they would always be in the foreground, and the worse-looking they were the farther back they'd be.

Lois: Well, we'd be under contract for the whole picture, and a picture would run three to six months. And the other girls were only brought in for the big big production numbers.

JK: How did you come out to Hollywood? Did you pay your own way, and was it a gamble?

Lois: I came with my family. My mother wanted to move out here. And we moved out here as a family.

JK: So if they hadn't you might never have come to Hollywood. They didn't come because of you?

Lois: No, although my mother was a Hollywood mother. She thought this would be the greatest thing in the world if I could work in the movies.

Melba: But I wanted to come and just took the chance.

Lois: And a lot of the girls just simply lived here – like Sheila Ray. Ethelreda came from New York.

Melba: She came originally from Chicago.

JK: Did the Depression affect you out here, too?

Madison: Yes, but later. It took two years to get here. The first part of the Depression started in New York in '29 and hit here about '32.

JK: There must have been tons of girls looking for a break out here . . .

Melba: Sure, it was a melting pot.

JK: If you were pretty, it was a better chance than almost anywhere else?

Lois: Sure. Right. To have a job paying $50 a week during the Depression was pretty good money.

JK: What film did you begin with?

Lois: I began with *Footlight Parade*. That was made in '33. I was hired as a dancer even though Buzz didn't ask me to dance. So I went to work every day and I wore my tap shoes. But we never tapped! We swam! And I still wore my tap shoes in the water! And I can remember going to my first costume fitting – these water number costumes were leotards. Made out of soufflé. And they fitted us without the diamonds and the covered parts. And I can remember running out to my mother in tears, saying: 'I don't want to work in the picture business!' I thought this leotard with nothing underneath it was my costume! But at the same time, do you realize how modest we were? And do you realize we never had any navels? The whole group of Berkeley girls never had navels! They covered them up with a little patch. The feathers would fall off, but our navel patches remained on. And I can remember when that number started to shoot, Buzz had the Wardrobe Dept. drag out a whole bunch of smocks, and all the girls had smocks on when they weren't in front of camera. And he had the doors closed. He wanted it to be just so for the girls. Because those were pretty racy costumes. They were nothing more than bikinis are today. Even in that 'Lullaby of Broadway' number they covered our navels.

JK: And no one objected because you didn't want to lose a job?

Lois: But there was a very relaxed atmosphere with Buzz –

Melba: And he had one of the best senses of humour I've ever known. He would break the tension immediately.

JK: How about when you were waterlogged?

Lois: Well, he would say halfway – dirty little things like: 'O.K. girls, now come on, spread your pretty little legs,' and it would get a giggle out of everybody. Now, on the piano number we had nothing to do. We sat at those pianos for days and days and days. But he would have us there for maybe two months on salary. And if the front office would call and say: 'What are you doing with all these people?' he'd say: 'O.K. girls. Jack Warner is coming down, and when he gets here I want you all to get up and do *tours jetés*.' So we'd all get up and do *tours jetés* like crazy. And the front office would come down and he'd say: This is what I've been working on.' And they'd say: 'Well, it's pretty bad.' But he'd be working it all out in his head. And many times we'd play poker, tell jokes all day long during rehearsals. Then when it came to shooting, we'd really work the long hours. He'd say: 'Stand here or stand there.' So we'd stand and wait for him to get his idea. I remember on 'The Lady in Red', the thing

with Dolores Del Rio, Buzz decided to rib the front office. He said: 'I'd really like to get some white horses for this number but I don't think the front office would let me have them.' So he told them he was doing a barnyard number and he wanted all the animals you'd find in a farmyard, cows, chickens, pigs, the lot. And they said: 'Oh no, that's impossible.' So he said: 'Well, in that case I'll settle for six horses.' And so he got what he wanted. And one day these horses, very high-strung horses, stampeded all over the lot, right out of the studio, and everybody was after them trying to catch them! That was a sight! That was when he was doing *In Caliente*.

JK: I'm curious. When you've been waving those flags in the 'Love and War' number for days on end, what goes through your mind?

Lois: I don't have the remotest idea. I was scared of heights, because he had us on those pedestals. Sheila Ray and I were his guinea pigs on those things. We cried when we were up on those, and Buzz personally came to take us down. We were strapped up there, there was a board up our back.

Madison: I could tell you a couple of stories about the executives when they were shooting these semi-nude numbers, but you couldn't use it in a broadcast.

Lois: Oh Mady, he doesn't want to hear that.

JK: Oh yes I do.

Madison: It was while they were doing the 'Shadow Waltz' number, and some of the girls were up high. The executives got wind of it and they'd come down on the set because the girls had very little on, and from down below you could look right up them. And some of the girls had had a drink, and these three up on top, they proceeded to urinate so that it hit just where the executives stood. That sent them scurrying off – of course nothing happened to them 'cause they knew them from the weekend trips. Everything with Buzz was standing and waiting for hours while the camera did the work.

Buzz invented this platform that the camera was mounted on and which was driven electrically, so it could go up and down and all around the stage. And then, on stage 7 they raised the roof for *Cain and Mabel*. Hearst paid for that. Where the girls were angels and went up into the sky.

Lois: I was in *Cain and Mabel*, but I wasn't an angel. Thank God! I was down on the floor. I remember one of the toughest numbers was when we had 200 girls for the 'Waterfall' number. Why there were so many times when many girls couldn't go into the water. And this got to be a thing. Some of them played that to the hilt, so the number would go overtime and we'd have to work extra days. It got to the point where they would have a roll-call every day, and the Assistant Director would keep track of the dating system so he would know if some girls hadn't gone in 28 days before. And there was one girl, we finally all ganged up on her because she'd managed to keep out of the water so much. We threw her in!

JK: It's very interesting how individual you all look in person when you seemed to have a sameness about you then. The same wig, the same make-up. Unlike stars, you weren't supposed to be individuals. But how many of you were content to be chorus girls and how many dreamt of becoming

stars or marrying a star?
Lois: I don't think we did really.
Melba: I think most of them did marry pretty well.
Madison: Vicki isn't exactly broke.
Lois: Actually, if we had been orientated towards it as people are today, I think we could have done very well. But nobody ever told us to study and learn acting. And we thought it was kind of corny to even try.

Madison: And every time you had to act, you'd burst into tears!
Lois: Because I didn't think I was up to it. But some were ambitious. Like Carole Landis. She fulfilled her ambition. And Mary Dees. She was a really beautiful girl, she was Harlow's double. As a matter of fact, she took over from Harlow when she died. I don't know what became of her after that. But many of us were just there because it was a job.

Madison: The Goldwyn girls went farther than the Berkeley girls because Sam Goldwyn pushed them into leading parts. And some of them married well, like Dotty Coonan, and Paulette Goddard and Lucille Ball, and the girl in the *Great Ziegfeld* number – Virginia Bruce – she started out with Buzz. Lynn Bari was another one who came out of the chorus.

Lois: Yes, definitely. But as far as most of us were concerned, we thought this was a world apart.

JK: Do you remember anything that was funny while it happened?

Madison: I remember on *Gold Diggers of Paris*, when we hadn't done a thing for three months, and Jack Warner said he wanted to come and see how we were getting on, and within half an hour Buzz had whipped up a number. And Jack was very pleased with the number! And when they finally came to film it, it was nothing like it!

Lois: I was seventeen when I started working. And some girls were sixteen. Now, today, if you were that age they'd have to have teachers on the set. But they didn't check up on us then.

JK: But you couldn't have led the sort of normal life of small town girls?

Lois: Why not? Sure we did. We used to go to a place on Vine Street where Louis Prima played – The Open Door. And Martha Raye would come in as a friend – she wasn't working there – and they'd have a jam session. We'd hang out there quite often after work. Because this was fun. We went as a group. We'd go to places where there was music and dancing.

JK: What kind of other places? The Mocambo?

Lois: Oh no, that was much too expensive for us. We'd go Dutch treat. We would go to little joints where there would be a combo, where there was someone we wanted to hear.

JK: $50. Was that much?

Lois: Oh, yes. I supported my family on that. I was the only one working. My stepfather was on WPA and so was my brother, and I was the only one bringing home a salary. And we were fortunate. Those that didn't have a family usually shared.

Melba: Well, I lived with two other girls for instance. A little house that we rented out here in the valley. A nice little home and the three of us split everything. We each had our own bedroom, and a gardener, and enough money was left over for a maid!

JK: Has your life gone the way you thought it would then?

Lois: That's a very good question. I don't think I had a plan and so I'm very happy. Not smug or self-satisfied, but it's been a very happy life.

JK: Looking back, as we have, what do you remember fondest?

Melba: We were very close in those days. I don't know any in that group that I wouldn't be happy to hear from. And I would feel almost like a sister to them.

Lois: I would, too.

Melba: It was a wonderful experience. I wish my children had had it.

In his unquenchable quest for 'kulture' Samuel Goldwyn, who had brought out Berkeley, hired the

Vera Zorina and William Dollar in *The Goldwyn Follies*. The choreographer was her husband, George Balanchine.

Below: Choreography by Leonidoff for Schubert's 'Serenade'. The film, *When You're in Love*, starred Grace Moore.

Norma Shearer in MGM's lavish production of *Romeo and Juliet*. Agnes de Mille was engaged as choreographer for the dances.

Jeanette MacDonald, in the bizarre modernistic finale of *Broadway Serenade*, to music adapted from Tchaikovsky, Berkeley's first commission from MGM.

Star and director. Ann Miller dances among the instruments in *Small Town Girl*. The musicians, and Busby Berkeley, are under the stage.

Russian-born George Balanchine and his wife, the glamorous Norwegian (born in Berlin) prima ballerina, Vera Zorina, to create a somewhat premature blend of pop-art for his lavish and technicolorful *The Goldwyn Follies* (1938). After that they went on to Warner Bros to recreate their famous Rodgers and Hart 'Slaughter on 10th Avenue' ballet for the film version of the stage success, *On Your Toes* (1939). Another classically trained ballet master briefly in Hollywood was the Radio City Music Hall's Leon Leonidoff for Grace Moore's *When You're In Love* (Columbia, 1937); while the distaff side, besides the ubiquitous Viennese-born Albertina Rasch (she was married to composer Dimitri Tiomkin), included Bronislava Nijinska (*A Midsummer Night's Dream* (Warner Bros, 1935) and the American-born, European-trained Agnes De Mille (*Romeo and Juliet* (MGM, 1936)). Born into one of the most celebrated of the film pioneer families, De Mille's strikingly original contribution to choreography was to come not from her work on films, but from the theatre. Her best-known work for films are merely re-stagings of some of her celebrated Broadway ballets for *Oklahoma* (1955) and *Carousel* (1956).

However opulent their speciality numbers were, these classically based artists did not beat Berkeley at his own game, and the public only flocked to his entertaining geometric and low-brow flesh displays. It must have seemed as if Berkeley's power to astonish was endless, but by 1939, Warners, in the throes of yet another economic drive, insisted he cut back on the expensive production numbers that had set his films apart, and so he left. Perhaps it was time. For the public had shown signs of turning against what John Betjeman once described as '. . . décors, which, while displaying great ingenuity, resembled more often than not a sort of drunkard's dream'. Without breaking in his stride Berkeley moved over to MGM to stage a spectacular finale for a Jeanette MacDonald solo to Tchaikovsky's 'None But The Lonely Heart', the dancers all in Benda Masks, and Jeanette high above them singing her heart out in the otherwise unmemorable *Broadway Serenade* (1939). This got him a contract with MGM, where he worked on and off for the next two decades, starting with the first of the very successful early Garland and Rooney 'putting on the show in the backyard barn' musicals, i.e.: *Babes in Arms* (1939), *Babes on Broadway* (1941), etc. While these films made enormous public favourites of the young stars, the numbers in them were generally modest by his standards. Besides working on the spectacular 'Fascinatin' Rhythm' with Eleanor Powell (whom he considered the greatest dancer he'd ever worked with) for *Lady Be Good* (1941), the numbers for two of the splashiest Esther Williams musicals, *Million Dollar Mermaid* (1952) and *Easy To Love* (1953), as well as creating an all-stops-out tap routine for Ann Miller in *Small Town Girl* (1953), and even re-uniting him with his former chorine, Betty Grable, here starring in the last of her big musicals with Dan Dailey, *Call Me Mister* (1951), his contributions, though never dull, and still fun, had lost their freshness. They had colour, but the old razzle dazzle was gone; the art deco palaces had been covered with black felt. Only once, in the 40s, and using colour to achieve hallucinatory effects as surprising as his former work in black and white, did Berkeley pull another trump out of his deck. That came on loan-out to Zanuck's 20th Century-Fox, where the studio chief whose faith in him years earlier had started it all, now gave him another opportunity to pull the stops out, and go over the kaleidoscope rainbow with the numbers he concocted for Carmen Miranda (a Berkeleyesque fantasy in her own right) in *The Gang's All Here* (1943). He did his stuff with acres of brown-skinned girls, gigantic bananas, melon-sized strawberries and the inevitable, inimitable, always wonderful Harry Warren numbers. Though his soaring camera almost brained the volatile Carmen Miranda during the strenuous rehearsals for 'The Lady with the Tutti-Fruiti Hat' and knocked her headgear off, relationships remained cordial and the results are deliriously unforgettable.

But, back at MGM the stars were all-important, and vehicles were built around them, not to drive over them. Louis B. Mayer was not about to allow Berkeley to submerge his valuable stars the way he had Ruby Keeler and Dick Powell. Besides, the war was on and such extravagance might have seemed in dubious taste.

When Berkeley stopped making them, nobody else came along who could or wanted to fill his shoes. The times, after all, were different, and whatever Berkeley did, its success, was unique to the man. Not every dance director for that matter was also a Patton. His numbers, like the one for 'Lullaby of Broadway', are deft and potentially chilling illustrations of the underlying tension in his best work – the perverse Jekyll and Hyde appeal they had.

There have been the inevitable attempts in the guise of a homage as when, in 1972, at the height of the first big Berkeley revival in art houses and at film festivals around the world, the British 'enfant' and pretty 'terrible' film-via-TV director, Ken Russell, took it into his head to take a sweet little stage musical, *The Boy Friend*, that had been a pastiche of 20s flappers, and turn it into his 'tribute' to 30s innocence. A waif-like, long-limbed model, Twiggy, made her debut as a Ruby Keeler naïve; as her Dick Powell surrogate, another newcomer, even longer of limb and fleeter of foot, a Texan boy named Tommy Tune (who would go on to become one of the Broadway musical's most startlingly gifted triple threat talents).* But a Ken Russell 'tribute' as he showed with his treatment of *Mahler* and poor Tchaikovsky in *The Music Lovers*, (so why not also with Berkeley?) are things to be avoided at all cost. In a sense he is not so unlike

* Twelve years later, Twiggy and Tommy Tune were reunited in a hit Broadway musical set in the 30s, built around a collection of Gershwin songs, entitled *My One and Only*.

Berkeley in that what they express emanates from adolescent fantasizing. But while Buzz's camera is content to roll happily between the pines of Rome, Russell shoots up the Appian Way and into the Vulva, leaving us there to fend for ourselves. Berkeley's work, on the other hand, stays in the mind, reappears of its own accord, and to unfailing wonder and delight.

The Dancer

Like Fred Astaire, so too Eleanor Powell. The arrival of 'The Queen of Tap' in Hollywood was the direct result of the musical revival sparked off by the success of Berkeley's work. Eleanor Powell was

Top: Busby Berkeley with his star, Eleanor Powell, on the set for 'Fascinating Rhythm' in *Lady be Good*.

Above: Eleanor Powell in *Rosalie*, the Ziegfeld musical filmed by MGM in 1937. Cole Porter wrote new songs for the film version.

Bottom right: Ken Russell did his Berkeley homage in *The Boy Friend*, in 1972.

Right: Carmen Miranda as 'The Lady in the Tutti-Frutti Hat'. One of Berkeley's numbers for *The Gang's All Here*.

Far right: Two scenes from *Stand Up and Cheer*, the film that made the movie public sit up – a glad rag-doll of a child named Shirley Temple who sang 'Baby Take a Bow'. Pat Paterson and James Dunn, and the chorus in the 'Broadway's Gone Hillbilly' number.

Below: Ethel Merman's 'High and Low' number in *Strike me Pink*. Choreography by Robert Alton; his first film after leaving Broadway.

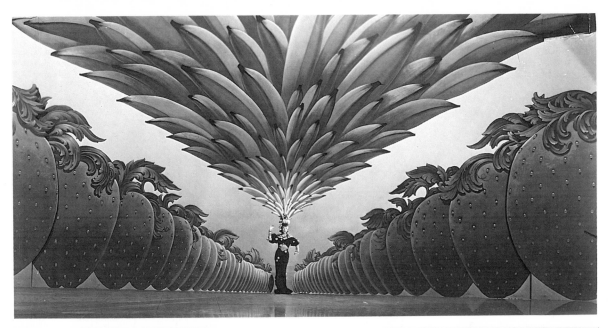

Left: Eleanor Powell during her Broadway career. A 1930 photograph, with the famous legs very much in evidence. Centre: In 1965, for her Las Vegas act, they were as shapely as ever. Right: During her Hollywood career, as one of MGM's top stars.

extraordinary; she was an artist, one of the few — possibly the only one – whose talent was such as to lift her above the spectacular sets and productions surrounding her.

Eleaner Powell was a dancer, but there was something electric about this woman, much as there was about Fred Astaire, which set her apart from the rest. Her film début owed much to the success of Berkeley and Astaire, and she worked with each one – once. Through her, MGM hoped to combine the two strands – showmanship and virtuoso dancing – into one astonishing spectacle.

After a hilarious false start in *George White's Scandals* of 1935, she recovered and tapped her way to legendary fame in a succession of carefully tailored revues; a little story, a little girl, a little romance, a little spot of bother and monumental terpsichorean fireworks designed to take one's breath away. Unlike similar Warner numbers to which singers and dancers were of minor importance (Ruby rarely danced more than a few steps), everything at Metro was designed as a setting for the star's particular talent. With a virtuoso like Eleanor Powell this system excelled itself. Not everybody enjoyed the results. Roger Edens, who worked with her on several films, found the production values surrounding her like '. . . that really monstrous epitome of nonsense, that big half-million dollar battleship with several thousand dancers and singing sailors with sequined cannons, and Eleanor Powell dancing on the decks', created for *Born To Dance* (1936) to Cole Porter's jazzy 'Swingin' the Jinx Away', 'an embarrassment of bad taste that would haunt [him] for years to come'. But not everybody shared his feelings.

When I met her she filled in the details of her work and her philosophy at a pace that left me only slightly less breathless than when we danced: 'I would rather dance than eat! Dancing to me is some sort of a God, like a Buddha. It encompasses you. Like jealousy. Very possessive, I really didn't know what the outside world was all about when I was making pictures. I couldn't have told you about the newspapers, what the current events were, anything.'

She was twelve when she went professional, doing the little acrobatic number she had learned for her dance school recital. At 17 she was a Broadway star in *Follow Through* because of a sensational tap routine, which turned out to be the standard routine taught by Jack Donohue (Marilyn Miller's partner). He taught her by tying her down with sandbags to keep her still. 'That's why I dance so close to the ground. Like a man, really. Fred's more aerial than I am.' From then on her career leapt forward. By the time of her film début she had had several more shows to her credit and had performed with every renowned big band of the day.

'Once I was identified as a tap dancer, that was it! Because nobody had ever seen that kind of thing before. When I hit it, the off-beat was just coming in. This was the big new thing and I used to practise all the time between shows to those records: Fats Waller, boogie woogie . . . oh honey! Because it's a black sound – a tap dancer is nothing but a frustrated drummer! You're a percussion instrument with your feet! You're a musician!'

She was in one of *George White's Scandals* on Broadway when White, out on the coast to make a film based on his formula, called her to come out for it. Her worst fears about Hollywood – all play and no work – were confirmed by this experience: 'I came out to do this picture and found that the rest of the cast – not Alice Faye, but the others, Ned Sparks, James Dunn – were all drinking away. Nobody worked before noon. I didn't know that this wasn't the ordinary way movies were being made because it's what I'd been told to expect.

'I was the heavy in the film – the one that takes Dunn away from Faye. I'm sitting around and days go by and nobody pays any attention to me. One of the actors was so stoned one day that he ate the artificial food that was set out on a table for a nightclub scene we had to play. . . . Then came the day George said to me, "Ellie, go and get made up. You're going to do your number." So I said, "Where do I go for make-up?" "Down the street past the cafeteria and you'll see it." Now I am shy, and I'd never been there and so when I pass a room saying 'Make-up' with three barber chairs and a line of people in front of each one and guys slapping this stuff on their faces, I joined the queue. They sit me down and this man says, "What are you wearing?" So I describe this costume and he starts slapping this stuff all over me. Well, these are the make-up men who make up the extras and they were making up Egyptians for a film and when he's finished all you can see is the whites of my eyes. I'm three shades darker than Pearl Bailey! Back on the set everybody is so stoned nobody notices anything.

'I'm back on Broadway, swearing "No more Hollywood" and Mr Mayer is sitting in the projection room at MGM looking at every banjo and harmonica player because they want to make musicals at MGM and they're looking for musical stars, and he sees my number and he says, "I love that girl but I can't use her as a star. She's coloured." Luckily one of the writers who knew me from Broadway was there and he told Mayer, "She's not coloured. That's Eleanor Powell." So Mayer said, "All right, we'll use her for one number."'

That 'number' was built into the star part in *Broadway Melody of 1936*: MGM had a new box-office favourite and an enormously successful cycle of films to go with her. Two more *Broadway Melodies* followed, and *Rosalie*, *Born To Dance*, *Honolulu*, *Lady Be Good* – all with dazzling exhibitions of her skill. Because she was expected to top herself with each film, and because these numbers took a long time to think up and prepare there weren't as many Eleanor Powell films as one might have wished, but those she made have ensured her reputation. For one of her numbers in *Broadway Melody of 1936* she did a point number with the Albertina Rasch Ballet.

'You're not supposed to be on your toes for more than three hours without a rest. Unfortunately, we had to keep on because of the set and everything. The blood came through our pink ballet slippers. And when we took our slippers off that night, they had big buckets of ice standing by. I lost four toe nails on the right foot on that picture. They grew a little, then I lost them again. Talk about stunts! When I went down in that gun-chute thing (*Born To Dance*) I didn't do it with the glove on and I got a burn all the way down my arm as I'm coming down. It took the skin right off.'

'Once I got into the studio I realized I had to learn about the camera if I was going to choreograph my own numbers. You almost design your own sets as well. You would get with the art director and you say, "I'd like a fountain and a staircase." He'd sketch something vaguely to fit with my idea because I was going to use that for an effect. First you would create the number. Then it has to be passed by the producer and the director and so forth – and that's frustrating because they are not looking at the number to see whether it's good or bad, whether they like it or not. If you go to a nightclub, and you see an act, you don't think about how many minutes it takes. But in Hollywood they say, "Okay, Ellie, start!" And they look a little while at you, then down at their stopwatch, and they've missed it, you know, and they say, "Honey, it's fine but it's just two minutes too long." Wow! You create a number so everything blends and gels and melds in and somebody comes along and tells you to take two minutes out! You can't just cut in the middle of the thing.

'I never had a choreographer, except for the background. I did all my own numbers. For my nightclub act, I had a choreographer who would just do the four boys – he'd bring them in for an entrance, and maybe he'd work out how to get them off. On *Born To Dance*, Dave Gould did all the numbers I wasn't in.

'I would try to think up something that is still tapping but with something else. After all, you can't just come out and tap. With *Born To Dance*, they had me up so high I was way up to the top of the roof of the tallest stage we had at MGM, and they had a big boom camera following me. And, y'know, the excitement of dum-da-da-da-dum coming down the stairs – da-da-da-dum: I had to learn from a fireman that if the pole's too long when you come down you twirl like firemen do when they come down. But I couldn't go round, I had to be lined up with the camera. And I also had to do it with one leg and one arm held out. Well, this is hard to do: after a while your gravity makes you go round. But they didn't

Vilma and Buddy Ebsen watch Eleanor Powell do her stuff on the rooftops of New York. A still from *The Broadway Melody of 1936*.

Eleanor Powell. Top, left to right: The finale of *Born to Dance*, 'Swingin' the Jinx Away'. 'I've Got a Feeling you're Fooling' in *The Broadway Melody of 1936* – Arthur Freed and Nacio Herb Brown wrote the songs. In *Lady be Good*, with a dog, obviously, of remarkable wit. Centre, left to right: The star in blackface in *Honolulu*. Performing a risky number in *Ship Ahoy*. Her matador number in the same film. Bottom, left to right: A skipping-rope number in *Honolulu*. The roping number in *I Dood It*, with Sam Garrett. Rehearsing with Bobby Connolly on the set of *Ship Ahoy*.

want me to go round. I didn't want to go round! I wanted to do it the hard way – one arm, one leg. These were the exciting things.

'Now the audience know I dance – that's set in their mind. But how to vary what I do. On the floor, on the ceiling, etc. So I have to utilize an art — whether it be juggling or roping – so that it's still tapping but it's done with a gimmick. When I did the matador number in *I Dood It*, the studio hired me a real matador. He studied with me in the rehearsal four hours a day prior to getting into rehearsal – the proper feet movements, all the expressions you need as a matador. I got books and read up on it. Usually my teachers got so involved with me that they forgot that I was going to put a number to it. When I did the roping number with Sam Garrett in *Ship Ahoy*, he said, "You gotta go into the rodeos! You're fabulous! Terrific! Forget all this and go into rodeos!" It was for the lasso thing: if you don't think that was rough! Those iron hondas on those ropes are thick, like a big pulley. And when you get the rope going up big, it's going about 55 mph. And to jump through that rope, through that big thing over and back, well . . . The inclination as this thing comes towards you is to duck. And then the honda would hit me on the head and knock me out – cold. So I had to practise in football shoulders and helmet. And I had to learn gradually. For the one trick, jumping through the big loop – there's got to be momentum but you've got to keep your arm straight, you can't bring your arm down. I developed such muscle – like fighters or golfers who pick up a softball and use it to make muscles. Now I got to put the difficult tap steps to it, and still keep this going. I perfected it. I could lasso with one finger and pull it back. There wasn't a thing I couldn't lasso. But Adrian, who was doing the clothes, had to take the right seam out of everything I wore and make a large sleeve because I had an arm that was mammoth!

'Or take the little dog number in *Lady Be Good*. I auditioned dogs. I had dogs of every size and shape till I finally found the right one which belonged to our prop man's little girl, and which had the right personality and those human eyes! I started working and training that dog. He's smart but he doesn't know anything. First I took him home with me and he slept in my bedroom and I fed him. After a time I put a rope around his neck and started in making the figure eight, saying, "Buttons, c'mon, Buttons," clicking my fingers, and I'd drag him a little bit and then give him some yummy. This went on until I could take the little leash off and he went with just a snap of the fingers; then next with no command. But he had to get used to my taps going and that threw his little ears at first. If you don't think that was a job! This dog was just an old house-dog; he'd fetch the papers but that was it. In this number he had to go over the sofa and then land on my chest and in the end knock me back on the thing. I taught him to stand on his legs, to walk behind me, to sway his little hips with the hula. Three months to create the things, whatever it was – roping, matador, dog – during my holidays. The studio gave me all the help I needed.

'I had to train with real cadets for *Rosalie*: they had about thirty-four West Point cadets. They embellished the rest with the chorus boys. The head man from West Point came down and taught me that drill. The drum number was my own. We went on the back lot at night to shoot that and it was slippery because the dew had settled on the drumheads. I took one step and slid from here to there! Ray Bolger and Nelson Eddy, as a gag, had an ambulance out there and Red Cross coats and bandages, so I'm thinking all the time that if I fall they'll be there to pick me up. We had to stop production and put corking on top of each drum because we'd forgotten all about the dampness. Well, on one take I got about a third of the way to

the end and a drum bounced me six feet in the air because they had put a thicker layer in. We had to go back and shoot that again.

'It was very dangerous; they were big drums. They couldn't use a double for me. I had to learn how to do a line of turns down those drums – turn and dip a little but not not break the flow of the turn. Oh, that was hard! The top drum was about 75 feet high and they had to hoist me up there. I could have done that number better but I was just holding back a little bit because I was afraid of the dew. That number was about two weeks in rehearsals. It took us four nights to film that, starting at eight o'clock until about two in the morning. We were two days in the sound room doing the music – eighteen hours each day. We had to take every one of those drums into the sound room when I recorded the music because how can you time the leap from drum to drum? There's no possible way I could get the tempo of the thing otherwise. In other words, the conductor used to have to follow *me*. And that wasn't the end of it because I'd have to go back and put the taps in at the end of the whole picture. Taps are *never* done on the set; they never pick up the taps as you're being photographed. I think that was the most difficult as far as the possibility of an accident happening. But you remember the number in *Ship Ahoy* when I went off the top of the diving board and landed in the middle of a swimming pool. There was a great big muscleman. I dive into his arms. I have to keep my body stiff, and he throws me like a bullet. I go from the water and there's a fella who catches me on the pool side. And I'm to be thrown some distance backwards. Of course, I've done adagio and acrobatic stuff before, so it's a regular thing.

'We go along in rehearsal and everything's fine. The fellow does it once. We rehearse it again for camera because it was very hard to follow all that. Second rehearsal – wonderful, just perfect. I get in my outfit now and get all fixed up for the camera. Roll 'em, action! What happened was that when the fellow threw me, he hadn't got quite enough umph and I can see that I'm not going to reach the concrete. To save my hair and face for make-up, I grabbed the edge of the pool and kept my head up out of the water. Now this other poor guy knows he's got a star and he's been warned by the director and everybody to protect her. He sees I'm hanging and instead of leaving me alone, he dives in, grabs me by the waist and pulls me down to the bottom. He's panicking, see. But in so doing he pulled all the ligaments in my arm. We couldn't do any more shooting that day.'

If Ellie's films lacked anything it was a suitable partner. That problem was solved when Louis B. Mayer had her paired off with Fred Astaire. The result was a summit meeting of two of the screen's greatest dancers. 'Every dancer in motion pictures,' said Ellie, 'owes a debt of gratitude to Fred Astaire, because he brought dancing to the screen in the right way. Prior to his films with Ginger, a dancer would come on in a nightclub scene and would go into a dance and two steps later there'd be Joan Crawford's hand over the screen and a voice saying, "Come and sit down." And then the leading man sits down and looks at her and they talk more and then suddenly everybody applauds and the dancer is bowing and that was it for him. Nothing! That is what the dancer had in films. Fred changed that.'

If any name deserves to be associated with Astaire's film career outside of his partners, then that person is the choreographer, Hermes Pan. Still active to-day, Pan began in films with Fred Astaire at RKO in 1932 on *Flying Down To Rio*.

Hermes Pan: *Flying Down To Rio*, which is when I began, was one of the first times that dancing as

Hermes Pan doubling for Ginger Rogers while working with Fred Astaire on one of the dance sequences for *Roberta*.

Chorus in sunlight. Hermes Pan rehearsing the girls for *Swing Time*.

such had ever been seen on the screen, an intimate dance number set to music, which you see from start to finish. Before then there weren't many things you could call routines.

When I arrived in Hollywood it was during the Berkeley era, all of those geometrical designs, top shots and huge numbers where the curtain would go up on a small stage and you'd go into a number that seemed to take place on a stage the size of a football field. This was something that was imaginative but you actually didn't see much dancing on the screen. I think it's true to say that Astaire and Rogers were the first ones to really do a dance routine in its own right. When I started, choreographers were still called dance directors. I think the first time the word choreography was used to designate our work was when Agnes De Mille did *Oklahoma*. Of course even in *Flying Down To Rio* we still had those big production numbers – all a bit more dancing than usual.

There wasn't much competition in my field, because there weren't too many dance directors out there – Sammy Lee, Dave Gould, Bobby Connolly, LeRoy Prinz – and they were making so many musicals. These men were still of the early school, one-two-three kick, you know – it was some years before anybody else came along, and that went for dancers. It was some time after Fred that people like Eleanor Whitney, Dorothy Lee, and Jack Whiting got into films, but even with a rash of dancers it seemed that very few clicked, until people of Eleanor Powell's calibre came along. And she of course virtually choreographed her own numbers, so she didn't really need anyone.

Even if I hadn't joined up with Fred, I doubt that I would have done the sort of work Sammy Lee or the rest were into, because that had never been my bag. I love dancing as such and I always liked to see the more intimate dancing, a few people rather than a

huge number where the dancing gets lost.

When I joined RKO Dave Gould did all the choreography. He was a very quiet man, Strangely enough he wasn't a dancer. He was really what you'd call a promoter. He promoted ideas that he couldn't begin to carry out in dance terms. That was fortunate for me because I was the only one on the production side for *Flying Down To Rio* that could dance. So, while Gould concerned himself with getting the big numbers on I was left to work with Fred. Dave was like a second-unit director, getting people to carry out his orders, and then I and my assistant had to get together and make up the routines. As a matter of fact I had to write the number with the girls on the aeroplane when I got the job, and I made up another routine to show him my conception of a dance, which we used in the film and called it 'The Carioca'.

I've often wondered what I'd have done if I hadn't met Fred, because I'm sure that consciously and subconsciously I've absorbed an awful lot from him and his style. On the other hand, I'm sure that he has gotten certain things from me. For instance, when we worked in *Silk Stockings*, I got him to do some slides on his hip which he would never have done otherwise, and to catch Cyd in a fall from a box. He's never been the physical type – he's not very strong you know, and so he wouldn't have thought up things like that. Of course there are always little tricks to help. Often he'd say to me, "No, I won't do that. I will not. No, I can't do that", and I'd have to sort of sneak it up on him. Like that thing in *Carefree*, for 'The Yam', in which I wanted him to throw Ginger over his leg on six different tables. You see, I grew up with the camera. Because outside of the time I danced in the chorus in New York, I hadn't done that much, and so I really started learning with the camera. (Pan was born in 1910 and won an Oscar for his work on *A Damsel In Distress*).

My first serious experience with dancing was working with Astaire. The way he moved contributed a lot to my subsequent thinking when I came to choreograph. In all of those films I did with him at RKO, we were always conscious of the camera. We'd rehearse in front of those big mirrors, and those were our cameras. If you travel across the screen you get a much better effect of movement than if you come straight down the middle because you don't see that motion. All you get is a figure getting larger. We designed things so that if you had a step that came from the back and you wanted to coming forward, instead of coming straight down we'd do it diagonally. Then you had motion and speed.

As a matter of fact, the dance directors of that era were the hard-boiled, slangy types with cigars in the corner of their mouths the whole time. They'd shout at the girls, 'Get your fannies on; get the lead out of it!' They were sort of the nasty type. Except for Fred, I don't think any of the dancers who came out after him, like Ray Bolger, who was what we'd call an eccentric dancer, or Buddy Ebsen who was another of the legs mania men – there was nobody else who did what he did. It's a strange thing, because just to dance on the screen, unless it has some meaning doesn't mean an awful lot. You have to have some relation to the story for the dance to really take off emotionally. When a person who is part of the plot suddenly goes into a beautiful dance, then you are captivated by that situation far more than by somebody, no matter how good they are, who just comes on and dances. For example, Fred and Ginger would have a fight, then, in a dance he would woo her back, and that was part of the story. The dances were usually indicated in the script. For example, in *Top Hat* they go to the park, and they will do a dance, which was 'Isn't it a Lovely Day to Be Caught in The Rain'. But then I would work with Astaire and we would figure out how to get into a number without jarring it, because people were then beginning to be horrified at the idea of somebody bursting into song or dance without a reason. So the main trick was to get into a dance before you realized they were doing it. Sort of like the business for 'Isn't It A Lovely Day' Berlin had the idea for the song, and we knew that when they went into the park it would take place there, and it would be raining. Do you suddenly start the rain, and they would suddenly be caught in it? It was horrible. Then it starts to pour, thunder, the works, and Ginger is furious with him, blaming him for getting her into this situation, but then the *thunder* makes her jump into his arms, and then she's embarrassed at having been so frightened, and he's loving it, and it thunders again, and then he starts, 'The thunder and the lightning . . . da.da.da . . .'. It was so beautifully blended, moving from the scene into the dance, that you were just transfixed.

By this time Fred and Ginger had become established as a tremendously popular team so people were dying to see them again in something. In the case of *Top Hat* the idea came about from several people – Pandro Berman, Mark Sandrich, Irving Berlin, Allen Scott, who wrote the dialogue – and they all wrote an original script with Astaire and Rogers in mind and with Irving doing the music. We already knew where some of the numbers would go in the plot before he even began writing the score, so he knew what sort of things were needed, like the rain number, and we knew that we had to have a big production number because everything then had to have at least one big production number, so that's where 'The Piccolino' was – a big finale. Astaire and I wanted to make it a dance saying, 'Do the Piccolino' rather than a song saying, 'Hear the Piccolino', but Berlin wouldn't change it. Most of the numbers were written like that, and through meetings it was decided where to work them into the script. Fred had quite a bit of influence in saying where in the story he wanted to do the numbers, and he would even cut some of the dialogue when he didn't like what he had to say – he was always adding or subtracting from the script, especially in the dialogue, whereas Ginger just came in and did a job. The chemistry between them was strictly an accident nobody could have foreseen. I think Ginger realized more than Fred that they had a professional chemistry the public responded to. He was a little tired of being known as a team. I think he'd had it with being a team after he and Adele split up. For a long time it was he who wanted to break away, but the public demanded them. It was impossible for them to split. It would have been like divorcing your wife. The public really got those things into their heads and didn't want to know any different.

Ginger was wonderful in that she came to rehearsals, and was agreeable, and she would work hard. She'd do anything you would tell tell her – until it came time for her to put on the dress. She used to wear dresses that were full of bugle beads that would whip around and smack him in the face. Remember 'Let's Face The Music And Dance'? (*Follow The Fleet*). That dress weighed forty pounds, and the sleeves were long and very loose, and one time she turned fast and the thing almost knocked Fred across the room. Basically Fred prefers being a solo artist. When Fred and Ginger separated the public accepted Ginger more easily at first than they did Fred. It used to make him furious. Even when he later danced with people like Joan Fontaine (the poor girl couldn't even walk, and naturally she was terrified to *dance*), or Paulette Goddard, and Joan Leslie, Marjorie Reynolds – and then there was Sarah Churchill (*Royal Wedding*). Fred was so delighted to be on his own that he wouldn't have cared who his partner was.

Mark Sandrich directed most of the films in the series. While he wasn't very musically orientated he certainly had a great appreciation for the musical feeling of the films; he had wonderful taste in stories and he had a wonderful style. But as a matter of fact we never showed him any of the numbers, or Berman or Berlin, or to anybody really until they were half finished because we didn't want any suggestions or interference until we had our work securely underway.

The set designer, Van Nest Polglase, would come to us and ask what we wanted for the number, and he'd design for us, rather than for the script. In fact I got that from Fred too. I've always worked very closely with the set designers. In *Kiss Me Kate*, for example, I wanted that archway specially made so that we could do things in it. So I had them put in three archways for me.

Often we'd create a number without having any real music for it – just our rehearsal pianist, Hal Borne, who was invaluable to us, who'd put some melody into the tempo we wanted the dance to be done to. One thing was the 'Waltz in Swing Time' number. We wanted to do a jazz waltz, and then we got so excited about the idea of doing a swing waltz that we told Kern about it and he wrote us a swing waltz. I think it was very difficult for him because he didn't quite understand what we really meant, and I must say that Hal really had a great deal to do with getting Kern's music into a waltz. Hal was really a tremendous influence on that particular number. Till we had the new Kern number, Hal used to transpose some of the other songs Kern had written for the score, which were really nothing in feel like a waltz. The rehearsal pianist is a most important person when you're creating a number. Because we'd usually take a song into different rhythms, or we'd paraphrase them to suit the dance, because you can't just go from verse to chorus, so you'd have to put in an interlude to help you get into that, and that's not written, and the pianist has to do that for you.

When I first started with Fred, we used to have to

dance to a piano track and then they would put in the music later, which was just horrible. Sometimes they would try to record the taps while they were shooting it. We finally overcame that. Then we had playbacks. After *Follow the Fleet* (1936) we started to put in the taps later. We would do them with earphones; we would watch the film on the screen and then, I would do Ginger's taps. We would do sections at a time, and you had to watch the screen while you were doing it, so it was a little difficult because you couldn't turn around, with those earphones on, and besides you'd lose sight of the screen. You had to keep watching closely to get the synch right.

When Ginger and Fred split up for good, after *The Story of Vernon and Irene Castle* and Fred left RKO, I felt that was the end of a chapter.

'I just put my feet in the air and move them around,' said Astaire, who dances sober the way most people think they dance when they're drunk.

In his autobiography, Astaire sets out to deflate the chi-chi surrounding the art of the dance: 'I have no desire to prove anything by it. I have never used it as an outlet or as a means of expressing myself. I just dance.' One might say, similarly, of Garbo, she just acted; or of Caruso, he just sang. Their genius lay in making what came naturally to them – dancing, acting, or singing – seem within easy reach of anyone. It needed only the succession of mini-Garbos that sprang up to show that what was inspiring in the original became a wearying pose in others.

Since Astaire made his first screen appearance there have been many exciting dancers on the screen. Some, like Donald O'Connor, Bill Robinson, Dan Dailey, Ray Bolger, Gower Champion and Bob Fosse, superb in their own right or, like Gene Kelly, pathfinders in screen choreography. Only Astaire, however, has been able to make dancing appear as effortless and natural as breathing, one of the normal functions of life. Choreographically there is nothing anyone has done that Astaire couldn't do, but his dancing has never succumbed to a display of athletic prowess.

In his last film as a dancer, *Finian's Rainbow* (1968), Astaire (born in the first year of this century) again dances into view, still as dapper and slim as ever, and any talk of age or waning powers becomes superfluous. He was born Fred Austerlitz in Omaha, Nebraska, and his parents were Austrian immigrants. While still youngsters, he and his sister, Adele, teamed up to dance, and by the early 20s had become two of the brightest musical stars on either side of the Atlantic. Several of their hit shows subsequently provided material for his films (*Band Wagon, Funny Face*, etc.). When his sister retired from the stage in 1932 to get married, Astaire continued alone, starring successfully in *The Gay Divorce* (he filmed it in 1934). Any doubts he may have had of his success as a single were dispelled by the acclaim hs received on Broadway and in London. His career was just beginning.

Astaire's solo film début came in 1933, playing himself opposite Crawford in *Dancing Lady*, the success of which gave him the confidence to accept RKO's *Flying Down to Rio* (1933). His dancing

'Look to the Rainbow'. Astaire and dancers in *Finian's Rainbow*. Choreography with Hermes Pan.

The start of a famous partnership. 'The Carioca' in *Flying Down to Rio*.

partner was the wisecracking blonde who had gained attention snapping out one-liners as 'Anytime Annie' in *42nd Street*, Ginger Rogers. Ginger had been in films since 1930, and had actually decided to give up making musicals when offered the job with Astaire. They had already met during their Broadway days, when he had been called in to choreograph the 'Embraceable You' number, written for Ginger by the Gershwins for the musical, *Girl Crazy* (1930). She accepted *Flying Down to Rio*, expecting it to be little more tha a one-time thing. She told Astaire at the time, 'I don't want to do any more musicals, but I guess it'll turn out all right. Anyway, we'll have some fun!'

Thus began one of the great partnerships of the movies. Their roles in *Flying Down to Rio* were subordinate – the star was Dolores del Rio – but they caught the public's imagination as two vulnerable sophisticates who meet and after a cautious start acknowledge their love in a succession of dances in which the world is their ballroom. Ginger was Fred's ideal partner, following him exactly, dancing almost like his shadow rather than his prima ballerina. She was a clever faker; when she danced with Astaire, one looked at her face for reactions, instead of her feet. Besides which she was pert, pretty and had an appealingly vulnerable quality which she disguised behind a facade of caustic repartee. Only William Powell and Myrna

During the filming of *Top Hat*. Astaire and Rogers, with director Mark Sandrich, left, chat with Irving Berlin outside the sound stage.

Astaire doing his own, inimitable tribute to the legendary Bill Robinson in the 'Bojangles' number in *Swing Time*.

Horton, Victor Moore, Alice Brady and Helen Broderick. In their films, there is a perfection of team playing that was developed by their many appearances together or in similar roles in other films.

The crest of the Astaire-Rogers popularity was reached with *Top Hat* in 1935 and maintained until they went their separate ways in 1939 after completing *The Story of Vernon and Irene Castle*. In 1936, the year of *Follow the Fleet* and *Swing Time*, they came third in the top box-office ten, preceded by Shirley Temple, and followed by Dick Powell (sixth) and Jeanette MacDonald (ninth).

Their greatly varied routines, the simplicity of which hides the thought and work that went into their evolvement, were usually performed on extremely simple sets. Their fast-moving, well-acted films created dance crazes that swept the country and the other film studios: the 'Carioca' in *Flying Down to Rio*, the 'Continental' in *The Gay Divorcee*, and the 'Piccolino' in *Top Hat*, provoked such imitations as 'The Hunkadola' in *George White's Scandals of 1935*, the 'La Bomba' in *The Big Broadcast of 1937* and Irving Berlin's own answer to his 'Cheek to Cheek' in 'Back to Back' in *Second Fiddle* (1939). And of course there were their classic ballroom dances.

All the foremost songwriters wrote for Astaire's films. Gershwin's score for *A Damsel in Distress* (1937) includes Nice Work If You Can Get It' and 'A Foggy Day'. For *Shall We Dance*, the same year, he composed 'They All Laughed', 'Shall We Dance', 'Let's Call The Whole Thing Off' and 'They Can't Take That Away From Me'. Astaire also had an old Gershwin score for *Funny Face* (1957). Cole Porter's score for *The Gay Divorcee* included 'Night and Day' and 'The Continental'. In *The Broadway Melody of 1940* he partnered Eleanor Powell in 'Begin the Beguine'; in *You'll Never Get Rich* (1941) there was 'So Near and Yet So Far' with Rita Hayworth and for *Silk Stockings* (1957) there was yet another Cole Porter score. Jerome Kern's first score for an Astaire-Rogers film was *Roberta* (1935), which had originated on Broadway but which had two new songs, 'Lovely to Look At' and 'I Won't Dance'. For *Swing Time* (1936) Kern wrote the score, which included 'The Way You Look Tonight' and 'A Fine Romance', and for *You Were Never Lovelier* (1942), there was 'I'm Old Fashioned', the title song, and 'Dearly Beloved'. Burton Lane, composer of *Finian's Rainbow* and *On a Clear Day* contributed 'Everything I Have is Yours' to *Dancing Lady*, and wrote the songs for *Royal Wedding* (1951). Vincent Youmans wrote the score for *Flying Down to Rio*, which included 'Orchids in the Moonlight', the title song and the 'Carioca'. Irving Berlin provided first-rate scores for *Top Hat*, *Follow the Fleet*, *Carefree*, *Holiday Inn* (1942) and *Blue Skies* (1946 – he co-starred with Crosby in the last two) and *Easter Parade* (1948). Bing Crosby wrote in his auto-biography, *Call Me Lucky*: 'I remember *Holiday Inn* because in it Fred Astaire danced himself so thin that I could almost spit through him. In the film he did one number thirty-eight times before he was satisfied with it. He started the picture weighing 140 pounds. When he finished it he weighed 126 . . . when you're in a picture with Fred Astaire, you've

Loy achieved a similar, smooth elegance as a team. But they didn't dance.

Ginger and Fred are the common turned into the rare; they were the Lunt and Fontanne of the dance. Other partners brought out the romantic, the classical and the technical aspects of the man, but Ginger was the end of the day, the affectionate look back at a life shared, a past remembered, and the value of lasting; in short, the rewards that come to two people who know from the outset that they will know each other always, warts and all, and whom living together has made into one. Rita Hayworth, on the other hand, with her youth and flowing beauty, was to be Fred's truly romantic partner, bringing out the secretly glimpsed poet in his nature; Cyd Charisse would prove to be his classical muse. Together they are elegiac, a line that flows from beginning to end; and Eleanor Powell was to provide his most exhilarating professional challenge; theirs was the meeting of two stunning techniques, who through their enjoyment and magnetic artistry, make the rare worth the striving for.

The supporting players in the RKO-made Astaire-Rogers films were masters of the art of sophisticated farce, with the comic playing of such regulars as Eric Blore, Franklyn Pangborn, Edward Everett

Far left: *The Gay Divorcee*. 'The Continental'.

Left: Fred Astaire with his co-star, Bing Crosby, on the set of *Holiday Inn*.

Far left, below: *Roberta*. 'Smoke Gets in Your Eyes'.

Below: *Top Hat*. 'The Piccolino'.

got rocks in your head if you do much dancing. He's so quick-footed and so light that it's impossible not to look like a hay-digger compared with him.'

Astaire, who worked on the choreography in all of his films – mostly with his friend and favourite collaborator, Hermes Pan (they were still working together on Fred's last film musical, *Finian's Rainbow*), usually got to work two months before filming started.

Fred Astaire: When an idea comes to me, I ask for a certain type of music, or I write it myself. (His composing credits include 'I'm Building Up To An Awful Letdown'). Ninety-nine times out of a hundred the music would be written before. I might say to Irving Berlin, I'd like to do a thing about this or that and he'd come up with a song which I either could or couldn't use. This happened with Gershwin and Porter. Gershwin did a thing called 'High Hat' in *Funny Face*, which my sister and I did on Broadway and then in London. Now, a few years later Irving wrote a thing called 'Top Hat' when I went into the movies. And I think he got a little of that idea from the Gershwin number that we had done. That was at the time when they wanted a new dance with every film so they'd have something to publicize. Irving used to call it 'Doing the *THE*'. He used to say: 'What you want is a "THE" song, isn't

From top left: *Swing Time*. 'The Waltz in Swing Time'. *Follow the Fleet*. 'Let's Face the Music and Dance' and 'Let Yourself Go'. *Carefree*. 'The Yam'. *Swing Time*. 'Never Gonna Dance' and 'Pick Yourself Up'.

it? Doing the "The Song".' And I'd say, 'Yeah, that's it.' And he would say, 'Well, what kind of a "THE"?' And that time he came up with 'The Yam', which sounds as though it might be all right, but it wasn't a hit tune. It wasn't his inspiration, and I'm sure he got disgusted with it. We had a step in it which we thought might catch on, but things were different then. When I see my old movies on TV, it seems much smoother to me than it did at the time, and I seem to see what everyone else saw then. I very seldom see one that I don't find is better than I expected it to be. Some of them I had no idea were as good as they were.

It's not a good idea to work with the same person all the time. I didn't do everything with Hermes Pan. I worked with Bob Alton. I worked with Nick Castle. Hermes did all the things I did with Ginger, except for *The Barkleys of Broadway*, which I did with Bob Alton.

Partners are very important for me. If the girl isn't right, it's very tough on her. There are people who have complained about a lot of the girls I've danced with because they weren't like the other one. The main thing is to make sure they're doing something they like to do. Cyd Charisse is tallish. I liked some

things I did with Cyd. I liked 'Dancing In The Dark', and – I forget what I did in the darn show – and I liked the shoeshine routine. I didn't think the book part of it worked out too well. There was a sequence at the beginning where I was supposed to be the over-the-hill actor, and he was watching his furnishings auctioned off, and the producer (Arthur Freed) thought this would be funny. In other words, this guy was on his way out. People said to me afterwards, 'But you're not through. What are they doing that to you for?' (But this wasn't the story of

my life, and people take these things so seriously.) But when Cyd got the heels and hair and all this kind of thing, she's up there. It was the same with Rita. She was a lovely gal, but Rita was even taller, and Audrey Hepburn is a little tall. And Barrie Chase is taller than Ginger. Ginger started out the right height but then she got taller and taller as her heels got higher and higher. I got a slap in the face a couple of times from Ginger! I think we did about 42 takes of this thing, and the take we used was the first one, when the thing she had on really hit me!

That was in 'Let's Face The Music and Dance'.

Ginger and I did it over and over, and there was always some little thing that we didn't like. I think we finished about 8 o'clock at night, and decided to come back and look at the rushes the next morning. You could get them quickly in those days. And when we looked at it, the very first take was fine. Perfect. I said, 'Well, that's the one where I got hit in the kisser with your sleeve.' Joan Fontaine wasn't a dancer, but I thought it would be fun because I'd just done some things with Ginger and we both

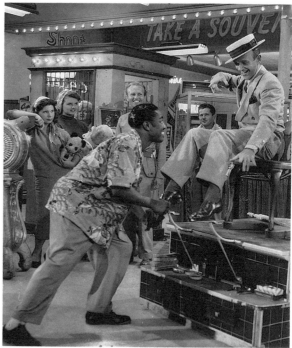

Above: The 'Limehouse Blues' number in *Ziegfeld Follies*. Astaire's partner was Arthur Freed's discovery, Lucille Bremer. The choreographer was Robert Alton.

Above right: Fred Astaire and LeRoy Daniel in *The Band Wagon*. 'Shine on Your Shoes'.

wanted to make a little change and so forth. Joan became an Academy Award winner, and all this kind of dramatic thing like all my dancing partners! But Joan always told me that the dance she did with me set her career back five years!

On the screen, as opposed to the stage, you can say, 'Well, I don't feel like shooting that today.' Athletes go through this too. You might say athletes don't dance but football players dance with all sorts of things in their arms. The funny part of it all is that 75% of the time you're hurting like hell somewhere when you're doing all that dancing. I've been through a number with a broken finger. I was putting on my sock or taking it off when I snapped this finger here. And I had to have it in a little cast. And while I was dancing with Rita Hayworth I was thinking about this damn finger! I've suffered from muscular spasms in my back for years.

In their first film together, *Flying Down to Rio* (RKO, 1933), Astaire (who'd made his film début in *Dancing Lady*, one of the first of the musicals produced in the wake of the Berkeley phenomenon) and Ginger were assigned the light comedy supporting roles, which in their subsequent films were usually taken by Helen Broderick (or Alice Brady) and Edward Everett Horton (or Victor Moore).

Fred Astaire: We had much better facilities at MGM. The equipment was much better. The stages were better, more modern, and the sound was newer.

Hermes and a girl and I would work to get Ginger's dances together, because we liked to have things set so she could walk in and learn them without going through all the problems we had in working them out. It's easier to do it that way. Sometimes we'd have to write our own music in addition to the song we were doing . . . interlude music sort of thing. We'd say to the arranger 'Apply this to the song'. So they'd put our music into the song and make it a part of it. I never thought about it while I was doing it. You just do it.

I enjoyed completely the field I was in, because I

didn't have any confidence in doing anything else, and I knew that the minute I did anything completely away from dancing, there'd be a big holler about it and they'd say: 'Well, when is he going to dance?' When I finally did do that with Stanley Kramer in *On the Beach* it was because I knew there was no way in which they could expect that fellow to dance. A nuclear scientist going into a dance never occurred to anybody. The picture unfortunately didn't do what I wished. After that I did a few others, like *The Pleasure of His Company*, and *Notorious Landlady*, which was a sort of come-and-goer. But I enjoyed all of them. They were like holidays to me to do something where I didn't have to dance.

I never had the attitude of wanting to say something in dance. Some people want there to be a message of some sort. But I was just doing it to tell a story. The reason I brought this up is that nowadays there is this big thing about 'what has he got to say?' or 'what's the meaning of this?' I don't think that every movie that's made has to be saying something. I think it can be doing something, like entertaining. I just tried to entertain. I never had that political outlook that some minds have had. You try to get a dimension across playing a role. You try to be a person of some sort.

Now, in *Finian's Rainbow* I had a very hard time in convincing the producers that I must dance a sizeable amount in the movie. They wanted me because they thought I was ripe for the role, because the role originally was not a musical role. He didn't even sing . . . he didn't do anything. But act. So they elaborated it into a musical role which was better. Now there was no music written for this fellow, so he had to take over something. And I took over the numbers I did do. And the big complaint in that movie was that I didn't dance enough. And the producers had been afraid that I was stepping out of the character of Finian.

I always remember *Top Hat* as being a big movie of mine. I guess the whole movie is what I think of a good deal. I did so many and I can't remember what a lot of them were about. I loved the 'Limehouse Blues' number. I did it again for my TV special, though in a different way. In the original we had the song, but we didn't know what it would be; then Minnelli suggested a plot, a touch of drama. That was a memorable one for me. Minnelli had two enormous stages for that whole thing. There were effects all over the place, and it was just wonderful. You know, you couldn't do that today. Not only would it cost too much, but it wouldn't be appreciated. If you made that movie today it wouldn't make it. But put it there, and it works. There are very few of them that you can bring back.

Then the 'Begin the Beguine' was a tough one, too. That whole picture was a kind of freak. It was so big, and it wasn't considered a success. Revues were out of fashion at the time and they have never come back. I know what I'd like to see . . . I'd like to see a real first class smash musical movie with Elvis Presley and Frank Sinatra together. Sinatra has never done on the screen what he can do best, not since way back. He doesn't want to be bothered. Too much rehearsing. Presley, to my mind, is one of the best talents there is. I think he's fantastic. He's a real talent.

Fred Astaire was speaking in 1971. If there's one thing that rankles with him to this day, as much if not more than people asking him for meanings in his dancing, it's that most of his films were in black and white.

Fred Astaire: I'll argue this point to my dying day. I don't see any reason why, if colour is available and it's good, that it shouldn't be used. I mean, do you go around looking at everything in black and white on the street?

Interestingly enough, considering Astaire's passionate feelings on the subject, one of his friends, Jock Whitney, was the man behind the first successful three-strip technicolor experiments. The musical short, *La Cucaracha*, and the feature, *Dancing Pirate*, both produced in 1935/36 were by Astaire's studio, RKO. But more than that, Astaire seems to ignore the fact that his classic 30s musicals were designed to take advantage of the screen's monotone range (like sculptors working with marble or ebony), with those dazzling black and white sets by Van Nest Polglase and Carroll Clark, and the wardrobes by Bernard Newman, Walter Plunkett, and Irene, that were the epitome of elegance, and together these created an aura of style to stimulate the visual senses. More than anything else, the look of those films, so complimentary to the stars' personalities, employed, extended and spread the influence of art deco throughout the land, *The Story of Vernon and Irene Castle*, a period subject, and those 40s musicals he made, but which were still filmed in black and white (though by then colour had become commonplace and designers no longer tried to emulate those stunning art deco palaces), would have benefited from colour. Certainly Astaire was to make enough films in colour with one of the movies leading colour artists, Vincente Minnelli; but their excellences and delights notwithstanding, they do not eclipse or in

any way lessen the great earlier works. The only strikingly designed black and white films of the 40s were not musicals but more likely to be *films noirs,* a genre which is very difficult to visualize in colour anyway.

'I've seen it from the daguerrotype things on. The difference between a colour still and a black and white one is just ridiculous. In colour it lives. I've done a number of pictures I've regretted were never made in colour. *Irene and Vernon Castle* – it's a crime that picture wasn't made in colour because it was a colourful subject.

'I did a picture I like called *Daddy Long Legs*. It was in its day a successful movie. I saw it on TV, and maybe it was ten minutes less than originally, and it was better! There is a better way to do things, and I hammered out at *Finian's Rainbow* and its length for the thing it was. It should have run for an hour and 50 minutes at the most. Things were too long drawn out. And it cost so darn much to blow it up for the TODD-A-O screen. And that cuts the feet off – and they jumped on that, saying they couldn't see Astaire's feet when he danced, and I thought Astaire's feet had been lost for so long what difference did it make!'

Running throughout his work, both in his early black and white days at RKO, and later, when his artistry was being applied to the formally choreographed, colourful routines of his masterful Metro musicals, he retains a virtuoso element that allows the choreographic structure of his dances space for those precious accidents which are the hallmark of a great artist. Fred Astaire was one of a rare breed. But: 'I'm not an isolated case at all', he says emphatically. Well the air is rare where he keeps his shoes.

The Directors

Musicals are not usually remembered for their directors. It's a fact, and a regrettable one, that while musicals had to have directors, with very few exceptions none of the outstanding directors of the day bothered themselves with this genre and, when they did, failed to treat it seriously. Which is to say lightly, lovingly, inventively – adding the last but all-important touch to the proceedings, creating out of all that available talent a whole that would be original to film. The directors who seemed to specialize in that sort of film were good craftsmen for the most part but seemed almost to be directing musicals because they weren't deemed good enough for anything else. The major producers, men like Pandro S. Berman, Joe Pasternak, Jack Cummings and Arthur Freed cared for their films, chose them, and put their stamp on their musicals more assuredly than the directors they usually employed.

Roy Del Ruth, Lloyd Bacon, David Butler, S. Sylvan Simon, Sidney Lanfield, George Sidney, Mervyn LeRoy – good workmen all – made a lot of musicals without realizing their true potential. One remembers Mervyn LeRoy's *Gold-diggers of 1933* for Busby Berkeley, Victor Fleming's *The Wizard of Oz* for Judy Garland, Roy Del Ruth's *The Broadway Melody of 1936* and *1938* for Eleanor Powell, Mark Sandrich's five films with Fred Astaire for Fred

Above: A dispirited group of law-breakers in Fritz Lang's *You and Me*, among them George E. Stone and Robert Cummings. The stars of the film were Sylvia Sidney and George Raft.

Right: Grace Moore and Walter Connolly enliven Sternberg's *The King Steps Out*.

Above right: The greatly underrated Victor Schertzinger on the set of *The Music Goes 'Round* with Rochelle Hudson and night club star Harry Richman. Even Schertzinger couldn't make Richman a film favourite.

Astaire, etc. Frank Borzage, Josef von Sternberg, Alfred Hitchcock, Fritz Lang, Billy Wilder, Cecil B. De Mille all made one musical each – none of which they would have considered memorable. While John Ford never made a musical at all, King Vidor, who made *Hallelujah*, told me once that he saw all films in *musical terms*. When they did do musicals the results were pretentious and that's why, with the exceptions of Frank Borzage and von Sternberg, these directors failed. Lewis Milestone's *Hallelujah, I'm a Bum* has already been cited. Fritz Lang's experience making *You and Me* (1938) is worth relating (the letter is dated 17 May 1969).

Dear Mr Kobal

When I was in Paris, before I went to London, I was asked by one or two interviewers if, to the best of my knowledge, I was ever influenced by a film or another director. After I thought it over I answered that I didn't think so, with one exception. This one exception was *You and Me*, and I certainly was influenced by my admiration for and friendship with Berthold Brecht. He called the plays he produced 'a Lehr-Stück', meaning *play* that was supposed to *teach* you something.

All the songs were supposed to be written by Kurt Weill, but as he unfortunately left during the shooting of the film some changes had to be made in the music by the Music Department of the studio, but they were always based on musical 'outlines' or 'sketches' by Kurt Weill.

I myself had very exact ideas about one special song, the one where the criminals on parole are sitting together on Christmas Eve, nursing a certain nostalgia for 'the good old days' in prison.

The music to this song should come out of the sounds the parolees make with their knuckles on the wooden table; first with their knuckles, then with their knives, then by using cups, mugs or glasses clashing on each other, the sound of knives

and forks rapping on glasses, and so on. The climax of the song should be the rat-a-tat-tat of the machine guns during the prison break.

Taking a lead from Brecht, Lang wanted to make a '*Lehr-film*', a film that should teach something, 'and I wound up with the worst film I ever made'.

Josef von Sternberg felt pretty much like that about his musical, *The King Steps Out*, but I disagree. In 1936 von Sternberg, who had begun the decade with *The Blue Angel* (1930), made his one and only screen operetta. The star was Grace Moore.

At the time she let everybody know she hated working with von Sternberg. Her comet-like ascent into film stardom two years earlier had already begun to burn out; filmed operettas had not regained their hold on the public, and the film was not a great success. It seems that everyone has accepted the director's cavalier dismissal of his own work, although Sternberg can hardly be accused of getting carried away about any of his films. However, it turns out to be a bright shaft of entertainment. In *The King Steps Out* von Sternberg presents a glorious current of quicksilver images from which emerge the Vienna of the woods and the waltz. Dorothy Fields put the lyrics to Fritz Kreisler's music. The screenplay by Sidney Buchman was based on a German original by the Marischka brothers, Hubert and Ernst. For once, Grace Moore was not cast in a backstage operatic story but in a charming tale of a royal romance in imperial Austria.

Like every woman directed by von Sternberg Moore looked radiant and her somewhat larger-than-life personality was so cleverly controlled and guided that she pulled the film along at a lively trot; everything and everyone in it was imbued with charm. Visually it is matchless; Columbia's back lot, home of many a *Lost Horizon*, never looked so rural and restful. The comic interpolations from the Duke (Walter Connolly), the irascible Raymond Walburn and from Herman Bing – tied up in knots by his own tongue with a hurdle of *terrrrrrrorrrrrs* that almost threatens to drown him and everyone in sight, are immaculately dropped into the overall scheme of von Sternberg's things so that the result is champagne, drunk to Fritz Kreisler's music, and leaving one exhilarated and without a headache. It's a treasure.

The catalogue has much to give us on Victor Schertzinger, who died in 1941 aged 51, at the height of his powers, but who is today almost totally forgotten. Yet he is probably one of the most significant contributors to some of Hollywood's most successful musicals. Schertzinger was one of the few, possibly the only, composer to become a film director. What his films lacked in an individual visual style they made up for in the music. They were as light, and delectable to watch as the songs he wrote were delightful to hear. Schertzinger, who also has the credit for writing one of the first, if not the first, original scores for a silent film, for Thomas H. Ince's 1916 anti-war epic, *Civilization*, also wrote the songs for Jeanette MacDonald to sing in Lubitsch's sound debut, *The Love Parade*. 'Dream Lover', and 'Paris, Stay the Same' were two of the hits. As director, Schertzinger created the perfect formulae for bringing outsize opera stars to the screen in a way both intimate and in keeping with their talents when he directed Grace Moore in the come-back that launched a host of imitations, *One Night of Love* (1934), for which he also wrote the popular title song. He also created the model for the *Road* films as director of *The Road to Singapore* and *The Road to Zanzibar*. Besides his score of films, his superbly-crafted songs are remembered more for the stars who introduced them than for their composer – a balance to be corrected. Some of the titles: 'Sand in My Shoes', 'I Don't Want to Cry Any More', 'Kiss the Boys Goodbye', 'Arthur Murray taught me dancing in a hurry', 'I Remember You' (revived in the 60s), and 'Tangerine' –

She may have the men in a whirl
But she's only fooling one girl
She's only fooling
Tangerine

Besides the afore-mentioned films he directed many other popular musicals, including Gilbert and Sullivan's *The Mikado*, filmed in England and in colour, and several of the better films starring Crosby. All his films are easy and good-natured and often witty in a dry, tongue-in-cheek way. Two of his films, while not masterpieces, are a darn sight better than a lot of the more highly-praised films of the 40s, and superior to any of the 60s and 70s musical Mega-Buck productions that lifted a show from Broadway and simply dumped it on celluloid. *Kiss the Boys Goodbye* (1941), a satirical dig at Hollywood by Broadway, was not as socially conscious as Preston Sturges' *Sullivan's Travels* made during the same year but full of chestnuts. *Rhythm on the River* (1940), a satire on Broadway, Tin Pan Alley and ghost writing, (the acceptable form of plagiarism), with a story whose antecedents can be traced back to Plautus, never misses a beat, with Crosby as the 'ghost' composer and Mary Martin as the 'ghost lyricist'. Fleet of foot and good in befuddlement, these two are films to enjoy and make one regret the loss of the man who made them. He died shortly after the completion of his last film, *The Fleet's In*, which is just as good, just as light, as tuneful and as attractive as the others. He was not a

Mary Martin and Bing Crosby in *Rhythm on the River*. The director was Victor Schertzinger.

man to let his personal problems affect his work. He was a lovely artist.

In 1931 George Cukor, another highly talented but unpretentious director, was just making his mark in the film world when Paramount entrusted him with the MacDonald-Chevalier team for *One Hour with You*. Lubitsch, having directed them either separately or as a team in three successive film musicals, and just them filming his pacifist war story, *The Man I Killed* (1932), was content initially to supervise *One Hour with You*. But the released version of the film had Cukor listed as 'dialogue director' and Lubitsch as 'director'.

The score of *One Hour with You* – from Oscar Straus with Leo Robin's lyrics – rose naturally from the action and furthered the story. Quite a large section of the dialogue is in rhyming couplets. Mitzi (an *éclair* performance by Genevieve Tobin) confides to her best friend, Collette (MacDonald), that, 'Unless you're well mated, this business of marriage is much over-rated!' Mitzi's husband, (Roland Young), doesn't trust his pretty blonde wife (with good reason) and tells the private detective he's hired to tail her: 'When I married her, she was a brunette; now you can't believe a word she says.' Jeanette, whether as trusting friend or suspicious wife, is delectable in her saucy wardrobe, ranging from the obligatory lingerie sequence (before MGM put the stays into her) or in her plunging evening gowns. The humour, in tune with the time, is often risqué but always good fun. As in most Lubitsch films, it was sexually very sophisticated. Lubitsch once said, 'I let the audience use their imagination. Can I help it if they misconstrue my suggestions?' Charles Ruggles, a desperate Lothario, dressing as Romeo for a dinner party, finds out that it's formal and not costume, as his butler had told him. When he asks 'Why did you tell me it was going to be a costume party?' the butler, with an admiring look at his employer's thighs, sighs, 'Ah Monsieur, I did so want to see you in tights!'

In his last musical (*The Merry Widow*, 1934), Lubitsch for the last time directed his favourite leading lady, Jeanette, once more with Chevalier.

Rouben Mamoulian's second film musical was the inimitable *Love Me Tonight*, with songs by Rodgers and Hart. Maurice Chevalier in 'The Poor Apache' number.

Right: Nino Martini sings – and saves his life in Mamoulian's quick-witted, fast-paced satire, *The Gay Desperado*. Italian tenor Martini never found another vehicle as effective as this and after one more film returned to the opera stage.

The part of the glamorous widow was a role for which Joan Crawford among others had pleaded with Louis B. Mayer. Chevalier, whose relations with MacDonald had never been overly fond, wanted Grace Moore – who wanted top billing, which put a damper on Chevalier's enthusiasm. Lubitsch, however, strongly backed by Metro's production genius, Irving Thalberg, insisted upon Jeanette, saying later, 'She had what it took to make the widow merry; without her, it would have been a very sad widow indeed.' In it Lubitsch's witty, highly personal signature was more prominent in his asides than in his handling of the stars. Under the credit titles of the film, one sees a dedicated geographer, with a magnifying glass, peering at a map of Europe, trying in vain to locate Marsovia, the country which Prince Danilo deserts for the blandishments of Paris. He gives up in despair.

But, even with three Lubitsch musicals behind her, the Mamoulian film capped her early career. Arthur Freed, Vincente Minnelli, and Charles Walters, three of the master-builders of the musical's golden years, were agreed that *Love Me Tonight* had the greatest influence on their own work. Mamoulian's best films possess the same superb flair, great panache and truly inspired treatment of conventional clichés. They are fun and imaginative; their sentiments are never allowed to cloy. The authors of *Love Me Tonight* were Leopold Marchand and Paul Armont; the scenarists, Samuel Hofenstein, Waldermar Young, George Marion Jr.

About the film, Mamoulian said 'The front office asked me to direct the next Jeanette MacDonald film. I said, "Why not Lubitsch?" He had already directed them a couple of times, and this was to be another of his. I kept refusing it but they put me on the spot. Then when I went ahead and did it, everybody thought, "What a thing for him to do, use MacDonald and Chevalier *after* Lubitsch!" By now I could use visual and aural images as I pleased. For instance when MacDonald's aunts open their mouths you hear the yapping of little dogs or the clucking of hens instead of their voices. Then there is a moment when one of the aunts exclaims to the family and guests at the castle that Chevalier is a tailor, and drops a vase: there I have the sound of dynamite exploding, because that, emotionally, is the size of it.

'I had no story when I began work on the film, and some hundred thousand dollars had already been spent. Leopold Marchand gave me the idea for the story, a modern fairy tale. I decided to make it lyrical, thoroughly stylized: a film in which the whole action of actors, as well as the movement of camera and cutting was rhythmic.

'Then I got Rodgers and Hart to write the music; they had been lingering at one of the studios. We finished the whole score before I began work on the script. We did the whole thing to a metronome, because we couldn't carry an orchestra round with us.'

Throughout the film rhythmic dialogue and verses are combined with music, and used to bridge dialogue with singing. The Rodgers and Hart songs were amongst the best they ever composed for film or stage – 'Mimi', 'Isn't It Romantic', 'Lover', 'The Son of a Gun is Nothing but a Tailor', 'The Song of Paree', and the lesser known but glorious title song.

'In the musicals I did, the architecture is a whole, and it is mine. On the stage, the writer gives you a ready-made play (and legally, at any rate, you cannot change a comma if he is against it). On the screen, a producing director is in complete control. I'd say that, as a rule, the best films are made by a director.

'There is a funny story about one of the film's songs, "Lover". That melody was my and Dick Rodger's favourite. Well, the film came out, and every song was a hit except "Lover". Four years later, the song began to creep in, and today it is the biggest hit from the film.'

'What survives best is myth, poetry. Realism dies. All arts aspire to the perfection of music. The medium of the film consists of both the screen and the audience. There must be a constant inter-reaction, it's the nature of the animal.'

It is this attitude which is behind *Love Me Tonight*'s roaring success: speech bursts into song; a walk becomes a dance. Mamoulian literally puts us on the wings of the song 'Isn't It Romantic?' to take us from the tailor's shop to the princess's castle. The tune, first sung by Maurice, is continued by a taxi driver, overheard by an artist who sings it in a train filled with soldiers. They march to it through the country-side where it's picked up by a gypsy in a nearby field. Each image blends into the next – as naturally as the song switches moods, from march time to a poetical strain of a violin – through the blurring of the images, double exposures and always lyrical camera movement. The gypsy's playing zings through the forest and settles on the balcony of the enchanting castle, where a sleepless Princess just happens to be dreaming in the moonlight.

In 1936, having meanwhile directed Garbo, Dietrich and Anna Sten, as well as Miriam Hopkins in colour, Mamoulian returned to musicals with *The Gay Desperado*, a lively satire on Mexican bandits and operatic film stars (Nino Martini). It is one of his own favourites. The New York film critics selected it as their favourite film for that year. Then came the Jerome Kern-Oscar Hammerstein *High, Wide and Handsome* (1937), a wonderfully evocative slice of early Americana, set in western Pennsylvania of the 1850s during the discovery of oil, and starring Irene Dunne, an all-round performer, peerless in comedy, romance, drama and musicals. She was a very special talent – never the broad gesture, never a hair out of place, but truth, tolerance, generosity of spirit and an irrefutable beauty about her which illuminates her work. In a role not too dissimilar in type from that of Magnolia in *Showboat*, she's Sally Waterson, daughter of the owner of a travelling medicine show, who meets and marries a young farmer, and tells him of the life she dreams of for them: 'The Folks Who Live on the Hill'. The epic-scaled musical has all the ingredients of that turbulent era – travelling medicine shows, shanty boats and girls of doubtful pasts and not much hope, circuses and raging all-out battles between the oilmen and the eastern railroad magnates. The story (choreographed by the film's dance director, LeRoy Prinz) climaxes in a regular donneybrook, a fight of furious action and excitement, that still manages to stay within the convention of the musical created by the earlier evocations of nostalgia and sentiment.

High, Wide and Handsome is another of those films which has been unaccountably neglected. It had verve, it had vitality, it had panache and songs by Kern sung by Dunne – yet even Mamoulian

Rouben Mamoulian, arm upraised, directing Irene Dunne in *High, Wide and Handsome*. The song is Jerome Kern's 'Can I Forget You?'. Irene Dunne and Randolph Scott in another scene, 'The Folks Who Live on the Hill'.

admirers find little to enthuse over. Their opinion was shared by the film's director and his star. Said Irene Dunne: 'It wasn't a happy film. It was very costly. Mamoulian was a very artistic director and I'd have to ride back and forth to Chino, California, where in January we'd sit around waiting for a cloud formation. The time it took! It couldn't happen today. We were way over budget and there'd be wrangles with the studio. It was an uncomfortable film to make with all that location work. Also, I lost my mother in the middle of it which was a shattering shock to me. I think I had two days off and had to go right back into making the film.

'I think I'll always remember the flavour of working on that film. Because this was a big budget film it had the full treatment, a première at the Cathay Circle. I went that night and sat directly in front of Helen Hayes. I was conscious of Helen Hayes breathing down my neck all evening.'

Mamoulian hadn't chosen this film for his project. It was pressed upon him, the last film he directed for Paramount.

Mamoulian: I had just finished *The Gay Desperado*, and I was tired. My agent sent me the script, even after I had told him I was against it. But they sent it anyway, asking me to read it – hoping that it would interest me. The stars were to be Gary Cooper and Irene Dunne. That also appealed to me; I'd never worked with them before. It was an interesting idea, but I knew I had to rewrite the script. This wasn't a matter of principle, I just usually like a subject, but not a script. And then the combination of oil and music isn't an easy one, as you can appreciate. It was a very tough picture to make, half dreams, half reality. Some things in it are good, but I don't feel that I succeeded.

When oilman Randolph Scott – we never got Gary Cooper – is trying to complete a pipeline by a certain date and get a much-needed contract, his railroad competitors send a gang of toughs with orders to break it up at all costs. For this climatic fight at the end, where we have Irene Dunne and her circus friends and elephants coming to the rescue, the property department built this whole mountain range out of papier maché. They completed it in advance of our arrival, and when we came to shoot the scene a few days later, the rains had got there before us. Our mountain range had gone soggy and had to be completely rebuilt. The river we'd built was gone, washed away, and our three trees were bare. Nobody says this, but the prop people are the unsung heroes of movies. In a day or two, they somehow got leaves and put them all back.

All the strands of the story are assimilated within the musical framework. Jerome Kern's songs convey the mood of America in the 1850s, and they are superb: the glorious title song; 'Can I Forget You?', 'The Folks Who Live on the Hill', 'The Things I Want' – an exquisite blues number, as memorable as Dorothy Lamour looked singing it; the peppy 'Allegheny Al' and the country-flavoured eightsome reel 'Will You Marry Me Tomorrow, Maria?', to which LeRoy Prinz brought an infectious, authentic and hip-slapping enthusiasm. In its rural setting, country feel, simple people, basic emotions, and glorious Kern tunes, it pre-dates the new type of integrated musicals to come. Broadway's celebrated *Oklahoma* is in the vein of this work. And Mamoulian directed that, too.

The Formulae

The great stars of the decade, popular idols like Bing Crosby, Mae West, Shirley Temple and Grace Moore, are, for most people, better known than any of the creators who directed their films and wrote their songs. It was around such potent personalities that Hollywood designed the 'star vehicle', a great and flexible formula that usually relies on yet another formula. The basic situations of the latter are used again and again with minor alterations that allow for the star's particular speciality. Thus, lavish all-star revues like *Paramount on Parade* (1930) were later revived as *The Big Broadcast of 1936, 37, 38*; while MGM resuscitated their smash hit, *The Broadway Melody* (1929), and gave it the kiss of life for three encores (1936, 38 and 40).

The one type of film that might seem made for the music is the biography of a famous musical personality, a Chopin, a Schubert, a Caruso or a Lanza.

Geraldine Farrar or Jerome Kern, or Judy Garland. Their lives allow for the natural integration of music into a story. Yet few of these musical biopics have so far proved to be very memorable. This type of musical flourished in Europe long before it reached the US shores – there such serious men as Beethoven, Mozart, Verdi, Tchaikovsky, Bellini, and Schubert, Schubert, Schubert were the subjects of films from France, Italy, Germany and England. A lot of them were dull, more were terrible. The leading players were usually good actors or great singers but unromantic as personalities. Abel Gance's *Un Grand Amour De Beethoven* (1936) gagged in the self-indulgent romanticism then permeating French pre-war cinema. They didn't just live, they *really* lived, and when they felt, they *really* felt and not even that great actor Harry Baur's profoundly sympathetic performance could wade through all that syrup without some of it sticking to him. Gance aspired to Beethoven or at any rate, to a film worthy of the man – and there were bound to be moments – Gance after all had directed *Napoléon* and other classics of French cinema. There is Beethoven strolling through the countryside, surrounded by bells, birds, rushing brooks, a village smithy at work, and he hears nothing. He is deaf. Only after he's passed by, does the screen pick up sound again. But most of the time, if he's sad he writes the *Pathétique* and if he's happy, it's *The Moonlight Sonata*. In later years, when Gance was being re-discovered by a new generation of French film buffs, François Truffaut wrote that for him Gance and Baur created an achievement comparable to bringing Rodin's Balzac statue to life in all its heaven-storming power and I suppose, glory. Bellini was struck dumb by his *Casta Diva*, Mozart was romantic and doomed. Puccini, Verdi, Tchaikovsky, et al, were romantic if not always doomed. None was more doomed than poor Schubert.

Perhaps no other composer, not even Schubert, was the excuse for so many films about his life and his family as 'The Waltz King', Johann Strauss and his father. The difference between Strauss *père* and Strauss *fils* was something few films about one or the other bothered to make clear, presumably on the assumption that one dead Strauss was the same as another dead Strauss. In England, Hitchcock made a one-time only diversion from suspense to musicals with Jessie Matthews. *Waltzes from Vienna* was a film about the Strausses; it did nothing for Strauss, Hitchcock or Matthews. But side by side with Forst's Schubert film there stands Duvivier's film about Johann Strauss, *The Great Waltz* (1939), made for MGM in Hollywood. It is a masterpiece.

Wit and screenwriter S. N. Behrman, who didn't care for this sort of film much, wrote funnily about the problems the film's producer, Gottfried Reinhardt, encountered when trying to sell the idea of *The Great Waltz* to the producer, Bernie Hyman: '. . . he brought him a recording of Miliza Korjus singing a Mozart aria with trills that soared to heaven. Mr Hyman was transported. "We'll put that in the picture," he said. Reinhardt, who wanted to keep this a film about Strauss, told him that this was impractical since the aria was by Mozart and the film was about Strauss. "Who the hell is going to

Throughout the years and all over the world the musical film made extensive use of the lives of the classical composers for biographies that played fast and loose with the facts of their lives. In chronological order. Richard Tauber as Schubert in *Blossom Time* (GB. 1934). Phillips Holmes as Bellini in *Casta Diva* (It-Ger. 1935). Fosco Grachetti with Gaby Morlay in *The Life of Giuseppe Verdi* (It. 1938). *Melodias Eternas* (Sp. 1940) had four ladies complicating the short life of Mozart. Left to right, Luisella Beghi, Maria Jacobini, Conchita Montenegro and Ione Salinas. Alan Curtis, (an American Schubert), with Ilona Massey in *New Wine* (1941). Cornel Wilde and Merle Oberon as Chopin and Georges Sand in *A Song to Remember* (1945). Stewart Granger as Paganini, with Jean Kent in the British *The Magic Bow* (1946). Katherine Hepburn as Clara Schumann in *Song of Love* (1947). H. Walter Kohl-Veltee as Beethoven in *Eroica* (Aus. 1949). Dirk Bogarde as Liszt, with Genevieve Page as a complication in *Song Without End* (1960).

stop me?" said Hyman, normally a mild man.'

Directed by the Frenchman, Julian Duvivier, during his Hollywood stay, *The Great Waltz* is an intoxicating flow of heady images dedicated to the spirit of Strauss, while letting the facts take care of themselves. It is not so much biography as glorious musical imagery in 3/4 time. According to Luise Rainer, who was one of the stars, another director, Victor Fleming, was brought in to re-shoot and expand Miliza Korjus' scenes to justify Metro's costly investment in bringing her over for this one film. It was well worth it. Fleming closely held to the spirit and beauty of the rest of the film; Joseph Rutterberg's camerawork was outstanding.

Unforgettable is the sequence where Strauss (Fernand Gravet) and Carla Donner (Miliza Korjus) drive through the woods at dawn in an open carriage; the rhythm of the trotting horse, the birds' trill, the shepherd's call, a postillion's horn, the sung interpolations of the soprano and carriage driver, all

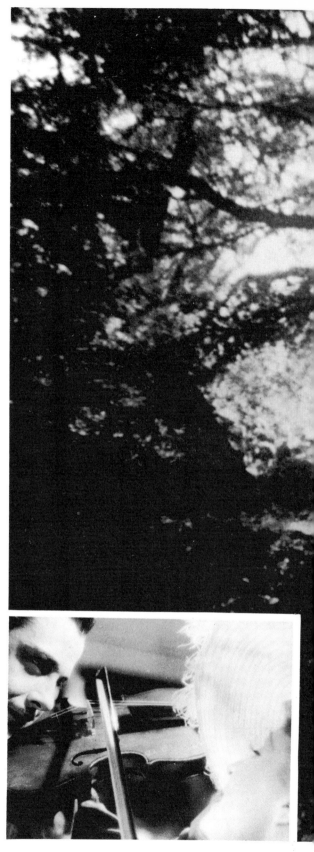

weave together to re-emerge from Strauss's head as the famous waltz, 'Tales from the Vienna Woods'. It is such a delightful scene that it would seem blasphemous to suggest Strauss composed it in any other way. Later, at a small inn, the camera swirls with and around the lovers in their waltz, dives on them from above and through the leafy trees, spins them faster and faster until the world is turned upside down.

Classical composers, unfortunately, weren't especially noted for their looks – one of those miscellaneous impressions that is generally accepted by people not necessarily familiar with their music. Perhaps it is because of the widespread belief that any classical composer dead for more than fifty-six years is *serious*: since dead men aren't much fun they can't have been good looking. Among the sexy exceptions are Cornel Wilde's Chopin in *A Song to Remember*, 1945, and Dirk Bogarde's Liszt in *Song without End*, 1960.

Most of the American music masters, contemporary enough to be alive, and thus collect huge royalties for their output, were glamorous, and therefore were played by *fun* actors, like Cary Grant, Robert Alda and Robert Walker. (MGM had such faith in Robert Walker's dramatic range that they had him play *fun* composer Jerome Kern one year, and the *serious* Brahms the next). Being *fun* people, they got the girl and had other romances that the scriptwriter cared to conjure up. Of course, they still suffered all the creative torments of the serious composers, and like them, still found a woman to be the best inspiration.

According to the Warners musical all-star biography of Cole Porter, *Night and Day* (1946), this master of lyrical wit had spent days and nights restlessly searching for the right words for the title song, when the helpful missus entered his study late at night, worried about the late hours he's keeping and the fact that he's not eating. He's bent over the piano, thinking. Muse Linda stands in dim-lit doorway, (back lighting gives her hair that halo look), and keeps her face and her thoughts in shadow. There's a tray with coffee and cookies in her hand. 'Cole,' she says. Up he looks. Sees her.

'You, you, you ... Do you realize, Linda, you're always there at the most important times.' Inspiration strikes, while she's busying herself unobtrusively. 'Night and Day, you are the one,' he says, and the fingers on the keyboard do the rest. If that's the way it really happened, it shouldn't have. It's awful. But the woman's role in the composer's life was usually reducible to that of a walking, talking thesaurus.

Florenz Ziegfeld was a producer who had so much fun in his real life that his 'reel' life, *The Great*

Ziegfeld (1936), was mild by comparison. It was one thing to be attractive enough to get the girl – maybe even two; however, an unending string of them might give people ideas that weren't commensurate with the lives of the great. Not as long as members of his family were still alive at any rate. His last wife, Miss Billie Burke, helped in the casting and generally advised on the details of her husband's life. Metro coyly admitted in their credits that the film was based more on spirit than fact.

Unfortunately, as a film, The Great Ziegfeld embodied many of the vices and few of the virtues of the musical biography genre. Besides the distorted facts, it was overlong, slow and self-indulgent. Its virtues were the Ziegfelds' good performances (Luise Rainer won an Oscar for making his first wife, Anna Held, a heart-wrencher), the appearance of a legendary name –'Fanny Brice, and, of course, the film's raison d'être, the all-girl production numbers. The only other thing to be said about it is that Ziegfeld's life was the first one to become a subject for an American film. The gargantuan 'A

Show business. From top left: Robert Alda as George Gershwin, with Oscar Levant as his friend Oscar Levant in *Rhapsody in Blue*. Cary Grant as Cole Porter, with Alexis Smith as his Mrs in *Night and Day*. Tom Drake as Richard Rodgers (at the piano), Mickey Rooney as Lorenz Hart and Marshall Thompson in *Words and Music*. Alice Faye as *Lillian Russell*, in the 'After the Ball' sequence. Kathryn Grayson as Grace Moore, with Merv Griffin in *The Grace Moore Story*. James Cagney was George M. Cohan, with Joan Leslie in *Yankee Doodle Dandy*. Luise Rainer as Anna Held and William Powell as Florenz Ziegfeld in *The Great Ziegfeld*.

Pretty Girl Is Like A Melody' number cost an astonishing 220,000 dollars. The tuxedo-clad singer, Stanley Morner, a tenor, was to become a famous 40s musical star at Warners as Dennis Morgan, but his voice was inexplicably dubbed by Allan Jones. The girl on top of the 32-feet-high revolving pyramid was a chorus girl in the long shots, but for close-ups they intercut shots of Virginia Bruce. Maybe they just didn't want to risk her costly neck. The set cost the earth but MGM made their money back by redraping it and trotting it out again and again for Eleanor Powell to dance over, down, around and under it, and when they filmed *Ziegfeld Girl* (1941), Hedy Lamarr, Lana Turner, Judy Garland and almost as many girls, singers and musicians as had been grouped around it the first time, 182 of them, were used to cover it up the second time. These musicals did well because of the stars, and there were more of them in the 30s than at any other time. The essence of the star is a mixture of many ingredients, of which acting talent is only one, and then not really the most important. Personality, magnetism, glamour, a capacity to stir the imagination of the audience, to radiate the impression that there is more than meets the eye and ear – these are what matter.

While star vehicles did not always make for *auteur* musicals, the vast studio resources at their disposal, the money lavished on them, the top production values – costumes, photographers, set designers, songwriters – ensured a sparkle for them all and stand for Hollywood's highest standard of craftsmanship.

Of all the crooners, Bing Crosby's tonsils lasted the longest. Unquestionably, if inexplicably, his was one of the few names that spelt sure-fire success for any musical he starred in during the better part of twenty-five years. In that time he starred in more successful films, recorded more songs, had more hits and sold more records than any singer before or since – including Sinatra, Al Jolson and the Beatles. Harry Lillis Crosby, as he was baptized, had been one of the 'Rhythm Boys' with Paul Whiteman's orchestra and made his film debut as such in *The King of Jazz* (1930). A popular series of musical shorts he made for Mack Sennett's company in 1930 added to his success as a radio vocalist, and had made him a star by the end of 1931, when Paramount toplined him in *The Big Broadcast*, the first of their revue films featuring well-known radio and recording personalities of the day. His unassuming, easy-going, congenial personality clicked with the public. He liked kids, went for the girls, looked more like the fellow that went to the movies than the one that starred in them. His image had family appeal. When he sang, he sounded like most men think they sound singing in the shower. For the next quarter of a century, he starred mostly for Paramount, and neither the changing musical trends nor the occsional slacking of public interest in musicals affected his films.

He could be seen as a riverboat gambler with Joan Bennett, all magnolia and old lace, as his love (*Mississippi*, 1935); as a mate on a luxury yacht, whose screwball heiress-owner (Carole Lombard) had her eye on him (*We're Not Dressing*, 1934, based on James Barrie's The Admirable Crichton); as the pipe-smoking college student, whose peace is interrupted by a chorus girl on the lam (Miriam Hopkins in *She Loves Me Not*, 1934); as a butler, a vagabond, Irish cop, priest and doctor. In Broadway hits (*Anything Goes*, 1936, and again in 1956); in biographical films (*The Birth of the Blues*, 1942, or *Dixie*, celebrating the old minstrel days, 1943); and 'putting on the show' in *Going Hollywood* (1933), with the easy-going underrated comedienne Marion Davies, where he introduced 'Temptation'. And he was always the relaxed singer of songs.

When surrounded by top comic talents (W. C. Fields, George Burns and Gracie Allen, Charles Ruggles, Jack Oakie, Bob Hope, etc.), he proved to be no mean comic himself. His leading ladies were amongst the most glamorous: Ida Lupino, Joan Blondell, Kitty Carlisle, Dorothy Lamour, Jane Wyman, Rhonda Fleming, Grace Kelly and almost every other top female star during his rule at

Bing Crosby and Cab Calloway in *The Big Broadcast of 1932*.

Paramount. The top songwriters composed more hits for him to sing than for anyone else (with the possible exception of Fred Astaire), and Crosby has the distinction of having introduced more of the Oscar-winning songs than anyone else ('Sweet Leilani' in *Waikiki Wedding*, 1937; 'White Christmas' in *Holiday Inn*, 1942; 'Would You Like to Swing on a Star?' in *Going My Way*, 1944; 'In the Cool, Cool, Cool of the Evening' in *Here Comes the Groom*, 1951).

In the early 50s, after twenty years at the top, his career – along with those of most of the older stars – suffered a dip, and Crosby broke his type-casting to play the alcoholic Broadway star in Clifford Odets' acid *The Country Girl* (1954) (for which he was nominated for the Oscar). But the part for which he had previously won the award, the likeable Father O'Malley in *Going My Way* (1944), contained the essence of his screen persona.

Another well-liked singer, John Boles, made his screen début as a Gloria Swanson discovery in the silent *The Love of Sunya* (1927). Having previously been a successful singer on Broadway, he was ideally fitted for the sound operettas that proliferated during the first years of the talkies. His voice was a clear tenor – or baritone, depending on which sound man was twiddling the knobs. (As the hero of *The Desert Song* (1929), *Photoplay* described his voice as a 'delightful baritone', while a few months later, the improved sound technique on *Rio Rita* had made him a tenor.) He was a star and featured leading man throughout the 30s and into the 40s.

Unassuming, reserved and pleasant-looking, John Boles was equally at home playing the father of such dimpled darlings as Shirley Temple and later, Kathryn Grayson, or supporting top dramatic actresses in sudsy dramas. He sang with Alice Faye (*George White's Scandals of 1934*), Bebe Daniels, Evelyn Laye (*One Heavenly Night*), Gladys Swarthout (*Rose of the Rancho*), Lilian Harvey (*My Lips Betray*), Gloria Swanson (*Music in the Air*) and many of the leading sopranos of the period.

For a time, Maurice Chevalier was another of those personalities whose name on any film spelt money. His American film début was in *Innocents of Paris* (1929). This film suffered woefully from the defects of the early sound musicals: weak plot, corny dialogue, twee mannerisms, and a catatonic camera. Nonetheless, Chevalier scored an immense personal success and introduced 'Louise' in it. He

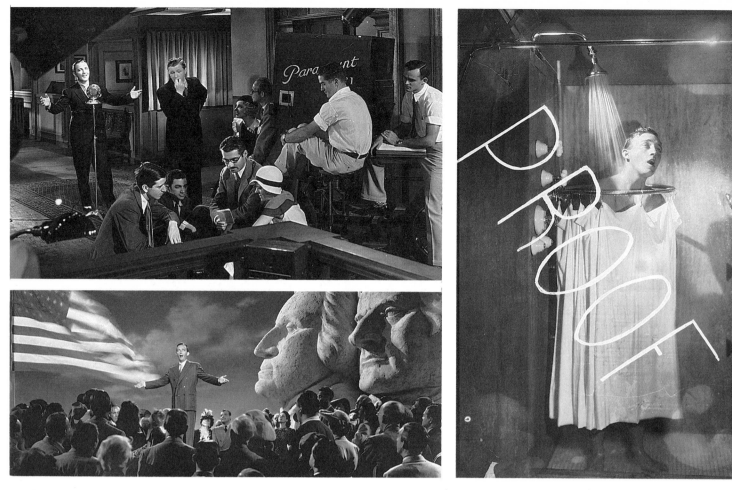

made four films that co-starred him with Jeanette MacDonald. And though he didn't like her and she didn't like him, the public liked them both.

Considering this was the heyday of the clean-cut collegiate boy, personified by crooner Charles 'Buddy' Rogers, Chevalier's impact is understandable. So anaemic was this early college hero that he has no present-day equivalent, unless it is Mickey Mouse. Other able exponents of this type besides Rogers were Charles Farrell, Rudy Vallee (*The Vagabond Lover*), Alexander Gray and Jack Oakie. Later Dick Powell revitalized this character through his own cheeky looks and charm.

Even before Geraldine Farrar's film début in 1915, opera singers had appeared in films. Farrar's great popularity, which her glamorous private life extended far beyond the normal confines of the opera house audiences, served to lend prestige to

Top left: On the set of *Too Much Harmony*. Bing Crosby at the microphone, with Stuart Erwin.

Above: An item from Bing Crosby's scrapbook, 1931.

Centre left: By 1943 Bing Crosby was an American institution, and contributed 'Old Glory' to *Star Spangled Rhythm*. The film was a series of numbers hung on a shred of plot, and provided, so they said, great entertainment for servicemen in World War II.

Operatic singers were sometimes in demand in Hollywood – but never for very long. From top left: Allan Jones in *The Firefly*. Gladys Swarthout in *Rose of the Rancho*. Lily Pons in *That Girl from Paris*. Kirsten Flagstad in *The Big Broadcast of 1938*, as Brünnhilde. Risë Stevens as Carmen: she sang the Habanera in Bing Crosby's *Going my Way*. Leonard Warren in *Irish Eyes are Smiling*. Ilona Massey in *Rosalie*.

Opposite, far left: Grace Moore and Frank Forest in the Love Duet in Act I of *Madame Butterfly* in her last Hollywood film, *I'll Take Romance*. Miss Moore showed that opera stars were just plain folk.

Left: The Sternberg presentation. Grace Moore in *The King Steps Out*, which had music by Fritz Kreisler.

Right: Grace Moore scored a stuning popular success in Victor Schertzinger's *One Night of Love* after three years' absence from the screen. She was nominated for an Oscar, and with one of the year's biggest box-office hits was responsible for launching an operatic invasion of films.

the new medium. She starred in more than a dozen films between 1916 and 1922, when she voluntarily left the screen. Her example and success brought Caruso, Mary Garden and the famed beauty, Lina Cavalieri, to the screen. But, like Lawrence Tibbett's in 1930, and Grace Moore's in 1934, Geraldine Farrar's triumph was a personal one and none who followed did as well.

Lawrence Tibbett's film début in *The Rogue Song* (1930) was a sensational success but it was shortlived. One year and three films later he was back at the Met, though a huge draw for having starred in films. In the initial response to the Tibbett hit, other opera stars were quickly signed up. Everett Marshall came out to play opposite Bebe Daniels in *Dixiana* (1930); the Irishman John McCormack made *Song O' My Heart* (1930, directed by Frank Borzage); Dennis King was *The Vagabond King*, and appeared in *Paramount on Parade*, as did Nino Martini; at Warners Alexander Gray was an early Nelson Eddy to Bernice Claire's MacDonald.

None of the men, and with the rare exception cited, few of the ladies of the high C's ever established themselves as successful screen personalities. Their faces were different, but they all sang the same song in pretty much the same story in which the little singer made good. Whether it was Lily Pons in *I Dream Too Much* (1935), Gladys Swarthout in *Romance in the Dark* (1938) or Risë Stevens in *Going My Way* (1945), they ended up on the stage of the Met pouring their song out to the thundering applause of extras. The unsuspecting layman might have wondered how the Met had time to give them all those débuts, one after the other. (Mamoulian satirized this vogue for opera stars in *The Gay Desperado* by turning the leading man, Nino Martini, into a hilarious ineffectual as soon as he stops singing.)

One of the few original operas in film was the little-known *Give us this Night* (1936), co-starring the glamorous American, Gladys Swarthout, with the wildly energetic Polish tenor, Jan Kiepura. The

Jeanette MacDonald, Hollywood's prima donna assoluta, enjoyed a film career that spanned twenty years.

principals' goal was, as usual, to get themselves on stage but the score was specially written for the film by Erich Wolfgang Korngold (who had won fame in Germany as the composer of the opera *Die tote Stadt* and later established himself in Hollywood with his symphonic scores for films like *King's Row, The Adventures of Robin Hood, Captain Blood,* etc.), and it was unpretentiously directed by Alexander Hall. What these films did accomplish was to revive a slackening interest in opera. Film stardom had given the singers glamour and wider exposure which brought an increase in opera audiences during the 30s. In Europe, where the operatic tradition was established and respected, this type of film was more popular, and golden-throated tenors had screen careers commensurate with their concert stage and operatic careers. Americans preferred their 'classical' music to come from the throats of stars they had seen develop on the screen.

Until the advent of Mario Lanza, no opera star enjoyed the affection given to MacDonald and Eddy.

Their first team-effort, *Naughty Marietta* (1935), made in the wake of the Grace Moore success, was not an expensive film, and the director, Woody 'One-Take' Van Dyke, was famed for finishing a film in the shortest time possible for the least amount. In this case he made the best of all that was offered to him, and surprised everybody by creating one of the year's biggest moneymakers. Its follow-up, *Rose Marie* (1936), re-teaming MacDonald-Eddy and Van Dyke, fared even better.

MGM, who knew a star team when they had one (Gilbert and Garbo, Loy and Powell, Gable and Crawford were also theirs), realized they had struck gold. The foremost technicians in the company were put to work on the MacDonald-Eddy films. Adrian dressed her, Guilaroff did her hair, great cameramen photographed them, and Cedric Gibbons did their sets. More and more of the scripts, however, sadly lacked opportunities for Jeanette to display her light touch, and the delicious sense of comedy she had shown early in her career when Lubitsch could say that 'In sophisticated comedy today, she has few equals. Underneath that red-gold hair is a very level head and a sense of humour not often found in beautiful women.'

'Charm', according to James Barrie, 'is the greatest gift in the world. If you have it, you don't need to have anything else; if you don't have it, it doesn't matter what else you have.' Jeanette MacDonald's chin may have been a bit too large for her face (though they corrected that by giving her a larger mouth), her shoulders too broad (but clothes dealt with that, and Nelson Eddy's were broader), her singing prone to too many tremolos, but she had enormous charm. This, plus large deep-green eyes, an abundance of red-gold hair, and a totally bewitching smile, made her one of the great musical stars of the decade. Their films were divided between directors Van Dyke (*Sweethearts*, 1938. *Bitter Sweet*, 1940, *I Married an Angel*, 1942) and Robert Z. Leonard (*Maytime*, 1937, *The Girl of the Golden West*, 1938, *New Moon*, 1940).

Maytime is the finest example of the MacDonald-Eddy team and of the studio teamwork. Originally

Below: MacDonald and Eddy in a production still for *Naughty Marietta*, the box-office hit that gave the romantic operetta musical a new lease of life. The director is W. S. Van Dyke.

Below right: The second MacDonald-Eddy film, *Rose Marie*, surpassed the success of the first.

MacDonald and Eddy in *Maytime*, one of the biggest money-makers of 1937. Allan Jones was the original choice as leading man but the public demanded the original team. Off the set, the stars post-synching songs from the film.

planned to co-star Allan Jones, the receipts on the MacDonald-Eddy films prompted the replacement of Jones and the scrapping of the expensive footage already shot. All the resources of the world's most powerful film studio were lavished on it. The 'Empress Eugenie' dresses, designed by Adrian, almost move themselves; Frederic Hope and Edwin B. Willis' reconstruction of some of the better homes and gardens of the last days of the Second Empire, chandeliered ballrooms, *intime* apartments, Parisian bohemian quarters, and the American small town at the turn of the century, are superb. And the story, based on the Sigmund Romberg operetta, or at least its title, gave MacDonald a part with greater range and depth than most of those she played at MGM.

She turns effortlessly from throw-away laughter to heartbreak with no need of wringing hands or gulping sobs. In her dramatic scenes, she had both the technique and the acting ability to compete with the hypnotic authority of the ageing John Barry-

more, who is superb as her psychotically jealous, brilliant Svengali-like mentor. But even when glossed up as a great movie star, she still exhibits a self-mocking fundamental honesty and integrity that is part of her charm.

Only one of the Romberg songs was retained in the film: 'Sweetheart' was the theme that bound the ardent lovers even in death. The film also contained cleverly interpolated operatic excerpts directed by William von Wymetal, far more engagingly introduced than was often the case.

Despite the enormous popularity of the team and of Jeanette's films without Eddy in the period between 1935 and 1942 (*The Firefly*, *San Francisco*) one regrets that Metro never gave her one of those wonderful screwball comedies that added new life to the career of soprano Irene Dunne. MacDonald might now be treasured as the delectable comedienne she had shown herself to be, and not simply for the 'camp' elements of her operettas.

Dear Jeanette – who, except a smart-ass sophisticate would begrudge or belittle her appeal to an enormous segment of the movie-going public? Yet this has been the fashionable attitude ever since she

Above: Jeanette in *San Francisco*, singing for Clark Gable. Also present, Ted Healy. An adroit comedienne and a favourite with Ernst Lubitsch, Jeanette MacDonald was no mean dramatic actress and could hold her own with the likes of Barrymore and Tracy.

Left: The 'Pretty as a Picture' number in *Sweethearts*.

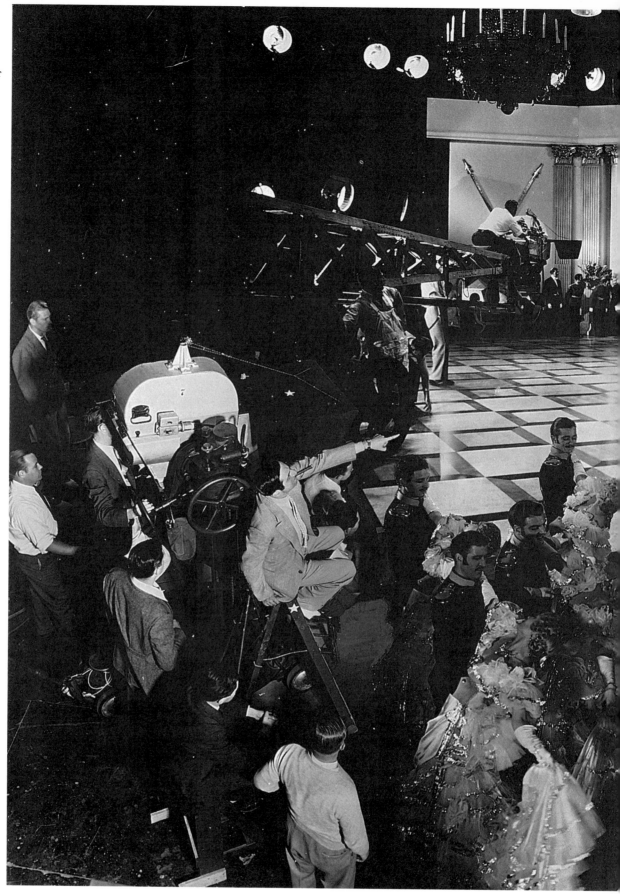

disappeared from the screen. What else is the success of Julie Andrews as Maria in *The Sound of Music*, but that of Jeanette MacDonald in *Maytime*? MacDonald's popularity wasn't a tribute to a great voice; she was no Grace Moore, Swarthout, Pons or Farrar. She embodied not the established favourite of the Met, but the girls singing in the church choirs who the young men would make their wives; the girl

proud parents in almost any town heard in their daughter who was pretty, popular and usually sang the lead in the local operetta productions; the mother children loved. The people loved these shows, and there were millions who came to an appreciation of great singing just this way.

Her singing was the excuse to relaunch a cycle of films that put Metro on the musical map in the 30s

and whose success more than anything else paved the way for the studio's full-scale entry into the musical field of the 40s. MacDonald Metro vehicles were long passé on Broadway and in Hollywood when she appeared to revitalize them on film; but though no longer deemed fashionable, Friml, Herbert and Romberg were staples of Orpheus Societies across the country, providing situations for attractive heroes and heroines, old-fashioned sentiments and gloriously lifting melodies – 'Ah, Sweet Mystery of Life' – that made them the *Oklahomas*, *The King and Is* and *Little Night Musics* of their day.

But if this were all, anyone else with a pretty voice and sweet face might have fared as well. Yet Gladys Swarthout, Lily Pons, Ilona Massey and Risë

Stevens could not strike the public chord. Only Jeanette did that. Though cloaked in gossamer and extravagantly lit to highlight her beauty, Jeanette was no prude. She really did sparkle, and she had bite. No less than Lubitsch chose her for four of his films. He dreamt of filming Richard Strauss's opera, *Der Rosenkavalier* with MacDonald as his Marschallin. Sadly, the project, delayed by trying to find the right actor to play Octavian, collapsed entirely when Lubitsch turned away because Strauss would not disassociate himself from the Nazi regime in Germany. Had that project been realized, it would have been MacDonald's finest hour. Another lost opportunity, all the sadder because there was no good reason for it, was Minnelli and Freed's failure to bring her back as the aunt or grandmother in *Gigi*. The emotional lift to be gained from re-teaming her with Chevalier in the musical's most memorable duet, sitting together on the verandah overlooking their past for 'I Remember it Well' would have been inspired.

Alas, nothing can be done about lost opportunities, except in that land of memory where MacDonald and Eddy so often wandered. But fashions changes are cruel and fast. Garland's ascent as a star in *The Wizard of Oz* marked the end of the era Jeanette had personified as definitely as the great Garbo's arrival had finished off the established stars before her. The underlying sensation of a contemporary emotional vulnerability in Garland's personality and in her voice was a breakthrough that marked a new era in musicals. To consolidate it, it became necessary to obliterate what had gone before, and the means used, as always, was ridicule. Nobody wanted to appear old-fashioned and everybody followed suit. MacDonald's appeal to her time was forgotten. Her

Irene Dunne singing 'You couldn't be cuter', written for her by Jerome Kern for *Joy of Living*.

vehicles were dismissed as upper-class fantasies for the lower classes and her style was relegated to the era her movies were set in instead of the time to which she appealed. When Garland, with the casual cruelty of one era's favourite about that of another, prefaced her version of MacDonald's *San Francisco* with a jokey verse about 'How that dear

Director William A. Seiter (at the camera, wearing a hat) preparing for Irene Dunne's 'Lovely to Look At' number in *Roberta*.

154

Work proceeds on the second film version of Jerome Kern's classic, *Show Boat*. Irene Dunne as Magnolia, on board, and director James Whale on the jetty, pointing.

Jeanette just stood there in the ruins and sang. And sa-a-a-a-a-ang', tossing the last off with a mock set of wobbly coloratura trills, audiences laughed uproariously at the artificiality implied on Mac-Donald's part. Fans who thought nothing of crying hysterically along with Judy Garland's emotional outpourings, commiserating with her modern angst, found nothing strange in laughing at the old-world sentiments that had made an earlier generation cry. After the first chorus the stage was set to laugh at Jeanette. This attitude became the standard approach, surviving even after the shifts of fashion that had caused it to matter had passed.

Dear Jeanette, she was nice while she lasted, and she deserved better than she got. So here's a toast to Lubitsch's Merry Widow. He knew what he was doing.

Jeanette's only real rival, once Moore had returned to the stage, as the Prima Donna Assoluta of films, was Irene Dunne. There were some slight similarities between the two ladies. Both came from the school of musical comedy and operetta (as had Grace Moore). Irene was the Magnolia of Ziegfeld's first touring production of *Show Boat*, where she was spotted by RKO's production chief, William LeBaron (who had previously re-launched Bebe Daniels' career in *Rio Rita*), and brought to Hollywood. She played opposite Richard Dix in another Edna Ferber (but non-musical) saga, *Cimarron*, and achieved immediate stardom. Jeanette had been starring on Broadway, where Richard Dix saw her

and suggested her to Paramount for a test as his leading lady, which she didn't play. However, Ernst Lubitsch saw the test when he was growing desperate trying to find a leading lady for his *The Love Parade* (he was about to sign Bebe Daniels) and the rest was wonderful. Both Irene and Jeanette were approximately the same age, both were good in comedy, and had a similar statuesque beauty, but there their similarities cease. Jeanette's triumphs lay in operetta, the worlds of Victor Herbert, Sigmund Romberg and Rudolf Friml (four of whose shows were the basis of her films – *The Vagabond King*, *The Lottery Bride*, *Rose Marie* and *The Firefly*), while Irene Dunne's appeal was quintessential Americana. Her music was the work of the master of American musicals, Jerome Kern, whose scores for *Show Boat* (1936), *High, Wide and Handsome* (1937), *Roberta* (1935), *Sweet Adeline* (1935) and *Joy of Living* (1938), marked the transition from operetta to musical comedy, for the old world to the new. Like Fred Astaire, like Vincente Minnelli, like so many of the greatest interpreters in the business, Dunne is not merely modest to the point of self-effacement, but difficult to get to talk about the why's and wherefore's of her work. It became a worthwhile challenge to try and persuade her do so: 'I wasn't mad about *Joy of Living*. Jerome Kern wrote a song for me called, "You Couldn't Be Cuter". But the thing I'm proudest of was the song he wrote for me for *Roberta*, "Lovely To Look At".

'To show you how the mind can play tricks, I got

so nervous over the song because I knew I'd have to be lovely to look at walking down that staircase, singing the song, that I got no sleep the night before and when I went in the next morning, the cameraman (Edward Cronjager) told the director (William Seiter), 'I'm not going to shoot her today. That's all there is to it. She'll have to go home to sleep'. We waited for a day or two, I rested up and then we shot it. I think that song has been used in more fashion shows than any other song ever written. You often wonder why a film misses or is a smash. I think *Roberta* turned out most how I envisaged it. I saw it a few weeks ago, and though the soundtrack had deteriorated, and though the story is really inane and silly (I didn't realize it at the time), the *entertainment* value is good. Astaire danced so beautifully with Rogers, the clothes' (Bernard Newman) 'were magnificent – it was an evening of entertainment and what more could you ask?

'Most of my numbers were dubbed, and I pride myself on that. First you record the number, then you shoot the scene and sing along to the recording. It's remarkable how you can do it. You can't really do it on the set because the sound engineers aren't really happy with the result.

'Of course, when I was studying at Chicago Musical College, I wanted to be in opera. Then when I got to New York and go to know some opera stars, I realized I didn't have quite the equipment to withstand all the rigours. But I did work quite a bit in opera. Both *Stingaree* and *The Great Lover* have operatic sequences. There was a very pretty song in *Stingaree*, I remember – but the song I'm known for – if I walk into some place where they know me, they play, "Smoke Gets In Your Eyes".

'I had nothing to do with the fact that all of my major film musicals had Kern scores. But there were not too many important musicals for singers – like *Show Boat*, *Roberta*, or *Sweet Adeline* – around at the time. And they all happened to be Kern. It was a sort of sequence of normal events after I'd taken over the lead at the end of *Showboat*, when it went on the road. But I played those roles the way I played all my parts. I studied a character very hard. If they gave me dialogue on the set I'd always ask to be excused for five or ten minutes so's I could find out why I was saying what I had to say, what relation it had to the character, what she was thinking while she said it. As a result the performance looks natural and easy and nobody realizes the amount of effort you've put in. Of course theyre not meant to. But it can be a disadvantage and that's why I was so pleased at the Academy Award nominations. You see, I was never flamboyant in a part, or eccentric, and that's the sort of performance that tends to catch the eye. Not that I'd stay awake nights worrying about it: I was always happy just to get nominated.' (She was nominated five times). 'But I was running against actresses like Bette Davis who, as you know, was all over the lot in those days – and tremendous I thought. But boy, you knew she was an actress! 'I'm still offered parts, but I think you tear yourself apart like that. Lerner and Loewe asked me to do something on the stage, and Rodgers and Hammerstein wanted me for *The King and I*, and I wish I had done that, but it would have meant

going back on the stage, but I'm afraid I'm not that much of a gambler, and I liked the things I was doing.

'But to get back to Kern. When I took over Magnolia in *Show Boat*, there was only one *Show Boat* company then. People don't realize that because since then there have been so many road companies. We were the only company and we had over one hundred Negroes in the cast, so it was a difficult company to travel with. We went to Chicago, Boston, and played one other place that's all. I still have the telegram Ziegfeld sent me after I took over the lead. You know he'd never come backstage and see you, but instead he'd send reams of telegrams. He said he couldn't remember when he'd had a more enjoyable evening at the theatre.

'James Whale wasn't the right director for the film. I really shouldn't say that, but to me the picture didn't come off as well as the stage play. There were a lot of interpolations that we didn't need at all, and I think the ending was stupid.' (For the 1936

Paul Robeson as Joe in *Show Boat*. Robeson's rendering of Jerome Kern's 'Ole Man River' was unforgettable.

Right: On the set of *It Started with Eve*. Next to the star is the producer, Joe Pasternak. Director Henry Koster is lower right; at the camera Rudolph Mate, director of photography. Pasternak and Koster were producer and director of *Three Smart Girls*, Deanna Durbin's first starring vehicle. It made all three of them famous.

Another classic performance from *Show Boat*. Helen Morgan, who created the part on Broadway, as Julie.

Deanna Durbin in *Three Smart Girls*.

Below: Deanna Durbin, the fifteen-year-old girl whose spirited charm and sweet singing voice saved a studio from bankruptcy.

version, the film decided on a much older Magnolia being re-united with a much older Ravenal, when she discovers him working as a backstage doorman at the theatre where their daughter is opening as the star of a new show.) 'He was more interested in atmosphere and lighting and he knew so little about that life. I could have put my foot down about it but there would have been no reason to do so because we had so many of the original people who'd done it on the stage' (Allan Jones, Paul Robeson and Dunne had been in touring productions; Charles Winninger, Sammy White and Helen Morgan had been in the original Broadway cast) 'that you could only expect the best. I knew the whole thing backwards. No. You see I should have put my foot down at the contract stage, but once the camera started turning I was an angel on the set. For me the stage production was one of the best things I was ever associated with. The score was marvellous, but even the book could have stood up on its own.'

The Jerome Kern-Edna Ferber classic of the Mississippi river boat days had already been filmed by Universal, with Laura La Plante as Magnolia. It would be one of Arthur Freed's productions for MGM in 1951, when the studio's singing sweethearts Kathryn Grayson and Howard Keel played Magnolia and Ravenal (Grayson also re-created another Dunne role in the re-make of *Roberta*, entitled *Lovely to Look At*, in 1952), and the broodingly beautiful Ava Gardner was the doomed Julie. Unlike the first version, the Dunne film had most of the original songs back, and included a new gem out of Kern's songchest – 'Ah Still Suits Me' as a duet between Paul Robeson and Hattie McDaniel. She accuses him of being a shiftless good for nothing; he's happy as he is. The song is light, but oh! that Hattie. The things she does just looking up and shaking that head while shelling those peas. Robeson's finest moment was 'Old Man River', a song that's the story of a generation, his powerful voice, rolling along, his spirit not containable by chains, behind him the heavy brooding skies, and silhouetted low against them were the bent, heavy-laden black men, carrying the load.

A different talent, but as great, was Helen Morgan's, whose inimitable rendition of 'Can't Help Lovin' That Man' in that shaky, wispy, will-she-make-it won't-she little voice is as effective. She and Robeson were the stuff of which legends are made. Irene Dunne was 35, playing a girl who for most of the story is just out of her teens. One never notices it, one never questions it – another contribution of magic to a film, which for those not associated with special memories such as hers, is so towering that not even the inane ending can spoil it. It just flows, like the river on whose banks and shores the characters live and grow.

The logical successor to the mantles of MacDonald and Dunne, in spite of the age difference, appeared to be Deanna Durbin, a teenager whose sweet, bell-like tones, pretty face, unspoilt personality and eye for fun made her a sensation after the release of *Three Smart Girls* (1937), a small musical Universal turned out after their lavish expenditure the year before. Overnight Durbin was the patron saint of the Universal lot, then reduced to the status of being a B company, with the occasional 'biggie' between their famous gallery of inexpensive Monster films. MGM had an impressive army of musical champions; Paramount had Mae West and Bing and Dottie; 20th Fox had the Blondes; Warner had Dick and Ruby and Busby, and now, with one fell swoop, Universal was in the top league with this brunette soprano. And they only got her by accident at that.

From her feature film début in 1937 until well into the mid-40s, any film she made was a guaranteed success. The first ten were produced by her mentor, Joseph Pasternak, and six of these were directed by Henry Koster. A European director of charm and taste, he made these six of her best films. Besides the first, there was the enduring *100 Men and a Girl* (1937), *Three Smart Girls Grow Up* (1939), *First Love* (1939), *Spring Parade* (1940), and *It Started with Eve* (1941).

Her career began in 1936 when Pasternak was shown a short film that Deanna Durbin and Judy Garland had made for MGM, *Every Sunday*. He decided Garland was the girl he wanted for the impish daughter in *Three Smart Girls*. Told that she was under contract to Metro, but that Durbin had just been signed by Universal, he cast the latter. As

A production still from *100 Men and a Girl*. Maestro Leopold Stokowski prepares to conduct an orchestra of out-of-work musicians (unseen). Deanna Durbin on the conductor's left.

work on the film progressed and it became apparent that there was a special talent in this stunning lyric soprano, her part was built up until she dominated the story. At this time, she was also appearing regularly on the Eddie Cantor show and fast becoming an enormous radio favourite aged only fifteen.

100 Men and a Girl (1937) was an even greater hit than *Three Smart Girls*. It co-starred her with the celebrated conductor, Leopold Stokowski. The combination of a cheerful, golden-voiced youngster, classical music and musical masters, popular standards and original songs, became known as the 'Pasternak special'. He was later to re-use the formula with Kathryn Grayson and Jane Powell, when he had his own unit at MGM in the forties.

Later, when she was old enough to be kissed, in *First Love* (1939), the public stayed faithful to her, which doesn't always happen. What Shirley Temple did for child actors, Deanna Durbin did for teenagers: her success automatically prompted studios to develop other young talents, the most successful of which was Durbin's former co-star, Judy Garland. MGM, awakening to the realization that they had lost one gold mine, set about devoting their studio's resources to building the other, and found that in Garland they had a unique legend all their own.

Deanna Durbin passed through her unkissable years, having to content herself with plots based on the Cinderella formula or as Little Miss Fix-It. The variations of themes for young stars that would retain the family trade were difficult to come by, but Deanna's youthful appeal and talent always proved sufficient. The public went to see her, and her presence assured the success of the film. This was the age of child-stars, little bundles of hope and

The happy ending of *100 Men and a Girl*. The great conductor and the musicians at Carnegie Hall – with the heroine who made it all happen.

cheer to lead the nation from its depression. Besides Temple, Durbin and Garland, there was another Eddie Cantor protégé, this one a sugary male child, Bobby Breen. Then there was spunky little Jane Withers who, when she wasn't making Shirley Temple's movie life hell, was the bright relief of Fox's more enjoyable B films. The multi-talented Mickey Rooney as Andy Hardy, Freddie 'Little Lord Fauntleroy' Bartholomew and the sceptical

Opposite, top left: Deanna Durbin nearly up to her waist in mud for *Can't Help Singing*. The songs were by Jerome Kern. Right: With her leading man, Robert Paige.

Centre: Dorothy (Judy Garland) and The Scarecrow (Ray Bolger) on the Yellow Brick Road in *The Wizard of Oz*. They are observed by The Witch (Margaret Hamilton).

Bottom: Tomorrow's stars in the MGM canteen in 1936. Left to right: Freddie Bartholomew, Virginia Weidler, Mickey Rooney, Deanna Durbin, Judy Garland and Jackie Cooper. The remarkable success of Durbin, Garland and Rooney shifted the emphasis: child stars gave way to teen-agers.

Virginia Weidler were all favourite child-stars. There were others, mostly justifying W. C. Fields' caustic philosophy: 'Any man who hates children and animals can't be *all* bad!' His own running feud

with the children in his films (Baby LeRoy, Gloria Jean and Jane Powell) is well known.

Durbin's versions of operatic arias swelled record sales; her fan club became the world's biggest, but she left Universal in 1949, saying 'I'm tired of playing little girls. I'm a woman now, I can't run around forever being the little Miss Fix-It who bursts into song. I want to get out of Hollywood and get a fresh approach.' She retired at the top.

Walter Plunkett designed the clothes for her only colour film, the *Oklahoma*-inspired *Can't Help Singing* (1944), which had another exhilarating Jerome Kern score. Plunkett, who was very fond of her, remembers: 'The entire Universal lot treated Deanna like an empress and anything she wanted was given her. She was about twenty-three then. Her dressing room on location (southern Utah) was a beautiful bungalow, almost a house, it was so large! I was told that Deanna would have the final word on everything concerning her and the film, which, of course, revolved around her. The first time I met her was to show her the sketches for her clothes. In the bungalow with us were the production manager, cameraman, director, set designer – the lot. She looked at the sketches and said, 'That's a lovely dress, I like that!' Then the production manager held the sketch up for the others to see and

Above: Donald O'Connor at the age of twelve in *Sing, You Sinners* (1938). The stars were Bing Crosby and Fred MacMurray. More durable than many child stars, O'Connor was a versatile dancer and, like Mickey Rooney, continues his film and stage career to the present.

Left: Judy Garland in 1937, a study by Laszlo Willinger.

Opposite, left: Child star to teenager. Jane Withers in *Pack up Your Troubles.*

Right: Children with singing voices were in demand after the success of *Three Smart Girls.* Gloria Jean in *The Underpup,* with C. Aubrey Smith.

said, 'Miss Durbin likes this sketch. If anybody has anything to say, now's the time.' Of course, they all said that they too thought it was great, and initialled it. Then the cameraman knew what lights were needed, and the set designer built his sets around the dresses she was wearing.

'A lot of the film was shot on location in June/July, and during one very hot period, we used to arrive on the location in the morning and find it covered by fog. Sitting around waiting for it to clear, Deanna asked us into her dressing room, where she had cartons of champagne and baskets of food. Later when the fog was lifted, her dress was too tight from all the food and champagne, so she said, "Let's go home for a rest, we can shoot it tomorrow." So the shooting was called off for the day, and there was this beautiful sunshine. Well, the next day, the same thing happened. We arrived and there would be this heavy fog, so into her dressing room we went for champagne and food, and by the time it had cleared

for shooting to begin, her dress was bulging again, and we went home for a rest. This went on for quite some time; and I don't know how we ever finished, but we did.

'The others – Fred and Ginger – they used to work their arses off rehearsing. Poor Debbie Reynolds used to be a puddle of sweat at the end of the day and say, "Do I have to go for a costume fitting now?" But she would come and then go back to rehearse. Donald O'Connor, Gene Kelly, Judy – they used to work for hours. Deanna just opened her pretty mouth and out would pour this lovely voice. She learnt her songs and just sang!

'When we got to the end, because the film was over-shooting, they wanted to cut a sequence. She had two left to shoot and I had designed an elaborate ball gown for each. They didn't know which sequence to cut, and anyway, they had to have her approval. So they hit on the idea of asking her which dress she preferred, and that was going

Right, centre: Bobby
Breen, another child with
a voice. Eight years old, in
Let's Sing Again, with
Henry Armetta.

to decide the sequence they would shoot. But
Deanna couldn't make up her mind; she liked them
both. So for the big musical finale with chorus and
all the trimmings, she wore both; first one, then for
the next verse the other. Nobody noticed, I don't
think, and anyway, that sort of thing is OK in a
musical!'

To the many types of stars connected with the
musicals the Wild West added another – the singing
cowboy. First there was Gene Autry and soon after,
Roy Rogers; both sang duets with their talented
horses, Champion or Trigger, or with the Sons of the
Pioneers. Roy Rogers ranged a bit farther afield
when songstress Dale Evans joined his corral. Song
favourites such as 'Tumbling Tumbleweeds', 'Ghost

Singing cowboys. Left:
Bob Baker on *Honour of
the West*. Right: Gene
Autry in *Carolina Moon*.
Centre: Roy Rogers in
Man from Oklahoma.

161

Riders in the Sky', Cole Porter's 'Don't Fence Me In' and many others first came from them.

Had she been born in Europe, Mae West would have inspired a Renoir or a Toulouse-Lautrec. Playwrights and poets would have vied for the privilege of supplying her with scripts. Fortunately, this exceptional woman wrote her own plays and few could have known better how to use her gifts as a performer. She was the good-natured and abundant sexual-symbol of the Depression generation, a buxom Joan of Arc leading the fight to waive the old conception of sex as a state of sin.

Significantly, most of Mae West's films of 1933–38 were set in the Gay Nineties: *Diamond Lil* (*She Done Him Wrong*), *It Ain't No Sin* (changed to *Belle of the Nineties*), *I'm No Angel* (1933), *Goin' to Town* (1935), *Every Day's a Holiday* (1938). She was born in Brooklyn when it was still part of the nineteenth century, which was to be the timesetting of much of her work. It isn't difficult to get her actual birth date, but neither is it important. Mae West was ageless.

She was well into her 40s when she arrived in Hollywood in the summer of 1932, already a legend on Broadway. On her arrival she informed the press, 'I'm not a little girl from a little town makin' good in a big town. I'm a big girl from a big town makin' good in a little town.' She rewrote the dialogue for what was a guest bit in *Night after Night*, and as far as the film's star, George Raft, was concerned, 'she stole everything but the cameras'. It was for this film that she wrote the line that became the title of her biography, when in response to a hat-check girl's open-mouthed look at her jewellery, 'Goodness, where did you get those beautiful diamonds?' Mae drawled, 'Goodness had nothing to do with it, dearie.'

In all her nine subsequent starring films, lively

Left: Mae West on Broadway. She became an entertainer at the age of five.

Below: After one film appearance – in *Night after Night* – Mae West was a star of movies as well as of the stage. 'I Wonder Where My Easy Rider's Gone' in *She Done Him Wrong*.

Right: Mae West in *I'm No Angel*, her third film. 'They call me Sister Honky-Tonk'.

The original title of *Belle of the Nineties*, Mae West's fourth film, was *It Ain't No Sin*. Here is Mae recalling 'My Old Flame' (below) and in 'The American Beauty Rose' number, above right.

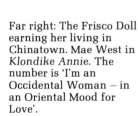

Far right: The Frisco Doll earning her living in Chinatown. Mae West in *Klondike Annie*. The number is 'I'm an Occidental Woman — in an Oriental Mood for Love'.

songs were an integral part of her image. *Variety*, writing of her numbers for *She Done him Wrong* (1933), a slightly modulated version of her rollicking stage success, *Diamond Lil*, said: 'Miss West . . . sings "Easy Rider", "A Guy What Takes His Time" and her own version of "Frankie and Johnny". All were somewhat cleaned up lyrically (from the stage versions) but Mae couldn't sing a lullaby without making it sexy.

In a niche of its own is Mae's essay into Grand Opera – a tongue-in-cheek nod to the box-office appeal of popular opera – *Goin' to Town* (1935), for which she sang an aria from *Samson and Delilah*

Left: *Every Day's a Holiday*. Right: *The Heat's On*.

Below, right: Mae West, still pink and ample, with the author. Los Angeles, 1972.

while suggestively fingering the tresses of her victim. The songs for her films were among the few things she didn't write herself; songwriters like Gene Austin and Sam Coslow wrote them for her. 'I was so busy writing the stories, the scripts – doing two people's work, writing them and half-directing them – I never had *time* on my hands. I got paid $400,000 a film then, while Gable got something like $75,000. I worked for it. But when Austin wrote me a song, like "Occidental Woman"' (for *Klondike Annie*, 1936) 'for instance, I always saw him beforehand to tell him the sort of song I needed for the film and the scene.'

The late Ann Sheridan recalled Mae West's manner of casting: 'rolling casually past rows of us Paramount starlets – on the arm of her manager, shrewdly looking us over – telling the prettiest to step back – these were either used for background in which you couldn't see them or not used at all. Not because she was jealous – nothing like that – she was a dear, but she knew what sold her films was herself and she didn't want to do anything that would make her look silly. She was one of the shrewdest women I've ever met and I wish I had learnt from her.'

Mae West died in 1980. When I met her in her Hollywood apartment she was in her seventies, and she was still pink and ample, with a fine layer of soft lines formed around her face and making spider tracks around her bright red lips. The humour remained. She wore an off-white, full-length silk

dressing-gown, and on her face and arms only a soft semi-transparent make-up; there was no great attempt to hide anything from anyone. Her skin was healthy, her eyes sharp and a very clear blue – with long, sweeping scimitar lashes and eyebrows carving their niche in her forehead, otherwise unlined. The hair was very blonde, rising high from her forehead and falling low below her shoulders. She sat, this Wagnerian of sex, still wise, still recording songs, still working, contributing to the continuing legend of her life, enjoying it and herself.

Mae recalled an actors' benefit one unspecified Sunday afternoon in New York, which featured the legendary French tragedienne, Sarah Bernhardt. Trying to put a date on it I asked if this was before or after Bernhardt had had her leg amputated and replaced it with a wooden one. "Oh yeah," said Mae, after she'd thought about it, 'that's right, dear, must have been after 'cause she was dragging things a bit. Of course she was an old lady. She just stood there a lot.' And what, I asked, had Bernhardt done. 'I don't know, dear, it wasn't English you know. But she was good.' And then Mae West, the most imitated woman in the world, lifted her arms in front of her, striking the declamatory pose of French actors, and went into an imitation of Sarah Bernhardt with a stately voice full of large rolled 'r's,' as it must have been on that stage in New York, sixty years earlier. After that I didn't question anything she told me about herself.

Of her singing style Mae said, 'I did the operatic bit just to show that I can sing, but I preferred to half-speak most of my songs, it gave them a more suggestive effect. I started out singing blues in vaudeville when I was a kid on the Bowery. First it was ragtime, then it was jazz, and later it was boogie-woogie – it was the black man's sound and we copied it because it was the greatest. They'd been developing it for years. But they had it. The same with sex-symbols. You need the roles to develop the image. Now all they do is to borrow some of my old tricks. But it's all wrong. If you have sex you don't have to be conscious of it, and that's what borrowing other people's tricks amounts to. If you don't have it, well, any cow can act it, but it shows through.'

When Mae West was still alive, it was said that a startling disclosure would be made at her death. This was widely gossiped to be nothing less than that Mae West had really been a man. Of course except for her great age there was no startling disclosure, and she certainly was *not* a man. For while any man in drag can, and usually does do a Mae West impersonation, for a woman to create such a liberated, androgynous creation, needing and wanting no one except her own totally self-absorbed self, that was and remains a truly remarkable triumph, on a par with Dietrich's, Garbo's and Monroe's. These women were not narcissists, but the real personifications of the Platonic ideal.

Of course musicals are based so much on fantasy and make-believe it is not surprising that dressing-up plays such a large part in them, whether used to heighten the sensation of glamour or of mystery, though nobody (except possibly Sternberg) would have thought of Plato as their springboard. As such, a sexual reversal, women in men's clothing, plays a subtle but telling part. Besides such obvious examples as the three versions of *Viktor und Viktoria*, there are countless numbers deploying this device – in *Broadway Through a Keyhole* (Constance Cummings), *Blonde Venus* (Marlene Dietrich), Eleanor Powell in most of her musicals at some stage or another, *Shipyard Sally* (Gracie Fields), *Irish Eyes are Smiling* (June Haver), *Two Girls and a Sailor* (June Allyson), *She Loves Me Not* (Miriam Hopkins), *Kiki* (Mary Pickford), *Down Argentine Way* (Betty Grable), *Nob Hill* (Vivian Blaine) – it is a long list. What one notices, taking Dietrich as the classic example in her musical numbers in Sternberg films and in Tay Garnett's *Seven Sinners*, is that a woman in drag hints at her secret strength and her potential independence from men, whereas a man in drag tends to reveal his

weakness; which is probably why a woman in a top hat and a man's tie can be both erotic and dangerous, while a man in a wig and a padded bra is a figure of pathos.

The more successful his transformation, the more disquieting the effect he creates. Note the difference between Jack Lemmon and Tony Curtis, both as variations on Monroe's type in *Some Like It Hot*. Whereas a woman in travesty can stand still, a man has to keep moving – fast, if he is not to be caught out. A confident, fully-rounded personality like Dietrich, her strength as much a part of her persona as her maternal streak, each aiding and enriching the other, can wear a man's dress suit or a sailor's cap to colossal effect, but she is accepted and applauded by men and women alike, because she softens the inherent threat of rejection with humour and tolerance. Although a warning is implied, she remains open and lets you know that the final choice she makes will be up to you. That is why she can be so effective in those moments in *Morocco*, and why we know that the right man, like Cooper, can redress her decision to leave us with his acceptance of all that she is, and not just a part of it. Dietrich's innate strength does not require a wardrobe to provide the clue. When Dietrich took to wearing men's trousers in public, she did not start a fashion. Women had been wearing them for some time. But she made them fashionable. By the evident comfort with which she wore them, by emphasizing her allure she showed women a sense of style without the fear of looking freakish or conspicuous. In the 70s and 80s when it became 'all go' this was no longer a problem, but I am speaking of one's parents' parents' day, when people were still bound by the image.

Of course the woman or actress without Marlene's sang-froid did not reach her heights. One thinks here of Katherine Hepburn's androgynous, unsettling boy role in *Sylvia Scarlett*, and of Garbo as *Queen Christina*, which only underlined the distance growing up between herself and her public. A man engaged in a sex-reversal role is rarely better than a grotesque, and if he doesn't mean to be funny and it goes on too long, he is in danger of revealing more about himself than he intended. A famous blonde sex-symbol was not at all put out, and even sympathetic when she was told the latest dirt her male co-star was spreading about her, 'Oh, that's all right,' she smiled, 'he's just jealous because I look better in a dress than he does.' One need never apologize for strength. This leads one to conclude that it's not women who are weak, but our image of them, and it's not men who are innately stronger, but the image we have of them. A woman can adapt an endless variety of disguises without ever becoming the less for it. For example, a woman dressed as a little girl, is amusing and provocative. A man as a little boy, all hairy arms and legs sticking from little jumpers and short pants, is grotesque. A woman as a sex symbol is glorious. A man as a sex symbol, as distinct from a *sexy* man, treads dangerous ground – narcissistic, infantile, potentially weak. A man disguised as anything except another man is vulnerable to ridicule. I have been speaking her of a wardrobe change, not a sex change. Transvestites are another matter

altogether; a man who becomes a woman acquires her strength, while the reverse route takes it away. But both are sterile and lack true mystery since they sacrifice a side of themselves. Perhaps it's this sterility, the fear it touches at the deepest level, that has accounted for the fact that the few roles for which transvestites have been cast have all been sinister. So far nothing has changed that, not even Dr Frankenfurter in *The Rocky Horror Picture Show* – which was also some kind of a musical, or *La Cage aux Folles*.

Marlene Dietrich was another star whose career will always be associated with great songs, though not necessarily in musicals as such. The musical moments in her Sternberg films, *The Blue Angel*, *Morocco* (1930), *Blonde Venus* (1932), *The Devil is a Woman* (1935), belong to the highlights of the era. The songs Friedrich Hollander composed for her to sing in *Desire* (1936), *Destry Rides Again* (1939), *Seven Sinners* (1940), *A Foreign Affair* (1948),

did as much for her as she for them, and the combination for the films. Together with Mae West, she led a new tradition that had sprung up with sound films, turning the siren into an occasional *lorelei*. From the day that Gloria Swanson introduced 'Love, Your Magic Spell Is Everywhere' in *The Trespasser*, songs became a heaven-sent opportunity for underlining a glamour star's allure, even if they weren't really singers, and, on the occasion where, instead, they danced, like Paulette Goddard, Joan Fontaine, Jean Harlow or Carole Lombard, when they really weren't dancers. That didn't matter. A nightclub provided atmosphere for introductions, convenient pillars and tables for striking poses, and a milieu, which, like station frontiers, were half-way houses for these ladies whom life hadn't treated fairly, to wait, hoping for the right man to come along, the man they could love, the man who'd be big and strong, and would rescue them from the mean, lean, oily, corrupt, teeth-picking, knife-twiddling, nattily-attired owner of the club who somehow always had them under his spell. These moments gave their public the opportunity to study and identify with, or covet or worship their idols. For, while the great star was singing, there was no need for her to move (dancing was also a means of striking exotic poses) and there would be a perfect excuse for the camera to pay homage to the beauty which the public had paid to see. Of course these numbers with the girl in the sleazy bar were in reality a secret celebration of

Top left: Dietrich in *The Blue Angel*. 'Falling in Love Again'.

Dietrich in Hollywood. In *Morocco* she appeared in her familiar guise in the 'What am I bid for my apples?' number, left. But in the same film she appeared for the first time *en travesti* when she performed 'When Love is Dead' (Quand l'amour meurt). The impact was remarkable and she repeated it to great effect in subsequent films.

the great Goddess, bane of the churches, burnt as a witch, stoned as adulterous, worshipped as mother, she was virgin and whore in one and in all her glory.

Not surprisingly, considering their effectiveness, these moments became *de rigeur* for every budding sex-star and fading *femme fatale*. Charged up with thousands of watts of electricity from the great lamps playing on their faces, they ignited or regenerated. Exotic new import Anna Sten, in *Nana* (dressed by Adrian, lit by Gregg Toland, singing Rodgers and Hart's 'That's Love'), Kay Francis in *Mandalay* (dressed by Orry Kelly, lit by Tony Gaudio, singing Kahal and Fain's 'When Tomorrow Comes'), Joan Crawford in *The Bride Wore Red* (dressed by Adrian, lit by George Folsey, singing Franz Waxman's 'Who Wants Love?'), Constance Bennett in *Moulin Rouge* (dressed by Travis Banton, lit by Charles Rosher, singing Warren & Dubin's 'Boulevard of Broken Dreams'), Marlene Dietrich in *Songs of Songs* (dressed by Travis Banton, lit by Victor Milner, singing Friedrich Hollander's 'Johnny', with English lyrics by Edward Heymann. Yes, Marlene, there were English lyrics written for it). Lamour, Lamarr, Lupino, the lot. Even Bette Davis joined in WB's all-star contribution to the war effort, *Thank Your Lucky Stars* (1943), where she bemoaned the plight of the girls left behind in 'They're Either Too Young or Too Old' and added some high kicks for good measure.

These musical celebrations were rarely the work of the film's director who left this nonsense to his dance director. When, of course, a director came along who understood what it was all about and worked it into his script, then something quite wonderful could occur. And in Josef von Sternberg, Marlene Dietrich – who could be erotic and stylish at once and had made her first talkie in Germany when she played the woman the leading man implored with the song, 'I Kiss Your Hand Madame' (*Ich küsse ihre Hand Madame*, 1929) – found such a man. The numbers Sternberg wove around her in *The Blue Angel* were his celebration of woman's special place and her inspiration to the artist. In this case, perhaps, he was also dealing with Dietrich's spell on him, for Sternberg was no Svengali, and Dietrich was certainly no Trilby sleep-walking to fame. In *The Blue Angel* (Ph: Gunther Rittau), *Morocco* (Ph: Lee Garmes), *Blonde Venus* (Ph: Bert Glennon) and, especially in *The Devil is a Woman* (Ph: J. von Sternberg), the woman is always on stage, whether it's as a cabaret singer or a hausfrau and mother.

'What Am I Bid For My Apples?' (by Leo Robin and Karl Hajos) she mockingly intones, having already supplied her own, bitterly weary reason 'Quand l'amour meurt' (When Love Is Dead, by Millandy and Crémieux), earlier in the same film, *Morocco* (1930). And love having died, or at least a part of her having been badly bruised by the experience, she wants nothing more to do with men. In case we miss the point she is dressed from head to foot in masculine attire, top hat, tuxedo and patent leather shoes. The night-club owner is worried before she goes on stage. For a moment it does seem his worst fears are confirmed as she steps insolently on stage, taking a last drag from a cigarette before tossing it away, and coolly ignoring catcalls and

jeers her clothes and her insolent demeanour provoke. Love her or hate her, it's all the same to her. One of the legionnaires in the crowded café appreciates her *élan*. His applause quells the others who now start to appreciate a joke even though they don't know what it is as yet. When they are silent, she starts, and sings the song as she had always intended, to the women in the audience. It's a challenge the men appreciate more than their dates. As she moves through the room, her cool mockery is matched with professional admiration by the legionnaire, Tom Brown. He understands her but doesn't buy her act, even when, her eyes never leaving his, he watches her lightly kissing a woman on the lips before she stops at his table, and taking the flower he threw her, gives it to his jealous date before moving on. Her act has been a comment on the way men like him have taken much more than kisses from women who loved them and then passed on. All this is conveyed in a musical number where Sternberg has Marlene do to legionnaire, Tom, what she is meant to do to the audience seeing her in her first American film – provoke, stimulate, and excite admiration and wonder. And since the audience could sense, as Tom does, what must have happened to her before, and because she has the courage to try again, to fall in love, to renounce her cynicism for hope, they fell in love with her.

Blonde Venus (1932) provides opportunities to shatter the composure of the most blasé member of the audience. Banalities are announced with trumpet fanfares. She flees with her child, hiding in the back of a wagonload of hay that is sculptured with lights to create a luxury nest that would rival a canopied featherbed in Versailles, as it must have felt to the child sheltered in his mother's arms. Clichés bare their breasts with the assurance of the great truths from which they sprang. Here Dietrich is the fallen women, outcast wife, unworthy mother for an indiscretion committed to save her husband's life. It is the fear of losing her child that forces her off on her spiralling road down railroad tracks to one-horse towns, with a song here and there to pay for a meal. For one of them, she's in a full-length beaded dress lit to create the illusion of near nudity (which must have given Dietrich the idea for her spectacular nightclub act later in her career). Sternberg's achievement with the numbers is to integrate them so fully into the heroine's character that one is often likely to forget them as isolated moments. Even so, there is one number that could be lifted out of the film and which would always rival anything that's been done in that line. It's the number built around the song, 'Hot Voodoo' (music by Ralph Rainger, lyrics by Sam Coslow).

In a nightclub, a line of scantily clad black girls with frizzy Afro hairdos, carrying shields and holding on to a chain, file on to the stage (sets by Wiard Ihnen), with a fierce gorilla as captive. At times the gorilla refuses to budge, glowering at a ringside table through its small slit eyes, and making threatening gestures with its long black hairy arms. The people at the nearby tables shy away from his reach, laugh nervously but with excitement, for the club has been advertising a new sensation making her début this evening as The Blonde Venus. At last the simian is on stage, the swaying girls no longer looking like his captors but more like the nubile sacrifices that might be offered up to soothe him. They sway in rows on either side, while he is rocking back and forth on his hind legs as if preparing for his next move, with his arms cradling his belly. Slowly he takes one arm away, as if perhaps to grasp a branch and swing over the audience, when, to one's astonishment, we see that he has removed the outer paw and that beneath his hairy ugliness is a woman's long, white, manicured hand. And then the other paw is removed, and now two shimmeringly phosphorescent white hands lift off the head. Revealed, is the Blonde Venus, attraction extraordinaire, with her mouth slightly parted in a mocking self-assurance that only Dietrich could evoke, a smile and her eyes wide open and apart, looking and laughing, as if to say, 'Nice trick, huh! I can do much better, kiddies, but this will do for now.' And then she steps out of the suit. One of the girls hands her an enormous blonde frizzy Afro wig, and another hands her a shield, and

Dietrich in *Blonde Venus*. Her films were not musicals but song was creatively used to raise the temperature in certain sequences. A frame shot, above, shows her shedding a gorilla skin in 'Hot Voodoo'. Left: Earning her supper in a night club, goddess of the gutters. Opposite: As the rage of Paris in a white tuxedo for 'You Little So-and-So'.

Overleaf: A succession of glamorous ladies appeared in films with music – and sometimes musicals – during their Hollywood careers. From top left: Clara Bow in *Love Among the Millionaires*. Garbo posing for a still in *Mata Hari* – she was only visibly Garbo in close-up. Ann Sothern in *Let's Fall in Love*, with Edmund Lowe. Jean Harlow in *Reckless* had songs by Jerome Kern. Carole Lombard in *Swing High, Swing Low*. Anna Sten in *Nana* had a song by Rodgers and Hart. Joan Crawford in *Dancing Lady*. Kay Francis in *Mandalay*. Lana Turner in *Ziegfeld Girl*. Hedy Lamarr in *White Cargo*: well, it was some sort of dance. Barbara Stanwyck in *Lady of Burlesque*.

she sings this perfectly silly little naughty jingle-jangle about some voodoo that makes men 'slay-ay-ayves'. The song is a throw-away. In fact, it's a little too obvious that Sternberg didn't care for it, or even for the audience, for it's as if he were saying, 'You didn't come here o hear her sing! You came here to get drunk and gawk at the lady's legs. OK, here are her legs.' But Sternberg, whatever his feelings might have been, and he wasn't happy to be making this film, simply cannot do something that is not memorable in the craft he has made his art. Extraordinary as this number has always seemed to me, it is clearly a number that could have been staged in a typical nightclub-sized stage, and yet, the effect is so astounding that it easily rivals any of the cast-of-thousands production numbers that filled a whole sound stage.

Later in the story he must have had second thoughts, for to a much better tune, 'You Little So and So', sung by the fallen woman, now resurrected as the sensation of Paris, Sternberg has Dietrich appear down a long runway through little more than floating chiffon, wearing an all white man's evening suit and top hat (for once again, she is through with love), and the effect is as startling as before.

At first they banned the film in Germany because Goebbels felt that the role was a slur on mother-hood, though there may have been other reasons, such as Dietrich's refusal to come back to work in her home land. And it wasn't one of Sternberg-Dietrich's biggest hits in America either. The critics said it was because it was too static, too stylish and too composed! I think it's because Sternberg's irritation with the studio for insisting he make the film when he didn't want to, with Dietrich for her increasing dependency on him, and with the public for their Dietrich obsession, created a negative undercurrent. Today any and all of these reasons no longer count. This 50-year-old film, a trifle tossed off to fulfil an obligation to give the studio a Dietrich film for their fall schedule, is clearly the work of a genius.

Sternberg also shot two musical numbers for their last collaborative effort, *The Devil is a Woman* (1935). But one number was cut before the film's release. Entitled, 'If It Isn't Pain, It Isn't Love', it just about says it all for the film's theme, and all that's left of that sequence is a shot of her going off stage on her way to an assignation with her latest conquest, which takes her past her older lover, knowing full well that he is suffering hell inside and enjoying the fact. Of course, that was what the whole film was about, pain, and love and the pain of love, and of parting. It was a bitter pill to swallow and by 1935 the public preferred something more

uplifting, like Shirley Temple on the good ship Lollipop. The remaining number is another of those ridiculous trifles by Ralph Rainger and Leo Robin, entitled 'Three Sweethearts Have I', one of whom is a farmer, another a baker and the third, a grocer, but it's plain from her delivery that the produce she likes them for isn't from the field, the oven or the shop. When the Spanish Government took time out from its Civil War to protest at the detrimental image this film gave to the Spaniard, and threatened to boycott all Paramount films if this one wasn't withdrawn, the studio cut their losses and pulled it, and Paramount said goodbye to Sternberg.

After their partnership was dissolved, Dietrich was still luckier than most of the glamorous songstresses with the songs she had to sing, and what her directors did with them, and for her, as in *Desire*, directed by Frank Borzage, and *Seven Sinners*, directed by Tay Garnett, both films with wonderful songs by Friedrich Hollander, who also wrote the score for *Destry Rides Again*, the adult-western in which she lost the man but won back the public. Dietrich was exceptional but moments like these, even without this sort of care, still worked their wonders with other stars, in other films. It was always a pleasant bonus when one of the glamour gals actually had a pleasing voice, usually a Dietrich mezzo. More commonly, not that it matters, the husky voice emanating from the slinky form belonged to one of the studio's stable of unseen singers, whose careers were based on their total adaptability to correspond with the star's image. It's known now for instance that Lauren Bacall's sultry singing début in *To Have and Have Not* (1944) was supposed to have been the work of male singer Andy Williams. Not that these dubbing decisions from on high always made sense. For example, Eleanor Powell sang for herself on Broadway, but

only in some, not all, of her films, and Ava Gardner was dubbed when she played Julie in *Show Boat*. But on the film's sound track album, released by the same studio, she used her own voice to great effect. Dramatic actress Ida Lupino, whose singing was dubbed first at Paramount, then at Warners, was finally allowed to use her own voice when she went to 20th Century-Fox to make *Road House* (1950), and introduced a song that became a standard, 'Again . . . don't let it happen again'. Lupino was talking about love of course, not dubbing!

In any case, dubbed or not, ever since sound, glamorous women have been slaying their men with a bold look and a low voice. Carole Lombard sang in *White Woman;* Veronica Lake, a seventeen-year-old femme fatale, sang in *I Wanted Wings;* Lana Turner sang and danced in several of her early films, while Metro was still searching for her definitive image. In the meantime her singing was dubbed. The list is endless. The immortal Greta Garbo hummed a few bars in *Grand Hotel* and did an exotic strip for *Mata Hari* (1932), her limitations as a dancer being concealed by the use of a real one, June Lang, in the long shots.* 'It' girl, Clara Bow, was developing as a likeable musical star in her early sound films when she retired. Others who 'also sang' in the 30s were Merle Oberon, Ann Sothern, Jane Wyman and Dorothy Lamour.

For imaginative lunacy, Dorothy Lamour's early films take the cake, or rather, the banana. An inspired stroke planted this radio songstress in the middle of the jungle, where her dimestore sultriness

Dietrich moves to a new studio, and to renewed success with Friedrich Hollander's 'See What the Boys in the Back Room Will Have' in *Destry Rides Again*.

---

* Interestingly enough, times might change but not old habits. It was revealed soon after the release of one of 1983's biggest musical hits, *Flashdance*, that the sensational dances by the film's star, Jennifer Beals, were actually performed by a professional dancer in the long shots.

Swing High, Swing Low was Dorothy Lamour's second film and she played Carole Lombard's rival for the affections of Fred MacMurray. She scored a hit with 'Panamania'.

Man About Town, and Dorothy dressed for 'Strange Enchantment', by Loesser and Hollander.

scored heavily with both the screen-natives and the public. She was usually discovered as a sarong-clad orphan in exotically titled jungle frolics. Here Hollywood could keep well within the confines of the Hays Code without sacrificing the sex appeal inherited from Mae West: the jungle provided an ideal setting for double-entendres and mini-skirts.

Making her début as Ulah, *The Jungle Princess* (1936), Lamour was variously known to the natives as *Aloma of the South Seas* (1941), Marmara, Tama, Mima, Dea and Manuela. There would be beautiful South Sea music, native ceremonies and sacred dances specially choreographed. Her singing soon took second place to the table-cloths she wore, a craze she inspired. Her studio, Paramount, never quite made up its mind whether she was a sexy siren, luring men to their due rewards with her throaty chanting and slow-flapping eyelids (*Johnny Apollo*, 1940) or a long-haired nature-lover, who appeared in the jungle to the never-ending surprise of her stock leading men: Ray Milland, Robert Preston, Richard Denning, Jon Hall.

Seen today, these films are high camp. Even at the time, she and her sarong soon became something of a joke, which she had humour enough to appreciate. She burlesqued her own image in the *Road* series, as a glamorous foil for Crosby and Hope, successfully continuing her career long after the novelty wore off

wanted to grow up, was one of the greatest stars of her day, and that's probably why her subsequent career in films is minimal – she really had no place else to go. Like Mae West, she was not only a star but also a symbol, and symbols tend to be locked in time. Her popularity as a child exceeded that of any mature contemporary. From 1934 and for the next four years, she was the World's Number One box-office attraction, the figurehead of the New America emerging from the Depression.

Her innocent and optimistic world of song and dance allowed adults in by the side door. Overnight, every child had to have Shirley Temple curls, and wear Shirley Temple frocks. Stage-struck mothers poured into Hollywood, helpless infants in tow, made up to look like her. The jealous mothers of unsuccessful children spread the stories that Shirley was not really a little girl, but a little boy, or alternatively, a precocious midget. The songs she sang, 'On The Good Ship Lollipop', 'Baby Take A Bow',

Top: Dorothy Lamour and a popular co-star in *Her Jungle Love.*

Between the Crosby-Lamour-Hope films Dorothy Lamour was kept very busy in movies like *Melody Inn* (right) and *The Fleet's In.*

and the table-cloths went out of the wardrobe and back on the table. The success of her films sparked off a series of similar hokum at other studios, featuring Yvonne de Carlo, Piper Laurie, Patricia Morison, Hedy Lamarr and Universal's own Latin-American siren queen of fantasy, Maria Montez. These women however, did not sing, having a hard enough time with the dialogue.

At the pinnacle of Mae West's box-office triumph, if anyone had wondered who her most logical successor might be, one would have been hard-put to come up with a name. Anyone who guessed correctly, that it would be a little six-year-old called Shirley Temple, would have been considered crazy. Yet such was the case. By the end of 1934, the West lights were dimming, and little Shirley Temple had become the astonishing box-office champion.

Shirley Temple, the child whom the public never

'Animal Crackers In My Soup', 'When I Grow Up', 'That's What I Want For Christmas' and more, are among the most vivid of the musical memories of the 30s. Her tap dances in many of her films with the masterful Negro dancer, Bill 'Bojangles' Robinson, had a delighting innocence hard to equal.

They were teamed in four films together: *The Little Colonel,* and *The Littlest Rebel,* both in 1935, and *Rebecca of Sunnybrook Farm* and *Just Around the Corner,* released in 1938, while he also did the choreography for *Dimples* (1936). It was regrettable, that, with a few exceptions, Hollywood did very little with the great wealth of black talent available all through those years, until the 50s, when Dorothy Dandridge and Harry Belafonte broke through the colour bar as major stars with *Carmen Jones* (20th Century-Fox, 1954). In the meantime, vaudeville and stage headliners like Robinson, Hattie McDaniel,

Shirley Temple was a seasoned player before she became a star, appearing in a series of 'Baby Burlesque' shorts. Here she is doing a spoof of the glamorous Dietrich as Morelegs Sweetrick in *Kid'in' Hollywood*.

Left: Shirley Temple at the age of nine, the world's biggest box-office attraction.

Below: By 1934 Shirley Temple was news and had made two very successful films for Paramount, whose idea this kitsch publicity photograph was. Baby LeRoy escorts Shirley to the movies – to see Mae West, the reigning queen of the box-office, in *It Ain't No Sin* (*Belle of the Nineties*). Within a year Shirley Temple had replaced Mae West at the top.

BABY LE ROY & SHIRLEY TEMPLE
in Paramount Pictures

the Nicholas Brothers, Ethel Waters, Louis Armstrong and, of course, Lena Horne, were relegated to supporting roles (excluding the very few all-black films, *Cabin in the Sky* and *Stormy Weather*) but which their talents always turned into the highlights of the films they appeared in. Sadly, their moments were few and far between, but what there was, was choice.

Meanwhile, Shirley Temple, who was seven years old when she first worked with Robinson, wouldn't have been aware of any of this, and her ease and happiness with Robinson have lost nothing with the years. Her film début was in *War Babies* (1932), when she was only four. It was one of at least fourteen short films she made before 1934. These 'Baby Burlesques' were one-reel take-offs on famous films and current stars, with tiny diapered children playing all the parts. Amongst others, she did Mae

West, and was a charmer as glamorous 'Morelegs Sweetrick', a take-off of Dietrich's success in *Morocco*. Shirley was not so much an over-powering talent as a radiator of contagious good humour and sweetness that never turned treacly, a rare quality in screen infants.

Her success in the name part of *Little Miss Marker* (1934), based on a Damon Runyan story, established her as the brightest new bet in the film world. She effortlessly stole the film from everyone, including star Adolphe Menjou, who called her a six-year-old Ethel Barrymore. Her 1934 films included *Carolina, Mandalay, Now I'll Tell* (with Alice Faye in an early part), *Change of Heart, Now and Forever*, and *Baby take a Bow* (made to cash in on her success in the all-star *Stand Up and Cheer*, 1934). Fifty years later the reason for this success is totally understandable. Dangling like a limp, raggedy doll in the crook of James Dunn's arm (he scoops her up at the end of her song), her face lit up by a million-watt smile that reaches across the

The wealth of black talent available to the film studios in the 30s and 40s was never properly used. Some notable artists appeared in tantalising glimpses. Left, from top: Maxine Sullivan in *St Louis Blues*, Oscar winner Hattie McDaniel in *Far Horizon*, and Bill Robinson in a Vitaphone short. Above: Buck and Bubbles in *Varsity Show*. Right, from top: Aunt Jemima in a Vitaphone short, *The Lease Breakers*, The Four Flash Devils in the British film revue *Soft Lights and Sweet Music*, and the Nicholas Brothers in *Orchestra Wives*. The Brothers were brilliant enough to stand out in Gene Kelly's company, in *The Pirate*.

Above: Whether the film was a musical or not Dorothy Lamour found it hard to stay out of a sarong for long. A production still from *Beyond the Blue Horizon*. Her leading man was Richard Denning.

Right: Ilonka Tolnay walks to market to sell a goat. On her journey she sings 'It's Foolish – But it's Fun'. Deanna Durbin in one of her biggest hits, *Spring Parade*. The songs were by Robert Stolz.

Far right: Eleanor Powell's 'Swingin' the Jinx Away' in *Born to Dance*.

Above: With James Dunn in *Stand up and Cheer*. Her 'Baby, Take a Bow' number led to the contract with Fox. Right: In *Curly Top* – 'When I Grow Up'.

Below: The last film Shirley Temple made for Fox (20th Century-Fox by then). With Jack Oakie and Charlotte Greenwood in *Young People*.

decades, it's no wonder that she became, for Americans, one which attained the unattainable. She was to her era what *E.T.* is to ours; it can't be explained, only accepted as a form of genius.

When the year's Oscars were being awarded, Shirley received a miniature one for bringing 'more happiness to millions of children and millions of grownups than any child of her years in the history of the world'. She was then just seven. Her films were entertainment, pure and simple.

In 1935 Zanuck's company, 20th Century, merged with Fox and Shirley Temple became the first of the golden blondes who founded the studio's prosperity. Until 1940, all her films were made for them,

most of them shrewdly cast, excellently produced, and not without their share of wit. In *Captain January*, she took part in an adorable spoof of the then popular grand opera invasion, when with Guy Kibbee and Slim Summerville, the three launched into the 'sextet' from *Lucia di Lammermoor*. In *Poor Little Rich Girl*, and again in *Stowaway* (both 1936) she was supported by the golden-voiced Alice Faye (soon herself to become the company's reigning blonde), thus inaugurating the shrewd Fox policy of promoting one up-and-coming blonde in the vehicles of the current Queen.

By 1937 her popularity was such that to obtain her services to play Dorothy in *The Wizard of Oz*, MGM's studio chief Louis B. Mayer agreed to lend Jean Harlow *and* Clark Gable to Zanuck for his planned epic *In Old Chicago*. When Temple left Fox in 1940, at the end of her seven-year contract (and only her last few films were unsuccessful), there was talk of her playing with Rooney and Garland in *Babes on Broadway*. This came to nothing. Her last film at her alma mater, *Young People* (1940, directed by Allan Dwan), had a plot not unlike those of the Garland-Rooney films. Temple, as the young adopted daughter of a couple of vaudevillians had the sparkle and spirit of old – with only one difference, she was no longer a little girl of infinite promise. Though continuing in films until 1949 (like Denna Durbin, who also retired then, and Judy Garland, who suffered a breakdown and whose career came to a temporary halt), Shirley Temple had long since passed her peak. In her heyday, 1934–40, she had earned five million dollars and appeared in twenty-two films (excluding those made for other companies, and her short films). Today she remains firmly entrenched as one of the legends of an era – the one that began with gold-diggers and ended on a note of diminutive blonde optimism.

Five years of unparalleled success in 22 films. From top left: With Alice Faye and Jack Haley in the 'Military Man' number in *The Poor Little Rich Girl*. With a baby pig in *Rebecca of Sunnybrook Farm*. With Slim Summerville in *Captain January*, launching the Sextet from *Lucia di Lammermoor*. In *Just Around the Corner* – 'I Love to Walk in the Rain'. 'The Parade of the Wooden Soldiers' with Bill Robinson in *Rebecca of Sunnybrook Farm*.

Manual of Arms

(AND LEGS)

ARMS by U. S. Army
LEGS by Betty Grable,
20th Century-Fox Star

1. ORDER ARMS:
*The butt of the rifle
Rests on the ground,*

*Eyes straight ahead—
Don't look—honor bound!*

2. RIGHT SHOULDER ARMS:
*Now raise the rifle
With the right hand.*

*Grasp it and balance
With left, steady stand!*

*Regrasp it, right hand
This time on the butt,*

*Now place the rifle
At shoulder. Don't strut!*

3. PORT ARMS:
*Now raise the rifle
With your right hand*

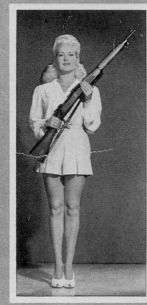

*Cross over, up right,
At left shoulder land!*

4. LEFT SHOULDER ARMS:
*Now release rifle
With the left hand,*

*Forearms horizontal!
Drop right. (A command!)*

5. INSPECTION ARMS:
*Seize the bolt action,
Look through magazine!*

*Raise head now, and eyes, too,
Your arms must be clean!*

*Now rest. Move your left foot,
Legs straight, weight between;*

*With left palm touch rifle!
At ease! That was keen!*

The Golden Years

Hermes Pan: You couldn't do much with Betty Grable outside of letting her be Betty Grable.

JK: What was Betty Grable?

Pan: Cover Girl; cute, a cute blonde who sang and danced.

JK: Jack Cole told me she could have done more than she was allowed to do.

Pan: I don't really agree. She really was not a good tap dancer, and she couldn't do ballet. I worked with Betty on so many films and I can't imagine her doing, well, say that number Cyd did in *Sombrero*, or anything very lyrical and flowing. She could move, and she had beautiful legs; her colour was beautiful; she was pleasant to watch, and when she was on the screen she had a certain magnetism.

JK: What was your brief when choreographing a number for her?

Pan: Make her do what she did best. Don't try to change her. If you try to change her then you're fighting a lost cause because it won't come out right. I'm not knocking her. She was a Number One at the Box-Office and nobody did what she did better, so we must have done something right.

The effect of the War in Europe and the Far East on Hollywood, in sunny California, had been the closure of valuable markets that had accounted for a large percentage of their earnings. Besides this initial loss in revenue, another danger loomed, closer to home, with direr consequences for the industry. The system by which theatres were forced to book 'blind' a studio's entire annual output, or do without the big guaranteed box-office hits, was broken up by the government and by 1945 pictures were sold in blocks of five, which had first to be seen by the exhibitors.

Almost simultaneously, the Attorney General's Office threatened to break the powerful studio monopolies, ensuring distribution for any and all of their year's product. The effect of these changes meant a tightening of the financial reins as even stars suffered salary cuts (though theirs, unlike those of the rest of the staff, would be replaced), and a greater reliance on scripts and directors who could come in under schedule. Yet these events coincided with a great technical improvement; special lacquers gave film prints an unrivalled sheen, and colour film showed a marked improvement which benefited from the subtler lighting that could now be employed. These benefits could be seen almost at once in the musicals, many of which were made in colour.

Just as the 30s had been dominated by the great stars, so in another, subtler way, the 40s would mark the decade of the great directors of musicals. During and after the war, the two most thriving genres were the *film noir* and the musical, where, to a great degree the director was the master. Of course there were still stars – there would always be stars – but the emphasis could be seen to shift.

The musical and the *film noir* were two sides of the same coin. In the latter there appeared a new hero on the horizon: the psychopathic hoodlum, sodden alcoholic and neurotic heroine who were domestic adaptations of the sadistic Nazis and perverted Orientals, whose presence in the propaganda war films streaming out of Hollywood at the height of the conflict had provided such a popular ingredient. With war villains gone, or reprogrammed into allies, their abnormal psychology was grafted on to the gangrenous elements in American society, bringing a monstrous new life to the flower. The musical thrived on sunshine. Shadows were banished. In the musicals, the love of one's mother (especially at Metro) was the sign of a good American.

When America entered the war in December 1941, people flocked to the movies in unprecedented numbers. The profits the American film industry feared had been lost with the closure of the European outlets doubled themselves with their own public. Musicals helped them forget their fears for a brief interlude, and were never more popular.

The Grables of Wrath

Although for the purists it was Metro who put the real gold into musicals, 20th Century-Fox's streamlined, fastpaced and tuneful vehicles woven around their bevy of blondes, shone just as bright for the public of those times. Fox's gold-plated blonde policy had begun in the 30s, when the films of reigning Queen, Shirley Temple, were used to launch Alice Faye. When she became Queen, Alice did for Betty Grable what Grable would do for June Haver and Haver in her turn did for Marilyn Monroe – hoist them up the ladder of public affection.

Undoubtedly Darryl F. (for Francis) Zanuck was one of Hollywood's foxiest judges when it came to knowing what the public wanted and giving it to them, even though it wasn't his cup of téa. It made him an ideal head of a studio, and it was in that capacity that his influential involvement with musicals saved the fortunes of one company and refilled the impoverished coffers of another. There's little about Zanuck in his capacity as an independent producer that suggests that he cared for the genre; his preferences outside his dogged but vain attempts to launch French starlets as American stars lay in hard hitting, large-scale action subjects, heavy with social realism and literary flavour: *The Grapes of Wrath*, *The Ox-Bow Incident*, *Gentleman's Agreement* and *Pinky* are notable examples. Musicals to him were like the

The 20th Century-Fox daisy chain. Shirley Temple, queen of the box-office, is given first-class support by Alice Faye in *Stowaway*, top left. Alice, now in top place, is seen with Betty Grable in *Tin Pan Alley*, top right. Betty in *The Dolly Sisters*, above left; the other sister is June Haver. June is approached by a prospective tenant, Marilyn Monroe, in *The Love Nest*, above right. Marilyn had no successors.

working man's girlie shows, a pleasant way to pass the time, but nothing more. MGM's producer, Arthur Freed, whose career spans the same length of time as Zanuck's, and whose musicals were also at their peak, wanted to and did show that they could be both entertainment *and* art. Zanuck wanted only that they should show a profit. Unquestionably, Freed's were more artistic, but Zanuck's made more money more consistently.

In 1934 Zanuck formed his own company, confidently called 20th Century. Shortly afterwards he merged his thriving concern with the ailing Fox Film Corporation. Immediately, he started revitalizing that studio's stable of stars, plush-lining the Temple films, while shrewdly foreseeing that she'd soon be too old to make others dream and using her films for all they were worth to showcase his next generation of stars. Out of their ranks arose sleepy-voiced, sleepy-eyed, zoftig-shaped blonde song-stress Alice Faye, whose career as a Jean Harlow look-alike had been languishing. With *In Old Chicago* (1938), the studio's biggest production of the year, Alice Faye, Zanuck's first Class A model, was given the part that made her a star and ascended the heavens of popularity. Alice, and

those who followed her, were the relaundered, Hays Office-approved version of the Warner Bros gold digger, the result of a dizzying cross-pollination of Mae West and Shirley Temple, the 30's two most successful female stars.

Zanuck kept the gold – all his musical stars were blondes, irrespective of their roots – and left the objectionable digging to the supporting cast. These girls could be the heroine's wise-cracking side-kick: Joan Davies, Martha Raye, June Havoc – or the rival in love: Ethel Merman, Louise Hovick (June Havoc's sister, better known and better served as burles-que's stripteaser and novelist, Gypsy Rose Lee) or Lynn Bari. Sad but true, brunettes did not fare well at the Zanuck paddock. He, who never knew what to do with the great Gypsy, had dropped another brunette when he took over Fox without giving her so much as a second glance. When his cast-off re-surfaced, transformed into an electrifying blaze of colour and emotion, he found himself in the embarrassing position of having to hire Rita Hayworth back at enormous cost for a role no-one under contract to him could play. In *Blood and Sand*, Rita Hayworth, Doña Sol, Queen of the Sun, toyed with the matador who knew a lot about bulls but little about women, bringing to it the spice of the victor. The pleasantly innocuous Fox musicals met with greater popular success than anything else he produced in all of his years in the business. Consider, when tempted to dismiss films like *Weekend in Havana, Moon over Miami, Coney Island*, etc. and so forth, that those *Grapes of Wrath* might never have reached maturity on the screen if it hadn't been for these technicolor resort-revues which the people of Steinbeck's saga paid hard earned nickels and dimes to see. Alice, Betty and Shirley underwrote 20th Century's social conscience, or, as Carl Denham might have said, 'Twasn't Zanuck but beauty that paid for the grapes of wrath.'

Later, when his crushed cast-off had sufficiently recovered to have her hair re-rooted a befitting strawberry blonde he was forced to hire her from a rival studio at enormous cost. In *Blood and Sand*, Rita Hayworth, pre-eminent as the Love Goddess of the decade, merely proved to the world what his brunettes had long known, that Zanuck was better with writers than with women.

Though Zanuck, having been a writer, laid great store by writers, great writers did not sit down to write great stories for his dimpled/dancing/singing/skating dolls. It was ironic that while the musicals Zanuck had initiated at Warners had been set in a hard, tough world of unemployment, poverty, hunger and want, it was in the buoyant way the protagonists tackled their lot that the life-enhancing spirit of the musical was successfully integrated. But in the war-time fantasies Zanuck inaugurated at Fox, this remarkable and powerful spirit was routed into the progressively emptier glitz and glamour package which wasn't far different in the end from the similar formulae Goebbels had come up with in Germany to lull the public into a tuneful but false sense of self-satisfaction. The blander the plot, the lusher the sets and costumes; the further the plots strayed from any sort of norm, the more exotic the locations in which the action was set. It comes as no surprise then that for German as for American film makers heading down the South American way was a ticket to a trouble-free plot location paradise. And everybody went to Rio – or Cuba: there was *Stern von Rio, That Night in Rio, La Habanera, Weekend in Havana* . . . Initially there was some pretence at stories with some conflict. Later, the shipping directions on a crate of oranges were about as much as the story could bear. Naturally the law of diminishing returns took its toll. But not at first, for the people in them were young and gay and lively and that was infectious. The plots might be re-hashes of the tried and the true or cobbled out of nursery stories, but the nurseries that Zanuck set them in were jaw-droppers – plush, flush, chintz and organdie penthouses, haciendas, casinos, chalets and patios that stretched from Cape Cod to Mar del Plata.

Critics didn't like these films. Their attitude, then as now, has ever been to take the serious too seriously and the light too lightly. But nobody who went to them could complain of having been misled for nobody pretended, even remotely, that a film starring a Foxy Blonde was meant to advance the

role of art in the musical.

Alice Faye, the prototype of the Foxy Blonde, had made her film start starring in *George White's Scandals*, the picture for which she had originally been signed as a singer. Alice got the lead, partly through the intercession of the film's star, crooner Rudy Vallee, who in the fan press of the day, was often linked romantically with Miss Faye. She had a throaty, bluesy voice that could belt out a rhythm number but really came into its own in poignant love songs. That may have been the main reason her characters were made to suffer. By the end of 1937, after four years in Hollywood, Alice had made fifteen films. On loan-outs to other studios, in Fox's own musicals. or supporting Shirley Temple, Alice Faye was built for stardom, but it wasn't until Zanuck cast her in *In Old Chicago* (1938) that she was in the big league.* As a singer in the saloons of the Chicago-loop era she had a chance to wear period clothes (suited to her romantic figure), sing two songs, have two popular male co-stars, play the

Alice Faye and the 'I've Taken a Fancy to You' number in *In Old Chicago*. The part was originally intended for Jean Harlow but Alice, who used to look like her, scored a great success in her new, softer guise.

* Her role was originally written for Jean Harlow, in exchange for whom Fox was to loan MGM Shirley Temple to star in *The Wizard of Oz*. Harlow's death cancelled that deal.

Above: The stars of *In Old Chicago* reunited. Don Ameche (piano) and Tyrone Power (violin) have to wrestle with the ragtime form but Alice Faye is clearly at home with it. Jack (the Tin Man) Haley on the drums. *Alexander's Ragtime Band.*

Right: Alice Faye during her Jean Harlow-look-alike phase. On loan to Paramount in 1935 she co-starred with George Raft in *Every Night at 8.* Songstress Frances Langford, Alice, and comedienne Patsy Kelly, aspiring to fame as singing 'sisters', at the microphone.

lead in an 'A' film, and become a star.

Following hot on its heels and re-uniting the same stars – Power, Faye, Ameche – and director Henry King, *Alexander's Ragtime Band* (1938) was little more than an Irving Berlin sing-along – he was almost a musical film trend on his own. Most of the songs were divided between Alice Faye and that vocal power-house, Ethel Merman, miscast as Faye's rival in love.*

But it is Faye's film all the way. As a singer with Power's band she loves, suffers and sings – all three exquisitely. The story supposedly spanned three decades, but since it was a musical and therefore none of the stars showed any signs of ageing, it was not always easy to recognize this. By 1939, Alice Faye was a box-office gold mine and when she starred in a musical it guaranteed that film's entertainment value, as was the case with Betty Grable and, in the 50s, Doris Day. The public knew that if Alice was the star, they could expect fun, music, dances and a slight plot that would ensure enough tears for a set of hankies. Tears were not an ingredient of the films of either Sonja Henie, June Haver or the early Grable personality, although in Betty's later films, co-starred with gangly Dan Dailey, Grable had a chance to shed a few tears over her footloose partner. When Faye no longer needed a male star to support her, the up-and-coming John Payne, Richard Greene, George Montgomery, and Cesar Romero were tried out. Grable inherited many of them, along with Dick Haymes and Victor Mature.

Alice did it by giving you lumps. Betty did it standing on pumps. And Henie kept it on ice. No matter how many circles the frosty blonde Nor-

wegian-born Olympic skating champion turned she couldn't cut through the plots any more than the rest – but the public enjoyed her wintry holidays as much as their sunshine excursions. Only one thing separated Henie from her colleagues and that was her appetite for making money – her skating acrobatics took second place to her financial wizardry. Her bargaining powers, recalling the screen's first blonde millionaire charmer, Mary Pickford, made her one of the richest women in the world. Her dimples were just another place for storing cash.

Almost as much a part of these musicals as their stars was Astaire's former shadow, Hermes Pan, who joined Fox in 1941, and stayed for the decade, choreographing numbers for all of their musical ladies including Alice Faye (*Weekend in Havana, That Night in Rio*), June Haver (*Irish Eyes are Smiling, I Wonder Who's Kissing Her Now*), Rita Hayworth (*My Gal Sal*) and ten films with Betty Grable, from *Moon over Miami* in 1941 to *That Lady in Ermine* in 1948. Besides which he also doubled as her dancing partner in *Moon over Miami, Coney Island, Sweet Rosy O'Grady* and *Pin-up Girl*, and did a turn around the ice rink with Sonja Henie in *Sun Valley Serenade*. 'The only problem I ever had, and it wasn't really my problem,' recalled Pan, 'was on a Sonja Henie picture: but she was giving everybody such a hard time, that the studio finally just said "No, that's it".'

'This was during the making of *Sun Valley Serenade*, when we were doing the black ice ballet which I'd created for her. I had this idea that I would like a reflection of black and white, so I got together with the set man and he said, "Well, we'll get that effect by flooding it with nicosin dye." So there was about half an inch of water on the ice.* Anyway, Henie was very difficult to work with. She wouldn't listen

* Although she was the greatest musical star on Broadway for over three decades Merman never really made it in movies, and with the exception of *Call Me Madam* (Fox-5, 1953), which came late in her career, her classic stage creations went to others. Ann Sothern was *Panama Hattie*, Lucille Ball was the star of *Dubarry was a Lady*, Betty Hutton of *Annie Get Your Gun* and Rosalind Russell of *Gypsy*.

* Back in 1936, when she made her first film the trouble with shooting ice was that it didn't photograph like ice, so for the skating scenes in *One In A Million* Henie skated on frozen milk.

Left: Alice Faye and Betty Grable in *Tin Pan Alley* perform a spoof grass skirt number, 'K-K-K-Katy'.

Other girls skated on smaller rinks for the smaller studios. Left: Vera Hruba Ralston in Republic's *Lake Placid Serenade* (1944). Below: Belita in Pathe-Monogram's *Suspense* (1946).

Above: Sonja Henie, the Olympic champion whose ice-show musicals started a trend and made a fortune for 20th Century-Fox. *Second Fiddle*, far left, and *Sun Valley Serenade*, above.

to you, and she would rather do what she wanted to do. Anytime she got into a good spin, she would stay in it for 5000 years. So, this day I was at the microphone and she got into a beautiful sit spin, and she was supposed to leave at the count of 8, and just get off, because there are 16 boys coming down the ice on their cue and if she doesn't move it's going to be a straight collision. I was counting, and the cue came, and she was still doing her spin, and, there was nothing anybody could have done about it, and they hit her, and she was down in the nicosin dye. She was black. Her face was covered in it.

'She was furious. She said she refused to work like this and walked out. That was in the morning. Zanuck called me into his office and said, "Tell Sonja Henie that if she doesn't finish the number tonight, that's it, there will be no finish to the number." I think everybody thought that her real reason for stalling was that the next day we would be going into overtime and she was already getting a fortune, and this way she'd get even more. I think she was the highest-priced star at the studio, in the country even. So I told her what Zanuck had said and she flew into a storm. She and her mother used

Far left: Rita Hayworth with Hermes Pan, working on a dance for *My Gal Sal*.

Left: Hermes Pan partners Carmen Miranda in *That Night in Rio*.

to swear in Norwegian, screaming and hollering. She said, "I won't come back." In the end she changed her mind and we did a few more shots, just to tidy it up. The next day the picture was closed down. Anyway there was enough film for us to cut the number together because, in a case like that, there's not really any continuity. You have wipes, and then you have a certain thing, and then you have another wipe. Those things are never shot in one take. I found when I worked on that film, having never done any skating before, just a little skiing, that it was quite easy to turn with a music of, say 1,2,3,4 1,2,3,4, turn, 2,3,4 . . . and I worked out a few things. Skating was a bit like dancing, so that you could do many things on skates that you could do with your feet.'

Pan had been seriously contemplating retiring from films for good after Astaire left RKO and he found himself without work. As far as he was concerned, the Oscar he won for *A Damsel in Distress* was a jinx.*

Hermes Pan: Then suddenly I got a call from Zanuck. He wanted me to do *That Night in Rio*. I was signed for just that one picture. Carmen Miranda did the 'Chica Chica Boom Chic' number, which was quite a success. That opened up a whole new era for me. Before I joined them they had Seymour Felix – I think. He did most of the numbers for Shirley Temple's films and for Alice Faye. He was of the Sammy Lee, staid New York dance

Betty Grable performs Cole Porter's 'Let's Knock Knees' with Edward Everett Horton in the Astaire-Rogers musical *The Gay Divorcee*. The choreographer was Hermes Pan. Looking on, right, Fred Astaire.

school. You would never have thought, looking at Sammy, that he was a dance director; he looked more like a shoe salesman. I worked with Betty an awful lot – *Coney Island* and practically every picture she made at 20th outside of *Down Argentine Way*, and the films she later did with Dan Dailey. I'd started with her at RKO, doing the 'Let's Knock Knees' number with her and Edward Everett Horton *(The Gay Divorcee)*. She wasn't what you'd call a good dancer. At one point, somebody thought of her as Fred's partner, but that came to nothing because, as he once told me, he wouldn't have done it with her if they asked him because she wasn't the

* For three years, from 1935 to 1937, the Academy of Motion Picture Arts and Sciences deemed the choreographer, then billed as dance director, worthy of an Oscar. The first one went to Dave Gould in 1935 for his numbers for *The Broadway Melody of 1936* and *Folies Bergère*; the second went to Seymour Felix, winning in 1936 for *The Great Ziegfeld*, and the third and last went to Hermes Pan. After that, until they started to call them choreographers, a dance director's screen credit was reduced to 'Dances By'. The important contribution the dance directors had made, more often than not stylistically and in every other way superior to the work of the director credited with making the film, went ignored. It helps to account for the fact that until 1951, no director of musicals had a chance for a nomination unless there was no dance director credited. It wasn't until 1951, with *An American In Paris*,

(16 years after *The Great Ziegfeld*), that a musical won an Oscar, and not until 1958, that a director won an Oscar for directing a musical, when Vincente Minnelli won for *Gigi*. As if everyone suddenly realized that the bell for the studio musicals had tolled, they awarded it 9 Oscars in all. With *West Side Story* (1962), the musical's choreographer, Jerome Robbins, shared the Oscar for Best Director with Robert Wise. Not until Bob Fosse, one of the age's most dynamic dance directors, combined the two tasks into one with the brilliant *Cabaret* (1971) was the vital importance of good choreography at last recognized with an Oscar. But as recognition by the Academy of the artistic contribution of men like Berkeley, Robert Alton, Jack Cole, Eugene Loring, Fred Astaire, Rod Alexander, LeRoy Prinz et al, it was embarrassingly late.

right partner for him. For me this time at Fox was a
nice era, because they had very glamorous sets, and
wonderful colour, which we didn't have at RKO.
Also the music had become much easier to record
and I had much more money and much more
freedom at Fox because the directors I worked with
at Fox weren't what I'd call especially musical –
Walter Lang, David Butler, Irving Cummings – these
weren't great ideas men and they left that pretty
much up to me so long as it didn't hurt anything.

The numbers I did for Betty were just things I
dreamt up – pretty much the way I dreamt up the
'Fun House' number, or something like the 'Frankie
and Johnny' number [for *Meet Me in Las Vegas*]. The
story just told you what you needed, and you went
ahead and thought 'Wouldn't this be fun to do in
dance form' or 'Nobody has ever done that, I wonder
why?' and so I'd try it. As long as the director and
the studio felt what you were doing didn't harm her
characterization, you could do pretty much what
you wanted to do. And those girls weren't any
trouble to work with – not Rita, or Carmen who was
a wonderfully funny gal to work with, and Betty
was easy. 'Just tell me what to do,' – like Ginger,
easy to work with. You just had to bear in mind
what she couldn't do.

There's only one number that stands out in my
mind from that time, because I was very unhappy

Betty Grable at Paramount in 1936, before she became a star.

Solo numbers in *Tin Pan Alley*, left, (1940) and *Moon over Miami*, right, (1941).

about it! It was a number I did with Betty Grable. It was the worst number that I've done, that Grable's ever done, that anybody has ever done! It was one of those horrible things which is just forced on you because of the song. It was during the war and it was called, 'I'll be Marching to a Love Song',* and it was just the most awful number.

The Fox colour processing was strikingly bold and gay, the tones vivid, the images razor sharp. The fiery furnace reds, pigeon-blues and peppermint greens, the yellows and oranges that seemingly burst from the screen, belonged to a deliberately hallucinatory colour scheme that heightened the fantastic effect of their gaudy musical numbers – with girls as artichokes, as snowflakes, as undulating petals of water lilies, and Carmen Miranda as a citrus grove. Their cameramen were among the best – Leon Shamroy, Ernest Palmer, Charles Clarke – as were their set designers – Boris Leven, Richard Day and Wiard Ihnen. The plot locations were exotic (*Down Argentine Way*, 1940, *Carnival in Costa Rica*, 1947, *Springtime in the Rockies*, 1942, *That Night in Rio*, 1941), with boats cruising along tropic shores, horses racing over South American pampas, planes flying over Miami, disclosing vistas of breathtaking landscape, and people dancing across their hotel suite for sheer joy (*Moon over Miami, Three Little Girls in Blue*). Their stable of stars, headed by Betty Grable, Alice Faye, Carmen Miranda, Don Ameche, Jack Oakie, Charlotte Greenwood, Phil Silvers, etc. ensured that the fun was kept to a maximum.

* *Footlight Serenade* (20th Century-Fox, 1941). 'I'll be Marching To a Love Song' was cut from the final release print but survives in a widely-distributed War Bond short.

The Betty Grable era began with *Down Argentine Way* (directed by Irving Cummings, 1940). Alice Faye's last minute cancellation due to illness (shades of *42nd Street*) got Betty the part, just as years before Alice had got her break when Lilian Harvey walked out of *George White's Scandals*. Grable was recalled from Broadway, where she had gone after appearing in numerous B films at most of the studios in the thirties and getting nowhere. She had made her début in the chorus of *Whoopee!* (1930) and moved steadily but unspectacularly to bits and and small parts. She appeared as a bubbly blonde in two Astaire musicals, *The Gay Divorcee* and *Follow the Fleet*, and eventually graduated to playing the college campus sweetheart for Paramount, who were then rehashing their Nancy Carroll-Buddy Rodgers campus frolics. By the end of the 30s, with her film career at a standstill, Grable, nothing if not a trouper, decided on New York to impress the producers back home. She accepted a part in Cole Porter's *Du Barry was a Lady*. Ethel Merman and Bert Lahr were top-lined. Choreographer Robert Alton staged it, and future MGM director Charles Walters was Betty's dancing partner. Tough little cream-puff Betty received her share of praise, enough for Darryl F. Zanuck to trust her with sharing in Alice Faye's workload, especially as Alice was beginning to complain about the sameness of her assignments. For Grable, eleven years of slogging away now paid off. If the public had failed to notice her before, they were about to make up for it. Starting with *Down Argentine Way* she zoomed ahead to become the top money-making star of the 40s, hailed as the girl with the million-dollars legs (they were insured for that much with Lloyds of London), sweetheart of the forces and wartime Pin-Up Queen. Of course success extracted a price. One will never know if Jack Cole was right. Since her fans, having failed to notice her while she was growing up, now refused to let her grow any further. But there is a zesty sample of her potential as a shrewd cookie in *Sweet Rosie O'Grady* (1943), the girl on the cover of the *Police Gazette*.

Down Argentine Way was the archetypal Fox vehicle, as suited to Grable as it would have been to Alice Faye or any of the others, with a slight adjustment to the gears to accommodate the star's speciality. Since Grable's was dancing, she danced where Faye would have sung or Henie skated. *Down Argentine Way* is perfect light entertainment with ravishing colour photography by Leon Shamroy, a glamorous wardrobe by Travis Banton, a superb supporting cast, an original score by Harry Warren and Mack Gordon, and directed by Irving Cummings at a pace that wasted nothing. Ameche sees Grable; they know they are made for each other, so that's out of the way. For dessert there is *bombe glace* in an explosive guest contribution by Carmen Miranda, decked out like a fiery cockatoo, singing 'South American Way'. The whole concoction is held together by a story about a confused horse reared to be a jumper when it is really a racer.

Miranda played herself and became overnight the most widely copied woman in America, while her exaggerated mannerisms and clothing became a female impersonator's delight. No war-time woman

On the set of *Song of the Islands* (1942). Betty with Jack Oakie, while her 'valuable' assets are being freshened up.

The girl who did so much for servicemen's morale selling Defense Savings Stamps.

was seen without the serviceable turbans she re-introduced, which kept Veronica Lake hair-styles out of the machinery at the factories. Her elevator pumps, lifting her several inches above sea-level, also became the fad. She rarely got the hero. Like such other likeable though less exotic viragos – Martha Raye, Virginia O'Brien and Betty Hutton – she was usually the hunter. Dick Haymes, John Payne, George Montgomery or Don Ameche went to the blonde leading lady. The good-natured indefatigable Miranda never seemed to care much anyway, and neither did the public who adored her hot tamale outbursts, and wildly funny knack chewing the English language around until it came out sounding like an ancient Inca dialect. Her last film appearance was a Martin and Lewis musical, *Scared Stiff* (1953), shortly before her death. In it she played a part like all her others and was still electric. Without a personality like Miranda the sameness of these films was less easy to disguise.

Betty Grable remade *Coney Island* (set in New York) as *Wabash Avenue* (set in Chicago). Her costumes were slightly different; her co-stars were

It was Carmen Miranda's fate to be aped as a 'turn', usually by men in drag. Tommy Trinder did his first one in a wartime Palladium revue. Bottom: Jerry Lewis in *Scared Stiff*. Mickey Rooney in *Babes on Broadway* – for which Carmen showed him how. A GI making the best of a shortage of drag in *Winged Victory*.

Opposite: The Brazilian bombshell, Carmen Miranda, in her second film, *That Night in Rio*. She was something new; she crackled with vitality and her presentation was a carnival coronation.

Top right: By the end of the decade Betty Grable's films became mere frameworks for her legs. *Wabash Avenue*, 1950, had been *Coney Island* in 1943.
Centre right: A number from *The Dolly Sisters*. Betty Grable and June Haver in a biopic which was virtually a remake of the fictional *Tin Pan Alley*.

slightly different; her choreographers were different but *Wabash Avenue* was not as good because Betty by now was justifiably bored. She had done it all too often. Take *Tin Pan Alley* and *The Dolly Sisters*.

Tin Pan Alley had a story that was very loosely based on the careers of the Dolly Sisters. Faye, being the bigger star, got the better songs and the leading man (John Payne); but the film served to spotlight a young, peppy and slim-trim Grable. Once Grable was established she co-starred with June Haver in *The Dolly Sisters* (1945) – *Tin Pan Alley* all over

again. Haver, like Grable, also co-starred with Dan Dailey, the Broadway hoofer who'd been a Metro gangster before the war, until, working with Grable, he was able to return to his first love, musicals. An all-round entertainer/actor (he made several films with director John Ford) Dailey recalls his time at Fox:

'Musicals were probably one of the biggest grossing things they had at Fox, but they always did the gay nineties musicals and they always wanted you to do the same dance in every picture. You could change the wardrobe and the music, but that's about all you could change.

'I got into films when I was playing in LA with a tour of *I Married An Angel*, in which I'd replaced Chuck Walters, and a man from MGM asked me to make a test. When I got back from the war, after four and a half years in the army, they'd signed so many new young leading men who'd been 4F that there were about sixty guys ahead of me in line. When I went in people like Gregory Peck and Van Johnson had never made a picture. When I got out they were big stars! There was nothing for me.

'One day my agent called and said, "Listen, how would you like to make a picture with Betty Grable?" I hung up on him because I thought he was kidding me. But they were serious and wanted to see a test of me in a musical. Well, I'd made a test with Eleanor Powell when I was supposed to be doing *For Me and My Gal*, which Gene Kelly made when I went into the army, but originally it was supposed to be Powell and me. After Zanuck saw the test and he'd only remembered me from little things I'd done at Metro, nothing to do with musicals, he told me, "We'll have to sign you to a contract because if you do this picture – *Mother Wore Tights* (1947), you're going to be valuable to us." Betty was very kind to me, because she was a tremendous star at Fox as you know. And one day while we were making *When My Baby Smiles at Me* (1948), which was based on the old play *Burlesque*, we were doing something and she said "Oh baby, go get it . . . this one's yours, I've got mine," and she kind of hung back and let me have the picture. It was the one I was nominated for an Oscar for.

'When we did those films we worked on the songs by ourselves. We'd go to this little rehearsal hall, and try to find ways in which we could make them look or sound a little different. I did one routine for years which I designed for *You Were Meant for Me*' (1948, with Jeanne Crain). 'It was a number I did with two boys, easy, laid back, with a straw hat, simple and clean and pretty.

'Of course I felt that we could have done more, better things, but Mr Zanuck didn't want us to do them. We had our routine and that was it, so we didn't do them, but of course we knew what was going on at the other studios, like over at MGM. Mind you, we had something they couldn't do because Warner's tried to imitate us all the time, you know, all those Dennis Morgan-Jack Carson things and they never succeeded.

'Our musicals usually took about six months to make including rehearsals and everything. But I was probably the tallest dancer there was, so the things I did weren't too like what others were doing. I had to develop my own style; I don't think anybody could ever say I stole it from anybody. Being big, I had to move big! I couldn't do little teeny things like some people can. Peter Gennaro and those people, they do those little things! They look all right but I couldn't get away with that. I'm 6' 4" and Grable was only 5' 2" and you had to make it look like it was all right. But she always looked taller than she was for some reason or other. She thought tall.

'One of the last musicals I did at Fox was *There's No Business Like Show Business* (1954). It was like all those films they'd been doing forever but we felt that this one was kind of ridiculous, because it was so overwhelming. I mean, how many jugglers can you see at one time? Mitzi Gaynor, Donald O'Connor, Johnny Ray, Marilyn Monroe, Ethel

Below, left: Dan Dailey in the 'Chattanooga Choo Choo' number repeat in *You're My Everything* (top). On set with choreographer Nick Castle and little Shari Robinson (bottom).

Merman . . . and everybody jumping around. Mind you, I liked working with Merman. I'd done a small part in a play with her on Broadway, *Stars in Your Eyes*. She was the biggest star on Broadway, and I danced with Tamara Toumanova. So it was kind of a kick for me, working as her co-star where I had been nothing. We've been calling each other 'Mom' and 'Pop' ever since.

'Marilyn had been in an earlier film of mine, *A Ticket to Tomahawk* (1950). She was in the background there, but I was as much responsible for her being in that picture as anyone. Because they wanted to fire her every minute. Later, when she became a star, people said she was always late because she was a star. No. That was Marilyn. She just couldn't help it. There was always something happening and she just couldn't get there on time. We had a delay one time because she got this rash. She was always hanging us up. And she was just a little stock girl at Fox, getting about 75 dollars a week. But I liked her. People got too serious with her, putting too much on her. But I didn't see anything that made me think she would become such a big star. All I saw was a distressed girl who needed a job. I used to think she should take her make-up off before she went to bed, and things like that, but she didn't display anything until I saw her in a picture that Huston did. Then I thought, "Yeah, she's got something going." When we worked

together again on *No Business*, then you couldn't have missed it. She had style, a way of moving. Whether the music was playing or not, she was moving to it!'

Faye, after years of feuding with Zanuck, left Fox in 1945; Henie had left in '43. Haver retired in 1953 and Grable hung up her pumps in 1955. Eventually Zanuck's vehicle ground to a halt. The miracle was that a product perfected for a war-time mentality outlasted the war by almost a decade. Of course, by the time Zanuck tried to do with Monroe what he had done with Alice, Betty, Carole, Jayne, June, Sheree, Sonja, Vera and Vivien, the old horse and buggy had had it and with *There's No Business like Show Business* the whole shebang collapsed into an awful mess; no fun, no sparkle. It was time to go home and watch the old ones with Alice and Betty on TV.

The Thalberg Legacy

The musical requires the harmonious blending of many talents. The co-ordination and creative use of these elements can be demanding. Few directors possess the special flair for integrating these elements. What so distinguished the 40s musical was the appearance of new directors who could.

MGM's reputation for musicals in the 40s is due to directors who could create a unity of expression through song and dance. Lyricist turned producer, Arthur Freed brought Broadway's and Hollywood's top creators to MGM and with them their ideas —

Previous pages, centre: Anything worth doing once was worth doing twice, or three times, or more, according to 20th Century-Fox. Below: *Three Little Girls in Blue* had already been *Moon over Miami*, centre left, and *How to Marry a Millionaire*, bottom left. The plot had, in any case, been around forever – *Three Blind Mice*, 1938. Below right: Alice Faye, Joan Davis and Marjorie Weaver in a remake of a silent which had starred Constance Bennett, Joan Crawford and Sally O'Neill, *Sally, Irene and Mary*. Bottom right: *The Pleasure Seekers* was set in Spain – when the setting was Venice it had been *Three Coins in the Fountain*, which was *How to.* . . .

Left: Fred Astaire in *Yolanda and the Thief*. Centre: Donald O'Connor in *Anything Goes*. Gene Kelly at Columbia, practising for *Cover Girl*, and Russ Tamblyn in the south of France for *Follow the Girls*. Bottom: Bobby Van in *The Affairs of Dobie Gillis*, Bob Fosse, Gower Champion and Kurt Kasznar in *Give a Girl a Break*, and Gene Nelson in *I Wonder Who's Kissing Her Now?*

Betty Grable and Dan Dailey, all dressed up for *Call me Mister*.

choreographers like Charles Walters, Eugene Loring, Robert Alton, Michael Kidd, Stanley Donen, Gower Champion and Bob Fosse. Writers – Betty Comden and Adolph Green, Kay Thompson, Alan Jay Lerner and Robert Edens. Art Directors – Jack Martin Smith, Lemuel Ayers and Oliver Smith. Costume Designers – Walter Plunkett and Irene Sharaff. Songwriters – Harold Arlen, E. Y. Harburg, Ralph Blane, Burton Lane, Hugh Martin, Frederick Loewe, Dietz and Schwarz, Jules Styne, Harry Warren, Cole Porter and Irving Berlin. Cameramen – Harold Rosson and Harry Stradling. Freed brought back neglected directors like Busby Berkeley and Rouben Mamoulian, talked Vincent Minnelli into returning to Hollywood and started Charles Walters, Gene Kelly, Stanley Donen and Robert Alton off on their directorial careers. The stars he brought out, brought back and brought up symbolized the glory of the musical – Gene Kelly from Broadway, Fred Astaire from retirement and Judy Garland who personified it.

From this stunning gathering of talent sprang such legendary musicals as *Meet Me in St Louis, Summer Holiday, The Pirate, An American in Paris, Yolanda and the Thief, The Band Wagon, Show Boat, Annie Get Your Gun, Babes on Broadway, Babes in Arms, The Wizard of Oz, Cabin in the Sky, Easter Parade, Good News, Gigi, Bells are Ringing, Singin' in the Rain, It's Always Fair Weather* and *On the Town*. To work for the Freed unit was

Judy Garland and Mickey Rooney in the modern style 'Hoe Down' number for *Babes on Broadway*.

understandably the ambition of Broadway and Hollywood's musical best.

The first time I met him I found an unprepossessing but genial man in his 70s, still working in his office at Metro, still planning and full of enthusiasm for his never to be realized project, *Say it with Music*, built around the songs of Irving

199

Right, below: Judy Garland on the set of *Meet Me in St Louis* with her future husband, director Vincente Minnelli.

Below: A moment from *Meet Me in St Louis*. The grown-up sisters, Judy Garland and Lucille Bremer, talk about boys.

Bottom: Baby sister Margaret O'Brien has an accident at Hallow'een in *Meet Me in St Louis*. Left to right, Marjorie Main, Judy Garland, Mary Astor, Harry Davenport and Lucille Bremer.

Right: Kensington Avenue, St Louis, the home of the Smith family in 1903. Vincente Minnelli and the production team filming on one of the most elaborate sets ever built at MGM.

Berlin. His faith in the future of the musical was quite unshaken: 'We all live in a certain amount of fantasy; perhaps nobody actually sings a song out loud, but they think a song.'

'I came out to Hollywood in '24. Crosby worked for me downtown in my shows in the Los Angeles Orange Grove Theatre. Brown composed melodies for the spasmodically produced musical shows on the West Coast, obtaining prominence with the "Doll Dance" written for Carter de Haven's "Music Box Revue" in Hollywood.'

Throughout these years as a lyricist, working mostly in collaboration with Nacio Herb Brown, he has been associated with standards such as 'Singin' in the Rain' from *Hollywood Revue of 1929* ('I don't think I spent more than an hour and a half writing the lyrics for that song'). He wrote the lyrics for 'The Wedding of the Painted Doll', 'You Were Meant for Me', and the title song for *The Broadway Melody*. Another of his hits was 'Pagan Love Song' ('We wrote that in one evening'). Bing Crosby first sang his 'Temptation' in *Going Hollywood*, while Joan Crawford introduced 'All I Do is Dream of You' in her Depression weepy, *Sadie McKee*. Eleanor Powell danced up a storm to his songs for *The Broadway Melody of 1936*, 'I've Got a Feeling You're Fooling' and 'You Are My Lucky Star'.

'I became a producer with *Babes in Arms* (1939), because Louis B. Mayer was strong on musicals. He needed a musical producer and so he asked me and that's how I started.

'I brought in a whole new crowd of people. I wanted a fresh start from what had been before, a combination of the new ideas that had been happening on the stage and what could be done with film. The early musicals were novelties, but few of them were *real* musicals.

Louis Mayer was very interested in musicals and that's why there was so much backing for MGM musicals. He already knew what I wanted to do from when I worked on *The Wizard of Oz*. I not only brought the property in; Goldwyn had it but didn't know what to do with it. I sent somebody to ask him if we could buy it. He said, "What is it?" We told him, "A Fantasy." He said, "Let them buy it." *The Wizard of Oz* was a very shaky proposition then because Nick Schenck in New York didn't like it at all. Fantasy was dead in movies. Originally Mervyn had put Dick Thorpe on to direct and he no more belonged to it than . . . So I got Victor Fleming. That man was a poet. One of the great unsung men of this business. I mean, apart from *Gone with the Wind*, his pictures have really stood up. I used to have bread and coffee with him every morning at the studio, feeling out his mind and the kind of things that he liked. If you go back over the things he did, I think he's even greater than John Ford, who was one of the masters. Someday someone's going to bring up what Fleming meant to this business.

'I waited a year after *Wizard* until I found the right property because there are too many people around who are ready to shoot you if you don't click right off, good friends of mine, like Eddie Mannix, who had no feeling for the kind of thing I wanted to do. So I made a bet on Judy Garland and Mickey with *Babes in Arms*. Well, that became the biggest picture Metro had that year, so I was in good shape.

The toughest one, though, was *Meet Me in St Louis*, which nobody liked. Finally we had a meeting and Mayer said, "Arthur's record has been so good, either he'll learn a lesson or we will, so go make the picture." And it was the biggest grossing picture they had for five years.

'I felt a lot of the stuff they were doing in musicals was stale. It had become a cliché. Being a songwriter myself I had no feeling for operetta. It's the difference between Victor Herbert and Jerome Kern. Both were great, but Kern revolutionized popular show music; he was the daddy of Dick Rodgers and Burton Lane and all that group. Even Gershwin. And that was more my sort of stuff. And Mayer encouraged me to bring out new talent. I already had Garland, and Berkeley worked for me. I brought him over to MGM because he had one great thing, a sense of the camera. Probably the best sense of anybody in that period. He was an unconscious surrealist. Astaire I brought over because I admired him from the time I was a kid. I had a helluva time bringing him over to Metro, because Eddie Mannix said, "How can you photograph him?" He said he was so ugly, and this was after he'd done all his films at RKO. Jack Cummings was making a picture with the Dorsey band with Frank Sinatra in it *(Ship Ahoy)*, and Frank sang two songs, and Mannix wanted to cut them both out after the preview because he said you can't photograph him.

'The others I brought out from New York as self protection. You take the old-time directors they had, like Jack Conway and Bob Leonard and those fellows. We didn't have the same kind of feeling for things. So that's why I brought out Minnelli and Bob Alton, Chuck Walters and Gene Kelly, Alan Jay Lerner, and Comden and Green. I'd seen the show they'd written, *On the Town*, and I felt a great fresh

Fred Astaire and Lucille Bremer in Arthur Freed and Vincente Minnelli's revue, *Ziegfeld Follies*. This number was actually cut from the released film.

Above: Lena Horne and a fearful swain in *Cabin in the Sky*. Eddie Anderson seated, left, has the Lord's general, Kenneth Spencer, trying to keep him from temptation. Rex Ingram as the Devil (right) looks like winning. 'Consequences'.

Right: Another loss from *Ziegfeld Follies* was the Gershwin number, 'Liza', particularly since it deprived audiences of Lena Horne. In this production still her partner is Broadway star Avon Long.

talent there. Nobody had asked them to come before because Hollywood didn't like stage people, but I wanted new faces, fresh ideas. I've got to give a lot of credit for the success of my unit to Mayer because he completely backed me. Absolutely.

'When I first brought Minnelli out I couldn't get him an assignment because they said, "Who the hell is Minnelli?" So I bought *Cabin in the Sky*. It was an all-coloured picture; there were no Metro stars in it, so Mannix and a couple of the others couldn't scream. Then after that picture everybody wanted Minnelli.

'Walters came out as a choreographer on *Du Barry was a Lady*, and then he did the choreography on *Meet me in St Louis*. Funny part of it was that I knew Chuck wanted to become a director, and I called him when I was doing *Easter Parade*, because

by then Judy and Vincente were on the complete outs, so I couldn't use Vincente on it. So I said: "Chuck, I'm going to give you *Easter Parade*, and he said, 'Do you think I can do it?' I said 'Of course you can." Then Irving [Berlin], who knew Walters from New York, as a dancer, came to me and said, "I don't like the idea of Walters doing this. I'm going to discuss it with Mr Mayer." I said, "Irving, go ahead. You're making the picture . . ." and he said, "Forget it." He went back to New York. When he came back we ran the stuff for him and he said, "You were right." Now I had a helluva fight with Mannix about putting Chevalier in *Gigi*. He said, "That old son of a gun – nobody will got to see the picture."

'If there's one thing that characterizes my films, it's an honesty in writing. I got that from Thalberg. He was my model for what I wanted to be. When I started out at Metro I had a lot of talks with Thalberg. He had two or three great qualities. First of all, he had great taste. Second, he had a great sense of women. Most of the stars on the lot at that time were women, and he was mainly responsible. The other thing was, even in those days of hack writing in most cases, he had a sense of reality in writing. Of honesty in writing. He didn't like trick things. There are certain fundamental things that all producers got from Irving. Character more than plot. Irving always said, "To hell with the plot." *Meet me in St Louis* was built on characters. The only story there was "There's No Place Like Home". Every producer is different, as every director is different. A creative producer like Irving Thalberg or David Selznick *made* the picture. It wasn't a question of hiring the writer and the director. They made the picture. As a producer I was primarily concerned with the end product. Then, who's going to write it; who's going to do the songs; who's going to do the choreography. To get all the top talents. In these things I did a lot of research myself. For example in *The Wizard of Oz*, how do you do the Munchkins? I said, "Get singer midgets." Whose going to do the lion? I said, "Bert Lahr is the lion."

'I remember one idea for *Easter Parade* to give it a twist. The fellow always sends the Easter bonnet. I said, for once let the girl send the Easter bonnet. So she sends him the silk hat with the flowers around it. But there are many producers work that way.

'Take *An American in Paris*. I've got a poolroom in my house. Ira [Gershwin] and I used to play pool a lot. So then, one evening after we'd finished playing we're sitting, and I got this flash. Now for years I'd been wanting to make a picture about Paris in the Lautrec period. Minnelli and I used to talk about it many times, but then Huston made *Moulin Rouge*. So I said to Ira, "How about selling me the title *An American in Paris?*" He said, "If you use all Gershwin music." I said, "I wouldn't use anything else." So we started talking about it and I said that what I wanted to do was take George's composition of *An American in Paris* and use it *in toto* for the finish as a ballet. Irving Berlin was here at the time as I was doing *Easter Parade* and he said, "Kid, I hope you know what you're doing. To do a 20-minute ballet in a picture!" Now I didn't know whether it would be Astaire or Kelly. So I told Vincente the idea and he was crazy about it, and we decided that Gene was more of a ballet dancer than

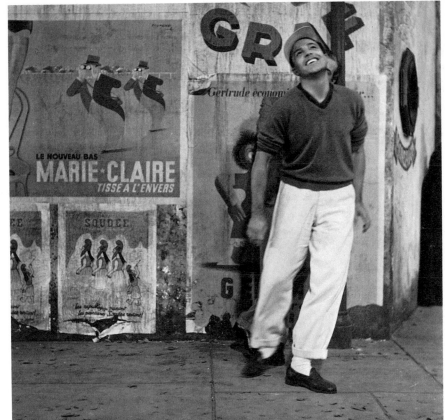

Above: Gene Kelly – *An American in Paris.*

Left: Gene Kelly and Leslie Caron. A number from *An American in Paris.*

Above left: Gene Kelly in *The Pirate*, on his perilous way by high wire to Judy Garland's room.

Fred. Now we looked over some French girls. The studio tried to get me to use Cyd Charisse because she was under contract but she wasn't right. There was a girl in Paris called Odile Versois, and I called Gene, who was on holiday in New York, to ask him to fly to Paris and make a test of this Versois girl, and, incidentally, there was this other little girl we looked at pictures of, who we referred to as the cat girl, and I told him to make a test of her as well. Then we looked at them and I asked Gene which one he liked. He said, "I won't tell you. You go down and see who you like." I asked Vince which one he liked. He said, "I won't tell you. Let's run them again and we'll write it down on a piece of paper." We ran the two tests again. Versois was pretty good. She was an experienced actress. But we both wrote down the other girl. That was Leslie Caron. She was a kid; she came over with her mother. I think we paid her $500 a week, which was more money than she'd ever seen and she probably still has 400 of that 500. Now came the question of who was going to write it. Ira was stuck on Alan Lerner, but I was afraid to approach Alan on it because he liked to write the songs himself and we had all Gershwin songs, but I told Alan the idea anyway and he said, "I'd like to write it." I thought he was kidding at first, but he won the Academy Award for it. Now there was a copy of *Life* Magazine about the fellows over there studying painting on the G.I. Bill of Rights so I said, "Let's make the character a painter because George Gershwin had been in Paris studying painting, and it gives a little feeling for the characters. And I gave Alan the idea for the Oscar Levant character, based on David Diamond, who was always broke and never had enough money to come back to America. But the rest of it was Alan of course.

'Then our original idea was to shoot the ballet on the streets in Paris. So, about the middle of the picture I got the idea that since the man was a painter, in his imagination he would see the paintings of Renoir, Rouault, all of them, and I called Vince and Gene up after shooting one day and told them my idea and they loved it and we cancelled our plane tickets and brought Irene Sharaff out to do the costumes for it and shot it here. So these are the steps in the making of a picture similar to most pictures.

'When I first told Mayer that I wanted to make a picture called *An American in Paris* he said, "Where did you get a title like that?" I said, "It's Gershwin." He said, "Make it." He didn't say, "Who's going to be in it? What's in it?" In the end, making a musical is a collaborative affair. It was Lerner, it was Minnelli, it was Gene. All of them. It's the total thing.

'Take today. Streisand is a big star. But *Hello Dolly* is a bust. Streisand was the biggest piece of miscasting in the world. And it's one of the reasons young Zanuck was out at Fox – spending $23 million on a little picture like that! But there are no rules. As Louis Mayer said: "Business is not an exact science." When I look back what I remember fondest is the people I worked with. The group I worked with – Alan Lerner and Fritz Loewe, Betty and Adolph, Judy, Minnelli, all these great people I worked with. Those are the great moments.' Probably the most significant of Freed's many decisions was the one that brought Vincente Minnelli back to Hollywood in 1940.

Minnelli was hardly new to the business, having been born into the theatrical life and having toured the mid-west as a child in the Minnelli Brothers tent show. His father, an Italian, was the orchestra leader; and his mother, of French origin, was the leading lady. From the grind of the tent shows the young Minnelli went to work as a sign painter (his flair for colour and design), then joined the Balaban and Katz theatrical chain as an assistant, helping to direct their stage shows and design their costumes and sets.

Inevitably it led him to New York where he became set designer at the Paramount Theatre where, amongst his other productions, he designed the enormously successful English adaptation of the German operetta, *Du Barry*, which starred Grace Moore and brought that artist back to Hollywood. Then he became the stage director at the Radio City Music Hall for three years. He also directed ballets like *El Amor Brujo* and several Broadway musicals, becoming one of the most talked about creative forces on the scene. His fame reached Hollywood's ears. Paramount signed him in 1937 and brought him to the coast but, except for designing and directing a black-faced Martha Raye and Louis Armstrong for the Harold Arlen and Ted Koehler 'Public Enemy Number One' sequence in *Artists and Models* (1937), they didn't know what to do with him. The day of their creative expansiveness was behind them. Hominy grits was the dish of the day.

His next bout with Hollywood was decisive. Freed, who knew of Minnelli's Broadway work, offered him a contract. 'I asked him to come out, and he came for the price of his hotel bill.' For some time he was kept at Metro without being given any specific directorial work. However, he did have the opportunity to absorb the atmosphere and study the work then going on in the various departments of the Freed unit. At this time, he directed and staged the Judy Garland musical sequences in *Babes on Broadway* (1941).

'When I arrived in Hollywood, I didn't look down on musicals as so many people who were doing them there did, treating them as a romp, a slapstick, nothing to be taken seriously. Busby Berkeley's large-scale numbers never moved me. I'm only interested in musical stories in which one can achieve a complete integration of dancing, singing, sound and vision. I would often look at Mamoulian's *Love Me Tonight*, as it was such a perfect example of how to make a musical.'

Minnelli talked about the method he has adhered to consistently in his film career: 'I don't have everything completely prepared before I go on a set. I know some directors work like that, and it seems to suit them, but for me this wouldn't be right. It's prepared as well as you can prepare it, but I always feel that you must leave quite a large area for improvisation. Things come out when you're working with personalities, so you make alterations as you go along.'

Minnelli, interviewed by Mark Shivas for *Movie No. 1*, adds: 'Each time I begin on a new film, I have to forget that I've ever made any before. It's an unconscious process – you must wait, hoarding impressions. As you mull it over, you begin to see a form, a style. This is the crucial moment – you have to resist all outside influences, for everything brings back memories of something else, and another style may superimpose itself on what you have in mind. This is the tricky point: you must wait until you are sure that you can hold on to the essential thing, the style you want. You can't see a single detail, you don't know how to put it together, but that doesn't matter. You can see this form, this style. I think it is largely a matter of intuition. I think with my stomach more than with my head.

'Initially I had great opposition to some of the things I had in mind to do. Especially from the art dept, which was then run by Cedric Gibbons. They were used to doing things a certain way and he could never understand what it was I was getting at. So I just held my ground, and eventually, when they saw that it seemed to work, they let me alone. I remember the problems we had with the fountain for the ballet in *An American*. I knew the man who was in charge of all the painting, a fantastic man; he got into the spirit of it and made it a sort of competition between all his artists, getting them to submit sketches in the style of different artists. And I worked out this central fountain idea with the man who did the sculptures, who was also marvellous. But Cedric Gibbons felt that the fountain should be solid, with things painted on it in the style of Dufy. I knew that wouldn't work because of when the lights would have to go out and then the silhouette would be horrible, while making it in metal, with all these apertures, and very sketchy, it would work whether there was light on it or not, and when there was light behind it it would still look like there were figures sketched in. But you have to compromise when you're working with a commercial studio. You just have to learn how to get a certain percentage of what you started out to get and to be satisfied with that. But I always have a very good idea of how I wanted things to be done, right from the beginning.

'Subconsciously, to some extent, when I read a script, especially for a musical, I see it in colour. And the camera is my paint brush. I generally shoot with just one camera. The most important elements to keep in mind when doing a musical are the property, the story and the score, and then the choreographer. Of course the score governs the whole quality of the film. It's as important as the written word. When I was a designer I had a morgue, boxes and boxes of clippings, and I'd go through them before I'd do a film, to find the sort of thing I had in mind for something. That helps an art director very much, even when sometimes it's something that has nothing to do with what they are looking for at all, but it shows a quality, a way of thinking. It's not to limit them, because you always work with people you have respect for, like Cecil Beaton. Working with Irene Sharaff you're working with a master. She really intellectualizes all these things. She has reasons for everything.'

Then came *Meet me in St Louis*, a timely and timeless classic. It was a showcase for all the virtues of a closely knit family – as would please Louis B. Mayer, who was personally responsible for the *Andy Hardy* series – depicting an American ideal that could quicken the heart of the man in the trenches. It is a perfectly constructed musical and great Americana.

'*Meet me in St Louis* was based on a series of original short stories written by Sally Benson which had appeared with great success in *The New Yorker*. When Freed asked me what I thought of the idea of doing a film based on these stories I was very excited, because I could see them as people.

'From the first, I wanted Judy [Garland] for it. At that time she was riding very high at MGM, and was against doing it. Everybody was telling her that it would kill her career. She came to me full of objections. She had already been to see Arthur Freed and hadn't got anywhere with him, but she thought she could make short shrift of me. When I finished explaining what I had in mind and how right she

would be for the film, she left my office bewildered, having agreed to do it.'

Minnelli achieves a meticulous sense of the past by exploring with his colour camera the magnificent set designed by Lemuel Ayres and Cedric Gibbons. The street and buildings give the cosy feeling of families living behind those doors, to be opened at the camera's touch.

All the songs arise spontaneously. At a party given in the family home, it is only natural for someone to lay the piano, and for the friends to dance and sing 'Skip to my Lou', a joyously choreographed number by Walters. The two youngest sisters creep down from their beds to look in on the party. Esther, (Judy), to entice them back to bed, agrees to do a number with her baby sister, Tootie (Margaret O'Brien). The two, strawhatted and with canes in hand, go into a cakewalk number that entertains friends and underlines the close affection that binds the family.

Garland is at her best, as she always was when directed by Minnelli (*The Pirate, Ziegfeld Follies, Till the Clouds Roll By*). Rarely has her singing, welcome as it always is, seemed so right. 'The Trolley Song', 'The Boy Next Door' and the infectious, lilting title song are a few of the gems.

At a time in Hollywood films when the mother of a girl as old as Garland would normally be played by a character actress, Minnelli cast Mary Astor. She proved the perfect choice, the quiet pillar of warmth and love at the centre of the family. The performance Minnelli draws out of Margaret O'Brien is one that momentarily alters any dubious feelings one might have about child actors. Garland, comforting her the night before Christmas, which is also the night before they move to New York, sings 'Have Yourself a Merry Little Christmas'. Six-year-old O'Brien,

Director and star of *The Pirate* on the set with their baby daughter. Liza Minnelli is in her father's arms.

Astair and Bremer were teamed again in *Yolanda and the Thief*, and their producer and director were again Arthur Freed and Vincente Minnelli. The stars in the swirling 'The Four by Five' number.

Opposite, top: The magnificently designed, dressed and costumed 'Limehouse Blues' number in *Ziegfield Follies*. Fred Astaire and Lucille Bremer.

Right: Fred Astaire and Cyd Charisse in *The Band Wagon*. The spectacular Mickey Spillane 'Girl Hunt' ballet.

faced pressed against the cold window pane, looks at her carefully built snowmen, and her tears well up and flow silently. The ending, resolving in the father's decision to stay in St Louis, is one of overwhelming happiness. It was Minnelli's third film, and a theme to which he never returned. It may well be his finest work.

He followed *St Louis* with *The Clock*, a non-musical starring Judy Garland (who would soon be his wife) and Robert Walker. Then he made as stylish a technicolor extravaganza as any director has ever made, *Ziegfield Follies* (1945). Minnelli shot the bulk of his sequences between May and July of 1944 but the film's release was held up until early in 1946. The name had proved profitable to Metro twice before with *The Great Ziegfield* (1936) and *Ziegfield Girl* (1941). It was the lavish revue film to end them all, in which five directors also shot sequences or parts of sequences while Minnelli was in overall charge. In *Ziegfield Follies*, Minnelli could do all the things he had been experimenting with

while working on the stage at Radio City Music Hall.

A quarter of a century later the film's elegance remains undimmed, its best numbers suffused with the grace, style and visual enchantment of the Minnelli hallmark. His own favourite sequence in the film was the 'Limehouse Blues' number.

'It had an interesting problem, and was made very much in the "Broken Blossom" style. "Limehouse Blues", as you may know, had a theatrical tradition.' (It was first sung in the 20s by Gertrude Lawrence in the André Charlot Revues.' 'First of all the "Limehouse Blues" ballet had been choreographed with a style designed by Irene Sharaff in the manner of French Chinoiserie, a fantasy. I shot that first, completely as a theatrical thing, with the lighting done in the theatrical way. Long stretches would be in blackness, then suddenly the entire set would appear and so on. Then it took up an entirely different style in the prologue and epilogue. They had to be done in very few days, so I found a set that was already standing. It was a set of an English street' (from *The Picture of Dorian Gray*). 'I made a few changes and turned it into Limehouse, planted a bunch of extras, selected costumes for the characters and then made up a story. I just used black, yellow and white with yellow lighting to give it some kind of style, and a lot of fog . . . and made an impression, that's all. But it was great fun to do; it was all improvised.'

Astaire and Kelly had a number in *Ziegfeld Follies* – the only time they appeared together on film – "The Babbit and The Bromide". 'We kept thinking about what we could do with them together: as they were both in the film it would have been a shame to waste the opportunity – so we found a story, but then the story became unimportant. They are quite different as dancers; Kelly is more earthy, and Astaire is more jaunty. Doing the number, they were so considerate of each other – like Alphonse and Gaston – neither intending to outdo the other.'

In 1945 Minnelli went to work on the least successful of his major musicals, the charming fantasy based on a story by Ludwig Bemelmans, *Yolanda and the Thief*. The stars were Astaire and Lucille Bremer, while Jack Martin Smith once again collaborated as designer, and Eugene Loring did the memorable choreography. For the first time, Minnelli did one of his great ballet sequences in a film, the surrealistically designed 'Dream Ballet' which foretells the plot of this fantasy, proving that ballet could be done successfully, when everybody had been saying that the public would never stand for it. (The enormous success of the English film, *The Red Shoes*, two years later completely refuted this old argument.) But the most memorable of all the Harry Warner-Arthur Freed numbers for the film was the four-by-five (the music is in four-by-four time, the dance is five-four) 'Coffee Time'. As hands clap and feet tap, Astaire partners Bremer on a swirling op-art parquet floor to a state of pure exhilaration. For its duration one can almost forget that the red-headed, button-faced Lucille Bremer is not Rita Hayworth.

Minnelli worked on another non-musical, the very *noir Undercurrent* and then returned to the genre with what remains and grows as one of the most energetic, stylishly colourful and bravura musicals made. Cole Porter wrote an original score that was one of his finest for a film, and which, like so much of his work, was initially considered inferior to his earlier achievements. The film was *The Pirate* (1947).

It had been done on the stage as a straight comedy by Alfred Lunt and Lynne Fontanne and had been written for them by S. N. Behrman. I was very pleased with the way the film turned out. Judy gave one of her best performances, and the Cole Porter songs were excellent. Unfortunately, the merchandising of the film was bad, and it failed to go over well when it was released.

Gene Kelly collaborated with Minnelli on the dance numbers, and if Kelly's strenuously athletic style is not to everybody's liking, he nevertheless gives the dance numbers an explosive energy that was unlike the Minnelli-Astaire films.

Late in 1952 *The Band Wagon*, starring Fred

Astaire and Cyd Charisse, was released. Minnelli and Astaire complemented each other here in an inspired way. Again it was Freed who brought them all together, as he recalled: 'I started out with the Howard Dietz and Schwartz music. Dietz was then one of our vice-presidents. Buchanan was an accident in the picture. I had wanted Clifton Webb

Leslie Caron and Isabel
Jeans in Minnelli's *Gigi*.

with second thoughts about his career. Tony Hunter,
like Astaire, is a former Broadway star who went
into films. Oscar Levant and Nanette Fabray lend
exuberant support as the two wise-cracking playwrights, not unlike Comden and Green, and Jack
Buchanan matches Astaire in a send-up of the outrageous Broadway actor-author-director genius, not
unlike José Ferrer at that time.

Astaire gives one of his finest performances. His
dancing has poetry and eloquence. In the story he
and Cyd Charisse soon find their patience strained
by the tension of rehearsals and a basic misunder-
standing between each other. They go for a late
night ride in Central Park; music reaches them from
a nearby bandstand, they start to walk in step.
Subconsciously, their bodies pick up the rhythm of
their feet; they melt into 'Dancing in the Dark',
expressing in motion all they feel for one another.
Minnelli's camera is the private eye that shows us
their heart.

Minnelli: *The Band Wagon* being about the theatre,
the ballet that would climax the story had to be on a
stage, and had to be something that was popular at
that time because the idea of the story was that the
director (Jack Buchanan), who was very artistic and
impractical, ruined the show.* Astaire picked it up,
made it popular, jazzy, and that's what the people
like. As Mickey Spillane's novels were very popular,
I made it a satire on those novels. They're almost a
satire in themselves. I made it in the spirit of Mickey
Spillane, with beautiful girls and killings and
private eyes.

The film was very smart. But the people were very
real. The feelings were true. One didn't have to be
smart to identify with and respond to all this talent
devoting their energy to entertain. It never smirked
or stooped, and the underlying honesty of emotion
that marks the appeal of Astaire and Rogers as
much as that of MacDonald and Eddy reached out to
entrance all.

Subsequently Minnelli's musicals turned more

Gene Kelly and Cyd
Charisse in *Brigadoon*.

originally, but he thought the character wasn't sar-
castic enough, and suggested I take [Jack]
Buchanan. Cyd Charisse was probably Fred's best
partner.'

Astaire and his sister Adele had starred in the
revue of the same name which 20th Century-Fox
bought and then didn't know what to do with,
though using some of the songs for *Dancing in the
Dark* (1949). For the Minnelli film MGM bought the
rights to the title and the songs but added a new and
wittily sophisticated storyline conceived by
Comden and Green. Said Minnelli, 'Astaire was
sporting enough to like it.'

Astaire accepted the part of Tony Hunter, failing
film hoofer who, encouraged by a couple of writer
friends, tries for a Broadway comeback. Super-
ficially the character of Tony Hunter had a lot in
common with Astaire, then fifty-two and possibly

towards the tried and true Broadway musicals. *Gigi* (1958), though based on a play inspired in turn by a French film starring Danielle Delorme, had not been a musical and proved the exception. But the three others of that decade, *Brigadoon* (1953), *Kismet* (1955) and *Bells are Ringing* (1960) were adapted from the stage with variable success. It was a time in his career when Minnelli had turned more to straight subjects and this conflict of interest showed, especially in the case of the very lack-lustre *Kismet*, a project he accepted on the insistence of Dore Schary against his own inclinations, being absorbed in the shooting of *Lust for Life* at the same time. Sadly what should, could so easily, have been an eye-opening Oriental fantasy was a dull smug listless bazaar trek enlivened only by Howard Keel's braggadocio beggar-poet and Dolores Gray's lusty harem queen. *Brigadoon*, set in a make-believe highland village, was only a little better. For one thing it didn't have Ann Blyth and Vic Damone as insipid lovers, instead there was Gene Kelly, his choreography and Cyd Charisse, who was always best when she was slightly other-world, and there was the great Lerner and Loewe score.

Only *Bells are Ringing*, made after the success of *Gigi*, seemed to revitalize Minnelli's interest in musicals. Charles O'Curran, Betty Hutton's ex, worked on the choreography. Judy Holliday, already something of a cult favourite, recreated her Broadway triumph in the Comden and Green show and Dean Martin was her acceptable if uninspiring leading man. Of course all these films showed the Minnelli touch but only the last of them had his flair, the intangible something that lifts the spirits. Even so, it is sub-Minnelli. Not so *Gigi*, the Gallic *My Fair Lady* with an original Lerner and Loewe score that won eight Oscars, including one for Minnelli. Visually it was ravishing and of a piece, Paris, the Belle Epoque, and a vintage Loewe score. Though he received no credit, when the film went into over-time, Chuck Walters was brought in by Freed to shoot two of the numbers back in Hollywood, 'The Night They Invented Champagne', and 'She's Not Thinking of Me.' This contribution takes no credit away from Minnelli's achievement.

Minnelli: *Gigi* was controlled by what we [Alan Jay Lerner] set out to do. A story of Paris by Colette in a period that had it's own visual style, the early 1900s. We tried to recreate it very much in the order of the Sem drawings, because Sem actually did caricatures in Maxim's of the people Colette was writing about. Lerner was very sensitive to this and so was I, and the way we showed Paris was completely dictated by the story and the period, everything was done within that frame.

Gigi, originally intended for magical Audrey Hepburn who had been brought out to Hollywood on the strength of creating the role on Broadway, was unavailable and the part was played by the garrulous gamine, Leslie Caron. Caron, who had repeatedly expressed her dissatisfaction with dancing in musicals(!) was here required only to sing, and back again with Minnelli who had given her the springboard to fame in *An American in Paris*, gave a respectable interpretation of the

tomboy groomed to become a courtesan. But the film's real acting surprise was Louis Jourdan, and its human treasures lay in the evergreen hands of Chevalier, Gingold and Isabel Jeans. But none of their contributions would have had the same effect without Minnelli. It is his triumph.

Minnelli: *Kismet* and *Brigadoon*, which were done about the same time, had both been stage musicals. Their difference from *Gigi* is a difference in the style of writing. The style of *Gigi* is the sort of thing Alan Lerner did in *My Fair Lady*, where the lyrics of the songs are practically dialogue. It's a completely different style from *An American in Paris* and *The Band Wagon*, where you use a song that had been a popular standard for years. But I have no preference amongst the various styles of my films. I like the freedom of *An American in Paris*, but I also like the discipline and control of a piece like *Gigi*, which is more of a play with musical accompaniment. The problem with *Bells are Ringing* was to get the same effects on the screen in a different way than was done on the stage. It is a dramatic story in which songs are used to advance the action; again, almost like dialogue.*

Since *Bells Are Ringing* Minnelli has made only one musical, although for a long time he worked on Freed's projected musical biography of Irving Berlin, *Say It With Music*. He returned in good form with *On A Clear Day* (1970), the musical adapted by Alan Jay Lerner from his stage show, with songs by Burton Lane, starring Barbra Streisand. It had Cecil Beaton for the costumes and psychiatry as its subject.

What made a Minnelli film more than just songs and dances cleverly interpolated into the plot was his use of the subconscious motivation that erupted into elation *with* a song and dance. This he brought into the open to make sense of song and dance to explain everyday emotions. Charles Walters and Bob Fosse would follow his lead; Minnelli had got his from the work of Rouben Mamoulian. Arthur Freed, like Minnelli, was a great admirer of Mamoulian's and so it was natural that he would try and get him to work for him. The result was *Summer Holiday* (1948).

Summer Holiday is a musical adaptation of Eugene O'Neill's play, *Ah, Wilderness!* But it is more than an adaptation, much more than a straight translation from the stage to the screen – as O'Neill discovered when Mamoulian first discussed his plan with him: 'I went to see O'Neill out of affectionate respect, to talk to him. Of course, I already knew him. Back in 1928 he had a play, *Marco Millions*, which the Theatre Guild was planning to do. I wasn't meant to direct it, but O'Neill saw my production of *Porgy* and insisted that I direct his play. They already had another director, but they all wanted to please O'Neill. I said I would do it with certain cuts. Now, O'Neill always refused to change a comma, so they just laughed and sent me to see him myself. He flushed red when I told him about the cuts I wanted

---

* In the past few years MGM have unearthed the cut numbers from some of their musicals, including those Minnelli filmed for *Brigadoon* and *Bells are Ringing*.

Another moment from the 'Girl Hunt' ballet in *The Band Wagon*. This time Astaire's partner, Cyd Charisse, is in blonde guise.

Rouben Mamoulian's *Summer Holiday*. The 4th of July picnic scene, choreographed by Charles Walters.

to make; he listened to my ideas and he approved all my cuts.

'Now we were very good friends, and when I was set for *Summer Holiday*, I wanted to explain to him what changes I intended on the script. We had a long talk. He asked, "Why do it as a musical? It's a good play!" I agreed with him.' (It had already been filmed as a straight play by MGM under its own title in 1935.) 'But I told him why I wanted to do it as a musical and that I had to make some changes. He flushed again and said, "You talk about respect and affection and you want to change it!" So I explained my ideas for filming it. I told him what I planned to do with the barroom scene, and how I wanted the audience to see what the boy felt. That was the scene between the boy' (Mickey Rooney) 'and the local bad girl' (Marilyn Maxwell) 'in which she grows gradually more and more glamorous as the boy becomes more and more intoxicated. O'Neill was very excited by my idea. He understood that what I was trying to do *was* out of my admiration, and he agreed with anything I wanted to do after that.

'In the film I had a series of scenes in the styles of famous American painters: Grant Wood, Thomas Benton, John Curry. From them I learned what marvellous things you can do by just using different shades of the same colour. On a colour musical, I work out a chromatic script. I get everybody connected with it together and tell them what colours I want for everything. If I had a yellow wall in a room, I'd make sure the costumes would be off-yellow, no strong reds or such. Gibbons' (Cedric Gibbons, head set designer for MGM) 'was very worried about this. He thought Mayer would be against it. So I spoke with Freed and told him what I wanted, and things were OK after that.'

Walter Plunkett's memories are infused with admiration: 'Mamoulian is a great example of the old-fashioned continental director-producer à la Max Reinhardt, having the script writer, cameraman, designer and musicians working together with him. For instance, he let us know that for the opening scene of the film he wanted a period feel like that of the Currier and Ives prints of turn-of-the-century America. I wanted to eliminate colours from the dresses and suits of the characters to give the washed, faded look of the prints. So all of the clothes were done in different shades of white, pearly grey, whitened pinks, etc. Then when you did want to use colour for a scene or a dress, it had some meaning. When Mamoulian described the honkey-tonk sequence to me' (Mickey Rooney and Marilyn Maxwell) 'I came up with the idea of dressing the girl in progressive shades of red, to match the effect his first drink was having on him. This probably wouldn't have happened if Mamoulian hadn't been so exactly sure of what he wanted or if he hadn't known how to communicate it so exactly. Another time, there was an "Arabian Nights" dream sequence.' (This number between Rooney and Gloria de Haven was cut from the final print). 'Mamoulian allowed me to adapt the whole number from Persian print miniatures in those exquisite colours.

'Rarely does the designer in a film know what the other craftsmen on a film are doing. They design their dresses without knowing what the art director

might be doing for a scene in which the clothes would be worn. But working on Mamoulian's or Minnelli's film is like making a watch; each cog had to fit. No one can be good if he is made to work by himself, and then doesn't fit into the final image required. To achieve this effect, you have to be a good watchmaker: Mamoulian, Minnelli, Selznick, Arthur Freed, Jack Cummings, etc. With these people, it was the film that came first, not the star.'

When it was released *Summer Holiday* was a failure and, ignominiously, had to be taken off in some cinemas because the audience was making more noise than the film. Its time would come. A

Top: The 'A Couple of Swells' number in *Easter Parade*, with Judy Garland and Fred Astaire. The choreographer was Robert Alton.

Above: Charles Walters as Judy Garland's dance partner in *Presenting Lily Mars*.

great contribution to the film's appeal were the dances, Charles Walter's last choreographic chore before becoming a fully fledged director in his own right.

Walters had been brought to Hollywood by Freed as choreographer on a Kelly film. After five years as choreographer and occasionally as dancer, partnering Judy Garland among others, in films like *Presenting Lily Mars, Du Barry was a Lady, Broadway Rhythm, Girl Crazy*, etc, he got his chance to direct the small-budgeted remake of *Good News*, to star June Allyson in yet another role first created on screen by Bessie Love. Here was a case where less was made more by its director, after which he never looked back. *Good News* was my first film as a director, and I did everything in it, including the choreography. In my other films, I had various choreographic collaborators, such as Bob Alton for *Easter Parade* and *The Barkleys of Broadway,* but in *Good News* I did the straight numbers and the dances myself.'

Good News proved such a success ('It made

nothing but money!'), that Freed rewarded Walters with two of the studio's most valuable star properties, Judy Garland and Gene Kelly, for Irving Berlin's *Easter Parade* (1948). Initially, Minnelli was supposed to direct this film, but both Judy and Minnelli's psychiatrists thought it advisable for them not to work together just then. When Kelly sprained his ankle, Astaire, who had gone into retirement after *Blue Skies* two years before, was wooed back.

'The first script I saw was terrible! The hero was a real heavy. But with Astaire in the film, the whole script was geared to his high points. Bob Alton had blocked out most of the dance numbers with Kelly when I got there, and they were changed very little for Astaire.'

The only potential working problem was not between the stars, or the star and the director, but with the choreographer, Robert Alton, for it was Alton who had given Chuck his start in Broadway and now here he was working for his former chorus boy. It was tough but the men's professionalism came first and friendship survived. Freed subsequently gave Alton a chance to direct a musical, *Pagan Love Song* (1950), but it was not a success.* Apart from the excitement of the surprisingly successful star-harmony of Garland and Astaire, and peppery Ann Miller doing her best to make her first appearance in an MGM film really count, *Easter Parade*, one of those Irving Berlin singalongs, is not Walters at his typical best.

Easter Parade is another triumph for Garland and Astaire, as they leap joyfully through a film that for most of its duration is true to the first principle of recording movement. The story, set in turn of the century New York, is short and sweet and the numbers come thick and fast. 'Just a Couple of Swells' has Astaire and Garland doing their celebrated comic routine as tramps. The smooth elegance of 'It only Happens when I Dance with You' enables

*He had previously directed the non-musical comedy, *Merton Of The Movies* (1947), with Red Skelton.

him to partner a surprisingly demure Ann Miller in a
dance in a living room that remains a living room
without hampering the dancers' ballroom smooth-
ness; and in her solo, Ann, as Garland's glamorous
rival for Astaire's attention, does a show-stopping
echt-Miller tap routine to 'Shaking the Blues Away'.
The dialogue has a nice snap and doesn't hold up the
footwork. Fred, after painfully teaching the inexper-
ienced Garland a few steps (her way of telling her
left foot from her right is by attaching a garter to one),
loses his cool:

'Miss Brown, what idiot ever told you you could
dance?'

'You did!'

The film established Charles Walters as a major
new figure in the musical pantheon.

'Most of the choreography for *Easter Parade* was
done with the camera in mind', he said, 'so that it
could involve the audience in the dance numbers to a
greater degree.' The film's opening is a perfect
example of the Walters flair for capturing movement
with the camera and for the unexpected camera
angle that suddenly gains the number a whole new
perspective. It begins with our first sight of Astaire –
from the knees down – as he breezes wittily through
the streets of New York on a sunny day (in colour by
Technicolor.) Walters confidently keeps his
camera in step, until at last Astaire enters a shop,
and we see him full length. Having cleverly and
charmingly introduced the star, all in rhythm and
without a word of dialogue, Walter explodes the
screen with the first number, 'Drum Crazy', in which
Astaire takes advantage of the toy shop's contents.

I met Walters in his cool white apartment over-

looking the Pacific. His home is surprisingly free of
mementoes of his career except for a few signed
photographs of stars he has worked with, including
Debbie Reynolds, Joan Crawford and Gloria
Swanson.

His dancer's training has kept him in shape; his
striking good looks have altered little. With the
exception of his last film, a non-musical, *Walk,
Don't Run* (1966), for Columbia, all his film credits
have been with MGM, where he arrived from New
York in 1942 as a choreographer.

Charles Walters: I have always done the 'stars'
numbers – the so-called 'intimate book' numbers
like all *High Society* and Harve Presnell's and
Debbie's numbers for *The Unsinkable Molly Brown*.
I did all of Judy's numbers for her last film at Metro,
Summer Stock, and all the numbers Kelly and Judy
did together. Kelly did his own singles; I only shot
them. I'll never understand why more choreographers haven't made it as directors; after all,
dialogue is movement and rhythm; but more have
blown it than made it, unfortunately.

I never knew from picture to picture what I was
going to be doing next. At least we had artistic heads
in those days; now we get stockholders hollering,
telling us what we should do. Freed never interfered
once he picked the person for the job. If he thought
something was wrong, he'd discuss it with you, but
when it came to the final decision, he gave the choice
to his directors. He had a respect for talent, and that
created a good atmosphere in which to work. You
felt there was someone who understood what you
were trying to do and let you do it.

Leslie Caron and the puppets, à la Lilian Harvey in Charles Walters' *Lili*.

easier to go back than waste money on covering everything.'

Walters' choreographic use of the camera, the way in which it takes us into his confidence and includes us in his own excitement with the dance, has been characteristic of his work, no matter who actually choreographed the numbers of his later films. Whether as a director or as a choreographer he had taken the dance to the audience.

I suppose one of the things that made Metro musicals so alive and inventive was that we didn't study other people's work or what was happening in the theatre then, even though most of us came from the stage. I don't remember seeing anyone else's films, so I don't know whether or not I was influenced by the people working around me.

Musicals are tougher to do than straight dramas or comedies, because of the rehearsals needed, the recording sessions, the choreography, etc., but there is no basic difference between the way I direct drama and the way I direct musicals.

What makes a Walters musical different is an intuitive sense of rhythm which infuses the picture from the shooting, planning through on to the cutting stages. 'I have always edited my flicks, straight or musical, and only shot what I felt was needed. It's

Almost from the moment he arrived in Hollywood, Gene Kelly made it clear that he was not satisfied to be just a star who danced. His training as a choreographer and instructor at his own dancing school, strongly influenced by the new trends taking place in dance on Broadway and outside, could be seen at work in the dance numbers he choreographed for himself. Perhaps this driving need to control, shape and guide his numbers (especially in the films he did not direct), though justified by itself, laid too heavy a burden on his supposedly 'Jolly Lad' star persona. This happy guy up there on the screen who was wooing Kathryn, Esther, Vera, June, all nice next-door girls, as if he might leap up and kick their pretty teeth in if they dared say 'No' just once too often. His underlying impatience is in some measure responsible for the dynamic but overloaded feeling of some of his dance routines. In the end, they become wearying, imaginative but not spontaneous; and when partnered, as he preferred to be, by children, a feeling of cuteness lurked beneath their cleverness. It was inevitable that he would play a pathetic, white-faced pierrot in his ambitious feature-length ballet film, *Invitation to the Dance* (1956). Nevertheless, as a film star, Kelly was a most important addition to the musical talents gathered at MGM. With Stanley Donen, who had begun his professional career as a dancer in the chorus of *Pal Joey* (starring Kelly), he choreographed and co-directed several classic musicals, beginning with *On the Town* (1949), and including *Singin' in the Rain* (1952), and *It's Always Fair Weather* (1955). Donen also directed *Seven Brides for Seven Brothers* (1954) and *Funny Face* (1956), and co-directed *Damn Yankees* (1959) and *The Pajama Game* (1957) with George Abbott. These are among the few exciting musicals made with flair in the 50s.

For sheer 4th-of-July exuberance, neither Kelly nor Donen ever made a better film than *On the Town*. It was based on a stage musical by Betty Comden and Adolph Green, with music by Leonard Bernstein, and inspired by the Jerome Robbins ballet *Fancy Free*. Robbins choreographed the 1944 stage musical, as he had the earlier ballet version.

Arthur Freed recalled: 'We owned the property for pictures because originally they were looking for some backing for the show on Broadway, and they asked me to hear it, played me a couple of the songs and told me the idea for the Jerry Robbins ballet about three sailors on one day in New York, and I OK'd it and the studio put up the money. Then when I wanted to do it Gene said, "But I just did a sailor in *Anchors Aweigh*." But I told him this was a different kind of sailor. I felt it was a very honest story – three sailors meet three girls and then they've got to leave them, and you don't know whether they're ever going to get together again or not. So it had warmth.

Gene Kelly and Stanley Donen, co-directors, going over the next step on the set of *Singin' in the Rain*.

It probably would have been better if all three men had danced because everything in the show was basically written around Jerry Robbins' dances. But we got by with it. Of course for the film we had other scenes for which we needed other songs, and some of the original ones no longer fitted. I had compunctions about cutting them but you can't make your show a Bible. Otherwise you're not making a motion picture. That was one of the problems with *My Fair Lady*. Maybe I made a mistake, but the songs for Sinatra and Garrett had to be written; there was nothing for them otherwise.' Freed brought in Roger Edens to produce the film as well as write an entirely new set of songs with Comden and Green. Thus the spirit of the original was kept and the freshness more than made up for the coy patches.

In *On The Town*, Kelly was at last the director, and it reflects in his performance. What is sometimes his insufferable excellence is here that particular American genius for hyped spontaneity that draws an audience to and participate in. New York is perfect for Kelly and his troupe: Betty Garrett chasing shy Sinatra, Kelly in pursuit of

Vera-Ellen, and Ann Miller after Jules Munshin. The best solo number in the film takes place in the anthropological section of New York's Natural History Museum, where Miller adopts cave-woman tactics for a prehistoric tap that brings the dinosaurs tumbling down à la *Bringing up Baby*.

To the directors, to their cameraman, Harold Rosson, and to what was left of the original Bernstein score, credit must go for a musical which had all the gaiety, the vitality and the animal spirits proper to contemporary popular art. *On The Town* broke with the Hollywood convention of what a musical should be and should look like, and proved that dance numbers could be effectively staged in actual locations. For Kelly and Donen it opened a new chapter.

Kelly's film début was *For Me And My Gal* (1942, produced by Arthur Freed and directed by Busby Berkeley), a story with a vaudeville background and the trenches of World War I, in which he starred with Judy Garland. He was loaned to Universal to co-star with Deanna Durbin in *Christmas Holiday* (1944), a murky thriller with songs, and to Columbia

Top left: Gene Kelly on the set of *For Me and My Gal* (1942). Rehearsing, he sails over the head of Judy Garland.

Top: Gene Kelly in his role as solo director-choreographer. On the set of *Invitation to the Dance*, rehearsing the *corps de ballet* at the MGM British studios.

Above: *On the Town*. Gene Kelly co-directed with Stanley Donen, and starred with Betty Garrett, Frank Sinatra, Gene Kelly, Jules Munshin. Ann Miller's back is visible, and Alice Pearce is under the table.

for one of his best-remembered parts, in *Cover Girl* opposite Rita Hayworth. *Cover Girl* is Rita Hayworth, but at that time it also made Kelly.

Though dance direction credit went to Seymour Felix, several numbers were choreographed by Kelly and Donen, and they stand out in sharp contrast to the rest of the film. Rita Hayworth, Virginia van Upp's screenplay, Jerome Kern's score, and Ira Gershwin's lyrics (including the Oscar-nominated 'Long Ago and Far Away') all contributed sophistication, gaiety and charm to Columbia's biggest money-maker of the year. The film marked another auspicious coming together in the shape of the brilliantly innovative, jazz-orientated choreographer, Jack Cole, who worked here with Hayworth for the first of several memorable times. Her work with Cole made Rita the dancing goddess of the decade. More of her later.

Kelly received choreographic credit on *Anchors Aweigh* (1945), where he teamed for the first time with band singer Frank Sinatra (Joe Pasternak produced it and George Sidney directed). Sinatra's screen persona, as a girl-shy, diffident lad, is ironical to say the least in light of his subsequent career, on screen and off. This misconceived image-typing at MGM may have been responsible for setting back his career for a long time.

Anchors Aweigh gave Kelly two of his most popular dance numbers. The first is a fairytale sequence cleverly blending animation with live action to partner him with cartoon favourites Tom and Jerry. It remains fresh and clever. The other was a charming Mexican hat dance he performed to cheer up a solemn little girl.

In 1952, Kelly and Donen got together again for *Singin' In The Rain*, an original by Adolphe Green and Betty Comden, and incorporating most of the well-loved songs of Arthur Freed and Nacio Herb Brown, based on many of the incidents in Freed's own career, the early transition to sound.

Kelly co-starred with crazy-legs Donald O'Connor and eager-beaver adolescent Debbie Reynolds, while the acting honours were stolen by Jean Hagen (as outrageously nasal 'I Can't Stand It' silent star

Lina Lamont), who talks with a mike in her bosom and a parakeet in her throat. With a voice and personality like hers Lina would have been a natural in 40s musicals. Individual dancing honours must go to O'Connor who, like Astaire, has been a professional since childhood, and never seems to be working when he does those intricate numbers. His 'Make 'Em Laugh' over couches, tables and chairs, and through walls is one of the true comical dance *tour de force* numbers in film musical history. But it was to be matched in the most celebrated number to come from the film – Kelly's rendition of the title tune. Danced in a downpour, it is a personal explosion of rapture after Debbie, the nice little mouse, admits she loves him. Leaving her at her

Phil Silvers, Rita Hayworth and Gene Kelly in *Cover Girl*. 'Make Way for Tomorrow'.

Below, left: The first time Kelly and Sinatra played sailor-buddies was in *Anchors Aweigh* (1945).

Three soldiers this time, and all of them dancers. Dan Dailey, Gene Kelly and Michael Kidd in the opening number from *It's Always Fair Weather*.

One of the classics of the film musical. Gene Kelly's 'Singin' in the Rain' from the film of the same name, which he co-directed with Stanley Donen. The producer was Arthur Freed.

front door as the rain begins, he dances past lighted windows and a rolling drunk. He juggles with a brolly and skips through the shower baths and flooding streets, until a policeman brings it to a halt. Off he goes along more pedestrian paths, as the camera cranes back, and the scene fades, but never to leave the memory. It is Kelly's great triumph.

Stanley Donen: Anybody who says that every picture is not a collaboration is an idiot. It's a question of how much you collaborate and who you collaborate with . . . nothing is more fun than finding someone who stimulates you, and who can be stimulated by you. The result, rather than just adding up to two and two, multiplies itself, and you find

Deep in My Heart. Cyd Charisse and James Mitchell in the 'One Alone' number, based on a song from Romberg's *The Desert Song.* The film was a biopic loosely based on Romberg's career. Choreography by Eugene Loring.

Gene Kelly in the 'Broadway Rhythm' finale in *Singin' in the Rain.*

Opposite, top: Marge and Gower Champion in *Give a Girl a Break,* one of Stanley Donen's directorial solos. This modest but very likeable backstage musical also starred Debbie Reynolds and Bob Fosse.

Bottom right: Michael Kidd rehearsing the 'Luck be a Lady Tonight' number on the set of *Guys and Dolls.*

yourself doing much better things – you are both carried away on the crest of excitement. The more you collaborate with everybody – the actors, the cutter, the cameraman, the sound man – the better it's going to be. That is all a director is really, a collaborator with all of these people.

Singin' In The Rain has become such a universal favourite that it has eclipsed the memory of another musical evocation of the 20s. Directed in the same year by Douglas Sirk, *Has Anybody Seen My Gal* (1952), though starring non-musical Rock Hudson and Piper Laurie, looks good, and the evocation of the roaring 20s and the songs of the era has a charm all of its own.

The next Donen-Kelly collaboration was *It's Always Fair Weather* (1955) – with much the same team as had made *On The Town*: Adolphe Green,

Betty Comden, and of course, Freed. This time, Dan Dailey (on loan-out from Fox), choreographer Michael Kidd and Kelly were the jolly GIs: the lissom, long-stemmed Cyd Charisse who had vamped Kelly so well in *Singin'* was the girl, and the bouncy song-belting Dolores Gray made a notable film début as a gushing TV hostess. The plot revolves around a disillusioning reunion of war-time buddies, and this bitter flavour surprised public and critics. It was fast-moving, decorated with sharp and cutting dialogue, and punctuated by some clever dancing. It was not a success when it came out, but few musicals made in 1955 were. It was the last time Donen and Kelly worked together.

Since 1955 Gene Kelly has left his acting career behind to involve himself more as a director. Aside from the ambitious but overly arty *Invitation To The Dance* (1956), his most recent musical, as a director, has been 20th Century-Fox's twenty-million dollar *Hello Dolly!* (1969), starring Barbra Streisand and choreographed by Michael Kidd: a thunderingly dated and heavy film. And as a performer he was last seen partnering Olivia Newton-John in *Xanadu* (1980), a pasty re-vamping of Hollywood's *Down To Earth*, with Kelly, sadly, playing a character named Danny McGuire, but nothing like his Danny in Rita's *Cover Girl*.

Donen had success on his own. His early musicals included *Royal Wedding* (1951), incongrously teaming Fred Astaire and Jane Powell (it had originally been meant for June Allyson and then Judy Garland), set in London and inspired by the real Royal Wedding of Princess Elizabeth to Prince Philip in much the same way as Grace Kelly's Royal Princess who renounces love for duty in *The Swan* (1956) took its lead from a page in Princess Margaret's life. Then there was the small-budgeted but delightful *Give A Girl A Break* (1953), with a cast of superb young musical performers that included Bob Fosse, Debbie Reynolds and Marge and Gower Champion. Gower, who like Fosse, was to make his real success as

Above: Stanley Donen directed and Michael Kidd choreographed one of the most high-spirited of all 50s musicals, *Seven Brides for Seven Brothers*. Jane Powell's 'Goin' Courting' with Russ Tamblyn. The other brothers were Howard Keel, Jeff Richards, Tommy Rall, Marc Platt, Matt Maddox and Jacques D'Amboise. The 'Barn Raising' number (above).

219

Above: Doris Day, Barbara Nichols and the girls in *The Pajama Game*. Co-directed by George Abbott and Stanley Donen the film, like the original Broadway production, boasted choreography by Bob Fosse, and some of the best singing and dancing in a 50s musical.

Right: Gwen Verdon, in *Damn Yankees*, is making it plain to the fast weakening Tab Hunter that 'Whatever Lola Wants – Lola Gets'.

Below right: Audrey Hepburn's 'Basal Metabolism' number in *Funny Face* reminded one that she had begun her career with a ballet scholarship in England.

director on Broadway, also choreographed the film's dances. In 1954 Donen directed the big-budgeted but awful Sigmund Romberg song-book, *Deep In My Heart*. Even with an all-star cast, great songs and Roger Edens producing, it was the dullest of all musicals.

After that, Donen made what is probably his best solo work – *Seven Brides For Seven Brothers* (1954). The dance numbers, choreographed by Michael Kidd, dominated this exuberant film, and the original score by Gene de Paul and Johnny Mercer was one great song after another, sung feelingly by the unlikely team of Howard Keel and Jane Powell, who rarely had it so good. Not even the obvious back-projection in much of the film and the bright but variable Ansco-colour photography could slow down the foot-tapping fun. It had been producer Jack Cummings' pet project for some time, and he produced with obvious care on a relatively small budget, for although it was in early Cinemascope, not much was expected from it. Blonde, small and pretty soprano Jane Powell revealed the required amount of grit and spunk beneath her winsome facade to play a woman who could handle seven lusty giants. Her clear, high, spring-water voice was just right for eulogizing 'When You're in Love' with the mountains to echo her.

Since becoming established as an independent producer-director Donen has made only a few more musicals: the very chi-chi, very elegant, very pink *Funny Face* (1957), produced by Roger Edens and starring Fred Astaire, Audrey Hepburn and Kay Thompson, with music by the Gershwins; *The Pajama Game* (1957), based on the effervescent Broadway hit and choreographed by Bob Fosse, with Doris Day in one of her best roles; and *Damn Yankees* (1959), again choreographed by Fosse, finally giving Gwen Verdon her only chance to display on the screen the brilliant dancing personality that has made her a Broadway legend. In films, mostly as Jack Cole's asistant at Columbia, and then at Fox, she was usually brought in for duets with Betty Grable and spent most of her energy making sure she didn't upstage the star. Donen's only other musicals, after a fifteen-year hiatus, was an original for the screen, *The Little*

Prince (1974), with songs by Lerner and Loewe, but oh, woe, all whimsy and no charm or much style, and the Busby Berkeley pastiche for *Movie, Movie* (1978).

'The biggest thing to happen to the MGM musical was the discovery of Judy Garland.' The words are Roger Edens'. Garland was actress, singer and star, and every director wanted to work with her. Though she appeared in several films for other studio units, her career is inextricably linked with the Freed group, where her directors included Busby Berkeley, Minnelli and Charles Walters. Her performances in the musicals of the 40s are for many the highlights of that era.

Judy was born Frances Ethel in Grand Rapids, Minnesota, the third and youngest daughter of Frank and Ethel Gumm. Her father owned the theatre at Grand Rapids and the three girls were brought up for the stage. Judy's début came un-expectedly at the age of three when she marched herself in front of the footlights at the end of an act and launched into a solo of 'Jingle Bells' – just like in the movies! Her parents enrolled her in a children's drama school when they moved to California and, with her sisters, she formed an act, The Gumm Sisters.

While on a bill with George Jessel he told her she was 'as pretty as a garland of flowers', and advised a change from Gumm to Garland. A year later, Hoagy Carmichael's song 'Judy' inspired the rest. Frances Gumm became Judy Garland. Judy went back to school after the job finished and stayed there until producer Lew Brown, of DeSylva, Brown and Henderson, heard her entertain and suggested she should approach the film studios. She was only twelve when she was signed by MGM, along with Deanna Durbin. It was Arthur Freed who signed her:

'Garland and her sisters came to audition for me. Her mother played the worst piano I had ever heard, so I said to the little girl, "You just sing by yourself." She sang "Zing Went The Strings of My Heart". That was it! You just couldn't mistake that talent. There was so much of it. Judy interpreted a song better than anybody else in the business. She could dance, she wasn't a great dancer but she could come in with Kelly or Fred Astaire and after about an hour's rehearsal, do it and give the appearance of a great dancer. She could play low comedy, had looks – everything. For years Judy was perfect. No problem at all. I just looked at part of Meet me in St Louis the other night and watched Judy sing, "Have Yourself A Merry Little Christmas", and there was nobody like her.' While talking about her Freed paused often, looking away, lost in his own memories before continuing, unprompted: 'She was every song-writer's favourite. The reason I got Irving Berlin to agree to do Easter Parade was on account of Judy. Because every songwriter there ever was – whether it was Kern or Irving or Cole Porter or Harold Arlen – wanted to write for Judy. Judy and Fred. They were the two they wanted their songs sung by.'

Garland's future was resolved when she sang a special version of 'You Made Me Love You' for Clark Gable's birthday party. As one of the galaxy of Metro-stars paying tribute to Hollywood's 'King' she sang specially added lyrics by Roger Edens. The song, now known as 'Dear Mr Gable' became the foundation of one of the musical's greatest legends. A brilliant stroke of fortune got her the part of Dorothy in The Wizard of Oz (1939), when Metro couldn't get Shirley Temple, and clinched Judy's position. As she was in her rapidly developing teens her breasts had to be bound, her dresses carefully designed, her hair in pigtails to achieve an illusion of fragile and wondering childhood. Her nose was fixed, and she was cleverly surrounded by tall co-stars. One of Hollywood's most sensitive directors of women, Victor Fleming, was brought in by Freed (although it was King Vidor who shot Over The Rainbow when Fleming was taken off to do Gone With The Wind). Oz was a great success and, at sixteen, Judy was a star.

Metro immediately re-teamed her with Mickey Rooney, with whom she had already made two films, and who, as 'Andy Hardy', had become one of their most profitable stars. Together, Mickey and Judy were an unbeatable combination. They could

Louis B. Mayer keeps an eye on two of his most valuable assets, Mickey Rooney and Judy Garland – whom he exploited to the limit, and beyond. Judy is wearing her costume for Dorothy in The Wizard of Oz.

Kay Thompson's 'Think Pink' number in *Funny Face*. As outrageously true-to-life high fashion editress Kay, better known for writing material and teaching other stars how to do it, at last has a chance to do it herself.

Judy Garland and Mickey Rooney in *Strike Up the Band*. This award-winning action still was taken by Ed Cronenweth.

do just about anything and do it well – sing, dance, play the piano, the drums, act, mime. They were brilliant exponents of all that Freed's unit at Metro was aiming at. With Rooney, Judy made two Andy Hardy films, *Love Finds Andy Hardy* (1938) and *Andy Hardy Meets a Debutante* (1940). Judy and Mickey had first appeared in *Thoroughbreds Don't Cry* (1937), but it was their work in those barnyard musicals, *Babes In Arms* (1939), *Strike Up The Band* (1940), *Babes On Broadway* (1941) and *Girl Crazy* (1943) that really took advantage of them as a team.

Roger Edens worked closely on most of Judy's films and wrote songs and special material for her. 'One of my favourite numbers in the film *Strike Up The Band* was "Nobody's Got Me". It's a scene in the library and Judy is alone there, putting books away. It's done very quietly and simply, with great camerawork. Busby Berkeley was in charge of this, and at the end of the scene he had the camera moving overhead and got a magnificent shot of Judy walking into oblivion among the bookshelves, looking about so high.'

Judy's *Little Nelly Kelly* (1940) was a first attempt to portray an adult. It was from the George M. Cohan play, and she sang some very good songs: 'It's a Great Day for the Irish' and 'A Pretty Girl Milking Her Cow' written for her by Roger Edens. It was a lot of blarney, but proved that Garland was as riveting on her own as she was with Rooney and all her later co-stars. Roger Edens said in an interview: 'Initially, studio executives weren't at all keen on the idea of Judy's growing up. Mr Mayer, a very sweet old guy, was in the centre of the debate about making Judy both the mother and the daughter. "We simply can't let that baby have a child", he'd say.'

She made three films in 1941 that included the

opulent *Ziegfeld Girl*, billing her *above* Hedy Lamarr and Lana Turner. Later that same year she married composer David Rose. She received her first solo star billing on *For Me And My Gal*, singing a memorable version of 'After You've Gone' à la Fanny Brice's 'My Man'. By 1944, when she was Esther Smith in *Meet Me In St Louis*, Garland was undeniably the most electric musical star in the business and Metro's biggest star. Under Minnelli's direction the young Garland glowed. They married in 1945.

Many of the songs she sang in her films were the hits of the 40s. In *Girl Crazy*, adapted from the 30s stage show, she gave new life to Gershwin's 'Bidin' My Time', 'Embraceable You', 'I Got Rhythm', 'But Not for Me', etc. In *The Harvey Girls* (1946), she sang the Oscar-winning 'On the Atchison, Topeka and the Santa Fe'. Despite the work-to-clock direction by George Sidney, Judy was the bounciest of a bevy of waitresses in the wild west, conquering the forces of evil in a corrupt western town.

Judy played Marilyn Miller in a guest appearance in the biography of Jerome Kern, *Till The Clouds Roll By* (1946), that had her singing two numbers, 'Look for the Silver Lining' and 'Who?' Her scenes were directed by her husband; the rest of the film wasn't, unfortunately. Both numbers had a special humorous place in Judy's memory. She discovered shortly before rehearsals that she was pregnant. The waist-line of her dress had to be continually altered and raised and she found it hilarious remembering running along a chorus line of men in tails asking, 'Who Stole My Heart Away?'

For her other number, 'Look for the Silver Lining', her pregnancy was so far advanced, that Minnelli hit upon the clever idea of having her sing the number à la Cinderella from behind a mountain of pots and pans which kept most of her body out of view.

The Pirate was her first film after the birth of

Above: On the set of *Girl Crazy*. Judy Garland with co-star Rooney and her hairdresser, Betty Lee.

Left: An avalanche of MGM players were roped in for *Till the Clouds Roll By*, in the hope of lifting the highly sentimentalized musical biography of Jerome Kern. Judy Garland as Marilyn Miller shone brightest, in 'Look for the Silver Lining'. The sequence was directed by Vincente Minnelli.

Above: Another musical hagiography, *Words and Music*, had Rooney as Lorenz Hart. For an up-tempo version of 'I Wish I Were in Love Again' he appeared with Judy Garland. Just how silly the idea was is underlined by a comparison of ages: Judy, who appeared as herself, would have to have been an astonishingly precocious ten-year-old to have done a number with Lorenz Hart when he was in Hollywood.

Above right: Judy with Charles Walters, her director for *Summer Stock*. The cycling routine each morning was part of the star's struggle with a weight problem.

Right: 'The Man that Got Away' in *A Star is Born*. The song was written for her by Harold ('Over the Rainbow') Arlen and the film was directed by George Cukor. A triumphant comeback, the film was the pinnacle of her movie career.

talented Liza. For *The Pirate*, Garland had the best of the Cole Porter songs: 'Love of My Life', 'Mack the Black', and 'Be a Clown' which she and Kelly tumbled their way through. She followed it with *Easter Parade*, but then nervous exhaustion forced her to withdraw from *The Barkleys of Broadway*. *Words and Music* had her raising the roof with 'Johnny One Note'. In Charles Walters' *Summer Stock* she was heavier and worn-looking but excellent when singing the oldie hit 'Get Happy'.

The strain of her years at the top began to tell. Walter Plunkett recalled: 'One day, when we were doing *Summer Stock*, Judy hadn't shown up and it was long past noon. At last a phone call came from her; she was down by the beach and said she was sorry not to have come in but was on her way to the set. When she arrived she was on the verge of tears as she explained her lateness. That morning, she'd arrived at the studio at 6 a.m. for make-up and instead of reading MGM over the studio gates, it read "The time has come". To her it meant that this was the day when she would go on the stage to film and the people would suddenly turn and point saying, 'Who the hell do you think you are? What makes you think you are a good dancer? or that you can sing?' She had been so petrified when she saw this that she turned the car around and drove until she reached the beach where she tried to sort herself out. Her career hasn't been easy. She's one person who

has paid for everything she's ever got out of life.'

The big pressure on Judy Garland was always having to live up to her own excellence. Because of her great talent, all the best people in Hollywood wanted to work with her. All eyes were always on her, and every night was opening night on the Garland set.

She was off the screen for four years after being taken off *Annie Get Your Gun*.* When at last she came back, having meanwhile scored a legendary series of triumphs on the stages of the London Palladium and New York's famed Palace, it was for *A Star is Born* (1954).

With her third husband, producer Sid Luft, she formed a production company, hiring fabled women's director George Cukor to direct her comeback. *A Star Is Born* is among Cukor's finest efforts. Broadway playwright Moss Hart updated the script from the first two versions, including scenes from George Cukor's earlier satire on the film industry, *What Price Hollywood?* (1932). Harold Arlen, who had written 'Over the Rainbow' for Judy in *The Wizard of Oz*, the song which was to be forever linked with her, repeated the gesture with a trunkful of hits including 'The Man That got Away'.

'Born in a Trunk'. Judy Garland in *A Star is Born*.

* Several of the numbers she shot for the film have since turned up in the MGM vaults and are planned for showing with other deleted musical numbers.

After Cukor had finished his job, it was thought advisable, considering Garland's reputation and her fans' expectations for the Garland musical, to add another musical sequence. Not Cukor but Leonard Gershe shot 'Born in a Trunk', an 18-minute-long show-stopping production number which, though effective, in fact only reprised the film's plot in song and dance. As a result of the great length of the final film, the distributors cut four sequences. To Cukor these had been vital. This is the one single tampering on any of his films that most rankled. Since his death part of these sequences have been found and restored for a 1983 re-release of the film.

Nervous tension had already become a hypnotic part of Garland's personality charging even the most superficial of her roles (i.e. *Summer Stock*, *In The Good Old Summertime*) with an urgency that gripped her audience. Nominated for an Oscar which, had she won, might have brought her back as a bankable film star, inexplicably, she lost to new-comer Grace Kelly. Garland did not appear in another film for six years, and then it was for a dramatic non-singing role in *Judgement at Nuremberg*. Movies would never recapture her again. Up to the time of her tragic, though not totally unexpected, premature death she divided her career between concert tours, TV specials, recordings, come-backs and occasional films like *I Could Go On Singing*, the latter something of a *film à clef*. Speaking to me shortly before his own death, Arthur Freed still spoke of his last project which was to have starred her still couldn't believe it was over. 'When she was on there wasn't anything she couldn't do. Do you know why? She was real. Unless you gave her something false to do, she would do it. This girl was real. There was never a mean thing in Judy. All this talk of oppression. . . . I had to take her out of *Annie Get Your Gun*. The girl just couldn't function. She couldn't get out of bed. . . . I don't know what it was. I'm not a psychiatrist. It was something within her. . . . I always thought that Judy would come back. I thought she was made out of iron. She came back so many times. She was going to play Irving Berlin's wife. Vincent was going to direct it. We'd be working together.'

The only 40s female talent at all comparable to Garland was Paramount's Betty Hutton. Arthur Freed had originally bought *Annie* for Garland as a plum, a reward, an incentive to overcome her problems. He offered the coveted directing job to Walters, who had worked so well with Judy. Since the deal hinged on Walters signing a new contract based on his old salary he refused and Busby Berkeley, whose own personal problems had forced his career into a wasteful decline, was brought on the film to begin shooting. His problems only exacerbated Judy's. After a mere two weeks with Berkeley Garland walked out in tears. Chuck Walters wrote me: 'I saw the rushes – they were awful. I was put on it; never shot an inch of film. Judy said, "I think it's too late. This monster [Berkeley] treats me the same as when I was 15!" She wouldn't show to finish a number they were on so she was finally suspended again. Much discussion on who to replace Judy ends up with Hutton who was doing a picture with Astaire at Paramount.' (Initially, scouring through Metro's contract list, Betty Garrett and June Allyson were considered and then dismissed.) 'While wait-

ing for Hutton I read in Hopper's columns that, "When shooting resumes on *Annie*, George Sidney will be megging." I called Freed, who denied it – but it was true. I was crushed. A perfect example of the Sidney steamroller. His father was a Vice-President at the studio; his wife, Lillian Burns, was the studio's drama coach and the closest person to Mayer. If

Opposite: Judy Garland as multitudes of fans prefer to remember her. The 'Get Happy' number was filmed two months after the rest of the film when the star had shed some of her problems and twenty pounds. *Summer Stock* was the last film she made for MGM.

Betty Hutton in *Annie Get Your Gun*. With J. Carroll Naish in 'I'm an Indian too'.

Judy Garland and Betty Hutton in costume tests for *Annie Get Your Gun*. Judy walked off the film because of nervous exhaustion and the part went to Betty Hutton, who made the most of it.

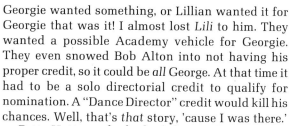

Georgie wanted something, or Lillian wanted it for Georgie that was it! I almost lost *Lili* to him. They wanted a possible Academy vehicle for Georgie. They even snowed Bob Alton into not having his proper credit, so it could be *all* George. At that time it had to be a solo directorial credit to qualify for nomination. A "Dance Director" credit would kill his chances. Well, that's *that* story, 'cause I was there.'

Betty Hutton, who had tried to get Paramount to buy the property for her and who never stopped believing she would end up playing the role, was often overly rumbustious, but she could belt a number in league with the best and was ideal for the part. As she said of herself, 'I didn't have the vocal equipment of Judy but I had the emotion. I sang from my heart.' She had been a sensation in nightclubs and on Broadway before her arrival in Hollywood to make her début in Victor Schertzinger's last film, *The Fleet's In* (1942). The film, starring a sarongless Lamour, had Betty in what would become her archetypal role, as a man-mad fury – a not-unusual war-time heroine considering the male shortage which made anything left in trousers desirable. Variations on this role occupied much of her early career at Paramount, where she was usually in pursuit of Eddie Bracken. The image of her as a frantic but good-natured screwball caught on. To establish a broader appeal for her Paramount softened her character but took no risk by casting her opposite Bing Crosby and Sonny Tufts in *Here Come the Waves* (1944). The new Hutton got Crosby, the loud one got Tufts. Thereafter Hutton alternated between the two extremes in films like *Cross My Heart* (1946), *Stork Club* (1945), and *Red, Hot and Blue* (1949), etc. She was 20s nightclub hostess Texan Guinan in *Incendiary Blonde* (1945), silent serial star Pearl White in *The Perils of Pauline* (1947), and for her last film at Paramount, she was vaudeville songstress Blossom Seeley in *Somebody Loves Me* (1952). Hutton was an all-round performer who could even hold her own opposite Fred Astaire in the light but amusing *Let's Dance* (1950), with a comedy routine between her and Astaire similar to the 'Couple of Swells' number he did with Garland in *Easter Parade*.

Throughout her career Betty was commandingly viewable, though she could easily become exhausting when the material was not up to her energy. Nervous temperament dogged her last few years on the screen, dissipating her triumphs as *Annie*, and in De Mille's *The Greatest Show On Earth*, so that

228

Director Charles O'Curran rehearsing his wife, Betty Hutton, in a number for *Somebody Loves Me*. The film, based on the career of vaudeville singer Blossom Seeley and her rocky marriage, finished Hutton's Paramount career.

much money and MGM were making so many musicals, and Mayer needed somebody like him to build Durbin-type films around their own newly acquired teenage soprano, Kathryn Grayson. Pasternak specialized in the glossy, conventional boy-meets-girl soprano films that were among the studio's biggest hits of the 40s. In the most enjoyable of these Kathryn Grayson was often the star: *Seven Sweethearts* (1942), *Thousands Cheer* (1943), *Anchors Aweigh* (1945), *Two Sisters from Boston* (1946), *That Midnight Kiss* (1949) and *The Toast of New Orleans* (1950). The latter two teamed her with Pasternak's triumphant discovery, tenor Mario Lanza. Lanza's short but volatile screen career reached its meteoric peak as *The Great Caruso* (1951). For a time he was the trimmest,

Above: Finale, George Sidney – Pasternak style, the lock, the stock and the barrel. Jane Powell in *Holiday in Mexico*, which also featured José and Amparo Iturbi, Walter Pidgeon, Ilona Massey, Xavier Cugat, a symphony orchestra and a 400-voice choir.

her disappearance after 1952 was perhaps not altogether surprising. (After many ups and downs she resurfaced on Broadway in 1981 as the alcoholic man-mad Miss Harrigan in the musical about a little orphan called *Annie*). Although like Garland, too much temperament has often been given as the reason for her departure, it also coincided with a general tightening of belts at the studios. Hutton's demise was just one of many now that the studios no longer needed them, whether they were as easy-going as Esther Williams or as temperamental as Hutton, though few disappeared as hard and fast as Betty.

Working at Metro, alongside the Arthur Freed unit, was the totally different Joe Pasternak unit. MGM had acquired Pasternak from Universal after his disagreement with that company about the future of the Deanna Durbin image, and the sort of films he wanted to make. Musicals were making so

certainly one of the comeliest, and undeniably the most successful of all operatic stars who have had a screen career. He was idolized. Studios filmed where he wanted. Despite sneering critics, the public would have no other. Now, more than twenty years after his death, the lionized tenor, Luciano Pavarotti, comes to the screen in *Yes, Giorgio* (1982), a role not unlike those Lanza once played, but without the Lanza big-screen appeal.

Grayson, the songstress with the heartshaped face and dimpled smile, made her film début as *Andy Hardy's Private Secretary* (1941). Her last musical was in the MacDonald role in *The Vagabond King* (1956), Paramount's belated attempt to revive operetta with Vista Vision. Although Grayson sang enchantingly this sort of film had long since had its day. Miss Grayson, a surprisingly realistic woman, had no illusions about her career: 'It was fun making films then. Everybody was so enthusiastic

Above: From Left to right Martha Raye, Miliza Korjus and Howard Keel listen while Kathryn Grayson delivers her contribution at MGM's party to celebrate the release of *That's Entertainment* in 1974.

Above right: Kathryn Grayson and Mario Lanza in the first of two films as the battling sweethearts. She's a soprano, he's a tenor – on the rocky road to musical romance in *That Midnight Kiss*.

Far right: Mario Lanza as Enrico Caruso. *The Great Caruso* was a whopping box-office success but Lanza, who reached his peak in this role, was another star whose career was bedevilled by artistic temperament and a weight problem. Joe Pasternak produced.

Right: Kathryn Grayson, resident MGM songstress for a number of years, in a production still from *Thousands Cheer*. The director was George Sidney.

and talented. I had marvellous actors like Mary Astor and John Boles playing my parents and there's so much one can learn from people like them.

'About my films – well, most of them were big budgeted and seemed to take forever to make. I didn't have very good directors on most of them. The only time I ever worked with Minnelli was when he came into shoot a musical number for *Lovely To Look At*. (Minnelli had also worked on Miss Grayson's sequence, 'There's Beauty Everywhere', in *Ziegfeld Follies*.) I think it was a favour to Mervyn LeRoy. Anyway, Adrian was going to design the clothes for that sequence and I had really been looking forward to it. Adrian was such a famous name to me, and because I arrived at Metro just as he left, he had never designed any of my clothes before. Well it turned out to be awful. Just awful. Adrian, you know, had been famous for his simple classic designs, and I thought he would make me one of those, but instead it was all frilly, and on my chest there was this enormous corsage of grapes. Now I have a very feminine body, and I certainly didn't need a cluster of grapes draped to emphasize it further. I asked them to take it off but Minnelli refused. It was terrible. I kept pressing myself against edges of tables and walls to bust them. They were furious with me, I suppose, but I hated that cluster.'

Ann Miller worked at almost every studio, playing in almost every sort of musical. She began with straight parts in *Stage Door* (1937) and Capra's *You Can't Take It With You* (1938), subsequent to going

Above left: Howard Keel and Kathryn Grayson sing Jerome Kern's 'Only Make Believe'. A moment from the third film version of *Show Boat*, directed by George Sidney and glowingly photographed in colour by Charles Roster.

Above: Cyd Charisse and John Brascia in 'Frankie and Johnny', choreographed by Hermes Pan for *Meet Me in Las Vegas*.

Left: Cole Porter's *Kiss Me Kate*, the only musical to be filmed in 3D (lots of flying cutlery), translated almost perfectly from stage to screen and gave Kathryn Grayson her best film role. Left to right, Howard Keel and Kathryn Grayson, Tommy Rall, Kurt Kasznar and Ann Miller in the finale. Produced by Jack Cummings, it was photographed by Charles Roster and had costumes by Walter Plunkett and art direction by Urie McLeary. It was a joy to behold.

to and returning from Broadway to star in such films as *Too Many Girls* (1940), *Hit Parade of 1941* and even a Gene Autry western, *Melody Ranch* (1940). There followed a seven-year stint at Columbia before she finally reached MGM and inheriting Eleanor Powell's tap dancing shoes though not Powell's crown.

That sort of fame would not be hers till long after her sort of musical ceased to be made in Hollywood and she went on Broadway, where audiences, hungry with nostalgia for the talent of her era, now cheered her skill and undimmed energy. Her film roles consisted of a non-stop succession of good-natured if not overly bright broads with a perpetual smile beaming away while she moved with incredible zest and vigour, alone or in and out of people's arms. Her presence lifted the otherwise lumbering *Deep In My Heart*, and she roused the wolves to whistle with her rendition of Kern's 'I'll Be Hard To Handle' in *Lovely To Look At* (1952). Her finest hour came almost at the end of the musical cycle with *Kiss Me Kate* (1953). Her old friend, Hermes Pan, who'd already worked with her back at RKO, created a superb series of numbers, one of which, 'Too Darn Hot' was the sort of solo with which she would have stopped the show had it been live, as well as five others, which partnered her with no less than three of the best male dancers around – Bobby Van, Tommy Rall and Bob Fosse. For 'From This Moment On' they were also joined by Carol Haney and Jeannie Coyne for a dancing feast of slides, leaps and ravishing rapid turns and twirls. It was ensemble dancing of the highest order.

On Broadway, as the last and arguably liveliest of the many *Mames*, there was a chance to talk to Ann Miller about her days at RKO, MGM, Republic, Columbia, and Monogram . . .

'Not Monogram! *Never* Monogram, *darlin'!* . . .

'Lucille Ball is the person who discovered me. She saw me dancing in a theatre and she was with a talent scout at the time, and she was responsible for my contract at RKO. I was thirteen years old. I was just a baby. Here I was with my hair dyed black, and pearls, and blood-red lipstick and long eyelashes and bust pads and high heels and nail polish and white fox stoles and I was a baby.' (At 5′ 6″, and Texan, she was always a rather big baby.) 'I had one fake birth certificate and one real one. It had to be faked.

'First I did *New Faces of 1937*, then I did *Life of the Party*, then *Stage Door*. I had two dance numbers in the first two films, and I had one or two speaking lines in *Stage Door* and I did a dance with Ginger. Then came *Radio City Revels*, *You Can't Take It With You*, *Room Service*, *Having A Wonderful Time*, and then I left RKO and went into the *Scandals* for a year and was a tremendous hit in that show. The Conga was all the rage at the time and I did the first tap conga and I came back to RKO at $3,000 a week, where before I'd been making only $250 a week. And then I did *Too Many Girls* for George Abbott with Lucille Ball. And then I went on to my Columbia career and did all the war musicals, one right after the other: *Reveille With Beverly*, *Time Out For Rhythm*, *What's Buzzin', Cousin?* – Ohhhhh! It was just wild! I went on and on! *Eadie Was A Lady*, *The Thrill Of Brazil*. . . .

'Six years with Harry Cohn. I got to know him quite well. He kept me as a sort of threat to Rita Hayworth, to keep her in line, because she was quite the glamour girl and she married Aly Khan. Every time she'd get married she'd leave her career, and he'd get terribly upset and he'd say: "If you don't behave yourself I'm going to put Ann Miller in that part." A film was being prepared for her called *The Petty Girl*, which was about Petty, the artist who drew beautiful long-legged girls on calendars – they were called the Petty Girls. It was being prepared as a colour film for Rita and she upped and married Aly Khan. And he said, "I'm going to give the part to Ann Miller," and then I upped and married and left my career at that point, and poor Harry Cohn was left with both of us gone and he was beside himself and didn't know what to do. He sued my husband for $150,000 and my husband paid off. Because I quit my career. I walked out. She married, and I married and we both walked out!' (peals of laughter).

'It was quite a thrill for Mr Cohn! When I did divorce my husband I had to go back to Columbia and Mr Cohn kept me sitting there until the contract just lapsed. But I had had marvellous choreographers. Jack Cole, the first thing he ever did at Columbia was with me. He rejuvenated the whole dance world. He was probably the greatest of them all. And I had Hermes Pan. Fred Astaire wouldn't make a move without Hermes. These were some of the greatest men in our business.

'Then I was lucky that Cyd Charisse fell and broke her leg – sad for Cyd – it meant they had to take her out of *Easter Parade* and replace her with me. And that's how I got my chance on the MGM lot. I was over there for almost ten years – and it was just a succession of movie, movie, movie. *On The Town* and right on down. I think, though, that *Kiss Me Kate* was the most amusing picture I did and rather satisfying from the standpoint that it was a great Cole Porter score and the photography was good and it's something that never dated. But I liked all my MGM pictures, I was very proud of them. And to think, I only became a dancer because I had rickets when I was a child and my legs were not good, and my

Opposite, top: Ann Miller's 'Prehistoric Man' number is a highlight of *On the Town*. With Gene Kelly, Frank Sinatra, Jules Munshin and Betty Garrett.

Bottom: Ann Miller with director Charles Barton and dance director Nick Castle (right) on the set of *What's Buzzin' Cousin* (1943).

Left: 'Shaking the Blues Away'. Ann Miller making her debut as an MGM star in one of her best numbers, in *Easter Parade*.

Ann Miller on her toes. A 1939 portrait by Columbia's A. L. (Whitey) Schaefer.

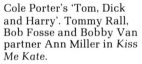

Cole Porter's 'Tom, Dick and Harry'. Tommy Rall, Bob Fosse and Bobby Van partner Ann Miller in *Kiss Me Kate*.

233

Right: Hermes Pan under water, rehearsing Esther Williams for a number in *Jupiter's Darling*.

Below: Esther Williams contributes her bit to MGM's *Ziegfeld Follies*.

mother gave me ballet to straighten my legs out.'

One of the reasons Ann never became MGM's reigning dancing queen had to do with the fact that after a long search, ever since Eleanor Powell's departure, they had finally found a dancer with the personality suitable for star grooming, Cyd Charisse. Prior to her arrival on the scene, the studio had tried but failed to establish Lucille Bremer as their answer to Rita Hayworth – despite several elaborately staged opportunities, two opposite Astaire in *Yolanda and the Thief* (1945) and *Ziegfeld Follies* (1946). With Charisse they were more fortunate, as she went on to become the quintessential romantic dancing heroine.

Cyd Charisse made her screen début in Columbia's *Something To Shout About* (1943). Robert Alton brought her to the attention of Arthur Freed. Carefully built up in small parts, this Circe in tights soon became noticed for her eloquent legs. Sometimes she had little more than a dance number – *Ziegfeld Follies*, *Till the Clouds Roll By*, and *Words and Music*. She had a tempestuous Hayworth-type number with Ricardo Montalban in *Fiesta* (1947), and again in *The Kissing Bandit* (1948) with Montalban and Ann Miller. But her true sphere was the classic, the graceful, the poetic. In Minnelli's *The Band Wagon* Charisse was at her peak, as she responded to Astaire's artistry – melting, yielding, answering his call; it even flowed into their non-musical exchanges. In these moments one was given an insight into what seemed a very private art. Freed teamed them again in Cole Porter's romantic soufflé, *Silk Stockings* (1957), with Mamoulian at the helm for what has been this maestro's last film. Though the chemistry with Astaire was still there, the acting demands of the role, Garbo's *Ninotchka*, were beyond her.

Charisse also partnered Gene Kelly in three of his films, *Brigadoon*, *It's Always Fair Weather*, and *Singin' In The Rain*, and worked with Dan Dailey in *Meet Me In Las Vegas* (1956), for which Hermes Pan dreamt up the duelling 'Frankie and Johnnie' ballet, having her and Liliane Montevechi dance it out for the favours of John Brascia. She was a sight to see in all and unforgettable as the lethal 'Louise Brooks' beauty of *Singin' In The Rain*'s climatic 'Broadway Rhythm Ballet'. Charisse moved through Metro's classiest musicals like a Greek goddess. Though at times there was a bit too much marble in her performance, she made up for it by resembling one too.

Rich as this gathering of star names and talents appears, it doesn't begin to take into account so many other, just as popular, Metro musical favourites. Esther Williams, whether as *Bathing Beauty*, *Jupiter's Darling* or *Neptune's Daughter*, for fourteen wet and wonderful years, dived where no man or woman had gone before, as she slipped adroitly out of the clutches of males overheated by her cool, to take a tuneful dip among the flora and the fauna of the deep. Van Johnson, another MGM import from the Broadway chorus, was poolside in four of her films, when his freckled grin wasn't being used to form a popular duo with his husky-voiced, bouncy little June Allyson who made her screen début repeating her Broadway role in *Best Foot Forward* with Gloria de Haven and Nancy Walker. Virginia O'Brien, Red Skelton, Ann Sothern, José

Iturbi, Lauritz Melchior, Vic Damone were others.
And among these was Lena Horne.

There have been many stars in musicals with less
talent than sultry Lena Horne, a stylish singer of love
songs with an erotic flavour that put her in the top of
her class. Yet her screen career was decidedly undistinguished. Most of it was spent rubbing up against
ornate lamps, doors, pillars and posts from MGM's
bulging prop department, while crooning the blues,
in which position she got to introduce 'Love' in
Ziegfeld Follies.

'I was discovered for the movies,' she related, 'by
Roger Edens who had heard me singing in New
York, and liked my work and told Arthur Freed, and

they brought me out to Los Angeles. I suppose I was
excited but I couldn't seriously believe anything
would come of it. Edens met me and my agent and
escorted us to Freed's office. I could tell from his
voice that he was a Southerner, but for some reason
I didn't feel that instant distrust a Southern accent
usually creates in me. Roger played and I sang,
"More Than You Know!" and Freed asked me to stay
and sing for Louis B. Mayer.

'While we were waiting to go see him, Vincente
Minnelli walked in. I had met him in New York
when he had been doing musicals and had thought
of me for a role in one of them. He was terribly
cordial to me. "Wouldn't it be wonderful if we could

'The Sping', a rumba number for Lena Horne in *Panama Hattie*.

'Honeysuckle Rose'. Lena Horne rehearsing with director George Sidney for her contribution to *Thousands Cheer*.

finally do something together," he said. Among all those strangers in Arthur Freed's big impressive office, it was good to get such a greeting, while waiting to see whether the great man would deign to see us.

'Then we got a call to go and see Mayer. He was a short, chubby man – on this occasion, as on most of the very few others that I dealt personally with him, he seemed very genial and fatherly to me. I sang for him and I remember him just sitting there, beaming at me through his round glasses. After I'd done a couple of songs for him he disappeared into some inner sanctum and came back with Marion Davies on his arm, and I had to sing for her too. By this time everybody was all charged up.

'It turned out that MGM had bought *Cabin In The Sky*, the all-Negro musical, though it was going to be some time before they could put it into production. At that time there were no Negroes under long-term contract at any of the studios. All the Negro actors in town were free-lancers, hired for jobs as the need arose. I wasn't too proud to play roles as maids or maybe even as some jungle type, which most Negroes were forced to play in movies at that time, but since I was starting out fresh I wanted to try and

establish a different kind of image for Negro women before I got typecast. The first part they offered me was a flippant, fresh maid in a Jeanette MacDonald musical [*Cairo*]. Well, they didn't make me into a maid [Ethel Walters played the part] but they didn't make me anything else either. I became a butterfly pinned to a column singing away.'

Her numbers were shot so as to be easily removable for the racially insensitive Southern distributors. MGM had initially planned to cash in on her rare beauty because of her light skin colour and thought to pass her off as an exotic Latin-American discovery. A make-up was even specially devised for her, the Light-Egyptian, Blend No: 5. It was her steadfast refusal to comply with this studio-image and so compromise her integrity as a Negro artist that resulted in her non-parts. The two films in which she had an integral role, *Stormy Weather* (1943) and *Cabin In The Sky* (1943), were all black musicals; for the rest, Metro's cowardice deprived the musical of a great personality. As for Egyptian No.: 5, it was subsequently used to darken the skin and accent the allure of Hedy Lamarr and Ava Gardner when playing the sultry exotics Lena could have played.

Lena Horne suffered the biggest disappointment of her film career when she failed to be cast as *Show Boat*'s Julie La Verne, the role she, and many others would have thought she was born to play. After all, in the tab version shot for the Kern hagiography, *Till the Clouds Roll By*, also produced by Arthur Freed, Lena was cast as Julie. Since Hollywood casting is not always predicated on the obvious, Lena's failure to get the part in the studio's full-fledged technicolor re-make of the theatrical musical milestone may not necessarily have been caused by front office fear of the Code's negative ruling on showing anything that smacked of miscegenation. Even with the all-white Ava Gardner, the fact that the character was meant to have coloured blood still created a tricky situation when it came to filming her love scenes with Robert Sterling. He could hold her in his arms, even kiss the blood on a cut on her arm, but nothing more extended.

But the real reason for not casting Lena, at least as far as Arthur Freed was concerned when we spoke of it, was not out of timidity but a case of getting the perfect actress for the part. For him that was always Ava Gardner. To get her he had to fight off studio head Dore Schary's choice, Dinah Shore.

'Julie' said Freed, 'had to look white. Julie had just that one drop of coloured blood, which was the biggest piece of injustice in the world against that girl. Lena would have been pure Negro. I brought her out here and I love her but you couldn't pass Lena off as white in a story that was set in a time and in a place where people would have known. With Ava you could believe she had a drop of coloured blood. I don't think anybody ever looked as beautiful as Ava did in that film. She was everything the part had to be. Like I told Dinah who was told to test for the part and who was sending me flowers and notes every day, when she finally said, "Why don't you give me the part?" "Because you're not a whore and Ava is. When Ava sings *Bill*, she's every streetwalker you ever saw." '

Considering Arthur Freed's track record, his

Dorothy Dandridge in *The Hit Parade of 1943*, more than ten years before her great success in *Carmen Jones*. Photograph by George Hommel.

explanation may very well be the truth of the matter. Still, casting Lena Horne in that part, in that film, at that moment in America, might have become one of Hollywood's more courageous and far-reaching moves. Instead it would be another six years before a white male was allowed to be seen kissing a coloured woman, when Zanuck cast Dorothy Dandridge in the all-star *Island in the Sun* (1957) opposite English actor John Justin, and it would be another decade after that breakthrough before guess who came to dinner, and married the daughter of the house.

More Who Aren't Less

The musical output and the stars of MGM and Fox dominated the 40s. Warners completely lost their former eminence and they had no directors with outstanding flair, though many of their contract directors, such as David Butler, Irving Rapper, Roy del Ruth and Mike Curtiz turned them out when called upon. Warners' musical biographies were all great box-office successes: *Yankee Doodle Dandy* (1942, in which James Cagney gave his Oscar-winning portrayal of George M. Cohan), *Shine on Harvest Moon* (1944, Ann Sheridan as Nora Bayes), *Rhapsody in Blue* (1945, Gershwin), *Night and Day* (1946, Cole Porter), and *I'll See You in My Dreams* (1951, lyricist Gus Kahn). Most of their other musicals, however, were updated versions of the least imaginative of their early films, rarely distinguished by stars, choreography or musical flair. Musicals were so popular in the 40s that Warners had successes but of their musical stars – Irene Manning, Arlene Dahl, Dennis Morgan, Jack Carson, Janis Paige, Patrice Wymore, Joan Leslie and, later, the living, breathing, lissom 'Pretty Girl' Virginia Mayo, cheerful, easy-to-watch dancer Gene Nelson and robust baritone Gordon MacRae – only Mayo reached the top ranks. Gene Nelson became a director later in his career, and guided Elvis Presley through *Kissin' Cousins* (1964) and *Harum Scarum* (1965).

Only at the end of the decade did Warners acquire

she was an outcome of the golden era.

Originally she had wanted to be a dancer, but a broken leg at 15 turned her to singing. By the time her leg was cured, her budding reputation as a singer had taken the place of any desire to dance. Bandleader Barney Rapp heard her and advised her to drop the Kappelhoff for Day. (People were forever telling the Kappelhoffs and Gumms of this world to change their names.)

She was 24 when she landed the starring part in her first film, *Romance on the High Seas* (1948, English title: *It's Magic*). The Warner Brothers had failed to get Mary Martin or Betty Hutton and the film was already in production without a lead singer. In 1952 Doris Day won the first of many awards as the world's most popular star. Her rendition of 'It's Magic' was the first of many hits, including 'Que Sera, Sera', 'I'll Never Stop Loving You', 'Pillow Talk' . . . Unfortunately, with few exceptions, her Warner musicals were little better than those they had been making without her. *Tea for Two* (1950) was a remake of *No, No, Nanette*. Others such as *Moonlight Bay* (1951) and its follow-up, *By the Light of the Silvery Moon* (1953), tried hard to establish the cosy, small-town atmosphere of the better Metro films, but it wasn't there. Gordon MacRae was her likeable vis-à-vis in many of them. Then there was *The West Point Story* (1950) and *The Lullaby of Broadway* (1951). The song was still great and so were the LeRoy Prinz numbers, but the story of a struggling singer wanting to make good on Broadway had lost any of its drive, and these films were too much, but not enough, like the Grable-Dailey Fox ones.

Then in 1953 she played the two-gun wild cat, *Calamity Jane*, sister under the saddle of Annie Oakley, in a lusty original that was one of the best musicals of the year and the best Doris Day made at Warners until *The Pajama Game*.

Howard Keel, in a repeat of his shrew-taming role in *Annie Get Your Gun*, was her co-star, and Day's

Top left: Gene Nelson and Virginia Mayo in *Painting the Clouds with Sunshine*.

Top right: Doris Day in her first feature film, *Romance on the High Seas*.

Above: Doris Day and Gordon Macrea, in *By the Light of the Silvery Moon*.

a star whose personality and talent were on a par with the Metro crowd. She was a tall blonde singer with the unlikely name of Doris Kappelhoff, who was already a successful singer (with bands like Fred Waring's and Bob Crosby's) and had made a few records. The description of 'the girl who looked as though she drank a pint of liquid sunshine every day' suited Doris Day to a T. She was the singer with the dream in her voice. Though she came into her own as one of the great in the relatively tuneless 50s,

rendition of 'Secret Love' made it her film. Warners then compromised her success by sticking her into two real musical duds, *April in Paris* and *Lucky Me*, both in 1954. She then went to MGM on a non-exclusive long-term contract, but by this time the musical trend was on its way out. Fewer were being made, and the great musical directors were leaving or making comedies and other types of film. Charles Vidor, who had earlier directed Rita Hayworth in films like *Gilda*, was assigned to helm the Ruth Etting biography, *Love Me or Leave Me* (1955). Doris Day's success as the hard-living torch singer of the jazz age, a part quite the opposite of any she had played to date, received good reviews and an Oscar nomination, and added encouragement to the trend for biographical films. After making *The Pajama Game* (1957), she wanted to play in the film of *South Pacific*, perfect for her, but the part went to Mitzi Gaynor.

For a star of her talents, she has had few great musical directors to work with. Ross Hunter's sophisticated comedy, *Pillow Talk* (1959), and similar films she made in the late 50s and 60s, placed her in the top box-office echelon. Her name was now synonymous with reliable entertainment. The only male star in the same position, Cary Grant, made a film with her, *That Touch of Mink*, which made a mint. Unfortunately, none of these later films were musicals.

There are many stars associated to some degree with 40s musicals, even if they weren't all as deservedly popular as Ann Sheridan, who had 'oomph' and saw the humour of it as she hoisted her 'bustle and corset' Warner Bros films out of their rut. There was velvet-voiced radio and record favourite Dinah Shore doing bits here and there, introducing 'I'll Walk Alone' in Universal's all-star contribution to the war effort, *Follow the Boys* (1944), and 'Now I Know' in Danny Kaye's feature film debut, *Up in Arms* (1944), which also featured the lissom Goldwyn Girls. Danny Kaye was a

Above, left: An exuberant Doris Day as *Calamity Jane*, her best role in years with great new songs like 'The Deadwood Stage'. Her co-star was Howard Keel, as Wild Bill Hicock.

Above: Doris Day as she appeared in her best film, as Ruth Etting in *Love Me or Leave Me*. Her co-star was James Cagney, who played Marty Snyder.

Left: Doris Day and Frank Sinatra in *Young at Heart* (1954). The film was a musical re-working of WB's *Four Daughters*, with Sinatra as the tortured pianist who makes life tough for Doris.

musical star, too, in all those Goldwyn films as the epileptic KID from here and there. No denying his popularity. Carrot-topped, strangly voiced, cartoon featured, the sight of a girl (Virginia Mayo in his first five films) produced slack-jawed infantilism. The sight of anything else was an excuse to tie himself into knots, literally. But he was *Hans Christian Andersen* (1952), with that wonderful Frank Loesser score for him to sing, and *The Court Jester* (1956) remains one of the most delicious spoofs, musical or otherwise, on days of yore and other things, since Mark Twain's *A Connecticut Yankee*. Kaye came from Broadway, as had Mary Martin. though she had not the same success in films. Whatever it was that made her an idol on Broadway, on the screen she was simply not there. Or maybe the problem was that she was there already – her bangs came from Margaret Sullavan (whose vocals she had dubbed for *Shopworn Angel* 1938) in her first assault on Hollywood. Her innocently knowing style was virtually a carbon copy of her friend, Jean Arthur, and her low, slow whispy way with a romantic ballad was Alice Faye. In films Miss Martin gave one the uncomfortable feeling of watching a human jig-saw puzzle. If part of Merman's problem was 'too much' then Mary Martin's problem was a case of too many but not enough of anyone. Even so, a sensational success on Broadway singing Cole Porter's 'My Heart Belongs to Daddy' brought her back to Hollywood, where Paramount certainly tried hard to showcase her, with the result that she was in several pleasant and two above average musicals. *Rhythm on the River* (1940), with Bing Crosby, and the even more entertaining spoof on the *Gone with the Wind* casting furore, *Kiss the Boys Goodbye* (1941) were both directed by Victor Schertzinger. He made her look good but he couldn't make her a film star. Paramount, like MGM, made many musicals and

Bandleaders featured in film musicals. Top: In *Dancing Co-Ed* (1939 – called *Every Other Inch a Lady* in Britain) Artie Shaw accompanies a rare appearance by wife-to-be Lana Turner as a dancer. Above: Louis Armstrong and a rare film appearance by Billie Holliday in *New Orleans* (1947). Left: Tommy Dorsey and one of his singers in Eleanor Powell's *Ship Ahoy* (1942). The singer's name is Frank Sinatra. Opposite, top: Glenn Miller in *Orchestra Wives*. Centre: Benny Goodman and his band were in *The Gang's All Here* (1943 – *The Girls he Left Behind* in Britain) with Alice Faye and Carmen Miranda. Bottom: Harry James and his band in *Two Girls and a Sailor* (1944). The chorus beauty fourth from the right is Ava Gardner.

much money and could afford the luxury of failures like Lucille Bremer and Mary Martin, since teaming them with Crosby and Astaire usually ensured that the film itself made money.

The B-Plus companies of the 40s had to be more cautious; even so, their musicals, usually budgeted as programmers, were often fast and lively, and featured a galaxy of favourites, like Janet Blair, Larry Parks, Jinx Falkenburg, Evelyn Keyes, Gloria Jean, Peggy Ryan, Ann Blyth, Judy Canova, and 'the Mexican Spitfire', Lupe Velez, who had a hit with the title tune from *Six Lessons from Madame La Zonga* (1941). And even Republic, Monogram and PDC made musicals on a shoestring, starring a barn-tent Betty Grable named Mary Beth Hughes. Their films were vehicles too: an occasional memorable song, some forgettable footwork, and no musical invention of their own. But while it is difficult to recall the names of the films that first bore many of the song hits of the era they did have an audience. And among the leaders of the bands were Glenn Miller, Woody Herman, Artie Shaw, the Dorsey Brothers, Xavier Cugat, Kay Kyser . . .

Of course, despite this great outpouring of musicals and the great creative talents employed at the major studios, in one important respect the genre still failed to attract great directors to try their hands at this most complex of subjects, thus driving the successful stars and choreographers to directing their own work, much as the Golden Age of Comedy was the result of its stars turning directors. For the musical, like the silent comedy which it replaced, required more than a good book, yet book directors is what it mostly got. To appreciate the special genius of a Minnelli, the graceful *savoir-faire* of a Charles Walters, the nonchalance of a Schertzinger, the drive and athleticism of a Kelly, imbuing every frame of their works, one has to separate the book from the number, the dressing from the foundation,

the star from the material, to judge just what if anything, the George Sidneys, Mark Sandrichs, Lloyd Bacons, Dave Butlers *et al.* brought to the proceedings. For example, Mark Sandrich directed more of the classic Astaire-Roger musicals than anybody else, five in all, but on his own, without that celebrated team, which included Van Nest Polglase, Irene, Walter Plunkett, and the song writers, working under the creative production umbrella of Pandro S. Berman, he is virtually forgotten. Which leads one to conclude that the qualities of those films must have had little to do with his contribution to the whole. Or take George Sidney, the Henry Koster of the MGM lot, inasmuch as the bulk of his 40s musicals were the Pasternak-Grayson/Powell/Williams musicals with orchestral interludes. Sidney's films are notable for the wild cranes flying all over the sets only to settle in the belly of a tuba or peering up beneath a glass piano. Unlike Koster, who brought a personal elegance and sparkle to his Durbin films, Sidney rarely rose to the occasion and even less often above the material, leaving his camera to do that, coming down from way back to embellish the art of José Iturbi. It was an effective device for aiding and abetting a sense of spectacle and excitement, as with 'On The Atchison, Topeka and the Santa Fe'

number for *The Harvey Girls*, or to herald the arrival of the river boat in *Show Boat*. But, other than the inevitable initial effect created by swooping over size and expenditure the result is little more than prettification. Decorative these shots could be, as they were with equal effect in his non-musicals, *The Three Musketeers* and *Scaramouche*, but they neither lift the plot nor lighten the load and they certainly don't tote that barge. The sheer repetition of the device becomes a cliché as opposed to the startling dramatic punch when used by a King Vidor for the climax of *Duel in the Sun*, or the final shot of Garland for *A Star is Born*. In the end, entertaining as the films he worked on could be, ravishing as the stars in them looked in close-up, he was like so many of the directors of musicals all over Hollywood, a corporate employee. If all the ingredients were there, in *Annie Get Your Gun*, *Show Boat* and *Kiss Me Kate*, it worked. If they weren't, it sank: *Jupiter's Darling*, *Pepe* and *The Swinger*. The following is a partial list of corporation directors of many musicals:

Henry (*Alexander's Ragtime Band*) King is stolid; Irving (*My Gal Sal*) Cummings is lumbering; Walter (*State Fair*) Lang is genial; Lloyd (*The French Line*) Bacon is fast but flimsy; Norman (*Words and Music*) Taurog is sloppy; Roy (*Born to Dance*) del Ruth was

Danny Kaye in his first feature film, *Up in Arms*. The Goldwyn girl, top row left, is Virginia Mayo, who later became a Goldwyn star, and made four more films with Danny Kaye.

at his best when Eleanor Powell was at hers and together they made beautiful movies; David (*Tea for Two*) Butler is uninspired; Ray (*Dames*) Enright is hopeless; Mervyn (*Rose Marie*, Ann Blyth version) LeRoy is one long cliché; S. Sylvan (*Rio Rita*) Simon showed up for work; Sidney (*You'll Never Get Rich*) Landfield stayed detached from it; H. Bruce (*Three Little Girls in Blue*) Humberstone is just plain; Archie (*Go Into Your Dance*) Mayo just wanted to get the film into the can; Allan (*Young People*) Dwan knew when and where and why to dolly; George (*Holiday in Mexico*) Sidney, dilly-dallied; George (*The Dolly Sisters*) Seaton was verbose; George (*Star-Spangled Rhythm*) Marshall was raucous; Robert Z. (*Broadway Serenade*) Leonard was moist; Mitchell (*Lady in the Dark*) Leisen got so fussy he ended up strangling in his own and his leading ladies' draperies; W. S. (*Bitter Sweet*) Van Dyke wasn't nick-named Woody 'One-Take' Van Dyke for nothing with results bland when they should have been blithe. These are by no means all, just some of the better-known directors. Perhaps that's why the Directors' Guild was so jealous about their screen credits, and if Donald O'Connor never got

Ginger Rogers starred in *Lady in the Dark* (1944), an elaborate but porridgy film version of the Kurt Weill Broadway hit, directed by Mitchell Leisen who should have known better.

243

Two of Jack Cole's numbers for Rita Hayworth in *Tonight and Every Night*. Above: The samba is 'You excite me'. Below: Her partner in 'What does an English girl think of a Yank?' is Jack Cole.

the credit he deserved for his Universal musicals it may have had more to do with the slightness of directors like Arthur Lubin (*Bowery to Broadway*) and Charles Lamont (*The Merry Monahans*) than the slightness of his vehicles.

The 40s represents the big musical burst from the big studios and the big stars. Having begun the era with one pin-up favourite it is fitting to finish with another – Rita Hayworth, the Latin from Manhattan. Rita was Columbia Studio's musical comedy queen and the Love Goddess of the era. If it hadn't been for her presence on his lot it's not likely that Harry Cohn would have risked many musicals, for, like Zanuck, his interests lay further afield.

The difference between Cohn and Mayer was summed up by Gene Kelly, whose one-time loan-out to Columbia for his co-starring role in Rita Hayworth's *Cover Girl*, catapulted him into the top ranks. As he told his biographer, Clive Hirschhorn, 'If the picture had flopped, Cohn would have kicked me in the *derrière*. That was the way Harry operated, and the reason I could never have been under long-term contract to him. He would have exhausted me long before I could have exhausted him. Mayer, on the other hand, would put on a veneer of benevolence and self-righteousness which fooled the innocent into believing he was a nice avuncular old man, when in fact he was just as ruthless as the worst of them. During the Communist witch-hunts in 1947 Mayer remarked to someone that I couldn't possibly be a Commie because I was a Catholic who loved his mother.'

Amazingly, considering her suitability for musicals, her impact in them, and their success at the box-office, Rita only made a handful of musicals, but these proved sufficient to ensure the studio's reputation as one of Hollywood's major film-producing companies. Hayworth's films are primarily memorable for her presence. Her achievement is entirely cinematic and would have been quite lost on the stage where there is no close-up to open out from. When she dances she unfolds an action through means that are purely visual and far more expressive than histrionics.

Victor Saville, director of *Tonight and Every Night* (1945), said: 'Hayworth is a most extraordinary creature. She looked like nothing in the world when she came on to a stage – but once she was on the screen one looked at nothing else. It just wouldn't have been possible to make her look uninteresting. It was a magic rapport she had with the camera. Absolutely no temperament – very easy to

Rita Hayworth in *Gilda*. 'Put the blame on Mame' was choreographed by Jack Cole.

work with her – very professional dancer. She believed every dumb line she ever had to say, so on the screen she came out all right, while the actors who thought about their lines looked silly next to her. She was a natural.'

Rita Hayworth was born Margarita Carmen Cansino. Her father was a well-known Spanish dancer and her mother, Volga Haworth, was of English-Irish blood. Rita made her stage début at the age of six, having trained from the age of four, and went professional at twelve. By 1933 she had become her father's dancing partner. Not yet sixteen, she signed with Fox and made her screen début as half of a dance team, seen in the background of *Dante's Inferno* (1935). A number of trivial but star-grooming roles followed, but came to nothing when

Fox merged with 20th Century Films, and Zanuck dropped her. Very young and determined to succeed, she made B's for all the small companies around. This way she continued to gain exposure in low-budget westerns, thrillers and musicals, until she was chosen for Howard Hawks' *Only Angels Have Wings* (1939).

She was twenty and had lost weight, raised her hair line through electrolysis, and changed her hair colour to the copper-red it's famed for. Her impact as a faithless wife who moved even while standing still was sensational and then she was a star. But style is not something that can be applied like make-up; she simply *had* style. She was a magnificent animal – and that made her inevitably a sex goddess – with that hypnotic half-awake quality that made her

245

Rita Hayworth in *Cover Girl*. The star is seen with suitor Lee Bowman – her co-star, Gene Kelly, is not in this shot – and, to her right, Jinx Falkenberg, Eve Arden and Anita Colby. With his back to the camera, Otto Kruger.

247

mysterious until the moment she kicked off her shoes and began to dance. Then she was a volcano.

It was the walk-out of another star, Fox's blonde Carole Landis, that gave Hayworth the role of the wilful, destructive and glamorous Doña Sol in *Blood and Sand* (1941) that clinched her rise to the top. It was her first film in colour and brought her together with Hermes Pan, who arranged a brief but erotic little dance for her. Mamoulian's psychological use of colour to heighten mood and character benefited her and she was a sensation. Doña Sol did what she liked and went after – and got – what she wanted, and in this guise Rita Hayworth was to be triumphant.

After *Blood and Sand* Rita's boss, Harry Cohn of Columbia, shrewdly concentrated the publicity on her. She was starred in five musicals over the next three years. *You'll Never Get Rich* (1941) and *You Were Never Lovelier* (1942) co-starred her with Fred Astaire. *My Gal Sal* (Fox, 1942) gave her numbers by Hermes Pan and the opportunity to wear stunning period clothes. In *Cover Girl* (1944) she came from the chorus to stardom on Broadway with a memorable score by Jerome Kern and fabulous dance numbers with Gene Kelly. In Saville's *Tonight and Every Night* Hayworth was an American dancer working in a wartime London revue that never missed a performance during the Blitz. The songs by Sammy Cahn and Jule Styne, and especially the rousing title song, deserved to be better remembered. 'You Excite Me' – a dance done to a Brazilian tempo is the sort of number Hayworth is best at. Her red hair flickers stormily around her face, and her supple undulations open up a Dionysian revel. Marc Platt, a dancer-choreographer who had come from the stage production of *Oklahoma*,

partnered her in this film, and again in *Down to Earth* (1947). But Rita's most celebrated moment came at the climax of an otherwise non-musical melodrama. As *Gilda* (1946) the siren who ensnared men with her looks and locks of her hair, she had been true to a man once, and after what had happened to her, 'Watch Out!'. As with *You Were Never Lovelier*, she was back in Buenos Aires, only this time it wasn't her father but her psychotic husband who owned a casino, and instead of a sunny Fred Astaire to woo her in dance she incited an already neurotic Glenn Ford to near lethal rage with a song and a dance that lived up to her declaration earlier in the film that if she had been a ranch they would have called her 'the Bar-Nothing'. She laughed at him, with her mouth wide open, and she would tilt her head back so that her hair seemed to spill about her shoulders like wanton flames flickering, careless of the consequences, a bombshell with a delayed action fuse. And all she did was to take off her slinky black evening gloves – was it her fault that she could look naked with only her shoulders bare? Jack Cole, the choreographer who revolutionized dance in films and on Broadway, understood the power she had, and how to harness it, and he created 'Put the Blame on Mame' for Rita.

Cole said: 'Of all the things I ever did for movies' (and he worked with Dietrich in *Kismet*, Grable at Fox, Ann Miller at Columbia, and Marilyn Monroe) 'that's one of the few I can really look at on the screen right now and say, "If you want to see a beautiful erotic woman, this is it!" It still remains first class. It could be done right now. Every time I see Rita do "Put the Blame on Mame" I feel it's absolutely great.'

It was only natural, given that those who saw it

Marc Platt partners Rita Hayworth as the muse, Terpsichore, who has come *Down to Earth* to give a Broadway musical a bit of class by injecting a Grecian-style ballet into it. Cole's task was to make it artsy without being boring, and yet not so good as to be successful – the type of challenge that amused him.

never forgot it, every time Rita came back from a marriage, her films, *Affair in Trinidad* (1952), and *Fire Down Below* (1957), would have her dancing up a storm. It was a measure of Hayworth's talents that, even without a Jack Cole, and reduced to going through motions more familiar to patrons of a burlesque house than a family audience, she could still thrill.

Her numbers for *Miss Sadie Thompson* (1954, Somerset Maugham's *Rain*) give a torrid lift to the proceedings. There was little to rival them in the 50s. Rita, surrounded by a room-full of drunken, sweating, lonely, tanked-up sex-starved marines, feeds their libidos with her steamy shaking and belting of 'The Heat is On'. Later, on her bed, a bottle of beer to keep her cool, a couple of marines to share the time, she sings of the blue, Pacific blues, the feeling you get, from real bad news. She adjusts her pillows, she stretches out a hand with the bottle in it, she tosses her head, dismissive like, half-raises herself up from the bed only to fall back from so much effort in that hot blue night, and an audience is left with an unforgettable reminder of the haunting, mysterious, sexy-symbol that Hayworth was.

Her last appearance in a musical was as the cynical, high-society dame, Vera Simpson, in the belated, considerably toned-down film adaptation of Rodgers and Hart's musical, *Pal Joey* (1957). A somewhat too-old-to-be-successful-as-a-gigolo Frank Sinatra played gigolo Joey, the role his good pal Gene Kelly had created on the stage 17 years earlier and Cohn had offered him back in the 40s, opposite Rita. As the little mouse Joey really loves Columbia cast Kim Novak. George Sidney, who usually did well by Broadway hits when they became films, directed. But the best moments came in the two numbers Hermes Pan choreographed for her, reuniting them 15 years after he danced with her in *My Gal Sal*. As 'Vera of the Vanishing Zipper' (a clever stroke on the screenwriters' part over the stage version was to reveal Vera to have had a past in burlesque, and to have it revealed by Joey at a gala society benefit). Hayworth, taking off gloves and twirling the loose panels of her sophisticated evening-dress like a stripper's tassels to 'Zip', was in her element. And later, to 'Bewitched, Bothered and Bewildered', sung as she wakes and dances from her bed to the shower, she was in her glory.

Hayworth's dresses were by Jean-Louis; her hair was styled by Helen Hunt; Jack Cole, Hermes Pan and Valerie Bettis created most of her numbers; she didn't write her dialogue or her films; somebody else directed them and, as everyone now knows, her singing voice was dubbed by some of the best background singers in the profession – but what does it all matter. Without Rita, their efforts could never have met with such success. Harry Cohn might have fumed and fretted and cursed and wished he could have wound her up and set her working as Zanuck did with Betty and the Blondes, but Rita was an original.

Working with Hermes, Rita was romantic, reflective, adoring. With Cole she was on the assault, racing down high, long ramps out of her subconscious straight into that of the viewer. Cole's work presages a physical, flaunting 70s spirit.

Experienced in a context of cheerful 40s film musicals, it is hardly surprising that his work still brings a rush to the mind. Unfortunately they severely strained the silly plots they were set in. Unlike Gene Kelly, Cole never did direct his own films, only the numbers in them, but these, sets, design, costume, cuts, camera angles, were all his. Yet this dichotomy, between his results and their context, between Rita in long-johns or scanties dancing with the velocity of a stallion in stud, drew powerfully on our subconscious and made for revolutionary imagery in motion. The 40s and 50s were still too early for movies to show males dancing like this, unless set safely among Michael Kidd's lovelorn backwoodsmen or Gene Kelly's jolly sailors, for the implications in a man doing an equivalent to 'Put the Blame on Mame' would have been too disturbing, overwhelming. In fact the results would probably have not been anywhere near as effective. In the end, the sight of a man stomping his heels in a disco is a bit like a hammer on an anvil – exhilaration soon turns to madness and waste. Yet it is that ever-present current of physical, mean anger banked deep in Gene Kelly's work, the threat of the jolly male turning into a randy stallion, that must account in some measure for the enormous appeal of his screen guise, as jolly guy next door, sailor on leave, American in Paris, or star on the lam. He was the always smiling, always cheerful, always nice to kids and all-round hail-fellow, well-met buddy-buddy kind of guy.

The non-musical version of *Kismet* (1944) required Marlene Dietrich, a non-dancer, to perform an alluring dance displaying gilded legs. Jack Cole takes Miss Dietrich through her paces.

A dance number by Jack Cole for Columbia's 'gay new Latin-American musical', *The Thrill of Brazil* (1946). His dancers included one of the best there was, Carol Haney. She went on to become one of Broadway's foremost choreographers.

Marge Champion and Pat Denise in one of Jack Cole's numbers for *Three for the Show* (1955). Cole not only choreographed, but controlled the visual design and camera movement for his numbers.

But of this trio, Pan, Cole and Kelly, all of whom danced on the screen, only Gene was a star as well. And interestingly enough, after a fairly successful start in films, playing the sort of heels that had brought him to fame as Broadway's *Pal Joey*, his career started to flag. It was about then that he did an about-face and came up smiling; as 'The Laughing Cavalier', he never looked back. *Singin' In The Rain* was merely his coronation. Angry, physical and far more aggressively erotic than in his subsequent guise, he had not been getting far. Passive, sweet and happily contented, Rita was doing OK. When these intrinsic qualities became subordinated, when, as it were, these two unlikely people exchanged images, the results couldn't have been other than, as Cole once put it to me, 'Mother's Night in a Turkish Bath'.

Jack Cole's continuing influence on modern dance reaches out beyond his own stage and screen work of the 40s and 50s through to the works of a new generation of choreographers via the incredible team of dancers he brought together and trained in his years at Columbia, when he was in charge of the choreography for all of that studio's musicals. Out of that group of gypsies came such celebrated dancers and choreographers as Bambi Linn, Carol 'Steam Heat' Haney, Gwen *Sweet Charity* Verdon (Carol worked with Bob Fosse and Verdon was married to him), Bob Hamilton and Rod Alexander (with the celebrated TV musical comedy variety, *Shows of Shows*), Mat Maddox and many others. But what concerns us is Cole's work for the screen and for ladies like Betty Grable, Mitzi Gaynor, Marlene Dietrich, Ann Miller, Marilyn Monroe, and, of course, Rita Hayworth.

I met Cole while researching my book about Hayworth. He talked of Rita and other things as well.

Jack Cole: I was brought in on *Cover Girl* because Val Rasset and Seymour Felix were very old-fashioned ballet and girlie dance directors, not used to doing the new style numbers Cohn wanted for this big new musical with which he hoped to out-Metro Mayer. I had a marvellous time with Cohn, because I had a very sharp tongue – when you were alone with him you could say anything to him. He'd start giving you a hard time and you'd scream and holler and he'd say, 'OK, OK, I just wanted to see if you knew what you were doing. Go ahead.' He was a very good executive; his way was to divide and conquer. Of course my background was theatre, so to me the director was the director, no matter what he was like. I mean, if Victor Saville had told me that the stage of the Windmill Theatre was the size of my bedroom I would have done very different things for *Tonight and Every Night*.

Cohn took my contract over from Metro. I had absolute control over sets and costumes on which I worked. I could say, 'NO'. That gave me a lot of power for a man in my position. My thing was not to do those kind of old-fashioned bits but to do coloured air. I'd always work with the designer and have the whole number, camera angles, movement, everything, worked out in advance with a sketch artist so that there'd be no mistakes. It's very funny; movies at that time were always about ten years

behind the theatre in a kind of a way. I used to tease Harry, because my contract stated that I was hired for my 'peculiar and unique talents', but they wanted you to do what they'd been doing, and hoped that in some magical way it would come out peculiar and unique. And I'd tell Harry, if I'm doing the same dumb thing, whether I'm unique and peculiar or not, it'll come out the same dumb way. My contract also stipulated that I didn't have to work on a picture unless the budget was a million and a half – a lot of money then – which practically reduced me to only doing Hayworth pictures. But I did a million Z musicals, Ann Miller, Jinx Falkenburg, all those things, because Cohn was quite willing, if he liked you, to let you design the sets, the costumes, cut the film, shoot it, clean up the John, anything so long as you didn't goof. He was an extraordinarily bright man – with a very vulgar tongue. Nasty to actors. He thought they were all a tub of shit. He could make them. Of course, he couldn't. But that's the way they all thought. Zanuck was no different.

Rita trusted me. Later on, she had Valerie Bettis (*Affair In Trinidad, Salome*). Bettis was a very good modern dancer, an expert in her line, who wanted to be an actress, so that always creates a problem. Already they were competitive ladies. She always did numbers for Rita that Valerie Bettis would do. But Rita isn't a dancer in that way. Nor did she wish to be, nor did she pretend to be. You had to treat her like the most beautiful show-girl who could move, but not like a dancer. She could dance, but she didn't go to class every day like the kids in my troupe; she only took classes when she was rehearsing for a number and she only made a musical every other year or so, and they were working all the time.

The main objective in movies in those days, which Valerie Bettis didn't understand, was not to prove your point but to make the star look *marvellous* – don't prove anything about dancing. I learnt my lesson from Miss Dietrich when I was still at MGM. I did the dance she had to do for a real piece of dumb shit – *Kismet* (1944), a dumb-dumb movie. It wasn't a musical but she had to do this dance, and that lady was *no* dancer. I had this idea for her to do a real oriental style dance, and I designed a costume for her to wear, all authentic, gold chain, her legs covered in black trousers, the real thing. But Miss Dietrich, who'd been making a big fuss about always having to show her legs, wouldn't have it. She pretended to agree but she'd always find a way to get the chains caught against the steps or on things, till finally I took the hint. The lady wanted it her way, and she was the star. So she got the transparent skirt, and she painted her legs in gold paint so you couldn't miss them, and we did it her way. It wasn't authentic, but I learnt my lesson. And she was right. After all, she was the one who was going to be doing it up there, not me.

Rita and I got along very well. She was always a very pleasant working lady, and if you worked with as many star ladies as I have, where the worst thing you could say to them after they did something was to tell them it was marvellous, but I think we can make it even better – then you know that that's the highest compliment you can pay them. Rita came in

254

Left: Marilyn Monroe in the 'Heat Wave' number in *There's no Business Like Show Business* arranged by Jack Cole.

Right: Sheree North and Jacques D'Amboise in 'The Birth of the Blues' ballet in *The Best Things in Life are Free*. Choreography by one of Cole's dancers, Rod Alexander.

with the rest of the kids in the morning; did her bit; no fuss; no star; just work. But when it was for real, then she let go. The only time I danced with Rita [*Tonight and Every Night*] because the boy we had sprained his ankle, and there was a tight budget, and the director said, 'You know it, you did it, you do it.' So I did. The camera turned, and it was like WOW! I was knocked six ways from Sunday. Suddenly there was this mass of red hair, and eyes rolling, and ninety-four more teeth than I'd ever seen in a woman's mouth before. The moment film was in the camera she was the most animated object I'd ever seen. The thing with her was that she was *wildly* suited to do what she was doing at the time she was doing it. Betty [Grable] as a matter of fact was a very talented lady, but she just *had* show-business, having been in it with her mother since childhood. She was the most old, tired gypsy as a young girl. Her problem was that she could do those pictures forward and backward. She never looked at the script. She'd come in, do her make-up, see her three pages of dialogue for the day, say, 'OK. Ready' and go through it in a haze, thinking of her horse running in the race that day. But Rita always did it for real. It makes a difference.

Most of that time spent at Columbia was a very happy situation for me because, besides doing those Hayworth films for four years, Cohn made it possible for me to work with my kids. He was very proud of us – he hired all those people and kept them on salary when they were not working on a picture, but just studying and training all day long

with me. They became very expert and everybody got to know about them in California and Metro wanted to hire us all. They all turned out absolutely marvellous because they all got very good training and Harry Cohn paid for it. It's not been done before or since. In terms of my own career as a choreographer I wasted a lot of time doing all those star things for people who are really not talented, where I was more a kind of handholder-brother-mother, because I happened to get on with those ladies. In film you can take people who are the right type, who have a cinematic quality, and make quite a lot of things happen. Believe me – it's not like the stage where it's all you.

Monroe was another very hard-working lady. Of course she was a very neurotic girl. And though she had a good voice and a good ear, she was totally unknowing about dancing. Once she came late with me, once, and I said 'Never do that to me again, baby – I don't care what you do to the others, but not this pussycat.'

It was very funny. Marilyn had done all those films at Fox and finally she was doing the test for *Gentlemen Prefer Blondes*.

I did this extraordinarily beautiful test with Marilyn for 'Diamonds are a Girl's Best Friend'. Beautiful. All red and pink, empire style. A great enormous empire bed with pale pink chiffon sheets, black satin covers with red Napoleonic eagles, a great mahogany tub, big black maids with 18th-century turbans, and Marilyn was in bed with this lady just doing diamonds, brushing them. It was

Below: Betty Grable in one of Cole's numbers in *Meet Me After the Show*, and opposite, partnered by his assistant, Gwen Verdon, in *The Farmer Takes a Wife*.

extraordinarily beautiful. And she was so beautiful! Because she wore nothing but diamonds, and a big horse's tail with a diamond horsefly on it, and because the cameraman who shot it, Artie Arling (like all famous cameramen, they can smell a new star), he knocked himself out for her. She was looking incredible – out of this world. Anyway, we didn't shoot that number till last, and by that time there had been a lot of trouble with the publicity releases, and the studio was getting reports that women's clubs weren't going to let their people see Marilyn Monroe's films because she was too flagrantly sexual. So Zanuck called me up and said, 'No way baby, you can't shoot the number like that.' Well, she almost had to be taken to the hospital when she was told we wouldn't do it for real. And then when they told her that Jane Russell's deal with Fox included her cameraman! Marilyn wasn't a woman-hater, she was just very sure of herself, and Jane is a very nice easy Californian lady, so there was no problem in that sense, but Marilyn, unconsciously would just walk into Russell's camera light, you know. In the test, Jane was nowhere, an ice man in drag next to Marilyn. A good-looking sexy ice man to be sure, but Marilyn was just so screamingly beautiful. She was different. Off screen she looked like the most attractive sex-maniac girl next door, just a little black eye shadow, no make-up at all. But they got at her, and later on the only thing she had any security in was in the way she looked.

Like Rita, Monroe did have a very peculiar cinematic thing. When they were on the screen they made a lot of very good actors look like they were standing still. Marilyn couldn't dance but she acted dancing. Marvellous. She just didn't have any technique – and that worried her. And so she didn't sleep, and that gave her a line on her forehead, so she phoned in to say she was sick, because the one thing she counted on was the way she looked 'cause she knew everybody would be looking at her. And when she finally did get into make-up she'd be combing her hair that one more time, because she was frightened of coming out. And then she was such a little girl that she didn't know how to apologize. If it were Mitchum or Grable who were waiting, she'd be besides herself with fear and remorse, and yet she couldn't bring herself to come out.

Marilyn was like Rita. She kept trusting you to do right by her. She had no problems with you showing her how to be Marilyn Monroe. Because she was instinctively, marvellously erotic. What Harry and Darryl were buying from these ladies was "female eroticism" and they knew it.

I developed a technique with Hayworth that I developed to an extreme degree later with Monroe. When we'd do close-ups of certain kinds of things, I'd get within three feet of her, and she really would mimic me – I'd wet my mouth; open it like I can't breathe; rub my belly and she'd look at me this way and we'd just have each other, going on and on, and she just did it. She didn't have any feeling about it at all. She didn't have any compunctions about somebody showing Rita Hayworth how to do her stupid eyelashes. They were·working ladies. What more can you say of anybody?'

Marilyn Monroe knew that she benefited from Jack Cole's direction. For ten years he did virtually all of her film musical numbers. Overleaf: 'Diamonds are a Girl's Best Friend' in *Gentlemen Prefer Blondes*. Left: Preparing a number in *Let's Make Love*.

The 40s had sparked off a new creative era in the musical field. It had produced new names in the ranks of the directors, choreographers and designers and created its own galaxy of memorable personalities. By the mid-50s, when the musical boom had waned, and Hollywood's production of film was diminishing daily, it was also obvious that whatever position the musical might again hold, it could never again be on as vast and carefree a scale. For versatility, the musicals of the 40s remain unchallenged. They emerge as more than a reflection of the popular whims of the period and have become the yardstick by which all successive musicals must be measured.

Opposite: Cyd Charisse
dancing in Mexican
costume for *Fiesta* (1947),
a lavish MGM musical
filmed entirely south of
the borner. Also starring
were Esther Williams and
Ricardo Montalban.
Photograph by Clarence
Sinclair Bull.

Razzle Dazzle em

The era of Minnelli, Walters, Donen and Kelly, Pan and Astaire, Hayworth and Cole, rose up in the 30s, dominated the 40s and stopped dead in the 50s. Though most of them were still with us in body, their spirit and legacy, and that of all the other great names in an age profuse with them, just disappeared. A genre that had seemed omnipotent vanished as if it had never been. Only the most inane – those cheaply shot beach-ball and rock n' roll quickies, or the gilt-edged stage adaptations reached the screens, and neither could be considered representative of this genre's capabilities.

Since the mid-60s, good, even great, musicals have been made, and new musical talents have appeared in movies, but the replacements for those of the past can still be counted on the fingers of the hand with little assurance that many of them will last longer than the flick of the calendar page or the time it takes for a poster to wrinkle.

In the past quarter of a century, except for the to-date isolated genius of Bob Fosse, the giants in the film musical firmament have nearly all been established on records, their progress uninterrupted by the occasional negligible film, living in a self-enclosed world, even on their tours; gangs of Princes for whom what happens on the large screen matters little. Most of the films I've written about were before their time. Talking to rock-superstars like David Essex and Pete Townshend, one finds that they saw hardly more than a dozen films in their lives and that those they saw offered them nothing to believe in, thus setting them out to create a world of their own, in which, as reported in *Esquire* (November 1982) there was 'unlimited wealth – sex and booze, turn on the tap, it flowed, it was free, served endlessly – it led to girls with syphilis and men with nervous breakdowns' – it did not lead to a resurgence in film musicals. Most of the 50s generation, out of which the largest proportion of today's stars came, had their first contact with the great old musicals, if they saw them, on the late-show slots on TV. Their size diminished, their colour bled, their story line shredded to fit into commercial interruptions, they were postage stamp reproductions of famous paintings. Sure, for the dedicated, films could still be seen in something of their original length, size and form in museums and revival houses, but those are primarily the hunting places of archivists, custodians, and others who wax nostalgic over the good old days, even as they help bury them with lectures of preservation for the winter of revelation that never comes when it is needed. Besides, the musicals having never been taken that seriously in their hey-day were the last genre on any film programme list for reappraisal (unless to disparage them). This attitude only began to change in the early 70s. I still recall the difficulty I had seeing many of these films when I first worked on this project in the 60s.

What this neglect of the musical meant can be seen when occasionally an original, dynamic work like Bob Fosse's *Sweet Charity*, appeared, surfacing in a vacuum, to be derided by those into nostalgia, and ignored by the general public, who had grown up without a context for a work as fresh, exciting and rich as this film was. The musicals preceding it, those over-produced, listless white elephants from Broadway, had seen to that. A film that sang with the close-up, danced with the camera and turned the dances into a vital participant of the drama confused people. In the 'I' generation, a film that dealt with us, you and them, was more than most could take. Since then there have been two more by Fosse, *Cabaret* and *All that Jazz*, and musical stars like Bette Midler, Liza Minnelli, Streisand and Diana Ross, and Rock stars like The Beatles and The Rolling Stones. But the larger proportion of musicals have been as awful as *Man of La Mancha* or *Annie*, and the only new development has been in the large-screen versions of touring rock concerts, inaugurated by the success of *Woodstock*, which mix the documentary approach with the modern equivalent of old vaudeville skits. Though busting with an explosive energy uniquely their own, one still awaits the proper harnessing of that frenzied freedom for works that inspire rather than exhaust. *The Rose*, for all its clichés, was such a work because it set off the uniquely gifted, exhilaratingly talented Bette Midler in a story that had a beginning, a middle and an end.

But I'm getting ahead of myself. More than any other genre, because of their cost, musicals were the major victim of the great and crippling defeat of movies by television in the 50s. Stars who no longer guaranteed a public were eased out, or dropped when it came to renew their contracts. Many disappeared for good. MGM, the studio where most of the major musical talents were gathered, allowed frustrated choreographers, directors and stars to sit around without work until their contract ran out, or used them up in films that wiped out any remaining box-office appeal they might have had. One way or another, they unloaded Fred Astaire, Gene Kelly, Howard Keel, Cyd Charisse, Judy Garland, Jane Powell, Kathryn Grayson, Esther Williams, Ann Miller, Marge and Gower Champion, Vera-Ellen, Ann Blyth, Donald O'Connor, and such recently acquired talents as Dolores Gray, Taina Elg, Liliane Montevechi, Russ Tamblyn, Tommy Rall, Bobby Vann and Bob Fosse. Warner Bros did the same with Gene Nelson, Gordon McCrea, Virginia Mayo and Doris Day. Betty Grable, 20th Century's major asset for 10 years, was let go. Also, June Haver, Dan Dailey, Mitzi Gaynor, Gloria de Haven, Sheree North. Paramount retired Crosby, Lamour, Betty Hutton, Eddie Bracken, Rosemary Clooney, Dean Martin. Columbia found no replacement for Rita Hayworth.

The stars who survived, Marilyn Monroe, Dean Martin, Doris Day, Frank Sinatra and Debbie Reynolds, did so in comedies or dramas. Doris Day, stifled in her last few years at Warner Bros., sang less and found a fortune in sugar-spun comedies where gloss simulated style. Sinatra, the world's oldest roué, became the owner of a best-selling record company and star of movies in which he sang the title song. Dean Martin played his friend. Debbie Reynolds stayed in the public eye by being discarded by her singer husband for her best friend. Monroe was a different phenomenon.

Only one important new musical personality surfaced in the 50s – his impact so powerful, his fans so numerous and devoted, the profits from his records and live appearances so phenomenal, that

Previous pages: Liza Minnelli as Sally Bowles in Bob Fosse's *Cabaret*.

Pages 264-5: A bland era for the film musical. Eisenhower in America, 'You've never had it so good' in Britain; peace, a consumer boom and the new delights of TV. A public which preferred to sleep got the musicals it deserved. From top left: Peter Gallagher plays a rock idol based on the real-life careers of 50s teenage favourites like Fabian and Frankie Avalon in *The Idolmaker*. Connie Francis, the nation's top female recording artist during the late 50s. Gogi Grant, recording star, with Buddy Bergman and his orchestra in *The Big Beat*. Frankie Avalon. Fabian in *Hound Dog Man*, one of the numerous attempts to cash in on the success of Elvis with other teenagers' recording favourites. Ricky Nelson, Paul Anka and Tuesday Weld in *The Private Lives of Adam and Eve*. Little Richard doing 'Tutti Frutti' in *Don't Knock the Rock*. Frankie Vaughan made his Hollywood début playing a teen-idol in *Let's Make Love* with Marilyn Monroe. Britain's Elvis, Cliff Richard. Frank Tashlin's sight-gag-rich spoof on the music scene, *The Girl Can't Help It* (1956) featured Tom Ewell, hired to turn a no-talent blonde would-be singer, Jayne Mansfield, into a musical superstar and, as was often the case in those days, succeeding. Ann-Margret and Jesse Pearson in *Bye Bye Birdie* which was long before *Grease* in dealing with 50s high school crushes on rock 'n' roll idols. Tommy Sands made his film début in *Sing Boy Sing*. Jerry Lee Lewis in *High School Confidential*. Bobby Darin. John Saxon was a teenage combo leader and Judy Meredith was his girl friend in a typical 50s ersatz musical, *Summer Love*. Edward 'Kookie' Byrnes and souped-up hot rod – a staple teenage commodity. Pat Boone and friends in *Bernardine*; for a time Boone rivalled Elvis in popularity. Tommy Steele, British favourite, in *Tommy the Toreador*.

Hollywood, shaky as it was, bid high to get him into films. That person was Elvis Presley, the King of Rock-and-Roll. His charisma drew on the exuberance of the boy in the body of the man, an innocence in the heart of the tempest he stirred up – a sort of Marilyn Monroe in fly-buttoned trousers and open-necked shirts. To Fred Astaire, Presley was a show business phenomenon he admired. To the outraged establishment elders who watched in horror as he flamed across the nation's record counters, radios and TV screens, he was a flagrant incitement to anarchy and ingratitude from their children. To the new breed of teeny-boppers, he was the whirlwind that baffled and enraged their complacent, pre-fab elders. Girls went into paroxysms at the sound of his voice; when he shook his legs they threw their arms around each other, or fainted. The boys followed his lead, wore skin-tight trousers, cut their hair like his, stood like he did, walked like he did, shook their legs, and took up the guitar. They gave monsyllabic responses to establishment rebukes as the two generations drifted farther apart. Parents forgot their own youthful ecstasies over Dick Haymes and Frank Sinatra. Presley was their kid's age, and their childrens unlocked energy made them aware that they were old and out of date with the times. But new idols are never born out of the dreams of the old. They arise to satisfy the needs which the old idols can't. Since movies, like the nation and the media were also in the hands of old people, once they had signed Elvis they were content to exploit the personality but never the reason for its appeal. Without exception he was cast in dried-out, remodelled old vehicles that converted a likeable hell-raiser into a plastic saint. Ten years of pap like *Loving You*, *Blue Hawaii*,

Elvis Presley.

Right Elvis Presley and the dancers in *Loving You*.

Left: Elvis Presley in *GI Blues*. Right: *Elvis: That's the Way It Is*, documentary account of preparation and performance by Presley in Las Vegas.

Below: Presley and Ann-Margret in a number from *Viva Las Vegas*. For a time Ann promised to become the 60s Hayworth, but her films didn't help and she was so wound up in most of them you couldn't see her for glitter dust.

Paradise Hawaiian Style, *Fun in Acapulco*, *Girls, Girls, Girls*, etc., succeeded in emasculating this Huck Finn. Not the needs of his fans but the calming of the fears of the establishment dictated the films he was given. Provocatively titled subjects like *Wild in the Country*, *Jailhouse Rock*, *King Creole* and *Roustabout* could have starred Bing Crosby. Within a few years Elvis, like Betty Grable, could have phoned in his contribution. No wonder he became surly and discontented with his lot, glad to be out of it. Presley was betrayed by his manager, advisors, the studios, and by his fans who should have shown their anger by boycotting his films until they got what they wanted. Instead of the trend promised by the music, he was given graveyard assignments directed by old tyros like Richard Thorpe and Norman Taurog, whose principal claims to fame lay in bringing in a film under budget and handling child stars.

After ten years, to a generation of his fans tricked into parenthood, Presley returned to the live stage, a shadow of what he had been, with a night-club act that premiered in that gilded heaven of show business mediocrity, Las Vegas. All of their screaming and all of his gyrations couldn't put the real Elvis together again — for that he would have had to go out into the market place. The Beatles and the Rolling Stones were all over the place. The Who were smashing up their stages in a rebellious rage. Alice Cooper, Tina Turner and the rest were pulling the jungle out of their guitars and throats, and all around Presley were the heirs of his legacy to whom he was now like some elder statesman. As safe as Bing, one had the sight of a 40-year-old man on drugs and pills dying to shake the blues away.

The most successful film adaptations from the stage were usually those bought with a specific film star already in mind: *Gentlemen Prefer Blondes* was bought as a vehicle for Monroe. It could be adapted

Left: Mick Jagger and Keith Richards. The Rolling Stones always played to huge audiences. In films like *Let's Spend the Night Together* the audience on screen was part of the attraction. A scene from Hal Ashby's film of the Stones' 1982 USA tour.

Above: The Beatles. *Let it Be.*

Below, left: Tina Turner in *Tommy.*

Below: Jimi Hendrix.

Bottom: Janis Joplin.

Frank Sinatra, in the background, watches the dancers in the 'Luck, be a Lady' number choreographed by Michael Kidd to enliven an otherwise lacklustre group of *Guys and Dolls*.

Gordon MacRae as Curly and Charlotte Greenwood as Aunt Eller in the film version of *Oklahoma!* The director was Fred Zinneman.

then cast to fit the parts. Musical landmarks like *Oklahoma*, *Guys and Dolls*, *South Pacific* and *My Fair Lady* reached the screen smelling of reverence and looking as if they had been stored in formaldehyde at Madame Tussauds.

Because Rodgers and Hammerstein, whose shows with each other and those they did with others made up the greater part of the musicals (*Carousel*, *Flower Drum Song*, *Oklahoma*, *South Pacific*, *The King and I*, *State Fair*, *The Sound of Music*, *Pal Joey*, *Jumbo*, *Carmen Jones* and *Rose Marie*) they fared worst.

Their landmark, *Oklahoma*, was directed by the conscientious Fred Zinneman with plodding sincerity which knocked the high kicking pins out from under and turned its celebration of the friendship between the farmer and the cowhand into a long wake. Not just poor Jud was dead. The promise of the sweeping opening with Gordon MacCrea riding across the horizon singing the title song was short lived. But then, all openings are promising. Frank Loesser's superb show based on Damon Runyan's *Guys and Dolls* came to the screen in the early, no close-up days of Cinemascope, with the camera as hampered as it had been in the first days of sound, directed by Joseph L. Mankiewitz as a lugubrious and miscast chatterbox, with Brando playing what should have been Sinatra's part and vice versa, and the whole thing, with its painted sets looking neither fish nor fowl. 'Ask Me How Do I Feel' indeed! While George Cukor, superb with the fine stitch, couldn't open out Lerner and Loewe's *My Fair Lady* from being more than a stately parade of hats, and while Audrey Hepburn couldn't be less than enchanting in the title role, the studio proceeded to dub her voice and thus rob her

perfectly to what she did well and what audiences wanted to see her do. *The King And I* was an obvious vehicle for Deborah Kerr, *Gypsy* was bought for Rosalind Russell, *Pal Joey* for Frank Sinatra, and *Funny Girl* for Barbra Streisand to make her film début re-creating her stage hit. It's not that these were necessarily better directed than the others, but at least they were adapted to the person who in the end had to carry the show in much the same way the original stage version was usually built around the talents of stars like Gertrude Lawrence, Ethel Merman and Gene Kelly. The least effective transpositions were those bought first and

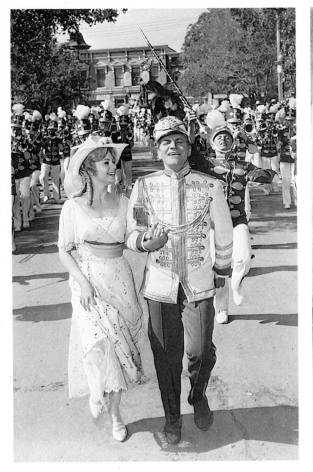

Above left: Robert Preston
repeated his Broadway
triumph as *The Music
Man*. His leading lady was
Shirley Jones.

Above: 'Shall we Dance?'
Yul Brynner's film career
took off with a bound
when he repeated his
Broadway success on film
in *The King and I*. Leading
lady, Deborah Kerr.

character of much of its charm. This was nothing compared to what Joshua Logan did to Rodgers and Hammerstein's Pulitzer prize-winning show, *South Pacific*, to Harold Rome's *Fanny*, or to Lerner and Loewe's enchanting *Camelot* and their gutsy *Paint Your Wagon*. Not many of the highly reputed stage directors have made a successful transition to movies – as a film director Robert Alton (*Merton of the Movies, The Pagan Love Song*), the legendary George Abbott (*Too Many Girls*, both *The Pajama Game* and *Damn Yankees* he co-directed with Stanley Donen) or Harold Prince (*A Little Night Music*) failed to repeat their theatrical triumphs. But Joshua Logan, who started out in films as a dialogue director on *Garden of Allah* (Selznick, 1936) before moving to Broadway and hit shows like *South Pacific, Picnic* and *Mr Roberts*, built up a reputation his musicals can't explain. The camera's scrutiny exposes pretensions both in front of and behind the lens far more swiftly and cruelly than the theatre. The theatre shows you what people think by what the author has them say and do; the camera, through the close-up lens, cuts through all that palaver and gets straight to the heart of the matter. It records what you say but it also reveals what you think and magnifies what you do. It is something Logan never seemed to have learnt – his large scenes lost in gaudy tricked-up effects, his intimate moments magnified to embarrass. *South Pacific* was an excuse for dubious muscular gyrations by the beach boy extras playing marines, while the romantic leads were lost in a wash of multi-coloured jells so that Mitzi Gaynor turned purple, Rossano Brazzi turned chartreuse and audiences turned green. Richard Harris's soliloquies in *Camelot* became deafening and Vanessa Redgrave's nasal

trickle ends up a torrential close-up. The scenes, whether in or out of doors, set in lagoons, tournaments, Marseilles waterfronts or the wide-open spaces of the West filmed in Cinemascope, Todd-AO and other wide-screen processes have the same cramped feeling, with the actors boxed in on themselves. With the exception of Mitzi Gaynor, none of the stars in his musicals – Rossano Brazzi, Lee Marvin, Clint Eastwood, Richard Harris, Jean Seberg, Vanessa Redgrave, Franco Nero – were singers or dancers, and it showed. You can get away with a lot in a musical as Deanna Durbin proved when she decided to wear two different dresses while singing the same song, because, as she said, it was a musical and nobody would notice the difference, but it's another matter to hire actors who neither sing nor dance for a musical. That may work in Broadway, where audiences have been known to thrill to the sight of Lauren Bacall and Katherine Hepburn doing just that, and being acclaimed for the outrage, but not on film. Lucille Ball learnt this to her cost when she evoked sad memories of *Sunset Boulevard*'s pitiful Norma Desmond instead of those of the zesty *Mame*, barely able to lift her leg while the gypsies danced their butts off all around her in an effort to disguise the fact that she was too old and too tired for the part. But it is easier to overlook this great star's self-delusion, since she has created so many wonderful memories, than it is to pass over Logan's pretensions.

If Logan is one of the worst he is by no means the only director to come a cropper when doing musicals – arguably the most complex genre and requiring the most skilful handling. At least a Henry King (*Carousel*) and Walter Lang (*King And I*) knew how to make a movie and didn't

try to improve on the original, but allowed the music, the cast, the sets and the costumes to flow unencumbered if unexcitingly. But what can be said for Arthur (*Love Story*, *Making Love*) Hiller's disastrous *Man of La Mancha*, in which Cervantes' noble knight of the woeful countenance (Peter O'Toole) met his killer windmill and the wonderful score lay buried in the O'Toole and Sophia Loren larynx. Norman Jewison showed no bias directing *Jesus Christ Superstar* and *Fiddler on the Roof* – both awful. Harold Prince buried Stephen Sondheim's *A Little Night Music* in the shadows thrown by Liz Taylor's ballooning shape. On the live stage Lauren Bacall might get away with being *The Woman of the Year* but on the screen considering the way she sang and danced it wasn't surprising when *The Fan* hit the. . . Frank L. Baum's little Dorothy became an anorexic neurotic when Diana Ross played her as a wailing school teacher in *The Wiz*, directed by Sidney Lumét, not one inch of whose screen credits gave one to believe he had ever seen or liked a musical, good as he is

with social dramas. *The Best Little Whorehouse in Texas* was a misnomer – only Dolly Parton's infectious good will and self-assurance were on a par with choreographer/dancer/director Tommy Tune's original Broadway staging. Milos Forman's *Hair* had none of the fresh ebullience of the 60s anti-war hit, or maybe it was just that the sight of

Left, above: Treat Williams in the film version of *Hair*. The director was Milos Forman.

Above: Richard Harris as King Arthur in Joshua Logan's film of *Camelot*.

Far left: Sophia Loren as Aldonza-Dulcinea in one of the Gillian Lynne numbers for *Man of La Mancha*. Not one of the film's three principals (the others were Peter O'Toole and James Coco) was a singer or a dancer.

Left: Lucille Ball in *Mame*, setting her party alight.

Opposite, top left: Audrey Hepburn in *My Fair Lady*. She had sung and danced in *Funny Face* but was dubbed for this.

Top right: Mitzi Gaynor as Nurse Nellie Forbush in Joshua Logan's film of *South Pacific*. In love with a wonderful guy, she sings 'Honey Bun'.

Above: Barbra Streisand in *Hello Dolly!* The film was directed by Gene Kelly and the choreography was by Michael Kidd. The title song, with Louis Armstrong.

Right: King Herod wants proof that Jesus is – what they say he is. Joshua Mostel in *Jesus Christ Superstar.*

Bottom: Len Cariou, Elizabeth Taylor, Laurence Guittard and Diana Rigg in *A Little Night Music.*

hippies getting high in Central Park was less endearing when it finally reached the big screen. And John Huston's first try at musicals at the age of 80 with the adventures of little orphan *Annie* was a $40 million dollar disaster that lacked modest virtues like charm, and had none to replace it.

Besides the mistakes in hiring totally unsuitable directors and casting the wrong people, a major share of the blame might lie in the large amounts of money invested to secure a hit. The responsibility imposed by these mammoth budgets – $24 million for *Hello Dolly!* and *The Wiz*; $22 million for *Darling Lili*, and a rumoured $40 million for *Annie* – would make mice of most men, since anticipation created by the knowledge of such sums spent would be hard to live up to, and few directors would be likely to stick their necks out for fear of having them cut off. Instead, like the girl in the story of *The Red Shoes*, so concerned with not getting them dirty that she steps on a loaf of bread to avoid a puddle, they stood in one spot, and sank.

Clearly these megaton productions, not just musicals, of the past few decades, illustrate one of

the oldest truths, namely that great works are not the results of huge sums of money at one's disposal and unlimited technical resources to draw on. It's the story of the emperor's nightingale all over again; the song from the heart of a plain bird is more beautiful than any mechanical marvel. Or, to quote Igor Stravinsky: 'The stained glass artists of Chartres had few colours, and the stained glass artists today have hundreds of colours but no Chartres. Organs, too, have more stops now than ever before, but no Bach.' Not enlarged resources then, but men and what they believe.

Fortunately, a few Chartres craftsmen like Robert Wise, and artists like Bob Fosse are always around to illuminate the uninspiring scene with their magic. To appreciate where they succeed when others fail it's best to let them speak for themselves.

Robert Wise was the RKO editor who worked on Orson Welles' *Citizen Kane*, and *The Magnificent Ambersons*, and as director has proved himself almost equally adept at every genre. Even so, his success with adapting two of the 50s most celebrated musicals, the Leonard Bernstein-Stephen Sondheim *West Side Story*, and the Rodgers and Hammerstein *The Sound of Music* is remarkable. For the filming of *West Side Story*, a great deal of whose initial success was attributable to Jerome Robbins' explosive staging of the dances, Wise shared the films' directing credit with the choreographer. Here was official recognition at last of the key contribution choreographers had made to the musical. For *The Sound of Music*, Wise had his work cut out. *West Side Story* was immediate and powerful with the explosive tension and rage of the crumbling ghettos it was set in. *The Sound of Music*, for all that it was set in Hitler's Austria, was really Ruritania – in fact, it could as easily have been set in the Napoleonic era of an operetta like *The Firefly*, or the France of *The Vagabond King*. It was as if Rodgers had never heard of Hart or

written *Pal Joey*. But if theatre audiences took to this syrupy wallow in dirndls and edelweiss replete with nuns and shepherds, Barons and Cinderellas as a respite from rock 'n' roll, there was no guarantee that there would be enough 'old' people to support it in sufficient numbers when it came to the screen. Wise had to re-think the whole project if it wasn't to suffer the fate of similar stage adaptations. Wise's solution, unlike such previous songbooks as *Brigadoon*, and *Silk Stockings*, was not to cast the film with dancers and re-write the show to their talents, nor, as with *Fanny* and *Irma La Douce*, throw out the songs altogether, using the music as incidental background score and film it as a straight old-fashioned drama, but to mix singers and actors and create the exhilaration the dancers provided in *West Side Story* through the camera and the editing. It worked superbly, rushing with the wind high up in the mountains where we first spot Maria, arms outstretched, running from speck-sized distance until she filled the hills and the camera with music; bouncing briskly down slopes and along narrow streets with the enthusiasm of artless children moving of their own high spirits and coming effortlessly to rest with the revitalized music. The film became a sensational success, earning over $100 million as well as winning Wise his second Oscar (he shared an Oscar with Robbins for *West Side Story*), and made Julie Andrews a colossal new star.

As Maria, the postulate nun who leaves the cloister to re-think her vocation in the outside world while working as the governess to the large motherless brood of children of the stern but dashing Baron von Trapp, she found the perfect role, at least so far as the public was concerned. Her diction was clean, crisp and flawless, her voice was clear and bright, her shingle-cut hair set off her large, fine, wholesome looks. There was no-nonsense to her manner and she exuded a real but benevolent authority that had all the hallmarks of such earlier

Far left: Aileen Quinn as Little Orphan Annie, with her dog Sandy and other orphans in John Huston's only musical, *Annie*.

Director Robert Wise, right, with choreographer Jerome Robbins, lines up a scene for *West Side Story*.

Opposite, top: Julie Andrews, perfectly cast, in the most successful box-office musical ever filmed. As Maria in *The Sound of Music*.

Below: Robert Wise on the set of *The Sound of Music*, directing Maria (Julie Andrews) and the children. 'My Favourite Things'.

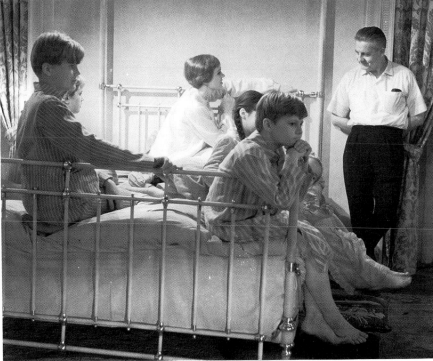

stars as Irene Dunne, Greer Garson and Deborah Kerr. Never for one moment did one fear that she would fail at anything she set out to do, whether it was climbing mountains, fording streams, comforting the small, fighting the wrong or marrying the Prince. She had been toasted as Broadway's *My Fair Lady*, and now became the screen's, even though she had lost out on the film when Jack Warner proved afraid to risk his $8 million investment on a screen unknown. When Warner Bros. set out to film another of her stage hits, *Camelot*, she could afford to turn up her nose at them. As long as she stayed true to this type her success was assured. Later tampering with it led her to a succession of flops, and a long hiatus in her career, but today, twenty years later, she's once again back in films like *Victor and Victoria*.

Wise: I wanted to make *The Sound of Music*, despite its various drawbacks. It was basically a good, warm, human story I felt could reach and move audiences around the world; and there was a fine score by Rodgers and Hammerstein. I hadn't seen the play when I took on the assignment. It came into my life unexpectedly while I was at 20th Century-Fox preparing another picture. William Wyler had been assigned to do the film but he had a conflict of interest which would have meant postponing *The Sound of Music*, which Fox didn't want to do because they had too much money tied up in it. I read Ernest Lehman's script (he'd done several films for me, including *West Side Story*) and felt he'd done a very good job of taking the material of the play, using the good stuff, moving other parts of it around, transposing songs to scenes or moods where they would be more effective in a film, basically enhancing the material. It was then that I also heard the score for the first time and realized that quite a few of the songs I'd recognized had come from this musical. I thought this might be an opportunity to put a different kind of musical on the screen, a fresh, warm, human story without letting it spill into mawkish sentimentality and sweetness.

I saw the show on my way through London to get to Salzburg to scout locations for the film. When I saw the show, despite its various faults, I found that I liked many of the basic qualities, though the pitfalls were more apparent on the stage than they'd been on reading the play and the script. It was always a major question how to give it life, colour, movement, reality, believability, a feeling of being there, *being real*, without getting too cute, too sweet. Of course we had a great advantage on the screen in that film is a much more real medium than the stage. Always, our aim was to find a way into the various songs or musical numbers, without the audience being aware of it until they find themselves caught up in a musical number. This worked very well with a number like 'My Favourite Things'. Of course, 'Do Re Me' is quite simple because it's a situation where Maria teaches the children how to sing. Our most difficult number to do without embarrassment was 'Climb Every Mountain' which the Mother Abbess sings to convince Maria to go back to the Captain and the children and find out if his love for her and hers for him is real. The stage requirements for a big and rousing first act curtain

Rita Moreno in a vivid purple dress in the 'I like to be in America' number in *West Side Story*. Choreographer Jerome Robbins co-directed with Robert Wise. Rita Morena won an Oscar for her performance.

Julie Andrews and Christopher Plummer in *The Sound of Music*. A sung love scene was the trickiest challenge of the film. Specially-designed filters helped establish a mood that encouraged belief that what we were hearing was what they were feeling. Robert Wise's handling of the scene made it seem the most natural thing in the world.

Above, right: As Gertrude Lawrence in *Star!* Julie Andrews re-created many of the best-remembered Lawrence numbers. One of these was Cole Porter's 'The Physician' which originally featured in the show *Nymph Errant*. Michael Kidd re-staged it for the film.

Far right: Julie Andrews in her film début, Walt Disney's Chim Chim Cheree-ous, *Mary Poppins*. Her partner is Dick Van Dyke.

Right: A 'new' Julie Andrews made her bow in *S.O.B.*

meant that they did the song in a rather large style, with a heavy operatic type of voice. Had we done it like that on the screen you wouldn't have been able to look at it. We decided on an entirely different kind of voice, an entirely different kind of treatment, via staging and lighting, to make it as simple and easy as we could, and avoid the kind of situation that would have the Mother Abbess looking directly at the camera and giving this message to the young postulate. I went for a very stylized form, with deep shadows, so that the song came as a symbolic thing rather than the advice from an older to a younger woman.

One of the traps we all fell into in the early days of Cinemascope was a feeling that just because it was a larger, bigger screen, that we should stay away from close-ups and shoot everything in medium shot, long shot, dolly shot or whatever, you know, handle everything in one angle. I treat it the way I

would have a 35mm frame. I cover the way I would shooting in 35mm. I think that accounts for the fact that one feels a sense of intimacy despite the fact that it is this large frame. Of course I had marvellous people working with me: McCord (the camera man); Boris Leven who was my designer on *West Side Story* and *Two for the Seesaw*. I had Morris Zuberanno, a sketch artist, with whom so many of the final effects on the screen had been worked out long in advance of filming. I worked in concert with these men, sketching, discussing, planning, long before I started shooting. I also had a marvellous cutter on the film, but of course a number like *Do Re Me* is planned way ahead and the cutting of that is in the script, starting at the picnic and then cutting to the Winkler's terrace, then cutting to the bicycles. All that was Ernie's idea, and all I and my people did was to translate Lehman's idea on to the film.

The casting for the film was my idea. It hadn't been set when I took over. At this time none of Julie's films were out yet. She'd finished *Mary Poppins*, and hadn't yet made *Americanization of Emily*, so her career was still in limbo. Ernie and another close associate of mine, Sollie Chaplin, talked about her, what we knew of her from the stage and one or two TV specials she'd done. Like anybody else we were a little reluctant to go out on a limb and insist on her to the studio for a $7–8 million picture without having seen her on film. So we prevailed on the Disney Studios to let us see a couple of sequences of their rough cut. The moment we saw her we knew, OHHHHHH!!! This was It. We were crazy about her. I went back to the studio and told young Zanuck that this was the girl we must have. She was perfect casting, natural, charming, everything. I convinced them that we could take a risk in our casting since what they had bought and paid for, and I think it was the biggest price paid for a musical up to the time of *My Fair Lady*, was the musical – *that* was our star. So we didn't need to support it by casting it with names that might not be right for the property. We had such a good time working together that I wanted to work with Julie again, which is how *Star!* came about.

Musical biopics had never been far away. They had had quite a vogue in the 50s and were just going through another phase, with films about Fanny Brice (*Funny Girl*) and Billie Holliday (*Lady Sings the Blues*) making a splash at the box-office. Wise had already made this sort of film in 1956 about the boxer, Rocky Marciano, and now turned to one with music. His biopic of the legendary British and American musical comedy star, Gertrude Lawrence, had one of the biggest budgets for any musical of the 60s – it also had colour, taste, period fidelity, costume authenticity, the classic songs by Coward, Cole Porter and Kurt Weill which Lawrence had first introduced. To stage the numbers Wise brought in Michael Kidd. As a story with music it was a lot better than many of the shows the real Gertrude Lawrence had brought to life with her radiant theatrical glamour and besides, Julie Andrews, with *Mary Poppins*, *The Sound of Music* and *Thoroughly Modern Millie* behind her, was just about impregnable at the box-office. The chirpy *Millie*, set in the carefree 20s milieu in which, in *The*

Boy Friend, Julie had scored her first big hit on the stage, brought together a great cast which included Lady Peel, the legendary Beatrice Lillie, friend and co-star of the real Gertrude Lawrence. Since the octogenarian Miss Lillie refused permission for anyone to play her 20s self except herself – unlike Noël Coward, who selected Daniel Massey for his youthful reincarnation – hers was about the only name that wasn't dropped into *Star!*

A lot of reasons can be found for the film's failure, just as much can be said in its favour. Moviegoers of the 60s weren't into 30s insouciance and theatrical glamour. Lawrence's sophisticated world was too far removed and her name was virtually forgotten. But probably the biggest error of all lay in casting Julie Andrews and having her play Lawrence as the brittle, selfish woman and mother she apparently was when not giving her all to her public – instead of going all out for the fabled Lawrence stage charm, which would have allowed an Andrews audience to succumb happily to Julie's charm. Audiences were not prepared to accept a highball from the woman they loved for giving their children a spoonful of sugar. This second Wise/Andrews teaming was killed in the clash with the Andrews image their first film had done so much to create.

There was the aforementioned *The King and I*, a MacDonald-Eddy operetta for the United Nations generation, that won Yul Brynner an Oscar for recreating the role he'd played on Broadway over 1000 times, but lost Deborah Kerr hers, for though she played the far more difficult role of the unsympathetic Victorian schoolmarm with radiant charm, her involvement in a messy divorce case lost her the voters' sympathy. Which says all there is to be said for the Oscars as an award of merit.

In 1962 Mervyn LeRoy made the Stephen Sondheim-Jules Styne musical *Gypsy*, the hard-knocks, early years of stripper Gypsy Rose Lee's life on the vaudeville circuit with her dragon of a mother. LeRoy, who had himself come out of vaudeville, and in the 30s directed hard-nosed musicals like *Gold Diggers of 1933*, gave this film all he had, and surprised one with this powerful, rousing paean to American get-up-and-go. If the dressing rooms were dingy, the back-stage alleys no place to raise a kid, the midnight railroad stations deserted, and the Depression grim, the people inhabiting them were anything but. Here was enough bazzaz and bravura spirits to enable them to bounce back from an endless round of knock-out blows and come back stronger each time. It also gave Rosalind Russell one of the finest moments of her career, her naked drive to win the Oscar she never got becoming the impetus behind Mama Rose's ferocious drive to make her children the star she hadn't been. Perhaps if Russell hadn't allowed the studio to get Lisa Kirk to dub her songs, creating the only jarring note since so much of Russell's bite is in her tongue, she might have won. But then, compromises like that in her own life kept Mama Rose in the wings while her daughters became successful. Warner Bros, who seemed to be doing most of the stage to screen adaptations of the 60s, let Morton da Costa bring the widely trumpeted *Music Man*, with Robert Preston re-creating his original role, to films. It was small-town Americana sorely in need of a Mickey Rooney and a Judy Garland, for 'Seventy-Six Trombones' blasting away in stereophonic sound couldn't lift that tired proscenium arch anymore than 'When The Parade Passes By' made one want to join in with serenading *Hello Dolly*. As Bob Fosse would say, 'In a film the only limitations are in the director's head . . .' Whatever the limitations Gene Kelly might have felt himself saddled with so that neither he, nor Michael Kidd, nor $24 million could make *Hello Dolly* a movie with more than one street to go down on and one reworked song to sing, they were not there to trouble newcomer Francis Ford Coppola, who leapt from schlock horror movies to big-budget, big-time, big-star musicals like *Finian's Rainbow* (1968) as if born to them. With the charming but dated Burton Lane-E. Y. Harburg 40s musical fable about Finian MacLornegan and his wild-haired daughter Sharon's search in the miscegenist South for the illusory pot of gold at the end of the Rainbow, Coppola established himself as one of the new breed of directorial giants come to shake-up Hollywood. Coppola's inventive and youthful imagination had flared forth the year before with the rollicking *You're A Big Boy Now*, which introduced a host of new faces both before and behind the screen with a score by The Loving Spoonful to appeal to the Haight-Ashbury generation. It was a modest but likeable film and ensured the bigger budget and the participation of the now legendary Fred Astaire, who broke his enforced absence from musicals to return to dance as Finian. It was right. It was good. It allowed him to sing and dance and act. He was old and grizzled and wonderful and Coppola knew just what had to be done. Instead of misguided reverence there was a proper appreciation and a welcome lack of sentimentality that set things off in a new light. Coppola, with the ignorance or the daring of youth moved his camera out into the fields and rolling hills with the confidence of the young Astaire. Along the way he revealed his gift for plumping film's ignored capacity for showing, shifting, and simultaneous realities. The old Astaire kept right up. The restless magic in his step had become a mite slower, the voice was a shade deeper but the richer in exchange and still tugged its peculiar way at the heart. In a similar situation, Richard Lester hired and then chopped up a cast of legendary clowns for his adaptation of *A Funny Thing Happened on the Way to the Forum*, reducing Buster Keaton, Phil Silvers and Zero Mostel to cardboard cut-outs that made nonsense of their participation. Nor were Coppola's treatment of classic standards – 'How Are Things in Glocca Morra', 'Look To The Rainbow', 'If This Isn't Love' and the wild and yearning 'Old Devil Moon' dropped in, as the numbers were in *Forum*, like hurdles to be avoided or covered up at all costs. *Finian* was also Petula Clark's first and only decent Hollywood musical. The others, like *Goodbye, Mr Chips*, sent her scurrying back to records. Despite the flaws (it got a bit stuck in those southern molasses and the casting was by no means perfect), Coppola showed what one might expect from the rising breed of directors, when – powered by a vision of the present and an appreciation of the past – they brought their own kind of spirit and

excitement into their musicals. In his wake came Martin Scorsese (*The Last Waltz*); Taylor Hackford (*The Idol Maker*); Robert Altman (*Nashville*); Gillian Armstrong (*Starstruck*); Mark Rydell (*The Rose*); Michael Ritchie (*The Divine Miss M*); Hal Ashby (*Let's Spend the Night Together*); even *Saturday Night Fever*, surely a fluke that landed on its feet and only started to disco, thanks to its charismatic star, John Travolta, and the music by the Bee Gees.

For all of these directors' variable results they have courage. What they lack seems to be an aesthetic to go with the super-realism made possible by the many new technical developments – the speed, light, the film itself – which have enabled directors to shoot anywhere, in any location, at any time of day or night. As a result the day of the musical love story is virtually over. Trying to re-create it, as with *One From the Heart* (Coppola), *At Long Last Love* (Peter Bogdanovitch) or *New York, New York*, virtually consigns them to failure, even when, as with *New York, New York*, there are so many good things in it. It's not enough to have accurate period sets and period costumes and period make-up, as was the case with *New York, New York*, when that sort of world was never a real world to begin with but a studio-bound world created in the 30s and 40s on the MGM backlot. It worked then because everyone accepted the convention to begin with. We know it wasn't the real Paris in *Maytime* or the real Broadway in *Babes on Broadway*, but back-drops were designed and lit for mood, and the actors in them created a reality in keeping with it which touched that part in our minds that felt rather than the part that dealt with

Rosalind Russell as fiercely ambitious Mama Rose and Diana Pace as Louise (Natalie Wood took over as Louise grew up), the game child actress who would become the legendary *Gypsy*.

Overleaf, top: A scene from the revolutionary 60s rock festival, *Woodstock*. Inset, the director, Michael Wadleigh, who used 20 cameras to cover an event in which 400,000 people took part. The first cultural event-documentary breakthrough to this market, suggesting a possible future direction film might take and still benefit from a new breed of entertainers and their music. Bottom left: Sid Vicious appeared with The Sex Pistols in *The Great Rock and Roll Swindle* which said, without beating around the bush, all there was to say about the Punk-Rock cult – which is why the film never became even a cult favourite. Right: The Village People in *Can't Stop the Music*.

Top: Bette Midler, electrifying as *The Rose*, one of those once-in-a-decade débuts. From centre left: Disco's queen, Donna Summer, got into movies just in time in *Thank God it's Friday*. John Travolta in *Saturday Night Fever* – the film and the star who spread disco fever around the world. Shimmering, talented Debbie Harry in *Roadie*. Barbara Harris, one of the most gifted stars of the American theatre, in Robert Altman's *Nashville*, a send-up of Country and Western – but a tribute, too, and one of the great ones of the decade. Altman's *Popeye* was based on the comic-strip character, and was almost a masterpiece too.

reality. As a result those films created the America people wanted to go to, for it offered hope, romance, laughter and opportunity. Whereas today, everyone knows that all those glamorous big cities are in fact every bit as grim and more so than their own home towns. Liza Minnelli and Robert de Niro were superb in *New York, New York*, but everything about them, their exchanges, their loving and fighting, had a modern anxiety about it which those airless spick and span studio-lit sets and sidewalks they inhabited did not. Robert Altman's quirky, exhilarating *Popeye* is a different kettle of fish, attempting something original, turning cartoons into living, breathing beings, and almost pulling it off. But Altman is one of the contemporary American cinema's most original talents and in Shelley Duval as Olive Oyl one had the near-impossible; hard to describe, but magical and unforgettable.

It is when the new breed of directors bring a contemporary approach to the new and improved tools to hand that the results have a dynamic force of their own which make their films powerful. And if most of them so far lack grace (one doesn't leave their films dancing so much as fighting) they do comment on the times in which they are living, through the means they use to achieve their effects. First anger. Then action. And then, perhaps, grace. Who knows what they might yet do; there's nothing like a nationwide depression to bring out the best in people and their artists.

In any age, at any time, Bob Fosse would shine. This acclaimed and controversial dancer, choreographer, director, innovator, author, the foremost talent in America today, having triumphed equally on stage, film and TV, is a pure product of the musical. Like Blondell, Minnelli, Hayworth, Kelly, Rooney, Astaire and Rose Lee he was born (Chicago, 1927) into the theatre: his father was a vaudevillian; his childhood was the one of endless tours on the Keith-Orpheum Circuit. At thirteen he was working in the chorus of musicals and burlesque shows. He came from the war to Broadway and nightclubs, where he worked with Mary Ann Niles (his first wife, a dancer like the others) and started to create his own specialities. His performance in the title role of a revival of *Pal Joey* led him to the attention of MGM.

When he got to Hollywood the musical comedy was giving out its last flames. Fosse arrived as the hope to fill the shoes of an earlier Mickey Rooney – the brash, idealistic, energetic, horse-powered college kid, full of ambitious dreams he can hardly wait to put into practice, but to which he added a modern, adult romantic quality that lifted this character into the present. But the sort of star vehicle for which this sort of personality was intended was no longer being made. By 1953, the year of his film debut in *Give a Girl a Break*, the era of the swansong had begun. When asked about this period in his life he wrote: 'When I first went there I had extremely high hopes. After all Metro had signed me and they made only the best musicals. I had fantasies of becoming the next Fred Astaire (my then idol) or Gene Kelly. However, as the size of my parts diminished with each picture, I decided to get the hell out of there and take a try at Broadway – so,

I asked for a release from my contract. This they gave me – rather quickly as I remember. It still stings me a little that they gave me an 'out' so easily.

'Actually, although I didn't know it at the time it was right near the end of their "big musical" period. They made *Band Wagon* while I was there, but I can't remember much else.

'Remember I was only a contract player at the time and therefore not privy to all the inside workings of the studio. However it seemed to me that Pasternak (at that time) made musicals that would cash in on the latest nightclub or record sensation, such as Vic Damone, etc. The classier ones would fall to Freed – such as the Kelly or Astaire ones. Cummings seemed to inherit all the ones that Freed

Bob Fosse and Janet Leigh in the second – musical – film version of *My Sister Eileen*, for which Fosse did the choreography. (A different musical version of *Eileen* called *Wonderful Town* was produced on Broadway.)

Above: Bob Fosse's choreography was one of the bright components in a good musical, *The Pajama Game*. Buzz Miller, Carol Haney and Kenneth LeRoy in the 'Steam Heat' number, as good on film as on the stage.

Bob Fosse rehearsing Shirley MacLaine for one of her numbers on the set of *Sweet Charity*.

couldn't do. Of course, even this generality has its flaws. After all Cummings did do *Seven Brides*, which I think is a great movie. And Pasternak did *Anchors Aweigh* – another terrific musical, in my opinion.

'Other than Cummings, whom I always liked and admired, I only worked with one other, Arthur Lowe Jr. He produced *The Affairs of Dobie Gillis*. It was the first black and white musical Metro had made in about twenty years and was shot in fifteen days – and looked it!

'The following is my total film experience up to the time of *Sweet Charity*. *Give a Girl a Break* (acted, sang, danced and contributed in a minor way to some of the choreography); *The Affairs of Dobie Gillis* (same as before); *Kiss Me Kate* (the same); *My Sister Eileen* (made at Columbia, same as before, except this time I choreographed the entire film); *Pajama Game* (Warners; choreographed); *Damn Yankees* (Warners, choreographed and danced). As a dancer I was always bothering the choreographer – asking to be allowed to make contributions. On *Girl* Stanley Donen allowed me to make minor contributions to the dances. But they were mostly his and Gower Champion's. On *Kate* Hermes Pan, the choreographer, allowed me to do a whole section of a number called 'From This Moment On'. It was the section I danced with Carol Haney. I guess I was a nuisance. I had nothing to do with the film version of *How to Succeed*. I sold

Mirish Bros my contribution to the property [Fosse had directed and choreographed the stage version]. They were allowed to make any alterations or deletions they felt were necessary. (Which they did.) I did *not* actively participate in the filming. An assistant of mine was hired for the job.

'I would have considered directing someone else's choreography had I been asked. I do, however, believe it would be a difficult position for the other choreographer to be in. I imagine also that I would have a bit of a problem in attempting not to "butt in" on the choreography.

'Seriously, it's a little too rough for me to say what I look for when viewing another's choregraphy without appearing to be pretentious. Which, above all else, I'm determined not to be. First, I watch to see if they have stolen anything from me. If they haven't, then I try to see what I can steal from them.'

To some degree Fosse's work, like that of Jerome Robbins and other modern choreographers, has been influenced by Jack Cole. After all, both Carol Haney and Gwen Verdon, two of Fosse's most dynamic partners, started out with Cole, and some of their background must have rubbed off. But Fosse took Cole's work to its conclusion, something Cole had not been able to do in his films. Fosse's dances arise out of the action, the action being an expression of the subconscious, and together they merged to create a unity in which song expresses mood and character, as naturally as turning a corner down a side street before rejoining the main road. Basically, all musicals are set in Ruritania, regardless of time or place, whether shot on studio sets or on location, whenever the subject is not set against a musical background – theatre, nightclubs, records – or the characters express their emotions outside of those settings. There's no getting away from that, and no need to. It's how it's done that makes the difference, that makes a musical contemporary, relevant, important. In one powerful leap Fosse revived the film musical and set it in the contemporary world. Since that first directorial effort he has gone from strength to strength, with *Cabaret*, *Lennie* and *All that Jazz*, each work tighter and more assured than its predecessor. But had his film career stopped with *Sweet Charity* his importance would still have been assured.

Adapted for the stage by Neil Simon from Fellini's non-musical film, *Notte di Cabiria*, starring Fellini's wife, Giulietta Masina, with a dynamic score by Cy Coleman and lyrics by Dorothy Fields, the Broadway version was intended to be a vehicle for Gwen Verdon, to be directed by her husband, Bob Fosse. *Charity* was a Cinderella story, except that the Prince got cold feet at the altar. What happy end there was came from our hope that Charity, with her incurable optimism, would be a survivor. But its power as a contemporary work lay in the energy behind the telling of her story and in the brilliantly choreographed dances. Fosse offers us an overabundance of fabulous solos, pas de deux; electrifying threesomes and spectacular production numbers which come hot on the heels of one another, for a chorus drilled to stop on cracks and tap on dimes, to grab audiences by the throat and shake them out of their molly-coddled state. By contrast, *West Side Story* (like *Lady Sings the Blues*, *Fame* and *Jesus*

Above: Bob Fosse partners his wife, the great dancing star Gwen Verdon in the 'Who's Got the Pain?' number in *Damn Yankees*. Though she had been in films for years, assisting Jack Cole and teaching people like Fernando Lamas to dance the Merry Widow Waltz, it needed Broadway to make her a star in her own right. She created the role of devil's advocate, Lola, on the stage.

Above right: Ann Reinking and Erzsebet Foldi in *All That Jazz*.

Christ Superstar) was safer since it was pretty predictable, set as it was among the flick-knife-slashing street gangs rumbling over crumbling ghettoes. Whereas Charity moved up-town, down-town, into Penthouses and dives, from the Fandango ballroom to the disco haunts of the super-rich; and everywhere that Charity went there was that urgent 'angst'-driven force prowling underneath it all, set to explode.

Fosse is a man so close to the ground that he can hear what people are feeling long before other people are thinking it out loud for them. These are the politics of artists, not of merchants, to know what is going on, to show what is wrong, and express it through their work. But from his first film, Fosse revealed himself as a conscientious artist who through the musical medium has gone further than any musical or most other films have gone in recent years. As it stands, with *Charity*, to be followed by *Lennie* and *All that Jazz*, he was saying that the

American way of life is not such a wonderful thing as *Andy Hardy* films and L. B. Mayer were saying, because we see what is really going on.

The controversy between art and politics, and artists in politics doesn't really interest me. What Lubitsch thought of Hitler, Eisenstein of Stalin, Minnelli of Roosevelt, Fosse of Nixon, or MacLaine, Fonda and Redgrave about Kennedy, Vietnam or the PLO commands our interest only out of consideration for what these people mean to our lives through their art. What they have to say is usually not much better or worse or any more perceptive than what the man next door has to say, except that he works with a handicap, lacking showbusiness glamour. Sometimes, of course, a performer or director will feel strong enough to put their ideas on the line, and make a film about their beliefs. But propaganda is rarely ever art, or even entertaining to more than a committed minority. The artist who steps outside his arena to talk about politics is using his or her name as window dressing. The artist, Lubitsch (*To Be Or Not To Be*) or Bob Fosse (*Cabaret, Lennie and All that Jazz*), through their art forces us to see how easily sucked in we are by window dressing. *Cabaret* is not an original statement by Fosse. It had been a Broadway musical adapted from the John Van Druten play *I am a Camera*, based on the Berlin diaries by Christopher Isherwood about an English boy like himself in the early 30s at the time of the rise of Nazism in Germany. Nevertheless he felt it contained something he wanted to say since he selected it as his second film; and while most of it, like the original show, is on the level of the life and mind of the dancers in the seedy Kit Kat Club, he brings to the film a moment that is all his own, a moment that is political film making at its most powerful in the justly singled-out and praised 'Tomorrow Belongs To Me'. In a beautiful landscape, a beautiful young boy sings a beautiful song. And then we realize *what* he is singing, as all the other people in the beer garden, except for one old man, join in the song and finish with the fist-clenched Nazi salute. It is not at all usual in American musicals, or any other musicals, to find that what you are seeing and hearing is beautiful but in which the *meaning* is awful. It sounds good; it looks good, but the meaning is terrible. That is new. That is powerful. That is the artist, through his art, pulling the blinkers off our eyes. Usually in musicals, the ugly people (from a moral point of view) are cast to look ugly (i.e. Rod Steiger as Jud in *Oklahoma*, Carol Burnett as Miss Hannigan in *Annie*) and they sing ugly, downbeat songs.

But if, except for this moment in *Cabaret* Fosse is talking about something that is outside himself, in his masterpiece, *All That Jazz*, he is talking about himself, and his worries, and his musical and human experiences. *Cabaret* could have been directed by somebody who isn't a dancer, though it's hard to think of any other director who could have achieved such a good mix of human interest, touching relationships between Sally and Issy Voo, and the political-social content, but *All That Jazz* cannot be done by anybody who is *not* a dancer. Thus he is able to go deeper and speak to a much wider audience. Through the problems of the tyrannical, chain-smoking, womanizing choreographer who must come to terms with death, he is able to bring us face to face with our own, and thus endlessly fascinating, obsessions and drives. The life of Joe Gideon (Fosse's alter-ego) becomes a metaphor for our lives. Fosse's art illuminates our own problems. Ay Ay Ay I don't like me very much, but if that is how I am and I don't like it then I'd better do something positive about it or stop whining. It probably makes it the first political musical. The forces that drive his brilliant louse are the ones that fuel his society – the universal obsession with death, the American obsessions with fame and power at whatever cost to one's private life and to the lives of the people, friends and family, around them, the time spent on analysis, and the frustration between the amount of things to be done and the physical limitations of our bodies. These all lead up to a catharsis. That is why this is one of the very few behind-the-scenes show-business films to become a popular hit. *Sweet Charity* showed what Fosse could do. *All That Jazz* showed us the man who did it, and what drove him to it. Art, unlike politics, illuminates us and gives us the courage to go on, pick ourselves up, dust ourselves off and start all over again. It's why people flocked to musicals during the Depression, during the war, and why they will do so again. In his work Fosse released the subconscious drive of his age into its conscious corollary through the medium of the dance. It has made him one of the foremost artists of his age. Could one do less than cheer?

Of course his films are musicals not because they have songs and dances but because his whole conception for a film is musical. His camera moves as if it's been attached to his own feverish, superbly disciplined body. His work is unashamedly erotic, secure in itself to stand naked and exultant. It is also too honest.

After Universal saw the finished print of *Charity* they felt the film, with Charity yet again the recipient of the wrong end of the stick, was too

downbeat. He had to change the ending and cut a quarter of an hour before they would release it in the States. Of course, by that time, we had been sucked in by the camera, gliding swiftly there, making spectacular roof-top leaps, pirouetting and swirling. And we also knew Charity and her kind, knew that she was no loser; could believe after hearing the plaintive "Where Am I Going?" turn into powerful self-assertion, that she too had grown and was ready to stand and fight, whether by entertaining the troops in Vietnam or by resisting the government who sent them there. Fosse had done all this and mastered another medium. Great camerawork needs a great subject to inspire it to greatness. Robert Surtees' colour photography takes fire from his director's ambitions. Being a man of the theatre, Fosse gave the film a glorious theatrical bravado, using the New York locations with the security of a studio set. The big musical numbers, 'Big Spender', with the hard and greedy ladies of the Fandango ballroom accosting customers to spend and dance, the number on the roof-top of the city with Charity and her pals insisting that 'There's Got To Be Something Better Than This' and the underground car-park revivalist meeting led by Sammy Davis Jr to the new gospel of 'The Rhythm Of Life' belong to the best of their kind. Others, Michael Kidd's for *Seven Brides*, the Kelly-Donen numbers for *On The Town*, and Fosse's for *The Pajama Game* and *Damn Yankees* are as good, but none are better. It doesn't make it the greatest musical there's ever been. For one thing, like a kid in a candy store, Fosse doesn't always know when to stop. For another, the role of Charity needed a Liza

Chita Rivera, Shirley MacLaine and Paula Kelly in Fosse's rooftop number, 'There's got to be something better than this' in *Sweet Charity*.

Overleaf: Bob Fosse's gifted ladies, and his alter ego. From top left: Gwen Verdon in *Damn Yankees*. Valerie Perrine in *Lennie*. Liza Minnelli in *Cabaret*. Roy Scheider in *All That Jazz*. Suzanne Charny and chorus in 'The Rich Man's Frug' in *Sweet Charity*. Ann Reinking in *All That Jazz*. Shirley MacLaine in *Sweet Charity*.

Minnelli or a Bette Middler, or the great Gwen Verdon herself, with legs to take wing or the will at least to get them there, for Charity's nature is a triumph over matter, and when Chita Rivera and Paula Kelly take off, MacLaine is left holding on to the floor.

But this does not alter the fact that this film is what great musicals are all about. Hard to believe, then, that Fosse had never directed a film before. Nor, in his own words, ever even had the ambition

to direct one: 'Hope, yes. Ambition, no. I love film – I think I've loved it since the first time I saw a film, which was most likely a "Tarzan" picture. I know you probably have heard this dozens of times but it is nevertheless how I feel: I see no limits to the possibilities of film except for the limits of the director's mind. Also, I think that for my whole life I've been a frustrated painter. The camera gives me a chance to finally do some "painting". I directed Charity more out of ignorance than courage.' When the time came for him to return to films, three years after the ignominious failure of Charity, nothing hindered him and no one cut him.

Liza Minnelli deserved to win her Oscar for Cabaret and become one of the new superstars, and that year Fosse won the Oscar for directing the film. He also won the Emmy for directing the best TV variety show, *Liza with a Z*, and the Tony for the best Broadway musical of the year, *Pippin*.

On Broadway, *Cabaret* had been a song book, with a score by John Kander and Fred Ebb. On the screen it became a song and dance book. With Liza as Sally Bowles, the kookie English performer at the KKK, the character became an American. Joel Grey recreated his Master of Ceremonies role. Because

both Joel and Liza are all-round entertainers, able to sing and dance, Fosse got them to do things in this seedy, sordid night club which were far and away superior to that sort of thing in that sort of place. People that good don't stay in run-down clubs for long. But it made for great entertainment which caught the feverish moth-like excitement of that moment in time as we watched them recklessly tossing about in the current of the heat from the flame, so close that it would soon consume them. From his own early background Fosse understood the bottom end of the show business world, these clubs and their entertainers, whether in Berlin, off Broadway, Chicago or anywhere else, better than any man and knew how to bring it alive in his work

The Fandango Ballroom girls in the 'Hey! Big Spender' number in Bob Fosse's directorial film debut, *Sweet Charity*. The three in the centre are Paula Kelly, Shirley MacLaine and Chita Rivera.

and make it a microcosm of the world outside. In *Cabaret* he took us inside those clubs, ringside.

In *Lennie* Fosse, (like Bruce, he shared a background in the club scene) takes us backstage and into the mind of the performer. It is black and white, and though not a musical, the film is a choreographed work. With *All That Jazz* Fosse has made his most personal work to date. We are taken inside the heart of the sort of man whose energy and whose very existence are fuelled by the need to create. We are shown achievement – and the cost. The greater the casualties, the greater the results. Each number is better than the last. Joe Gideon drives himself hardest, and drives his friends away; he is virtually alone when his life-style leads to a race with death. The film is totally without indulgence and makes no excuses. Joe Gideon is driven because he is an artist: an artist is neither a nobler, nor a better, kinder, or more attractive human being than anyone else. The contrary, if anything. Only saints and martyrs, agents and sycophants can put up with them from day to day. But when, as Fosse shows us in *All That Jazz*, we see the results of that man's work and the achievements he bullies, cajoles and inspires others to, one isn't surprised that after every parting they come back for more, ready to start again. With him they scale the heights, and that's worth the price.

Back in 1969 I wrote to ask Fosse what he felt the dances should achieve. He replied:

'Another tough one but I'll try. They should, in my opinion achieve one of the following:

1. Set the environment or atmosphere or character-behaviour of a particular locale or particular set of characters, e.g. (please forgive me for using my own numbers as examples) but I believe "Big Spender" accomplishes this.
2. Further the action – the best example that comes to mind at this moment is Jerry Robbins'

"Rumble" in *West Side Story* – which is another of my favourite film musicals.
3. Express a particular emotion. This does not necessarily move the story along but does elaborate on the particular feeling of the moment. Dances of "love" would fall into this group. Also dances of "elation". "Brass Band" is a combination. It's meant to be a dance of sheer elation and joy. "Someone Loves Me!" etc.
4. The last group that comes to mind are really what could be called just "entertainment". A lot of critics of musicals feel that these are the least desirable. However I enjoy them and have some luck with them. "Steam Heat" [*The Pyjama Game*] I would consider a plain entertainment number.
5. Of course all of the above should be accomplished with some beauty. They should be handsome to look at. And, somehow, emotionally affect the audience.

All this he has done, and more.

The Musical Biopic

Filmed biographies of show people have been around since sound, and because they really aren't musicals, but dramas about people who sang or danced for a living, anybody can direct them. Most people have, and if they are well cast, and life was really hard on them, they can be sure-fire box-office. The 50s was a great period for them – as blues singers, band-leaders, radio crooners, composers, opera stars and swimming beauties vied with each other with sagas of booze and heartbreak, pills, religion and sex, and if those were missing and you were basically a good, uninterested egg, the war would shoot you down, polio would get you, the plane would crash, and if none of those worked, dying of old age was made out to be a tragedy.

In the 50s Susan Hayward was Jane Froman in

With a Song in My Heart (1952). She was lovely, the songs were lovely, her clothes were lovely, and there was a happy end for Jane with the man who rescued her, though in real life they divorced. Susan Hayward was also Lillian Roth in I'll Cry Tomorrow (1955). It was a tough story about a girl who had it all and drank it all away; it was shot in black and white. Susan Hayward insisted on doing her own singing and, drama being raw meat to this actress, she was nominated for an Oscar. Doris Day shook off her stereotyped goody-two-shoes image in Love Me or Leave Me (1955) as prohibition songstress Ruth Etting, married to a jealous gangster she doesn't love, who shoots the pianist she does love. Doris singing Etting's songs like 'Ten Cents a Dance' and supported by Cagney as Marty 'the Gimp' Schneider moved her career into a higher gear. Betty Hutton was Blossom Seeley and Ralph Meeker her husband, Benny Fields, in Somebody Loves Me (1952), which marked the end of Betty Hutton's film career. Ann Blyth was the star of The Helen Morgan Story (1954), but her songs were dubbed by Gogi Grant. Esther Williams was Annette Kellerman in Million Dollar Mermaid (1952), playing the silent film swimming star. There were no songs identified with Miss Kellerman – as there are not that many songs identified with Esther Williams, though that did not prevent the latter from being in almost

Joel Grey as the MC, recreating his stage role, in Bob Fosse's Cabaret. 'Wilkommen..!'

Tommy Tune in Ken Russell's The Boy Friend. The Texan triple threat in his film debut, before carving a triumphant niche on Broadway as choreographer, director and star, the latest in a line of musical wizards electrifying the scene.

nothing but musicals. There were musical numbers in this film, too, since Miss Kellerman's life was basically happy (she was around during the filming), except for a skirmish with the police for wearing a one-piece bathing suit on the beach at the turn of the century. And a tank she swam in broke, once.

The enormous success of Jimmy Stewart as trombonist and bandleader in The Glenn Miller

Right: Susan Hayward as early film-musical star Lillian Roth in *I'll Cry Tomorrow*. Miss Hayward sang herself; the number is 'Sing, you Sinners'.

Far right: Tyrone Power and Kim Novak as the lushly beautiful Mr and Mrs in *The Eddie Duchin Story*.

Below: Bob Hope and James Cagney in *The Seven Little Foys*. Cagney re-created his George M. Cohan role in a guest spot.

Bottom: Barbra Streisand continued her funny Fanny Brice portrayal in *Funny Lady* (1975).

Story (1954) prompted *The Benny Goodman Story* (1955) about the equally famous and still surviving clarinettist. Lushly handsome Tyrone Power was matched with champagne blonde Kim Novak in *The Eddie Duchin Story* (1956), about the society favourite pianist and his society beauty wife, whose death was the great tragedy of his life. Danny Kaye was jazz trumpeter Red Nichols in *The Five Pennies* (1958). The high point of Sal Mineo's starring career as a teenage favourite was playing the drug-addicted drummer in *The Gene Krupa Story* (1959). Bob Hope was vaudevillian Eddie Foy in *The Seven Little Foys* (1955) and Mayor Jimmy Walker in *Beau James* (1957), which also brought Jimmy Cagney on to re-create his George M. Cohan character. José Ferrer was surely the dullest composer or the composer of the dullest film as Sigmund Romberg in *Deep in My Heart* (1954). Fred Astaire and Red Skelton played the bickering team of Bert Kalmar and Harry Ruby, one of whose greatest hits became the film's title, *Three Little Words* (1950). The success of *Singin' in the Rain* may have been behind the belief at 20th Century-Fox that 20s songwriters De Sylva, Brown and Henderson, whose songs included, 'The Moon Belongs to Everyone . . .' But *The Best Things in Life are Free* (1956), could be a hit played by Gordon MacRae, Dan Dailey and Ernest Borgnine. As nightclub comic Joe E. Lewis (the Lennie of his day) Frank Sinatra in *The Joker is Wild* (1957) went dramatic, but still got to sing the year's Oscar-winning song, 'All The Way'. Probably the most successful musical biopic of them all had been Mario Lanza as *The Great Caruso* (1951), and this encouraged Warners to cast Kathryn Grayson as Grace Moore in *So This is Love* (1953). The Metropolitan's Patrice Munsel played the Victorian Diva Nellie *Melba* (1953), but only Eleanor Parker, whose singing was dubbed by Eileen Farrell for her role as the Metropolitan's Wagnerian soprano, Marjorie Lawrence, in *Interrupted Melody* (1955), was a hit with the public. Dirk Bogarde was Liszt; Alan Badel was Wagner; a lot of people were being Schubert. In most of these, as in those that had come before and the bulk of those that came after, songs and dances, snatches of arias and concerts, served the function that microscopes, test tubes and tense hours over the laboratory burner did in the biographies of scientists and explorers - something to do between loving and leaving or being left and unloved, and they usually came at just the right

moment in the story. When everything was going well our heroine would be singing 'Hallelujah Come On Get Happy' – and when things were bad it was bound to be 'Why Was I Born, Why Am I Living?' A pretentious note entered them in the 60s with films like *Star!*, *Funny Girl* and especially Diana Ross's screen debut as Billie Holliday in *Lady Sings the Blues*. It was the era of black consciousness in the country and white guilt. As an opportunity for former Supreme Diana Ross to show off her abilities as a dramatic actress and singer the film was good. As a film about the life and times of a great artist it was slick and tricky and dishonest. Apparently Billie Holliday never smiled – except nervously; the sun never shone where she was; the only time people laughed was when they were drunk; and the white man in her life got Billie hooked on drugs. But to paraphrase Deanna Durbin, it's only a musical, so who's gonna notice it anyway.

Top left: Danny Kaye as Red Nichols and Louis Armstrong as himself in *The Five Pennies*. Right: James Stewart as the celebrated bandleader in *The Glenn Miller Story*.

Above: Gary Busey in the title role in *The Buddy Holly Story*.

Diana Ross in *Lady Sings the Blues*.

Streisand, Midler and Minnelli as once Garland, Hutton and Miranda, three big little girls, blue for you, they feel, they belt, they bellow laughter, tears, chagrin and self-pity. Streisand would like us to believe that she is really 'Lady Cool' underneath it all but who does she think she is kidding? Jeannette MacDonald she's not, and who isn't cool when they are alone and there is no one to hear? If these three show-business giants had a tough start in life, as it seems they did, certainly in the looks department (and for little girls in looks-conscious America, plainness must have been Hell) Liza had it worse. Her mother was Judy Garland. Hysteria ran out of the family tap. Other families get warm or cold, her tap had only one temperature – all emotion and scalding. Liza had more than a legend to live up to. She had a legend to live with in Judy Garland. 'I can do anything I want,' she told Liza, then a child, after leaving a hotel without paying her bill. Yet this supermarionette, all legs, arms and eyes threatening to burst from their sockets, is unquenchable. Midler is the only one to come along who could if she wished slip on the mantle of Mae West without requiring alterations. Like West, Midler is an original. A Fellini film bundled into hips, eyes and larynx. Whilst I find her voice moving and cheerful, I would say to those to whom purity of sound and vocal range are the criteria for a great singer, that here is a great singer because here is a great artist who chooses to sing. Her versions are definitive, like West's, like Dietrich's. Imagine their songs sung by someone else. The magic would be gone. Yet Sinatra can sing 'New York, New York', written for Liza Minelli, and have as big a hit, while Streisand's 'Hello Dolly' fails to nudge any of the Dollies who preceded her. Nor is Streisand's performance in On a Clear Day as good as Barbara Harris's who created the role on Broadway. I'll venture so far as to say that for all the glory of her voice, Streisand's are not the definitive versions of her songs. They have artistry but no soul. It's the difference between a Birgit Nilsson and a Maria Callas. Liza is driven in a way few others of this generation have been, or if they have, have survived. Liza, always on, always striving to excel, daring to stupefy. Every natural defect has been stripped, examined and turned into an asset. There is nothing she could not do if she set her mind to it. To find her precedent one looks not to her mother, but to Joan Crawford, the Joan of Our Dancing Daughters. A fire cracker set to explode by the friction of her own metabolism. Like Joan, Liza burns with ambition and may never realize that she has already succeeded and could start to enjoy herself. When her mother married for the fifth and last time Liza cabled her regrets. 'Sorry I can't make it this time. I promise to come to your next.' We don't know what Garland replied but Crawford would have applauded. Her performance in Cabaret, unlike anything Streisand has done, is definitive. Bette Midler is hors concours. Originals don't compete. New York, New York, the first, and to date, only film role written exclusively for Liza's talents confirms her as actress, show stopper, singer, star. (If only the director had left it there the

Diana Ross pulled all the stops out for her film debut as the legendary Billie Holiday in *Lady Sings the Blues*. Her performance vindicated the film.

film might have been the musical success he hoped for.) The film medium, with its opportunity for endless takes, is the perfect one for Liza, allowing her to establish peaks which, when she reaches for them on stage, can trip her up.

Bette Midler does not have those problems. She may not have Streisand's voice or Liza's technique, but Bette throws a feast. She started out making her name performing in gay bath houses and conquered a public of men and women in every stratum of society with her irreverent, irresistible, inimitable artistry. She is Clara Bow for vivacity, Mae West for generosity and Monroe for radiance. The girl's skin glows. A gift to mimics and an inspiration to photographers – could anybody have ever thought she was plain or ordinary? Her talent flows so generously, whether on stage, screen or records, that its hard to conceive of it being faked. Her film debut as *The Rose* is one of those rare events which reaffirms and explains the uniqueness of movies on the big screen as a primal pool, reflecting and encompassing all. *Divine Madness* reveals her as the greatest actress of the 80s.

In the end, one can't get away from the basic fact that, tough though she can make it, Streisand has an incredibly beautiful vocal talent. It has taken twenty years for that talent just to flow forth, exquisitely maintained and perfected, proudly served, and humbly offered. It wasn't always like that with Streisand. Not at first. Not for me. Not in *Funny Girl* (1968), and not in the other musicals she made following the huge hit she had, for her gift was thrown at one. She was a cutesy Brooklyn Antoinette tossing croissants like stale bread, and how

From top left: Liza Minnelli in *New York, New York* and *Cabaret*. Bette Midler in *The Rose*. Barbra Streisand in *Funny Girl* and *A Star is Born*. Dolly Parton in *The Best Luttle Whorehouse in Texas*.

would we know the difference anyway. The reason for this cold, off-putting attitude might lie in her plainness. One is never again as plain as when one is plain as a child. And Streisand has certainly made her *looks* an issue – even if *Vogue* tried to say it was the new Nefertiti look! – which is why I feel free to bring it up. From the moment she first appeared on the screen, re-creating her stage triumph as the Ziegfeld star, Fannie Brice (who wasn't a beauty either, but she had heart, and it never mattered with her) in *Funny Girl*. 'Look at me, the ugly duckling, a SWAN!' Of course we know that inside there was a swan. The world of movies is full of swans who started off as ugly ducklings. But real unattractiveness has rarely all that much to do with outward physical manifestations, like large noses, big lips, unruly red hair, clefts in the chin,

eyes crossed or of different colours. Those are the sort of things kids tend to pick on each other about, but it's only really said to hurt if the kid with the red hair, big nose, or crossed-eyes, happens to be an ornery little cuss. I would guess that Barbra (born Barbara) wasn't the nicest kid on her block, not easy to like, because she must have always considered herself to be better, to be apart. And she was. A talent like hers does that to you. Had she been born a regular little conventional Wasp beauty, kids would still have found things to dislike about her. She would have seen to that. By the time she came to the stage (the place where ugly ducklings with talent usually go to become swans) and from there to the movies, where people with her talent usually end up. After all, most (if not all) the classic screen beauties have been women who as

children could not have felt themselves pretty – Shearer (cross-eyed and knock-kneed), Crawford (all those freckles), Davis (bug-eyed), Garbo (so awkwardly large), Dietrich . . . haven't we all heard by now that the legendary beauty that is Dietrich was originally a fat dumpling nobody had time for till Sternberg saw the swan, and showed it to the world?

Except for Vincente Minnelli (remember how beautiful he made her look in *On A Clear Day*?) none of Streisand's other directors were exactly what you'd call men who could do much more with a handful of flour except add water, leave it out in the sun and hope it turned into bread. Pastry, not at all. Not William Wyler, not Bogdanovitch, not Herbert Ross, *The Owl and the Pussycat* (1970), not Pollack, *The Way We Were* (1973), not Kelly. But for films, even more than in the theatre, that's what Streisand needed, someone to give her confidence, to flatter her ego, to reassure her, like her, do whatever it needed, the way Victor Saville did for Jessie Matthews, to make the artist relax enough to stop fighting. 'Look at me, I'm plain. Laugh you jerks. But inside I'm beautiful!' OK, one says, fine. But then she'd crack, 'So what do I care what you think.' And you say, OK. But she'd come up with another twist, 'Screw the lot you. You want me, beg.' And people did. Audiences did. For a long time, who else was there? The result was a series of increasingly less popular films. If it hadn't been that, throughout, there was this talent, this extraordinarily affecting beauty that slipped through and kept bringing one back, audiences and producers might have given up on her long before they did. As it was, many of her most costly films, even in the ones where she sang, *Hello Dolly* (1961), *On A Clear Day* (1970), failed miserably at the box-office. It would be five years before anyone risked making another expensive musical starring her, and that was a sequel to her first, *Funny Lady* (1975). Hardly a real risk. On her recordings, where one

could listen and dream, there was never that problem in quite the same way. For Streisand, who could be so obnoxious about everything else, was always true to the gifts she must have known she had from the start, and which she always respected. If only one could have seen more of the Streisand working on a song, we might have glimpsed her true nature, long before now, and a marvellous relationship could have grown between the public and her. Today, twenty years later, though she still plays her 'Oh shucks, how could a good-looking guy like you . . . I mean, . . . You mean it? You really like . . . Oh no, you're just having me on . . .' schtick, she has grown older. She has grown rich. She has had men who loved her (one of whom, Elliott Gould, was her husband for a while), and she has had children. She has matured. She has learnt not to waste her energy any more on attacking and punishing the people who pay because they too want to benefit from her talent, but whom she treated as compensation for the lack of love, or appreciation, or understanding, or what have you. And now, this new star sings, sings, pours forth sounds so smooth, so generous, so illuminating with its sensitivity, and warmth with kindness, that in truth, hearing her, one sees only beauty, feels the way she sounds, floating free through long streaks of space and peacefulness. And so, too, finally, without resorting to exotic make-up, fancy hair-dos, ethnic or other schticks to catch the eye, she has become a true beauty. Whatever the reasons, and I'm just guessing, she has thrown away her crutches. She never needed those schticks anyway.

The European Connection

Even as Hollywood, the Rome of musicals, was crumbling from within, it still came up with such classics as *Damn Yankees*, *The Pajama Game*, *Gigi* and *Funny Face* (for some, one of the high spots of the American Cinema in the 50s). England, America's Athens, produced only the dreariest series of

Musicals from Britain, France and Russia. From top left: Cliff Richard, the Peter Pan of British musicals, in *Summer Holiday*. The girl is Una Stubbs. Meanwhile, in Russia, sturdy booted butchers break into a number in *Melodii Veriiskogo Kvartala* (Melodies of the Verysky Neighbourhood, 1974). Catherine Deneuve in *Les Parapluies de Cherbourg*, left, and director Jacques Demy, right. Paul Jones in Peter Watkins' 1984 cautionary tale, *Privilege*, about a 60s pop star whom the media try to turn into a Messiah to help them manipulate the masses. Catherine Deneuve and Françoise Dorleac, sisters as a sister act in Demy's *Les Demoiselles de Rochefort*, pay homage to Monroe and Russell.

pop-exploitation musicals. France had never been in the race. Germany was non-existent. The British-made musicals of the 50s and 60s were barely on a par with the American-International spate of similar teen films starring Frankie Avalon and Annette Funicello. British recording favourites like Frankie Vaughan, Tommy Steele, Joe Brown, Helen Shapiro, Adam Faith and Cliff Richard all brought their ersatz appeal to a lacklustre group of movies that were clearly designed as record spin-offs. In content as parochial as the Anna Neagle, Gracie Fields films that had gone before, they could not match those in spirit or in production. While the mounting of films starring Cliff Richard, Britain's Elvis Presley, was a notch above the rest in keeping with his larger teen appeal, their mindless naivety was no compensation for the winds of change already apparent on the recording scene. Films like *The Young Ones*, *Summer Holiday*, and *Wonderful Life* were acclaimed by the press with pardonable jingoistic self-congratulation but a total lack of critical perspective. Made on shoe-string budgets, few of the other films attracted enough of an audience to make a revival, never mind their survival, more than wishful thinking.

Sidney (*Lady Sings The Blues*) Furie directed the first few Richard films, in which frenzied camera tricks were no substitute for talent. Among the new directors, raised on a TV diet, the dire influence of 'commercials' could be clearly seen in their films, as tricks with zoom cuts and dissolves became a substitute for character and plot. In this method emotion was one of the first things to be discarded in favour of quick results by shocks to the viewers' systems. While this can be enjoyable when imposed on a three minute promo film for a record it exhausted itself when stretched over an hour and a half. If it was true that the young audiences who bought the records and for whom these films were intended would no longer sit patiently, it was equally true that they would tire just as fast of films that exploited their interest in a particular star or group without offering some substitute for the underlying cause that had made them buy those records in the first place. People were not just young and restless, they were also angry with being used. They showed their frustrations and concerns through the records they bought, and through the stars they sought out, whose music spoke of their shared interests and whom they made into cult heroes the establishment had to take notice of. There was too much money out there to be made for them to ignore it. But records can be cut and released before the heat of the moment has worn off and interest has changed. Movies are costly, take time to plan, and when geared to capitalize on a moment, often find themselves out of date by the time they are released. Rarely did the mood and the moment meet on the screen.

Only once in the 60s did the subject and the style join successfully in a film that became something of a cult favourite, when Richard Lester, who learnt his craft making commercials for British television, joined up with the Beatles and came up with *A Hard Day's Night*. The story, about a day in the life of the fabulous four as they tried to make their way to a concert without being devoured by their fans, was just larky and truthful enough to hold the attention. And, of course, the Beatles were at that moment probably the four most popular figures in the Western world. The subject of mad chases and narrow misses, leading to exhausted drops in barricaded hotel rooms, was suited to silent comedy speed, fast cuts, stop frames, high speed, hiding behind trees – all that craziness associated with the home movies Chaplin and Fairbanks had made. Here Lester could use all his tricks to translate the impact of the four unconventional pop stars into visually soaring camera ideas. It wasn't about the Beatles, any equally famous group or individual would have done as well, though the Liverpudlians' own sense of cheeky fun added immeasurably to the spirit of the thing. But Lester's cutting caught the spirit, the zest and the hectic energy of youth; his stop-frame and slow motion photography as they leapt up to sail through the air were welcome oases of rest, before the knockabout Keystone comedy

chase was on again. But such was the real speed of the Beatles' fame that, by the time they joined with Lester for their second film, *Help!*, they had become known as individuals in the public's mind and to treat them again as a group of Sennet's faceless clowns was a mistake. Though the Rolling Stones were second only to the Beatles in popularity there was no attempt to try to put them into a film. Lead singer Mick Jagger was in several dramatic roles his fans didn't bother to see. Since writers and directors failed to come up with any workable formula it was left to the performers themselves to come up with subjects for stories and for characters suited to them. The most famous of these was of course *Tommy*. Townshend, one of rock music's most original talents, subsequently also wrote and

Top: The Beatles in their second film, *Help!* (1965), directed by Richard Lester. Above: Ken Russell's maniacal film about the composer, Franz Liszt, *Lisztomania*.

Tim Curry in drag for cult favourite *The Rocky Horror Picture Show.*

Pete Townshend. Who – What – Where.

Townshend: My background in art college was a training in watching films, old musicals. I realized quite early on that the writing style that you develop in music – even on a three-minute single – is a picture-painting process. And when I started to get to grips, particularly with *Tommy*, I realized that I was dealing with something that was getting close to cinema technique, in that the atmosphere of the overall story, the mood that one had to set, was roughly the same that you would have to do with a straight musical film of the old tradition, of the 30s and 40s. You had to deal with the same beginning, middle and end of problems. At the same time anything portrayed musically is preposterous anyway. And in a sense it's like trying to create a new reality, a new basis of storytelling, of which the primary requirement is that it should entertain first and be didactic later. I've always felt that was what rock 'n' roll was about – to entertain first, and then contain its message, whether it was a lighthearted message or a doom-laden message or a message about teenage frustration or impending nuclear war or unemployment or even suffering in the ghetto.

I think in a way that rock concerts – partcularly the larger rock concerts – have actually taken the place of the light-hearted musical event. The kind of rock concerts that The Who are doing at the moment, which admittedly are very grandiose affairs, are celebrations, things with audience participation. The idea of going to a concert and having a good time is almost more important than which band is playing and which stage of their career the band is in; it's almost a celebration of rock 'n' roll.

There are really two distinct areas. One is like *Quadrophenia*, where I actually used a literal, cinematic technique when I put the songs together, so I was literally cutting it like a film, with great big lumpy cuts, or *Tommy* which was an abstract series of songs mainly put around a sort of Messianic storyline, and out of those two ideas I've actually come to the decision – I don't know whether it's true or false at the moment – that the film, or the future of music in film (and I know I could be wrong but this is my experience) – really depends on the extent to which writers like myself (who, let's face it, have got the clout to raise the money in the first place) are willing to sublimate their music for the images. The problem you have with a film like *Quadrophenia* is that it pushed the music right into the background and took the story that the music originally told, and tried to re-create the very subtle atmosphere that the music created on the record, whereupon the music becomes incidental; or do what Ken Russell tried to do with *Tommy*, which was to remain totally faithful to the music. I think both were frustrating in the extreme and both were flawed because of that. So, for me at the moment, I'm still looking for a new language. A new way of approaching the film script, a new way of developing musical ideas.

When I dealt with the meat and potatoes of *Quadrophenia*, I was writing the whole thing from the hero's sub-conscious. Every image was dependent on the listener in that they were getting a sneak

New Wave rock star Hazel O'Connor in *Breaking Glass.* Playing rough but nice girl who makes good, she ends up as a robot à la Fritz Lang's *Metropolis.*

produced *Quadrophenia* for the screen. He is the only rock composer to have his music directly translated to the film medium in a manner comparable to the early musicals and composers.

With the Beatles and the Rolling Stones, The Who were one of the biggest and longest-surviving groups to emerge in the 60s. Despite a triumphant 1982 American tour they are thinking of disbanding and looking for new directions. Pete Townshend, the band's lead guitar and songwriter/composer, was the creative writing force behind *Tommy* and *Quadrophenia*, two of the highlights of Rock culture during the 70s. To understand their generation and what motivated their careers, and to find out where their careers were going, I spoke to Pete Townshend.

look, a voyeuristic look into this kid's screwed-up mind. The people that you meet now have been weaned on music rather than movies, and they've rejected TV as well. Although they're TV babies and have probably seen a hell of a lot of old films, and some of them might be tremendous enthusiasts, they're weaned away by music because it allows them in a sense to go through their own subconscious. They're creating their own movies. Now when you then try to jump in and illustrate against a

Below: Pete Townshend, front left, with The Who in the Pinball Wizard sequence for the film of his rock opera, *Tommy*. Bottom: Elton John's appearance in the film.

backdrop of modern music – we're almost at a point now where . . . as far as I can see, it's never been successfully done. In other words, we've found a way of translating the novel into film terms quite successfully, but we've never actually achieved it with cohesive pieces of musical work.

TV and film in a way are a complete cohesive experience of the first order. What happens in my work is that I communicate with people on two levels. One is the intimacy of me sitting at home writing out an idea, working it up on a guitar or a piano, trying to create a mood, something personal and something that is elevatory if possible, but whatever it is, it's something that is directly from me to the listener. To the point where the listener goes out to a record store, buys the record, sits at home sometimes with a pair of earphones on in complete privacy, and exposes himself full frontal to my exposing myself full frontal. It's as pure as you can get. The other side of it is the affirmative experience you get at a concert, the celebration of the fact that that communication has taken place. Hey, you know, we all know that we're on the same level. They're obviously all waving their arms about saying that they all know, but in actual fact each individual has had a different experience. So the difference is that the record or music is the first order, and the concert is the second order in experience. Now, that is not the case with the film musical. That is a homogeneous, first order experience. In my fantasy, and I say fantasy because it's something I've been working on since 1972 when I started with a filmscript called *Lighthouse*, which was the idea of filming a concert with a fictional aegis of some sort or a fictional umbrella, whereupon the person who went to the cinema would feel as it were a first order experience. They would be exposed to the music they were hearing for the first time. The songs wouldn't be known to them. . . . Even when I've worked with people who've tried to develop scripts – like Ken Russell and Nick Roeg and Alan Parker – all of whom have worked with music at some point in their career and have done all kinds of other things as well – what I found with all of them is that until the idea is theirs, there's no move. If Nick Roeg could himself say what he wanted to communicate, I'm sure he'd be a far happier man. The problem, I suppose, is coming to grips with what kind of an event and what kind of experience, that first order cinema thing should be. I mean, if you look at *The Wall*, that is a third order experience. The record came first, the concerts came next, and the film came last. The whole thing is almost like the wrong way round. By the time the film got out to the audience, each individual in the audience had their own idea of how the film should look. And the only line of continuity in there was that Roger Daltrey played the central figure.

For my own solo recording career, I use a producer, somebody that organizes the sound and to some extent directs me. . . . What happened on a record is like opera – you might get a pretty daft story, but they hold water because the story is not the important part. But with *Tommy* it seemed that some of the things we got away with on the record just weren't acceptable in dramatic terms. Perhaps it's because of preconceptions, perhaps it's because people do expect cohesive stories. Certain things had to be followed through, things had to fit into a particular scheme, a particular flow. Even to the point where Ken and I were discussing about when people were going through that door and all the audience wondering where the hell they went to, I said: 'When the lover arrives and kills the father, we don't see what they do to the body.' And Ken went: 'Oh, no! Oh, no! You know, this is it. The audience are all going to be wondering right the way through the picture what's been done with the body.' I said that perhaps we shouldn't panic at this point. In fact, nobody did ask what they did with the body. But his fear was as a film maker – that you can't afford that kind of thing thrown in too often, because it distracts people too much. I did not have much control over Ken Russell. I did about two weeks work with him, working up ideas from the script, and then off he went. And very little control over the *Quadrophenia* film either, which again I'd worked on the script with a friend of mine. We handed over our script to Frank Roddam and David Humphreys, who then worked it up for their own purposes. I feel, in a way, that I am now at a point where – just in my own musical career – I just have to re-acquaint myself with certain of the principles of the work that I'm doing. As a song writer, I can approach what I do from a dozen different angles. I can scribble some words on a piece of paper, and I can live with those for a week or two, and I can then sit down at a piano and try and bring something forth. I can sit at a music computer and let it come at me, let that spark words off; I can confront myself with an audience, and in my case it might be a very small audience in a recording studio of two or three people, and just literally make something up as I go along, and then walk into the control room and they say: 'Oh, that's great. When did you write that?' And I say: 'Just now.' All those different things I have to closely examine: which of those areas is working most effectively, which I'm most comfortable with, which one has to be controlled on what level or edited on what level; and when you bring in yet another parameter, the most incredible catalystic parameter of visuals, which are at work in an abstract and mobile, ever-changing manner, when you're working with music. The actual discipline, really start to become so vast and so challenging . . .

In my own work I'm really looking now to regroup and minimalize, so I can improve my scope, have a better control over what I'm doing, and look at a potential which so many young musicians are looking at. Take Steve Strange, who's actually concerned with altering images, in other words, with how he looks and presents himself to the world as a public figure, and music being purely a sublimated image which allows him to then visualize. Whether it be for the photo session for the album sleeve with Helmut Newton or the film which he's currently doing and The Anvil album which he's shooting himself in America, and he's probably spending ten times as much money on the video promotion films as he's spent on actually making the record. Now that kind of creative through-put, as it were, means he's looking further, he's looking deeper and looking wider. My problem, I suppose, is

that at bottom I was working in a straight line. You don't actually try to write in images, or adjust to images, you allow them to occur at the other end. That's music. That's the way music has always been and probably will always be. But the potential for the audio-visual entertainment medium to entertain depends on somebody creating something. *Who* are the audience, *where* are the audience, and *what* are you trying to touch them with? Those seem to be the questions which I'm sitting and asking myself all the time. When I go to something like *Cats* – which I thought was wonderful, there were things that it was sparking off in my head that I knew were very different to the people around me, because the music itself was creating an aura which was enabling me to superimpose images on what was happening in front of me.

In exactly the same way that I know damn well in a Who concert, I go up there, I wear the same clothes every day, I sing the same material, but according to the mood and the atmosphere and the receptivity of the audience, people see different things. We can go on and do a tremendously powerful show in our opinion, and walk off and receive a batch of letters from people who said they thought the whole thing stank because from where they were sitting they couldn't see a thing. Or perhaps the video screen was out of synch with the band. On another occasion you can go on and think you've had a terrible time on the stage; you've been getting electric shocks off the mike, and people are ecstatic. They felt some magic. One of the guys that's most expert at using the audience's energy to create an aura, is Springsteen. There's a magic that happens ever seen him work? There's a magic that happens in the audience, and it's the audience's own energy that creates it. Which is something that makes people like me frustrated about their inability to come fully to grips with cinema, because a cinematic event is one where, at its best, you're in a theatre with 2,000 other people and you're all sharing in the experience, and maybe you're seeing it in different ways. But the atmosphere and the mood and the presence of all those other people is a vital, vital force.

It's interesting now, that in The Who's career they've become so introverted and so self-analytical, that they've lost the ability to touch and entertain intuitively. On the other hand, you've got people who are force-feeding pap. But The Who are giving a concert in Toronto in December [1982]. This is one of the first big satellited concerts. It's going out firstly as a concert, with an audience of about 15,000 people; simultaneously it's going out on Home Box-Office. People are paying to view it probably in about a million homes on TV as it happens. At the same time it is also going on to college campuses, where they are putting in large screens and heavy-duty sound equipment, and selling seats to seven or eight thousand people. And they are experiencing that concert as it happens, as a group of people. After that, there's a fourth phase, which is that the whole thing goes out on video cassette and is then sold like potato chips. So it's very interesting to see the four channels that it's going out on, and how effective each one will be that it touches. Because it seems to me that when we're talking about the

importance of that mass experience that the college thing is the thing to look at. The fact that people will be looking at a screen and hearing music, and there will be a mass of people there. It's a concert experience, not a film. . . .

We formed a film company originally because we hoped to pursue, not so much the evolution of music in film, but to grasp where we stand at the moment. If there's a direct line between what we do and the cinema.

I suppose I went through the same art school process as everybody else. I saw a film the other day, and one thing the video revolution is doing for me is to go back to the art school situation where films were accessible. I've been watching quite a few films on tape, and watching them again and again and again, to the point where there was a degree of analysis going on, of getting past the first emotional reaction. A film I saw the other day that really struck me in the way that I remember perceiving films at college was *In Cold Blood*. And there was one image in that of the guy talking to the preacher before he is to go to his hanging. A young man. He's

just telling his life story, he's not being particularly maudlin or sorry for himself or anything, he's just telling about his relationship with his father and how it screwed up, and it's raining outside and they shot it through a sheet of glass and there's water running down the glass distorting the image of his face that literally looks like his whole face is crying, and that was the way that I used to perceive films. I was looking for artistic images. I wasn't really ready to be entertained by a film.

At art school, I suppose I perceived any images the way I listened to music — it was always art first, it was always looking for something that was new to me. I don't know really how you define art, but my feeling about what I've done in my work is the fact that it has always defined itself to me, it's demanded the next step. I suppose the point at which I turned away from dealing with visual images or even thinking about them was when I wrote the first song that the band recorded, and it was called 'Can't Explain'. And I wrote it because at that time in 1964, bands like the Beatles were writing their own material, and the record companies had decided that they would only sign groups that wrote their own material. And we were playing rhythm and blues stuff like The Rolling Stones. We had our sights fairly low, and they said we're not going to get a record deal unless someone in the band writes a song. Who can do it? So I said: 'Well, I think I can do it.' So I sat down and wrote a fairly simple song, which six weeks later was in the British charts, being written about in the music papers and talked about by the fans as being something which had communicated to them. People were reacting to what I'd written. It was a turning point in my life. I had suddenly discovered this root. I hadn't had a hell of a lot of musical training. I started when I was quite young, but I was never trained to write.

What I got out of the whole nebulous thing was the idea that I was perhaps going to be in a group for a few years, and might make a bit of money, and might get on TV, might find me a pretty girl friend once or twice, might get me a car to ride around in for a few years, and then I would have to go back to the real world and get a real job at the ad agency or whatever it was I was going to do. But this discovery that I could write and communicate through it was a discovery of what I felt immediately and recognized as art. There was no

question about it. I did something over there. A response occurred. I had no control over that response, but I did something and a reaction happened.

Performing is the discovery process. It's the discovery of scope of achievement; the discovery that performance is a thrilling event, and moving even when it's bad, and how devastating it can be to feel that you've not come through in some way. And how that in some way is a whole experience, and a temporal one, because unlike film which goes out there frozen, a performance comes and goes and you've always got another chance. You've got a chance to grow and learn from your mistakes. And, all right, you get to my age and you've been doing it for quite a long time and you tend to cover your tracks to a great extent, and when you go into a performance you avoid making the pitfalls you've done before, so you don't have to live on quite such a razor's edge, but you do learn how dangerously you can afford to behave. How much you can expose, how much to the left or the right you can swing the pendulum, plumbing deep personal abstract things, psychoanalysing yourself in song, to purveying commercial pap. And there's a pendulum swings from one side to the other. Both ends of which I've been involved in. And I see the explosion

'The Sorcerer's Apprentice' sequence in Walt Disney's *Fantasia* (1940).

Scott Wilson and John
Forsythe (right) in *In Cold
Blood* (1967).

which I believe is eventually going to happen, as
young musicians and young creative people are
being straitjacketed, as audiences are becoming
disenchanted with arenas, with large-scale events,
the same way that cinema audiences became
disenchanted with being offered a different kind of
intimate performance. With the video disc performance, you get to see a more complete picture of what
it is the artist is trying to get across. If one thing is
going to need the other, you have to start to deal
with the kinds of balance, not just between music
and image, but all the other factors that are part of
it. If you look away from my work to the current
music exploration, it's all becoming smooth, it's all
becoming experienced and wise. When a young
band comes to talk to me these days about how
they're going to get their break, they don't talk
about how they're going to get their dates at the
local pub, they talk about how they're going to
afford to get their 10-kilowatt PA system, their two
pantechnicons full of equipment and their laser
light show. Or where they're going to get access to
their music computer. Or their digital recording
studio. So this kind of sophistication in approach
does tend to domino down.

The cinema, and to a lesser extent TV, which I
think has done a tremendous amount of damage,
has carried on treading, to a point where I think the
best film I've seen for some time – although I didn't
like it very much and felt a little bit condescended
to, a little bit manipulated – was E.T., and I thought:
why is a film like E.T., made by a young man like
Spielberg, who no doubt was brought up on The
Who, The Band and Bill Hailey, why has he got John
Williams writing the music? It's because he's
working with the old language. And *Star Wars* is
the same thing. It is just Flash Gordon, really. The
language is the same. The new language of communication, the intimacy and the depth, the

profundity of the experience which people now
expect from their entertainment medium, because
they've been brought up on an entertainment
medium called music, is so big that film has to start
to operate on a different deeper more complete and
all-consuming level. That's what I look to in the film
experience both at the creative input and someone
who sits back and wants to see it. I think, hell, if I
put on a record, whether it be Keith Jarrett piddling
about on the piano for two hours, or the new Bruce
Springsteen record, and I close the record lid after
an hour of listening to it and I feel like a different
person, I feel elevated and moved, what *should*
happen to me when I walk into a cinema? And why
doesn't it? And why are the two languages so
completely different and where is this crosspoint?
You really beat *The Wizard of Oz* in this respect.
Fame they'll watch once or twice, *The Wizard of Oz*
they've watched a thousand times, and for them it's
theirs. I feel it's mine. Obviously we're talking
classics now, and *Bugsy Malone* is not a classic. It's
a nice film, a good film and an effective film. I
thought *The Wall* was okay. A look – if a kind of a
bit of a dark look – at the introversion of what rock
stars go through when they're trying to wrangle
with what they see as art and the outside world sees
as rubbish. You know, this is entertainment for
unthinking kids. This is rock'n'roll. This isn't art.
The tension that this causes in individuals, knowing that I've been through it myself. I mean, I was
able to look at it and laugh and think, ha-ha-ha,
where is the happy ending, there must be one, or
there is one for me, or there was one for me, or I'm
still working on it . . . you can't close a chapter the
way they closed a chapter in *The Wall*, with a
couple of kids playing in the street. It's what you
give to children, what you provide children with
that is the real hope of the future. And that's what
one waits to see all the time, the skill that goes into a
film like *Star Wars*, the emotional skill that
Spielberg is so good at; using relationships like
mother-child relationships that tear at the heart-
strings, and the skills that people like myself have in
dealing in straight lines to people on direct, serious,
emotional subjects without anybody going pink in
the face. I mean, let's talk about: Do we masturbate?
Let's talk about: Are we homosexual? Let's talk
about: Are we worried about being blown to bits by
the nuclear bomb? All in a kind of a doo-what doo-
what framework. And while we're doing it, dancing
down the discotheque. Or having fun in an arena. I
mean, that to me is a good way to deal with life. It's
cathartic. When people go to war and they're given
a machine gun, one of the only things that gets them
through – apart from the fact that they have to be
told to do their job – is humour. Humour is a
wonderful leveller. And then we come back to the
question of balance. I believe there's a tremendous
appetite, a tremendous demand – I notice it in my
kids and they're in their early teens. There is a
dissatisfaction with *both* music and film. English
kids have been brought up on slightly higher
quality TV, but they're also being exposed to quite
sensational film events now. And they can also go,
as my kids have, and see a band like Haircut 100,
which is some teeny-bopper stuff, or come to a
concert like The Who and see a tremendous football

crowd thing. They're wondering where do they find themselves in this audience; where does it address itself to the mass; where does it all come together? Where is their *Fantasia*?

But what I think is important is a great awareness among young musicians that, despite the fact that they've all chosen music they still value the fact that pop music has a vitality and an innocence and a naiveté and a purity of line *still*, despite everything, and they now realize that there's a potential cross-over door-opening, I suppose, in terms of visualization of ideas. It comes through with the use of video in promotion films and stuff like that. People are starting to learn the language a lot earlier. People 16 or 17 years old are putting a group together, and when they come to do their first recording they already know what they want their video to look like. Now, those are people who are going to grow up with those particular skills. Quite how they allow them to blossom I don't know. But it's exciting to see that happen. When you hear the music for the first time, you will also see the images for the first time. A good bit of those images will be a performance process. And you will become involved in sharing the thrill of the discovery, the moment of discovery, like those valuable moments in cinema where somebody has done something crazy or exciting or dangerous and it's been captured because the machine has been there to capture it and yet it touches you in a special way. That is something which I think is going to happen. It's inevitable. . . .

I first saw *Fantasia* when I was about seven and I was still going to see it when I was about fourteen. I must have seen it about a hundred times. What was disturbing is that it was such an exciting proposition, but I couldn't work out why it worked and why it didn't work at the same time. It was like a challenge to me, and that was at a point where I was just a kid. And the next thing was when I was subjected to what I thought was rock 'n' roll initially; it was the Bill Hailey onslaught. My father used to be a dance musician in a band called The Squadronaires. They were very much like a Glenn Miller outfit, with a British audience. They were very successful, and I used to follow my Dad around, and I always wanted to be in a band, because I used to see the girls looking at him and this sort of thing. I didn't want to be a superstar, I didn't want to write music, I just wanted to be in a band. We were on the Isle of Man and I was about eleven, and his band did a summer season. And the people that owned the ballroom that he worked in also owned a lot of the cinemas, and they had a Saturday morning preview of *Rock Around the Clock*. I remember going in with my Dad and a few other guys in the band and two or three people from the press. It was very exclusive, no audience. Me and my friend, Jimpy, who was the same age as me – 11 – saw the film and understood it – and we knew that these other guys didn't. And that was when I realized something about this new language, which at that time wasn't even a new language. Bill Hailey was basically dealing with dance band, be-bop, swing; it was Presley that came along and brought in that black music influence with 'That's all Right, Mama' and 'Heartbreak Hotel' and stuff like that, and actually giving a kind

of strange, quirky cross-pollinated feeling, bringing in the blues, which after all was music that was meant to be cathartic. You sing about your problems in order to get them out. And rock'n'roll is sung over your problems in order to dance over them. That's the difference. It's a dance medium. And the thing about *Rock Around the Clock* was that there was some line of communication specifically to me. I know it's a trite film – this funny old man and this funny old band – but it was a new language. And it touched me in a new way.

Two of the best films about the musical explosion that shook Britain and from there, the world, were both written by the pop columnist, Ray Connolly, *That'll Be The Day*, and its sequel, *Stardust*. Not only did they introduce David Essex, who went on to become one of England's most versatile and talented singers, but they offered a fascinating statement of their time and the struggles the in-fighting, the merchandising and destruction of personalities that took place behind the scenes of the making of these new Gods. In *Privilege*, the first feature of documentary film maker Peter Watkins, we were treated to that director's over-stimulated fantasy in which he saw an Orwellian future where governments perverted these performers' crowd-swaying charisma to political ends, climaxing in Nuremberg style rallies. Watkins borrowed heavily from Leni Riefenstehl's work. He ignored the shifting sands of these idols' popularity when they project themselves out of their own arena. It was just such obvious propaganda that had turned audiences off. Far more subversive was what we saw in *Stardust*, where J.R. Ewing-like moguls (Larry Hagman among them, ten-gallon hat and all as the prototype for his subsequent *Dallas* role) bought groups like so many sacks of wheat, with commercialism triumphant, and the status quo maintained.

The other musicals produced in England, usually

'We don't need no education.' A number from Alan Parker's film, *Pink Floyd The Wall*.

financed with American coin, have been along the lines of Hollywood's own. *Half A Sixpence* (director, George Sidney), Tommy Steele's stage hit based on H. G. Wells' novel *Kipps* was flat. Carol Reed made a film of Lionel Bart's musical, *Oliver* (which won six Oscars). *Goodbye, Mr Chips*, *Scrooge*, and *Chitty, Chitty Bang-Bang* (with an original score by the *Mary Poppins* team, Richard and Sherman) have all cost millions to make, starred American performers or British performers with an American reputation, and employed British craftsmen, but might just as well have been shot in Hollywood.

Ken Russell, the *enfant terrible* of British television, for which he made films about Isadora Duncan and Delius among others, moved to the big screen with a gross series of biographies about safely dead classical composers whose lives and works he proceeded to vandalize. Confronted by the spectacle of such shuddering stupidity expended on such infantile pretensions, it's best to avoid the subject altogether and let Wagner, Mahler, Liszt and Tchaikovsky rest in peace. Only in Karel Reisz's engrossing biographical treatment of the life of the revolutionary American dancer and choreographer *Isadora*, and in Richard Attenborough's screen adaptation of Joan Littlewood's *Oh What A Lovely War* is real pleasure to be found.

France's contribution to the genre in the past twenty-five years is primarily the work of one man, director Jacques Demy. A self-confessed fan of the American musicals, he first revealed his obsession with the genre in *Lola* (1960), a pixical view of a day in the life of a faithful prostitute which cheerfully mingled songs, dances and homages to Dietrich's *The Blue Angel*. His flair developed in *Les Parapluies de Cherbourg* (1962), creating a popular work in which *all* the dialogue was sung, almost a light opera. With Michael Legrand's tirelessly revolving score, pastel-coloured painterly compositions and a lot of pretty young faces Demy contrived a world of naive charm that caught the mood of the moment. Like all those 30s operettas, his characters were recognizable in reality. Their problems – housing, money, and such were real. Since then he has steadily continued

his quest for finding the film equivalent for opera, a style and a rhythm of filming that would be in accordance with people who sing and dance their every thought. Since sound, film pacing has been primarily dictated by the spoken word. The goal has ever been to integrate the song into that without the too jarring effect it usually creates. It required the creation of a state of mind that once seemed prevalent so that it was no problem in the audience's mind to accept the transition from conversation to song. But this art was lost with the loss of innocence that came with Hiroshima. By the 60s, hardly anyone seemed to know how to introduce a lyrical moment into the proceedings without raising a laugh. Audiences had lost their childish wonder at movies, which enabled them, like children, to believe anything was possible so long as one kept an open heart and mind, and they hadn't gained the wisdom that no longer requires 'facts' to prove a truth or achieve a miracle. From *Umbrellas* up to his most recent work, *Une Chambre en Ville* (1982) Demy's films have primarily continued in the tradition of operetta, leavened with the political concerns of his

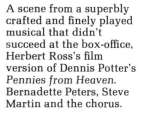

A scene from a superbly crafted and finely played musical that didn't succeed at the box-office, Herbert Ross's film version of Dennis Potter's *Pennies from Heaven*. Bernadette Peters, Steve Martin and the chorus.

John Travolta and Olivia Newton-John in the 70s smash about 50s high-school rockers, *Grease*.

Flashdance. Jennifer Beals as woman's answer to Travolta in *Saturday Night Fever.*

Contributions from the theatre continue to be a primary staple of 70s and 80s film musicals. Galvanising, dashing, Kevin Cline as the pirate king in Gilbert and Sullivan's *The Pirates of Penzance,* a big stage hit in Joseph Papp's production.

age; but none of the others has matched the success of the first.

Still riding the crest, Demy's *The Young Girls of Rochefort* (1966), his 'homage' to the American musical, was awaited with much excitement. The first success led to the second's larger budget. There was American interest behind it. He was able to afford international stars – Gene Kelly, a tireless American back in France where he meets and falls for Françoise Dorleac, the older of two beautiful sisters (the other is Catherine Deneuve), whose mother, played by Danielle Darrieux, was almost as youthful in her charm. George Chakiris, fresh from his success in *West Side Story*, and Grover Dale were others who danced into their lives. But the slender plot of two small-town sisters and the endless coincidences that occur in their world, simply couldn't support the weight of past, present and future that it took on, with in-jokes and self-amused asides pushing relentlessly into the main plot. So much of the film was irrelevant. While

producing nice images for a tourist office poster it simply never became one thing or another. It is often the problem with 'homages'. Subsequently his films became even more cloying and derivative. What might have been a lyrical fairy-tale, *Peau d'Ane* becomes another misguided 'homage' – this time not to the American musical, but to Jean Cocteau's *La Belle et la Bête* in which he tries to mix a Perrault princess with a space-age fairy-godmother, and a time of donkey skins with telephones – producing a long quote without context. Like Bogdanovitch's movies, Demy's are the work of a movie fan who forgets to put the things he likes into the films he makes, with the result that a homage ends up a fromage. He followed this with one of the best known of all musical legends, *The Pied Piper*, starring England's ballad singer Donovan, as a medieval parable for the anti-war anti-establishment youth of the day. But a lot of the power of the flower generation had already waned, and the film was listless, lost and painfully effete. Yet his work possesses many felicities, enough to show that *Les Parapluies* and *Lola* were not flukes, merely that he needs the right subject for his style. Demy has shown that he has the imagination, the eye, the intelligence and the desire to make the musicals that his genre needs. If he can also find fun in it all and not take himself so seriously, he might yet make a film as good as his early ones.

Where Do We Go From Here?

In the 70s records and rock concerts were the biggest thing on the entertainment horizon. Concerts given before thousands of foot-stomping, cheering people in baseball arenas and Olympic stadiums requiring small armies of police to control them, grew in size and in the revenues they brought in. If ever there was an expression of a popular folk art as basic as any tribal ritual out of which music, dance and colour would be born, this was it. Yet only a few films, like *The Rose*, and the Streisand-Kris Kristofferson remake of *A Star Is Born*, had the

sense to integrate these concert performances into the mainstream of their stories. The success of these films proved something epic film-makers had always known, namely that one of the things people really love is to look at other people having a good time, and the sight of thousands gathered in the open air to share a common experience attracted millions to the cinemas. There was quite a spate of other films using record-selling giants as a lure. For one reason or another these fell as flat as all such previous attempts to cash in.

Sgt. Pepper's Lonely Heart Club Band starred the Bee Gees (the brothers Gibb), Peter Frampton and Alice Cooper, and took as its starting point the rights to 29 Beatles songs owned by the Australian impresario, Robert Stigwood. Instead of a concert, he hit upon the idea of making a fantasy set in the 60s, the hey-day of the Beatles craze. The story set the action in a Utopian American community called Heartland, where people went around with a perpetual smile because they loved the music so. The sets were giant toys; a yacht-length limousine, a seven-storey balloon and a 20-feet high hamburger, and all of it shot in psychedelic colours. But fantasy has nearly always been a big turn-off on film, and the sight of some of the most popular recording stars of the day behaving like a lot of Walt Disney cartoon animals while singing songs they were not identified with, pleased neither their fans nor the Beatles' fans, who wanted their own heroes together again singing the songs they created.

American Hot Wax was about the week in the life of top 50's disc jockey, Alan Freed, that culminated in the birth of rock'n'roll, bringing on the original but now aged stars, Jerry Lee Lewis, Chuck Berry and Screamin' Jack Hawkins. *Thank God It's Friday* was set in the 70s disco scene and starred the 70s disco queen, Donna Summer. *Can't Stop The Music* had producer Alan Carr trying to capitalize on his earlier success with the youth market (*Saturday Night Fever* and *Grease*). But by the time it came to the screen, the gay-orientated pop group, The Village People, a 70s novelty act along the lines of

Alvin and the Chipmunks, had already been reduced to touring in Australia, and the film was an embarrassing mess best forgotten. *The Blues Brothers*, starring numerous recording favourites, was so ineptly directed by John Landis that if there was a wrong camera angle, he would find it, and performers like Aretha Franklin might just as well have stayed at home. *Xanadu* starred Olivia Newton-John (with Gene Kelly) in a remake of *Down to Earth*, with Olivia on roller skates. For his film début, middle-of-the-road singer Neil Diamond selected an even hoarier old story, nothing less than *The Jazz Singer*. This third remake looked like one long, slickly-put-together TV commercial with singer Diamond, bathed in goodness and light, photographed in a succession of pretty sweaters against lush California sunsets. But despite his enormous record sales (the film's sound track was the only thing that made a profit), Diamond on film was no 'Sound' for novelty and it fared as badly as the 1952 Danny Thomas and Peggy Lee version.

More conventional musicals fared little better. *The Little Prince* had the last score written by Lerner and Loewe for the St Exupéry fantasy about the little extra-terrestrial on a far-away planet, and was directed by Stanley Donen whose sophistication needed a more earth-based subject. *Lost Horizon* was a lost cause from the start. Shangri-La, the mythical haven high up in the Himalayas where all was peace and tranquillity and people lived into their hundreds without ageing, needed the most delicate, skilful touch for it to even have a chance in the hyper-realistic 70s. Its director, Charles Jarrott, was completely lacking in it. The large cast of actors, with the exception of Bobby Van, lacked a single personality who might have provided the lightness and charm to make this setting or these people and

their other-worldly serenity even remotely conceivable, with Norwegian actress Liv Ullman like some oatmeal queen devoid of her Northern Light, shrivelling all before her in the California sunshine. As leaden as she were Peter Finch, Olivia Hussey and Michael York. The singing and dancing wrecked a score by Bert Bacharach and Hal David that really deserved better. None of these films had that essential style and deftness of directorial touch that once made whimsy palatable, in films like *The Pirate, Cabin In the Sky, Damn Yankees* or *Mary Poppins*. Yet Herbert Ross, the choreographer of *Funny Girl* and *Goodbye, Mr Chips* who turned director (*Funny Lady, The Turning Point, Nijinsky*), without ever suggesting a recognizable personality or style throughout his work, pulled off a brilliant job of mimicry with *Pennies from Heaven* (1982). Budgeted in the tens of millions to pay for the stunningly evocative Edward Horner-inspired studio sets for a story set in the heart of the Depression 30s, it had a terrific script by British playwright Dennis Potter, who had first conceived it as a black-and-white series for British TV. The story of a song-sheet salesman, whose grim existence was relieved by a fantasy world invoked through the songs of the period, the film was as much an art director's (Fred Tuch and Bernie Cutler), costumier's (Bob Mackie) and cinematographer's (Gordon Willis) triumph as anything else. But the pastiche of 30s-style songs and dances was in keeping with the overall conception.

While the film would probably have gained a stronger emotional rapport with the audience if his cast of talented performers, including Steve Martin, Bernadette Peters and Christopher Walken, had also done their own singing instead of performing and lip-synching to the original 30s recordings, this was a justifiable if perhaps unwise decision to remain faithful to the playwright's idea. TV could never have done it so opulently, though it pointed up the basic disparity between TV, a writer's medium, and the movies, a director's medium. As an example of money spent to achieve a meticulous and impressive recreation of another time and place, it would have run for years as an exhibition at the Metropolitan Museum. Unfortunately there were not enough museum-goers to make the film a success, dooming it to the archives and retrospectives of 30s musicals which at last, fifty year late, depict the world that playwrights like Donald Ogden Stewart saw but Hollywood chose to ignore in favour of films that would lighten the lot of their audiences.

David Essex was the charismatic star of *That'll be the Day* and *Stardust*, the films which made him one of the idols of the musicals scene. His interests are now turning towards the legitimate theatre, but he became a star of both stage and screen by the early 70s and a conversation with him was bound to be illuminating.

David Essex

I didn't have an inkling to do a thing in music or theatre or cinema or anything when I was a kid. I was born in 1947. I lived in a working class background. My Dad was a docker and he got ill, he got TB. My mother and I became destitute – we were put into an institution with a curtained cubicle, and then when Dad came out of hospital – this is when I was about four – he was moved into another wing of the same place. Gradually he got better and we eventually got a council prefab. Have you ever seen those round buildings? You can't hang pictures up because the walls are curved. But we loved it – we had a garden. And my first real awareness of music was of my Mum, who used to play a piano in a pub at night, and scrub it out in the morning. And I'd be allowed just inside the door, and I'd listen to that. But I had no inkling of what was to come. As far as theatre goes, it was then a very middle class thing. So I never went to the theatre or anything like that. I watched shows on TV and I listened to music, and I worked down a street market on the fruit stall. Which I didn't find particularly interesting, except it was next door to the record stall. And those big 78s used to be in these boxes, and they'd play Frankie Laine. So I would listen and sell apples at the same time. It was all just magic to me. I think the first record I bought was 'See you later, Alligator', and I played it and it was just unbelievable. 'Cause at first I couldn't work out how the sound got on that bit of plastic. I remember looking for ages at the grooves and thinking: I can't work how that has got there. And then my interest in music started to develop. I was very good at football and I played in the West End Boys' team, which was quite a big football team, and I wasn't particularly worried about school. But I adored playing football. I failed my eleven-plus on purpose because I wanted to go to this school with a good football team. So I drew Popeye all over my exam sheet! But, anyway, I went on these adventures to Soho – this was when I was 14. It was like a different world. Because in the East End it's docks and it's a different feeling. But the West End is all lights and people, out late at night.

So I was walking along Wardour Street with a friend of mine called Jim, and I heard this music coming out of the basement. It was like the star over Bethlehem. I thought: What's that? It was about 11 o'clock at night – and it was the Flamingo Club. And they had what was called an all-nighter. So Jimmy and I paid up, and we went downstairs, and it was the most miraculous thing I've ever seen. It was full of black American GIs, and it was pounding R and B music. And there were live bands, and there was a live black R and B singer. And I think at that time it was 'Do the Dog'! And he was there in white hot pants, and it was like wonderland. Magic. I sat and I watched and I knew I had to be a musician. I just had to be a musician. And the next step was which instrument could I get and learn to play the quickest. Well, if you banged a drum it answered back immediately. So from the bits and pieces of money I'd made from the market, and with a bit of wheeling and dealing, I went off and bought my first snare drum. And my ambition – which is what I never realized – is that I never really have ambitions now, because I really can't realize that all this stuff has happened to me. The mixture of horror and ecstasy going down into that basement which was lit with a red light, full of very sinister-looking people, and I was only a 14-year-old boy was incredible. It was full of drugs and stuff. The courage it took – I know we walked back and forth past it about four times before we went in. That was a big step. So I started to learn the drums, and I got my first job which was in a dance band. I had to wear these bow ties and play waltzes and foxtrots, which was all right. But my ambition was to be a jazz drummer. And I started to listen to the most obscure music I could, because to me the more obscure it was the more credible it was. I had in my mind that anything that was black and obscure and blues-orientated or jazz-orientated was authentic. And things like the pop charts at the time – except for rock 'n' roll – was all a bit suspicious. Like Eve

Boswell. I had no time for that. Initially it was the music that drew me, and then it was just the feeling and the atmosphere . . . I just wanted to be a part of that. I wanted to play until 4 o'clock in the morning. I wanted to go home as the sun came up, and I wanted to know friends of a different colour. From different places. And people that talked with American accents. I wanted to be a part of it, I wanted to know it all. So I played in this dance band, which I didn't want to do, but it was my first job, and then there was a job going in a R and B band. And I played in that until it moved its musical policy to a point where our gig started to dissolve. It was quite depressing, because we were playing in pubs singing things like: 'The first time I met the blues . . . yeah, yeah . . .' And the pub owner would come up and say: 'Will you play something lively?' And we'd say: 'No, man.' And we'd pack up our stuff and go. We were so adamant about our art. We'd just stand on our principles and wouldn't move from it. So at this time our rhythm guitar player had worked as what was called – and is called – a cooper. They make barrels. And the owner man was a Jewish man of about 63 I suppose, and pop groups like the Beatles had started to make huge money. So the cooper had heard about this group and thought: Well, I'll get one. He didn't know much about Show Biz, but he had a friend who was a writer, journalist, critic – his name is Derek Bowman – and he collared Derek to come along to this pub where we played, and Derek was very struck with the group. Primarily I think he was struck with me; I was still playing drums and singing. I started singing when the lead guitar said he couldn't play effective guitar and sing at the same time. 'And you smoke a lot of cigarettes, you've got a husky voice, you ---- well sing!' I said: 'I don't want to sing – I'm playing the drums.' But somebody had to sing, and it was me. I was the only one who could sound relatively authentic. So I started to sing. He just got more and more introverted into his own guitar. He became a milkman, bless him. So by this time we had developed our own sort of R and B sound, and Mr Murray and Mr Bowman brought down various people. Not with much success, except that some people who came down said the boy on the drums is good, you should get him up at the front. So basically, to cut a long story short, the band fell to bits. Somebody got married and somebody argued with somebody else, and we were playing in Germany – you know those famous clubs. We were doing three shows a night. And the Germans hated it! They just thought it was the thing to have an English group. It was like Welcome to Death. I think it was their way of getting back at us for the Second World War. But that was an eye-opener. I was now about 16 and dealing with prostitutes. That never bothered me, but I think I've always been like an observer. Not totally a part of anything. I don't know why I'm like that. I put it down to maybe because it's I'm an only child, but I've never felt completely a part of anything. It's like there's another person there all the time. So we went off to Italy, and that's when the band started to dissolve. They came back and I stayed. I played in this cabaret club with Italian jugglers and all that. It was funny, because I couldn't speak Italian and hey couldn't speak English. So eventually I came back and met with Derek, and he said: 'What do you want to do?' Because I didn't have any real motivation. I knew I loved music, jazz – and I was kind of sure in my own mind that I would become a jazz player at Ronnie Scott's club or something like that. That's really all I wanted out of life.

So Derek said: 'What do you want to do?' I said, 'I dunno.' So he said: 'What about you becoming a solo singer?' I said: 'I dunno. What do I do?' He said: 'Well, we'll get in the studio and do some demos.' So I got this recording contract as a singer. And I'd never written a song. I kind of worked out arrangements for the band. But you don't know you're a songwriter until you write a song and it's a hit. So I didn't know I was a songwriter. I made a couple of shocking records in the 60s that were always sort of second-hand versions of successful songs at that time. They were just caricatures. At the time it was thrilling. My only regret is that I believed in people that maybe I shouldn't have. You don't know, it's something you have to live through. And then I started to meet people with big Rolls Royces. Funny-coloured clothes. And whatever they say goes. And I believed adamantly in every word they said. So I went on like that for a while without much success, and I started to tour as a singer with a band backing me, Derek still managing me. And then a fateful thing happened. I was in Manchester, and the way it used to work is that half of us would take it in turns to go and get bed and breakfast, and the other half would sleep in the van. And I'd been very ill for about a week, and it was my night to spend in the van in Manchester, and it was pissing down with rain. It was really awful. And it was the final straw. I got pneumonia, I came back to London, and I was ill in bed and Derek came to see me and I said there didn't seem much point in doing these one-night stands. It seemed to me like trying to win the pools. It didn't have much to do with whether you could sing or whether you had what's called talent, it was all too hit and miss. What about working in the theatre? So he got me some tickets, and when I got better I went off and saw my first play, which was *Juno and the Paycock*. Which I didn't understand at all, but the contact between the players and the audience, and the manners and the feeling of respect I felt in the auditorium which I didn't get in the other places I worked. I couldn't believe it – people would say: 'I'm sorry' and 'Excuse me.' In the other places, if you played a song you'd made up, people would walk off the floor. It was always hard, full of violence, actually. Most nights we played people would be punching each other sick. And we'd just keep playing! And your first thought was . . . the equipment was God. Everything you owned in life was the PA and the amplifier and the drums. So always we'd try and protect the stuff! You'd much rather have a bottle hit you on the head than go through your drum-kit! It was all like that.

Derek said: 'What do you think?' I said: 'It's great. I'd like to be part of that,' meaning the theatre. So Derek said: 'O.K. We'll have to see if we can find some repertory company where you can go and work.' Now I had a *very* East End accent. It's worn off and rounded off a little bit, simply because

David Essex and 'The Stray Cats' in *Stardust.*

nobody could understand a word I was saying. But I like to think I've still got a London accent. But at the time it was a major worry. Because everybody else sounded a bit like a BBC announcer. There was an ad in *The Stage* for a touring rep. Young, progressive actors wanted. I went along, and I've got a naturally big voice anyway, so I auditioned and I sang this song, and then I read a piece of script – which must have been shocking – and I got the job. It was kind of the junior lead in this touring rep. So there I was in a theatre company, and then it was a different kind of worry. I felt patronized a bit. Because of the way I talked and where I came from. But there were different kinds of people in this rep. There was the classic kind of rep actor with a wooden head and nothing else, no spirituality, a professional. Then there were some other interesting people who were actually good, and I learned things from them.

But the great thing for me at that time is that I spent eighteen months in this touring rep playing pissholes on the ends of piers to audiences of fourteen old ladies at the matinee, and just making the biggest mistakes and being invisible in a way. Walking over to the church spire and leaning on it, and stuff like that! It was great, I learned a lot. I was shook up at the time, and I had a great deal of trouble talking to these people, because I was so aware of my accent and my background. I couldn't converse; I never said anything. And I'd think everything over five times before I'd say: 'Shall we stop and have a cup of tea?' That was my first initiation into theatre. Then followed a few bleak years.

Most rock musicians have a different kind of fire from actors. I find actors generally really quite bland. Rock people have a sort of danger about them. Because they're dealing with channelled violence . . . and energy, a lot of the time. Even an unknown musician can be – I've seen it – they take on a . . . creative outline. I was at Ronnie Scott's last night, for instance, and there was a superb sax player in a band called Afro-Cuba, and I saw him at the bar before, and there was absolutely nothing about him. I know musicians who'd have a problem saying why they do what they do, how they do what they do, except when they pick up an instrument the spirituality of the contact that comes to them just says volumes. It's really the instrument and the music and the spirituality that makes it wonderful. Being an actor is a very comfortable thing. In many ways actors are workmen. Acting is really an extension of yourself. But the instrument sounds like it comes from somewhere else. When I play the drums it's like a force comes and takes me over. It's quite interesting. There seems to be an intangible thing in music, something which fires people. If you go to see a rock concert, it's so dramatic that it borders on pure theatre. A good concert lives for that moment, although there is obviously a reper-

JK: But not every flame will reach all the moths. mean, you have to have more. . . .

Essex: Oh, yeah. You want to be in the position t sell a few records, so you keep doing what you'r doing. But for myself, I try to walk a borderlin between being there for what I consider the righ reasons – which is to play my music the best way can – and at the same time not really losing the audience.

I never used to go to movies. But nowadays when see these old film musicals I like them a lot. But it's weird. I don't like what I call in-between films. I like

Diana Ross (wearing a dress) leads the happy Winkies in *The Wiz*. Choreographer, Louis Johnson.

toire and a shape, but there is freedom inside that. And just the kind of . . . indifference in a way, to the adulation is interesting. I think the thing that counts is the music and the song that you are doing. That is the God. I want to get it right. I want it to be the best song that I've written. I want to play it well and I want to sing it right. I want to create the atmosphere or the backdrop around that song. So if the audience relates, it's great. If they don't then the hell with them. Quite honestly. The audience becomes a moth, and the music and the song and the lights and the imagery is the flame. And the flame burns for itself, anyway. And that's why it's attractive.

real films – or very unreal films. And mainly the films from Hollywood, the musicals, which are beautiful and dreamlike. I love that. And the other kind of film I like are British films. Like *Brief Encounter* – great film – and *The Knack*, and *Up The Junction* . . . films like that. But the stuff in between – Westerns, John Wayne and Robert Mitchum and all that – I really can't be bothered with. But the musicals, they'd never put them on where I lived as a kid. That's a West End camp taste. They'd have *Bridge Over The River Kwai* and all that!

When I started performing I saw a few things like *Ferry Across The Mersey* but cinema I never enjoyed. I didn't like going into cinemas. It just seemed such a long time. I know that's ridiculous. But I always have had this problem that today is in the way of tomorrow, and I could not wait to get around that next corner. It's still with me now, but as a younger lad it was incredible. I just couldn't stay in one place. I've moved house, it must be sixteen times, since I left home. I'm just restless. Just to sit in a cinema, to go there for what would be two films, four hours' worth of stuff, I just felt I was missing something. Unless it was a fantasy. Then it seemed like something wonderful. Or if it was real good realism, that was good. Because that

my first break, as they say. And I hadn't gone back to records at that time. So the irony was that all of a sudden there was this film that basically – with a few reservations – was about me.

The way it all came together, really, was that through the success of *Godspell* I was able to go back to music on my own terms. And my terms were that I would write a tune for *TWBTD* that would be reflective in lyric, but with a modern sound. So I wrote 'Rock On' and played it for David Puttnam who thought it wah too weird. He didn't want it in

made me feel that there I was, up on the screen.
JK: Do any of the films about the music business capture it, or do they romanticize it?
Essex: You mean *That'll Be The Day* and *Stardust*? Well, Ray [Connolly] was a journalist in Liverpool, and Liverpool was the big centre for English 60s music. So I think he drew from that. And the way I got *That'll Be The Day* – after being on the road, doing what the character in *TWBTD* and *Stardust* did – was because I was the new young actor in *Godspell* playing Jesus. David Puttnam and Ray Connolly came along, saw me, and asked me to do a screen test, as an actor, for a film. They didn't particularly know about my musical background. Because I'd been adopted by the theatre. That was

the film. I said I wanted to do music my way. I'd done that 60s thing. So I turned round and did a deal with CBS and that song went to number one in America and number one over here. And it wasn't in the film. And there was this incredible last three weeks of *Godspell*. I had this incredible situation where *TWBTD* was the biggest box-office film, 'Rock On' was no. 1 in the charts, and *Godspell* was a real hot ticket. There were these three areas, and me pretty mystified. But especially thrilled about 'Rock On'. Because I still feel like a musician who acts.

The fact that it did sort of relate to people was quite odd. Very odd. Uncanny, really. And of course at the time of doing *TWBTD* they made me sign for a second film if *TWBTD* was successful. To me it was

Alan Parker's *Fame* was loosely based on New York's School of the Performing Arts, which launched a hugely popular TV series of the same name, sold millions of leg warmers, and started similar schools in American cities like Chicago. The film was a new version of the old story about aspiring youngsters, and differed from earlier versions primarily in its prolific use of four-letter words, presumably to show how contemporary it was. Choreographer, Louis Falco.

David Essex and Ringo Starr in *That'll be the Day.*

just pie in the sky. I didn't expect *Stardust* to be made, but then we made it and again it was very odd because it was happening to me in real life – I had become a teen idol. Before doing *Stardust* I had had lots of hits and sell-out concerts and all the rest of it. And in *Stardust* I had this sort of unpleasant situation where I was mirroring some of the things that were happening to me in real life that were pretty distasteful, and then fictionalizing it and recalling it on the screen, and there was quite honestly an identity crisis going on which took me three or four months to get over.

In a way I am my own audience. There is this mysterious third eye. I'm not ordinary or anything like that, but I don't think I'm completely besotted by fame and fortune. I think one of the reasons is that I've always looked upon it as a member of audience, but also looking at the project and doing it in the hope that it relates to me as opposed to only worrying about it *relating.* I think you've got to try and satisfy yourself initially. I think in the stuff I've done there's an element of danger, a dangerous path to tread. It's the easiest thing for a critic to shoot somebody down who comes from one area and makes a step into another. Journalists particularly and probably people en masse like to put you into a compartment which they really don't like to have you move out of. And I think some of the stick I've had is because I do do a lot of different things. And most of them seem to succeed. And people don't like that. Because they seem to feel that somehow there's a lack of authenticity. But I do a lot of things that

they think I wouldn't be likely to do . . . but what would I be likely to do? I loved *Byron*, it was wonderful. It was a thrill to do it. And I loved Che Guevara. I only do people that I really want to do. I can't piss around with stockbrokers, you know!

The thing about the movies is that they were pretty close to the truth because the people in them were living a life style not dissimilar from the characters they played. We were drawing on life as we knew it, so fundamentally the characters and the feelings of the principals were accurate. And the situations were very feasible. But life can be boring even for the world's biggest rock star. There are boring days, and in a two-hour film you have to eliminate those. So a kind of veneer does creep in; you don't get the full picture. I think *TWBTD* was a very good film, because in its own way it's a classic film of the working-class boy wanting to be different, and looking for an avenue, looking for somewhere to go, so he won't be a plumber like his dad. It's the beginning of the kind of person that made up the British explosion in the 60s. Through art and music. It was that kind of mentality. We couldn't have made that film before. The 50s was America. Everything was American. Any record that came out in England was a joke as far as we were concerned. I don't know why I was a fashionable or aware kid but the East End at that period was historically a hotbed of fashion. I mean, mods came from there. The blue beat thing really took off from there. So I was in an environment that was breaking down barriers. I used to have friends

A scene from *Stardust*. 'The Stray Cats' disembark from the plane during a successful tour. David Essex, Danielle, Adam Faith and, in the background in dark glasses, Keith Moon of The Who.

in the early 60s that had orange hair and shaved eyebrows – can you imagine what that was like in the mid-60s? And all that's been going on over the past few years – we've done it. I learned everything after leaving school, and I stopped going there when I was fourteen. The minute I started going up to the West End into music and stuff and getting into the adventures with the band, that to me was life. I know so many intellectuals and university graduates that are blockheads, because they don't have that common sense and logic of being able to adapt to life. Being able to put a plug on whatever it is.

I wanted to prove to myself that I could buy a Rolls Royce. But I hate pretence. I can't stand pretence. So the fact that I could go in and buy a Rolls Royce is one thing, but the fact of going out on the streets with it is a completely different thing! And I think that's ingrained in me. That working-class attitude.

When I played Earl's Court, which is an 18,000 seater, there was a circus there, in essence I was the ringmaster, because I stage my shows myself. I do the lights and I talk through it. I finished the whole thing with dancers and circus. It shocks me sometimes to think back on what I've done, because it's right over the top! At the Palladium there was a famous show always on Sunday nights, and they always went round on that thing at the end. So I got all these men dancers into fishnet tights and plumes on their heads, all with their hairy chests, in low-cut things, on this revolve with cardboard cut-outs, and the show opened up with that.

What makes me laugh is that when they do a show in the West End there are giant bills, and huge problematical things that can't be done. But rock people do it. I've got an army of forty people and we go on the road and we do it. We do outrageous things. At the Palladium, for instance, all the in-staff walked away and said: 'Won't do that – can't be done.' Because we had a complete scaffold and wooden set on wheels that was like a building site, so that you had all the glamour at the beginning, with the carnival cut-outs and dogs and things going round on this thing, and that would go down, and then we'd wheel this huge scaffold in and it would turn into all kinds of green lights and smoke, and the rock thing would come through. And they'd never seen anything like the way it was done. It is breaking new ground. It's drama, really. The whole thing about a rock tour is very special. It has to be filmed properly. It's like gypsies, a roving band or army of gypsies that goes to a town like a task force. The roadies go in – they're the spearhead. They go in at nine in the morning, and they deal with the problems with the County Council and all that stuff, and then they stick this stuff up, and it's so bizarre to be there. And then the band comes in at four o'clock to sound-check, and we go through all the lights, and the set goes up for that night only, and people come in off the street and see this extravaganza. It's like a circus. And the roadies break it down after the show, and they put it into the lorries, and they drive to the next hotel which they get to at three in the morning, and they go to bed and they're up at nine, and they're putting it up again. It's modern circus. It's a mixture of trying to give experiences to your audience, because they're walking in from Bradford and Leeds and stuff like that, and also trying to bring out all those little pictures that were in your mind when you wrote the song. And sometimes pictures that arrive in your mind after you've written the song. I don't know how anybody else puts their songs together. The last tour, which is the one I enjoyed the most, because I'm less aggressive now and starting to enjoy today a little bit more, I thought it would be nice to draw up flaps and have a backdrop with pure theatrical images on. Like a real piece of scenery. We drew pictures of a magician, and a man being blown out of a cannon, a bearded lady, and the masks of comedy and tragedy, dancing girls, a ballet dancer, a clown . . . the strongest images that come to mind, and we put them on this real scenery. And that was the 'Stagestruck' tour. It didn't seem to me that we needed more than that. It's a mind trip. I don't pull ideas from places, I don't consciously do that. It's all a mystery to me how I can write songs. It's a mystery about the performance thing . . . it is, and I'm not being modest or anything. I'm totally confused by the whole process. All I know is that I made up things and . . . you see, I'm constantly in the situation when I see something I've done and it surprises me. I listen to my album, which is written by me, and produced by me, and more or less arranged by me with the help of the band, and I listen to it and I think: it's great. I can't believe I've done this. When I go in and do things, I never think about them before. I walk in completely without ideas. I have a sort of shape, but I walk in and it will happen. There. I always consciously under-rehearse things. It's a mixture of being lazy – or maybe fright – and not wanting to finish it off. It's only the going there that makes you do it. I walk in very loose with things. Never work it out.

JK: Have you seen things like *The Last Waltz* and *Divine Madness* and those things?

Essex: No. I tell you, I've only seen fifteen or twenty films.

JK: In your life?

Essex: Yeah. I don't feel I'm in the same business. I don't really feel any major connection with all that. I don't feel it's a big village that we all live in. I go to the theatre a lot. I love theatre. It makes me feel humble that people are up there trying to convey emotion and move me. But for me cinema is detached. Because of what it is, it's studied. Obvious. Edited and a little bit more technical in a way. I'd like to feel the same sort of excitement others do when they see a film.

But I've never experienced it. I've only experienced half-full cinemas smelling of piss and stuff like that. And I wouldn't want to go there. It's funny, because when I go to New York I *feel like* going to the cinema. Much more than in LA. But in New York there are always people in the cinemas. And I think that really is the key.

I always set the attitude and the shape for the promo films for my records. I always do that. I think you've got to, because fundamentally you know more about that song than anybody else. And there are lines that are completely obscure to people, and quite rightly so. The only statement I could make to a 16-year-old boy who wanted to do what I do is that we stand or fall individually. Develop yourself and your own attitude towards music or theatre or whatever you're involved in, and don't be derivative. However bad, be original.

I was lucky. I was given a second shot because of the theatrical thing. I was burning to go back to music on my own terms, and it was really the success of *Godspell* and the theatre world that gave me that second chance.

I think the key thing for me about why films aren't particularly interesting is that there is very little danger in a film. They're not spontaneous in any way. I know it's a performance that's being filmed. But the way it has to be channelled through this endless technical process to me turns me off. I've never seen James Dean, or Presley. But Gene Vincent, Little Richard . . . they had impact. But I've never seen them, just heard the records.

Staying Alive

It is 1983. One of the recent record hits was called *Video Killed the Radio Stars*. The new generation of kids are into video games. The Beatles' fans have mortgages; Elvis Presley fans have grandchildren. Nobody seems to be coming up with anything more exciting than Pack Man. Even as I write this the once-omnipotent record industry is in the doldrums movies found themselves in during the 50s. Rock is stagnant, disco is dead. John Travolta, whose subsequent career never matched his initial impact, is making a sequel to *Saturday Night Fever* entitled *Staying Alive* (1983). There is a fear that records may go the way of player pianos as kids with calluses on their fingers from playing video games are turning to drugs that ensure you don't have to go out to have a good time. You can look at the laundry swirling in the laundromat machine, creating a light show all of its own. But every year there are at least one or two Broadway hits. As long as that happens there will be a producer out there waiting to adapt them for the mass international audience. At the moment Broadway's biggest hits include *Chorus Line*, *A Little Shop of Horrors*, *Dream Girls*, *Evita*, *9*, *Cats*, a smash revival of Jerome Kern's 1927 *Show Boat*, and a musical based on the big Dubin and Warren song hits from the Berkeley musicals, entitled *42nd Street*. So stay tuned. . . .

Acknowledgments

This book would have been impossible had it not been for the helpfulness and generosity of many people. Wherever possible, I have tried to get the facts from the people who made the films – the stars, directors, writers and designers – and to these I am especially indebted. Their patience, kindness and hospitality have made the period I've worked on this book a time to treasure.

I am indebted to Philip Jenkinson, David Bradley, William K. Everson, MCA-Universal Pictures, the British Film Institute, the staff of the Stiftung Deutsche Kinemathek Berlin and Bill Kenly – a man who always does more than any of his friends could ask for – for the opportunity of seeing many of the rare films discussed in this book.

In America, the kindness of Tallulah Bankhead and George Cukor, giving not only their own time, but opening doors to the homes of others who proved of great help, leaves me with a fond debt of gratitude. I am also grateful to Bea and Mark Miller, Lady Sylvia Ashley, Zsa Zsa Gabor, Ruth and Carl Esmond, Herman G. Weinberg, Nick Vanoff, Ruth Waterbury, Loretta Young, Gloria Swanson, Veronica Lake, Anita Loos, Josef von Sternberg, Miliza Korjus, and Leslie Wallwork; and to Richard Buban for making me feel at home while my head was still spinning with song and dance and I was no fit company for anyone. Also thanks to: Mark Shivas, Gene Archer, John Gillett, Gillian Hartnell, Pierre Savage, Robert Benayoun, and Keith Brownlow. Invaluable assistance was given to me about foreign films by Guillermo Cabrera Infante, José Miguel Rodriguez and Pam Cullen.

I would also like to extend my sincere thanks for their help to Mr N. Kaphan, MGM New York, and Eddie Patnam and Carol Fleming of MGM London, to Jennifer Arrowsmith, MCA-Universal London, and Alex Black, MCA-Universal New York; Jo Wimshurst, 20th Century-Fox London, and Joel Coler of the New York Office for their patience and forbearance with my requests on their time and services in the search for rare and unusual film stills for the book. Also to the courtesies of Warner Brothers-Seven Arts; to Hy Smith and Miss Terry Hamill of United-Artists.

For other stills I am indebted to: Dr Fritz Güttinger, Kevin Brownlow, Janus Barfoed of the Danish Film Archive; Sheila Whittacker of the British Film Institute; the Belgian Film Archive, Mark Ricci's Memory Shop, Pam Cullen, Peter Magdowski, Stiftung Deutsche Kinemathek Berlin, Herbert Wiemer of the Staatliches Film Archiv der DDR, Bill Kenly, Hermes Pan, Fred Sill, Michelle Snapes of the British Film Institute and Mary Corliss of the Museum of Modern Art.

Grateful acknowledgment is made to the authors who are quoted in this book and to the publishers and agents who granted permission to reproduce the excerpts. Most of the source material is listed below.

And finally my very special thanks are due to Juliet Colman, who acted as reader, writer, incentive and inspiration. This book could not have been produced without her help.

John Kobal. London, 1969.

Fourteen years later I have had a marvellous opportunity not merely to update but to re-think, re-write and add to the original work which enabled me to take advantage of the marvellous memories of the many people I met after the early version of this book first came out. Besides taking me back to Fred Astaire and Joan Blondell, it opened up a whole new world of friends, like the late Eleanor Powell, of whose wonderful spirit something is, I hope, forever captured here. There are many others whom I cannot really thank enough. Fourteen years is a long time and people who have come along who have corrected me in this and that – to all of them I am indebted, for as anyone who has ever written a book like this knows, research is endless, dates are incorrigible, and just when you think you have got it right, a typesetter might put it all into Roman numerals. But I would not like to finish this without remembering, very gratefully, these people who have done so much to keep me on the right track: Simon Crocker who miraculously managed to schedule my life to fit in everything else so I did not have to worry; Victoria Wilson who is not just a great editor but a good friend; Bill Gibb, Bill Douglas, Ross Woodman and John Russell Taylor, incisive, insightful, and always encouraging; the staff of The Kobal Collection, especially Alexandra Lascelles who did more than help me collect stills, but was always perceptive about what was good when I got muddled; Peter de Rone, who transcribed most of the interviews, and to Bill Kenly and Howard Mandelbaum who read it, corrected it, argued with me. They all helped me to make it what it is, which, I hope, is a tribute to the kind of films and the talents that make life the better for their existence.

The books, magazine and newspaper articles, and passages from the author's correspondence that were used included:

Agate, James. *Around Cinemas*. London: Home & van Thal, 1946.

Astaire, Fred. *Steps in Time*. New York: Harper and Bros., 1959. London: Heinemann, 1959.

Bankhead, Tallulah. *Tallulah. My Autobiography*. New York: Harper and Bros., 1952. London: Gollancz, 1952.

Biamonte, S. G. *Musica e Film*. Rome: Edizioni dell'Ateneo, 1959.

Burton, Jack. *The Blue Book of Hollywood Musicals*. New York: Century House, 1953.

Cantor, Eddie as told to David Freedman. *My Life Is in Your Hands*. New York: Harper and Bros., 1928.

Cantor, Eddie with Jane Kesner Ardmore. *Take My Life*. New York: Doubleday, 1957.

Clair, René. *Reflections on the Cinema*. London: William Kimber, 1953.

Crosby, Bing. *Call Me Lucky*. New York: Simon and Schuster, 1953. London: Muller, 1953.

Crosby, Ted. *Story of Bing Crosby*. Cleveland: World Publishing Co., 1946.

Eby, Lois. *Shirley Temple*. Derby, Conn: Monarch Books, 1962.

Eells, George. *Cole Porter: The Life That Late He Led*. New York: G. P. Putnam's Sons, 1967. London: W. H. Allen, 1967.

Film Daily Year Book, numbers 27, 28, 31, 60, 62, 65.

Film India: Looking Back 1896-1960. The Directorate of Film Festivals, 1962.

Fosse, Bob. Letter to the author, 29 April 1969.

Fowler, Gene. *Schnozzola, The Story of Jimmy Durante*. New York: Viking. London: Hammond, Hammond & Co., 1952.

Green, Stanley. *Encyclopedia of the Musical Film*. London & New York: Oxford University Press, 1981.

Griffith, Richard and Arthur Mayer. *The Movies*. New York: Simon and Schuster, 1957. London: Spring Books, 1963.

Hanisch, Michael. *Vom Singen in Regen*. Berlin: Henschelverlag, 1980.

Higham, Charles and Joel Greenberg. *Hollywood in the Forties*. London: Zwemmer, 1968. New York: A. S. Barnes, 1968.

Hollaender, Friedrich. *Von Kopf Bis Fuss*. Berlin: Henschelverlag, 1967.

Horne, Lena and Richard Schickel. *Lena*. New York: Doubleday, 1965.

Jacobs, Lewis. *The Rise of the American Film*. New York: Harcourt Brace, 1939. Teacher's College Press, Columbia University, 1970.

Kael, Pauline. *I Lost It at the Movies*. Boston: Little, Brown and Co., 1965. London: Jonathan Cape, 1966. *Kiss Kiss Bang Bang*. Boston: Little, Brown and Co., 1968.

Kalbus, Dr Oskar. *Vom Werden Deutscher Filmkunst*, Vols 1 and 2. Altona-Bahrenfeld, 1935.

Knight, Arthur. *The Liveliest Art*. New York: Macmillan Co., 1957. London: Muller, 1959.

Lake, Veronica with Donald Bain. *Veronica*. London: W. H. Allen, 1969.

Lang, Fritz. Letter to the author, 17 May 1969.

Leander, Zarah & Gabrielsson, Jan. *Es War So Wunderbar: Zarah Leander – Mein Leben*. Hoffmann & Campe, 1973.

Levant, Oscar. *Memoirs of an Amnesiac*. New York: G. P. Putnam's Sons, 1965.

McVay, Douglas. *The Musical Film*. London: Zwemmer, 1967. New York: A. S. Barnes, 1967.

Marx, Groucho. *Groucho and Me*. New York: Random House, 1959. London: Gollancz, 1959.

Marx, Harpo, with Roland Barber. *Harpo Speaks*. New York: Bernard Geis, 1961.

Merman, Ethel as told to Pete Martin. *Who Can Ask for Anything More*. New York: Doubleday, 1955.

Moore, Colleen. *Silent Star*. New York: Doubleday, 1968.

Moore, Grace. *You're Only Human Once*. London: Latimer House, 1947.

Michael, Paul. *The Academy Awards, A Pictorial History*. New York: Bobbs Merrill, 1964.

Meeker, David. *Jazz in the Movies: A Guide to Jazz Musicians 1917-1977*. Godalming: Talisman-LSP Books, 1977.

New York Post, The, 13 January 1978. 'Goodbye, Dolly! Hello, Donna Summer!'

Pan, Hermes. Letters to the author, 2 November 1980 and 16 October 1982

Pasternak, Joe as told to David Chandler. *Easy the Hard Way*. New York: G. P. Putnam's Sons, 1956. London: W. H. Allen, 1956.

Photoplay, June 1959.

Rock 'n' Roll Yearbook, The.

Rooney, Mickey. *i.e. an Autobiography*. New York: G. P. Putnam's Sons, 1965.

Roth, Lillian with Mike Conolly and Gerald Frank. *I'll Cry Tomorrow*. New York: Frederick Fell, 1954. London: Arthur Barker, 1957.

Sieben, Pearl. *The Immortal Jolson*. New York: Frederick Fell, 1962.

Springer, John. *All Talking! All Singing! All Dancing!* New York: Citadel Press, 1966.

Stravinsky, Igor & Craft, Robert. *Dialogues and a Diary*. New York: Alfred A. Knopf. London: Faber & Faber, 1968.

Taylor, Deems. *A Pictorial History of the Movies*. New York: Citadel Press, 1966.

Taylor, John Russell & Jackson, Arthur. *The Hollywood Musical*. London: Secker & Warburg. New York: McGraw Hill, 1971.

Time, 23 January 1983. 'The Yellow Brick Road to Profit'.

Vidor, King. *A Tree Is A Tree*. New York: Harcourt, Brace and World. London: Longmans, 1954.

Von Sternberg. *Fun in a Chinese Laundry*. New York: Macmillan Co., 1965. London: Secker & Warburg, 1966.

Waldekranz, Rune and Verner Arpe. *Knaurs Buch vom Film*. Munich/Zurich: Droemersche Verlagsanstalt, 1956.

Walters, Charles. Letters to the author, 19 March 1969 and 7 May 1969.

Warner, Jack with Dean Jennings. *My First Hundred Years in Hollywood*. New York: Random House, 1965.

Weinberg, Herman G. *The Lubitsch Touch*. New York: E. P. Dutton, 1968.

West, Mae. *Goodness Had Nothing to Do With It*. Englewood Cliffs, N.J.: Prentice-Hall, 1959. London: (Mae West) W. H. Allen, 1960.

Wilcox, Herbert. *Twenty-five Thousand Sunsets*. London: Bodley Head, 1967.

Zolotow, Maurice. *Marilyn Monroe*. London: W. H. Allen, 1961.

Zukor, Adolph with Dale Kramer. *The Public Is Never Wrong*. New York: G. P. Putnam's Sons, 1953. London: Cassell, 1954.

The following magazines were valuable in research: Photoplay, Screen Romance, Picture Show, Modern Screen, Films in Review, Screen Facts, Cinema Arts, Dance Magazine, Cinema, Films and Filming, Bioscope, Variety, Motion Picture Herald, Movie, Film-Kurier.

Index

Figures in bold type refer to captions

316

317